PROFESSIONAL WORDPRESS®

INTRODUCTION xxv

CHAPTER 1   First Post 1

CHAPTER 2   Functional Overview 19

CHAPTER 3   Code Overview 49

CHAPTER 4   Tour of the Core 65

CHAPTER 5   The Loop 79

CHAPTER 6   Data Management 103

CHAPTER 7   Plugin Development 121

CHAPTER 8   Theme Development 183

CHAPTER 9   Content Aggregation 229

CHAPTER 10   Crafting a User Experience 249

CHAPTER 11   Statistics, Scalability, Security, and Spam 273

CHAPTER 12   WordPress as a Content Management System 299

CHAPTER 13   WordPress in the Enterprise 317

CHAPTER 14   Migrating To WordPress 329

CHAPTER 15   WordPress Developer Community 351

INDEX 365

PROFESSIONAL

WordPress®

Quality Plugins

Cart 66
Social Media Widget
Theme My Login
Tweet, Like, Google +1, & Share
Widget Logic
WP Google Fonts
WP Slim Stat
WP Touch
Web Comic

PROFESSIONAL

WordPress®

DESIGN AND DEVELOPMENT

Hal Stern, David Damstra, and Brad Williams

WILEY

Wiley Publishing, Inc.

Professional WordPress®: Design and Development

Published by
Wiley Publishing, Inc.
10475 Crosspoint Boulevard
Indianapolis, IN 46256
www.wiley.com

Published by Wiley Publishing, Inc., Indianapolis, Indiana

Published simultaneously in Canada

ISBN: 978-0-470-56054-9

Manufactured in the United States of America

10 9 8 7 6 5 4 3 2 1

For general information on our other products and services please contact our Customer Care Department within the United States at (877) 762-2974, outside the United States at (317) 572-3993 or fax (317) 572-4002.

Wiley also publishes its books in a variety of electronic formats. Some content that appears in print may not be available in electronic books.

Library of Congress Control Number: 2010921230

ABOUT THE AUTHORS

HAL STERN is a Vice President with a major technology company where he focuses on cloud computing, security, large-scale data management, and building technical communities. Hal began blogging about five years ago as a way to share customer interactions and technology observations, and eventually began using WordPress as an outlet for more personal thoughts on music, food, life in New Jersey, ice hockey, and the flailings known as his golf game. You can follow Hal online at `porkrollandfriends.com` and `snowmanonfire.com`.

DAVID DAMSTRA is the Manager of Web Services for CU*Answers, a credit union service organization. David manages a team of developers to create web sites and web applications for the financial industry. David's team uses WordPress as the foundation for many web projects. David is also a Zend Certified Engineer for PHP5. You can find David online professionally at `ws.cuanswers.com` and personally at `mirmillo.com`.

BRAD WILLIAMS is the CEO and Co-Founder of WebDevStudios.com. He is also a co-host on the SitePoint Podcast and an Advisor on SitePoint Forums. He was one of the original co-hosts on the WordPress Weekly Podcast and still joins the show on occasion. Brad has been developing web sites for over 14 years, including the last four, where he has focused on open-source technologies like WordPress. You can follow Brad online on his personal blog at `strangework.com`.

ABOUT THE TECHNICAL EDITOR

MIKE LITTLE is the co-founding developer of the WordPress project. He started WordPress in 2003 with Matt Mullenweg (now of Automattic Inc.) and has been developing with and using it ever since. He now runs `zed1.com`, his web development and consultancy company, which specializes in WordPress. He recently worked on a number of government WordPress sites, most notably a Law Commission consultation site, and now develops and supports a site for a large Cabinet Office client. He is a published author and a member of the Usability Professionals Association.

CREDITS

EXECUTIVE EDITOR
Carol Long

PROJECT EDITOR
Brian MacDonald

TECHNICAL EDITOR
Mike Little

PRODUCTION EDITOR
Daniel Scribner

COPY EDITOR
Kim Cofer

EDITORIAL DIRECTOR
Robyn B. Siesky

EDITORIAL MANAGER
Mary Beth Wakefield

ASSOCIATE DIRECTOR OF MARKETING
David Mayhew

PRODUCTION MANAGER
Tim Tate

VICE PRESIDENT AND EXECUTIVE GROUP PUBLISHER
Richard Swadley

VICE PRESIDENT AND EXECUTIVE PUBLISHER
Barry Pruett

ASSOCIATE PUBLISHER
Jim Minatel

PROJECT COORDINATOR, COVER
Lynsey Stanford

PROOFREADER
Publication Services, Inc.

INDEXER
Robert Swanson

COVER DESIGNER
Michael E. Trent

COVER IMAGE
© Karen Phillips/istockphoto

ACKNOWLEDGMENTS

THIS BOOK IDEA STARTED WHEN Jonathan Dingman remembered a conversation we had about this book idea at WordCamp NYC 2008, and connected me with Carol Long at Wiley. Thanks to Carol for agreeing to endure another project with me, and to editor Brian MacDonald for turning meandering streams of thought into something powerful. Mike Little's technical review of the book was equally insightful and invaluable. Various co-workers in the MySQL and Sun Microsystems communities contributed to my passion for blogging and understanding how things work, among them Tim Bray, Rich Zippel, Dave Douglas, Brian Aker, Bob Sokol, Jeremy Barnish, Hansjoerg Klimetzki, and the divas, Candace LoMonaco and Maria Buoy. Co-authors Brad and David have made this project as much fun as a challenge, and their ability to edit as a group is only one small artifact of their immense developer talents. Finally, my wife Toby, and children Elana and Ben stopped asking why my laptop was appearing at odd times like weekends and vacations, and I appreciate the time and space given to me to finish my scribbles.

— HAL STERN

I'D LIKE TO THANK EVERYONE at Wiley, particularly Carol Long for putting her faith in a first time author and encouraging me to join this writing team, and editors Brian MacDonald and Mike Little for their valuable insights, suggestions, and quick responses to our changes. I am also indebted to my co-authors, Hal Stern and Brad Williams, who were able to turn this book around on such a tight schedule. Thanks to my family, specifically, Holly, Jack, Justin, and Jonah for their love and support while I was writing away. I'd also like to thank my parents, family, friends, and coworkers who have all helped in some way and encouraged me to write this book. Finally, I would like to thank the entire WordPress community for creating such a robust and powerful application.

— DAVID DAMSTRA

THANK YOU APRIL FOR putting up with my nerdy ways. Thank you Dad for being such an amazing person and role model. Thank you to my sister Brittany, her husband Alistair, and my niece Indiana Brooke. Thanks to Hal Stern for guiding me in this endeavor, David Damstra for being a great co-author, Mike Little for his expertise, Brian MacDonald for his amazing editorial skills, and Carol Long for believing in me. Thanks to Brian Messenlehner for getting me out to Jersey and helping make WDS a reality. Thanks to Matt Martz, Michael Torbert, and Scott Basgaard for reviewing the plugin development chapter. Thanks to Jeff (Fizzypop) Chandler for letting me be a part of the WordPress Weekly Podcast. Thanks to Margaret Roach for her mentoring and friendship. Thanks to all of my WordPress friends, including Lisa Sabin-Wilson, Brian Gardner, Craig Tuller (oohrah!), Travis Ballard, Corey Miller, Jonathan Dingman, Dre Armeda, Andy Peatling, Matt Mullenweg, Mark Jaquith, Jane Wells, Andrea and Ron, Aaron Brazell, Carl Hancock, Dan Milward, Ryan Imel, Shane (margarita) F., Daisy Olsen, Jeremy Clarke, Steve Bruner, Michael Myers, and many more. Thanks to Jeff Abshire and Jeff Gray for being awesome friends. Thanks to my podcast buddies Patrick O'Keefe, Stephan Segraves, and Kevin Yank. Last but not least thank you to my zoo: Lecter, Clarice, and Squeaks the Cat for your endless love and ridiculous ways.

— BRAD WILLIAMS

ACKNOWLEDGMENTS

CONTENTS

INTRODUCTION   *xxv*

CHAPTER 1: FIRST POST   **1**

What Is WordPress?   **1**
A Short History: WordPress and Friends   2
Current State   2
Intersecting the Community   3
WordPress and the GPL   4
Content and Conversation   **5**
WordPress as a Content Management System   5
Creating Conversation   6
Getting Started   **7**
Hosting Options   7
Do It Yourself Installation   9
Installing WordPress Files   9
Database Configuration   12
Finishing Up   **16**
First-Time Administration   16
First Post   17

CHAPTER 2: FUNCTIONAL OVERVIEW   **19**

The Dashboard   **19**
Dashboard Widgets   20
Customizing the Dashboard   21
Screen Options   21
Admin Menu   22
Creating and Managing Content   **22**
Creating Posts   22
Managing Posts   24
Creating Pages   25
Managing Pages   25
Links   25
Trash   26
Categorizing Your Content   **26**
Categories versus Tags   26
Post Categories   27

Tagging Posts   27
Categorizing Links   28
Working with Media   **28**
Media Library   28
Uploading Media   28
Inserting Media   29
Managing Media   30
Edit Media   30
Comments and Discussion   **31**
Managing Comments   31
Moderating Comments   32
Handling Comment Spam   32
Working with Users   **33**
Creating New Users   33
Managing Users   33
User Roles and Permissions   34
User Images   34
Extending User Profiles   35
Extending WordPress   **35**
Themes   35
Managing Themes   35
Adding New Themes   36
Upgrading a Theme   36
Using the Theme Editor   37
Working with Widgets   37
Plugins   38
Managing Plugins   38
Adding New Plugins   38
Upgrading a Plugin   38
Using the Plugin Editor   39
Content Tools   **39**
Importing Content   39
Exporting Content   40
Turbo   40
Upgrading WordPress   40
Configuring WordPress   **41**
General Settings   41
Writing and Reading   42
Discussion   44
Media   44

Privacy   45
Permalinks   45
Miscellaneous   46

CHAPTER 3: CODE OVERVIEW   **49**

Downloading   **49**
Download Locations   49
Available Formats   50
Release Archive   50
Exploring the Code   **50**
Configuring Key Files   **51**
wp-config.php file   52
Advanced wp-config Options   53
.htaccess   58
   Enabling Permalinks   58
   .htaccess Rewriting Rules   59
   Configuration Control Through .htaccess   60
The .maintenance File   61
WP-Content User Playground   **61**
Plugins   61
Themes   62
Uploads and Media Directory   62
Upgrade Directory   63
Custom Directories   63

CHAPTER 4: TOUR OF THE CORE   **65**

What's in the Core?   **65**
Using the Core as a Reference   **66**
Inline Documentation   67
Finding Functions   67
Exploring the Code   70
   Functions.php   70
   Formatting.php   70
   Pluggable.php   70
   Plugin.php   71
   Post.php   71
   Category.php   71
WordPress Codex and Resources   **72**
What Is the Codex?   72
Using the Codex   72

Function Reference   73
WordPress APIs   74
Codex Controversy   75
Don't Hack Core!   **76**
Why Not?   76
Alternatives to Hacking Core   76

CHAPTER 5: THE LOOP   **79**

Understanding the Loop   **80**
Putting the Loop in Context   **81**
Flow of the Loop   **81**
Template Tags   **84**
Commonly Used Template Tags   84
Tag Parameters   85
Customizing the Loop   **86**
Using the WP_Query Object   86
Building A Custom Query   87
Post Parameters   87
Page Parameters   88
Category, Tag, and Author Parameters   88
Time, Date, Ordering, and Custom Parameters   88
Putting It Together   89
Adding Paging To A Loop   89
Using query_posts()   90
Using get_posts()   92
Resetting a Query   93
More Than One Loop   94
Nested Loops   94
Multi-Pass Loops   95
Global Variables   **95**
Post Data   95
Author Data   96
User Data   96
Environmental Data   97
Global Variables or Template Tags?   98
Working Outside the Loop   **98**

CHAPTER 6: DATA MANAGEMENT   **103**

Database Schema   **103**
Table Structure   104

Table Details **105**

WordPress Database Class 107

Simple Database Queries 107

Complex Database Operations 108

Dealing With Errors 110

Direct Database Manipulation **111**

WordPress Taxonomy **114**

Default Taxonomies 114

Taxonomy Table Structure 115

Understanding Taxonomy Relationships 115

Building Your Own Taxonomies **116**

Custom Taxonomy Overview 116

Building Custom Taxonomies 116

Using Your Custom Taxonomy 119

CHAPTER 7: PLUGIN DEVELOPMENT **121**

Plugin Packaging **121**

Create a Plugin File 122

Creating the Plugin Header 122

Plugin License 123

Activate and Deactivate Functions 123

Internationalization 124

Directory Constants 126

Know Your Hooks: Actions and Filters **127**

Actions and Filters 127

Popular Filter Hooks 129

Popular Action Hooks 130

Plugin Settings **132**

Saving Plugin Options 132

Array of Options 133

Create a Menu and Submenus 134

Creating a Top-Level Menu 134

Adding To An Existing Menu 135

Create an Options Page 136

WordPress Integration **143**

Create a Meta Box 143

Shortcodes 147

Create a Widget 148

Create a Dashboard Widget 152

Creating Custom Tables   153
Uninstall Your Plugin   155

Plugin Security   **157**
Nonces   157
Data Validation   158

Creating a Plugin Example   **160**
Publish to the Plugin Directory   **175**
Restrictions   175
Submit Your Plugin   175
Create a readme.txt File   176
Setup SVN   179
Publish to the Plugin Directory   180
Releasing a New Version   181

CHAPTER 8: THEME DEVELOPMENT   **183**

Why Use a Theme?   **183**
Installing a Theme   **184**
FTP Installation   184
Theme Installer   185

What Is a Theme?   **185**
Template Files   185
CSS   186
Images and Assets   186
Plugins   186

Creating Your Own Theme   **187**
Starting from a Working Theme   187
Starting with the Sandbox Theme   187

Creating Your Own Theme: Getting Started   **189**
Essential File: Style.css   190
Showing Your Content: Index.php   191
Showing Your Content in Different Ways: Index.php   193

Creating Your Own Theme: DRY   **193**
Header.php   194
Footer.php   195
Sidebar.php   195
Deviations from the Norm: Conditional Tags   196

Creating Your Own Theme: Content Display   **197**

Customizing Your Homepage: home.php   197

Show Your Older Posts by Date: Archive.php   200

Showing Only One Category: Category.php   201

Show Posts of a Specific Tag: Tag.php   202

How to Show a Single Post: single.php   203

Display a Page: Page.php   204

Display an Image from Your Gallery: Image.php   206

Template Hierarchy   206

Creating Your Own Theme: Additional Files   **208**

Handle 404 Errors: 404.php   208

Attachment.php   209

Author.php   210

Comments.php   210

Add Functionality to Your Templates: Functions.php   211

Search.php   214

SearchForm.php   215

Other Files   215

Custom Page Templates   **216**

When to Use Custom Page Templates   216

How to Use Custom Page Templates   217

Stock Sandbox Page Templates   218

Theme Hierarchy and Child Themes   **219**

Premium Themes and Other Theme Frameworks   **224**

Revolution Theme   225

Hybrid Theme   225

Thematic Theme   226

Thesis Theme   226

Sandbox Theme   226

Partial Themes   226

CHAPTER 9: CONTENT AGGREGATION   **229**

What is a Lifestream?   **229**

Getting Noticed   **230**

Social Media Buttons   **231**

Simple Social Networking Badges   **232**

Collecting External Content — **233**

Generic XML Feed — 233

Integrating Twitter — 236

Google Maps — 238

Integrating RSS and ATOM Feeds — 239

Pushing Content from WordPress to Other Sites — **240**

Feeding RSS into Other Sites — 240

Feeding WordPress into Facebook — 241

Advertising — **242**

Monetizing Your Site — 242

Setting Up Advertising — 243

Using Advertising Plugins — 243

Manual Advertising Placement — 245

Dealing With Conflict — 246

Privacy and History — **247**

CHAPTER 10: CRAFTING A USER EXPERIENCE — **249**

User Experience Principles — **249**

Consistent Navigation — 250

Visual Design Elements — 251

Making Content Easy to Find — 253

Site Load Times — 254

Using JavaScript — 255

Usability and Usability Testing — **256**

Structuring Your Information — **257**

Getting Your Site Found — **259**

Duplicate Content — 261

Trackbacks and Pings — 263

Tags and Content Sharing Sites — 264

How Web Standards Get Your Data Discovered — **264**

Semantic HTML — 264

Valid HTML — 266

Microformats — 267

Searching Your Own Site — **269**

Weaknesses of the Default Search — 269

Alternatives and Plugins to Help — 270

Mobile Access — **271**

CHAPTER 11: STATISTICS, SCALABILITY, SECURITY, AND SPAM 273

Statistics Counters 273
AWStats 274
Statcounter 275
Mint 276
Google Analytics 276
Cache Management 278
WordPress System Complexity 279
Web Server Caching and Optimization 281
WordPress Object Caching 283
MySQL Query Cache 284
Load Balancing Your WordPress Site 284
Dealing With Spam 286
Comment Moderation and CAPTCHAs 286
Automating Spam Detection 287
Securing Your WordPress Site 288
Stay Up-to-Date 288
Hiding WordPress Version Information 289
Don't Use the Admin Account 289
Change Your Table Prefix 290
Move Your Configuration File 290
Move Your Content Directory 290
Use the Secret Key Feature 291
Force SSL on Login and Admin 291
Apache Permissions 291
MySQL Credentials 292
Recommended Security Plugins 292
WP Security Scan 292
WordPress Exploit Scanner 292
WordPress File Monitor 293
Using WordPress Roles 294
Subscriber Role 295
Contributor Role 295
Author Role 295
Editor Role 295
Administrator Role 296

Role Overview   296
Extending Roles   297

CHAPTER 12: WORDPRESS AS A CONTENT MANAGEMENT SYSTEM   299

Defining Content Management   **299**
Workflow and Delegation   **301**
User Roles and Delegation   301
Workflow   302
Content Organization   **303**
Theme and Widget Support   304
Homepages   305
Featured Content Pages   306
Content Hierarchy   308
Interactivity Features   **312**
Forums   312
Forms   313
E-Commerce   313
Other Content Management Systems   **313**
WordPress Integration   314
Where Not to Use WordPress   314

CHAPTER 13: WORDPRESS IN THE ENTERPRISE   317

Is WordPress Right for Your Enterprise?   **317**
When WordPress Isn't Right for You   **319**
Scalability   **319**
Performance Tuning   320
Caching   321
Regular Maintenance   322
Hardware Scaling   322
Integration with Enterprise Identity Management   **324**
LDAP and Active Directory   324
OpenID   325
Content Integration via Feeds   **326**

CHAPTER 14: MIGRATING TO WORDPRESS   329

Planning a Migration   **330**
Content Sources   330
Migration Checklist   331
Site Preparation   332

Content Identification **332**

   Migrating Text Documents 333

   Built-In WordPress Import Tools 333

      Blog Conversion 333

      Using WordPress eXtended RSS Files 334

   Building a Custom Import Script 335

Media Migration **344**

Moving Metadata **345**

Moving Authors and Users **345**

Theme and Presentation **346**

Unique Functionality **346**

Cleaning Up **346**

   Manual Fine-Tuning 347

   Import Limitations 347

   Updating URLs 347

   Redirection 348

Launching **349**

CHAPTER 15: WORDPRESS DEVELOPER COMMUNITY **351**

Contributing to WordPress **351**

   Understanding Trac 351

      Bug Reporting 352

      Trac Keywords 353

      View and Search Tickets 353

      Trac Timeline 354

      Browsing Source 354

   Working on the Core 355

      Understanding Subversion (SVN) 355

      Hook into WordPress Core 355

      Create a patch/diff File 355

   Submitting Plugins and Themes 356

   Documentation 356

Sister Projects **357**

   WordPress MU 357

   BuddyPress 357

   bbPress 357

   Future Projects 358

Resources **358**

   Codex 358

   Support Forums 358

WordPress Chat   359
Mailing Lists   359
External Resources   361
WordCamp and Meetups   361
WordPress.TV   361
Theme/Plugin Directories   362
WordPress Ideas   362
WordPress Development Updates   362
WordPress Podcasts   362
  WordPress Weekly   362
  WordCast Podcast   363
  The WordPress Podcast   363
  Plugins: The WordPress Plugins Podcast   363
WordPress News Sites   363
  WPTavern.com   363
  WPVibe.com   363
  WeblogToolsCollection.com   363
  WPEngineer.com   364
  WordPress Alltop   364
  WordPress Planet   364
  Planet WordPress   364

INDEX   **365**

INTRODUCTION

DEAR READER, thank you for picking up this book. WordPress is the most popular self-hosted blogging software in use today. It is available as an open source project, licensed under the GPL, and is built largely on top of the MySQL database and PHP programming language. Any server environment that supports that simple combination can run WordPress, making it remarkably portable as well as simple to install and operate. You don't need to be a systems administrator, developer, HTML expert, or design aesthete to use WordPress. On the other hand, because WordPress has been developed using a powerful set of Internet standard platforms, it can be extended and tailored for a wide variety of applications. WordPress is the publishing mechanism underneath thousands of individual blog voices and the engine that powers high-volume, high-profile sites such as CNN's blogs. It was designed for anyone comfortable navigating a browser, but is accessible to web designers as well. Key contributor Matt Mullenweg described the wide dynamic range of WordPress users and uses in his keynote at WordCamp NYC 2008 by noting that the WordPress team chose simple but powerful tools — PHP and MySQL — to build WordPress, making it simple to use but also powerful for developers.

Given that range of applications and capabilities, it can prove hard to know where to start if you want to make use of the power of WordPress for your specific purposes. Should you first study the database models and relationships of content and metadata, or the presentation mechanics that generate the HTML output? This book was designed for readers to develop a knowledge of WordPress from the inside out, focusing on the internal structure and flow of the core code as well as the data model on which that code operates. Knowing how something works often makes you more adept at working with it, extending it, or fixing it when it breaks. Just as a race car driver benefits from a fundamental knowledge of combustion engines, aerodynamics, and the mechanics of automobile suspension, someone driving WordPress through its full dynamic range will be significantly more adept once acquainted with the underlying software physics.

WHO IS THIS BOOK FOR?

It was the dichotomy between the almost trivial effort required to create a WordPress-based blog and publish a "first post" to the world and the much more detailed, broad understanding required to effect mass customization that led us to write this book. Many books on the market provide guidance to beginning bloggers by walking you through the typical functions of creating, configuring, and caring for your WordPress site. Our goal was to bridge the gap between an expert PHP developer who is comfortable reading the WordPress Codex in lieu of a manual and the casual WordPress user creating a public persona integrated with social networking sites and advertising services, with a tailored look and feel.

In short, we hope to appeal to a range of developers, from the person looking to fine-tune a WordPress theme to a more advanced developer with a plugin concept or who is using WordPress in a large enterprise integrated into a content management system. We do this by exploring WordPress from the inside out. Our goal for this book is to describe the basic operation of a function, and then offer guidance and examples that highlight how to take it apart and reassemble that function to fit a number of needs. WordPress users who are not hardened PHP developers may want to skim through the developer-centric section, whereas coders looking for specific patterns to implement new WordPress functionality can start in the middle and work toward the end.

HOW THIS BOOK IS STRUCTURED

This book is divided into three major sections: Chapters 1 through 4 are an overview of the WordPress system, its major functional elements, and a top-level description of what happens when a WordPress-generated web page is displayed. Chapters 5 through 8 build on this foundation and dive into the core of WordPress, describing internal code flow and data structures. This middle section is strongly developer-oriented, and describes how to extend WordPress through plug-ins and customize it via themes. The last section, Chapters 9 through 15, combines a developer view of user experience and optimization with the deployer requirements for performance, security, and enterprise integration.

The following is a detailed chapter-by-chapter overview of what you can expect to find in this book.

Chapter 1, "First Post," contains a brief summary of the history of the WordPress software core, explores some popular hosting options, why community matters in a content-centric world, and concludes with the basics of do-it-yourself WordPress installation and debugging.

Chapter 2, "Functional Overview," examines each of the major sections of the WordPress system as seen by a typical user in the course of writing, editing, and managing a blog. This chapter covers the basic mechanics of the WordPress Dashboard, plugins, settings, permissions and users, and content management features, laying the foundation for dissecting their internals in later chapters. If you're a beginning WordPress user, you should find this overview sufficient to develop proficiency in basic WordPress authoring and management tasks.

Chapter 3, "Code Overview," starts with the mechanics of downloading the WordPress distribution and describes its basic contents and filesystem layout. A top-to-bottom code flow walks you from an index or specific post URL, through the process of selecting posts, assembling content, and generating the displayed HTML. This chapter is a map for the more detailed code tours in the developer-focused section.

Chapter 4, "Tour of the Core," examines the essential PHP functions comprising the basic WordPress engine. It serves as an introduction to the developer-focused middle section of the book and also lays the foundation for the deployment-, integration-, and experience-focused chapters in the last section. This chapter also covers using the core as a reference guide, and why it is best not to hack the core code to achieve desired customizations.

Chapter 5, "The Loop," is the basis for the developer-centric core of this book. The WordPress main loop drives the functions of creating and storing content in the MySQL database, as well as extracting appropriate chunks of it to be sorted, decorated, and nested under banners or next to sidebars, in both cases generating something a web browser consumes. This chapter disassembles those processes of creating, saving, and publishing a new post as well as displaying content that has been stored in the WordPress MySQL databases. The underlying database functions and the management of content metadata are covered in more detail to complete a thorough view of WordPress's internal operation.

Chapter 6, "Data Management," is the MySQL-based counterpart to Chapter 5. The core functions create, update, and manipulate entries in multiple MySQL database tables, and this chapter covers the database schema, data and metadata taxonomies used, and the basic relations that exist between WordPress elements. It also includes an overview of the basic query functions used to select and extract content from MySQL, forming a basis for extensions and custom code that needs to be able to examine the individual data underlying a blog.

Chapter 7, "Plugin Development," starts with the basic plugin architecture and then explores the hook, action, and filter interfaces that integrate new functionality around the WordPress core. This chapter demonstrates the interposition of functions into the page composition or content management streams and how to save plugin data. Examples of building a plugin using a simple framework outline the necessary functionality of any plugin. This chapter also covers creation of widgets, simpler-to-use plugins that typically add decoration, additional images, or content to a blog sidebar; many plugins also have a widget for easier management. Publishing a plugin to the WordPress repository and pitfalls of plugin conflict round out the discussion of WordPress's functional extensions.

Chapter 8, "Theme Development," is the display and rendering counterpart to Chapter 7. Plugins add new features and functions to the core, whereas themes and CSS page templates change the way that content is shown to readers. Starting with the basic Sandbox theme, this chapter covers writing a theme, building custom page templates, theme installation, and how thematic elements are used by the functions described in previous chapters. This chapter ends the deep developer-focused middle section of the book.

Chapter 9, "Content Aggregation," looks at WordPress from a services point of view. If a blog represents your public persona or online presence, it has to pull content from a variety of tools and content sources. This chapter delves into web services interfaces, WordPress APIs, feeds into and out of WordPress, and making WordPress entries show up in Facebook pages.

Chapter 10, "Crafting the User Experience," looks at a WordPress installation from the perspective of a regular or potential reader. Usability, testing, and the ease of finding information within a WordPress blog form the basics, with added emphasis on web standards for metadata and search engine optimization so a blog, or a specific blog post, can be found through an appropriate Google search. Whereas Chapter 9 covers pulling external content into your WordPress instance, this chapter shows how to get your content to show up elsewhere on the Web. Alternatives for adding search functionality, one of WordPress's weaknesses, are discussed, along with content accessibility and delivery to mobile devices.

Chapter 11, "Scalability, Statistics, Security, and Spam," deals with good and bad popularity. Keeping a WordPress installation safe from inevitable comment spammers as well as malicious attackers is a key part of configuration and management, and this chapter covers the more popular security and anti-spam plugins and features. Traffic analysis tools indicate how well certain content types, functions, ad campaigns, promotions, or links are driving readership and how this informs traffic management.

Chapter 12, "WordPress as a Content Management System," goes beyond blogging to examples of WordPress as a system for managing the life cycle, integration, and distribution of networked content. Integration with other open source content management systems including Drupal and Joomla rounds out this chapter.

Chapter 13, "WordPress in the Enterprise," tackles issues of scale and integration. WordPress may address deficiencies in "enterprise scale" content management tools, and building on the mechanisms covered in Chapter 12, this chapter shows how to use WordPress with a variety of enterprise facilities ranging from identity management to Microsoft ASP/.NET services.

Chapter 14, "Migrating to WordPress," provides an overview of moving content from an existing blog or content management system into WordPress, and examines issues of importing media such as images, video, or formatted data. This chapter also covers mechanisms for redirecting existing sites to a WordPress installation.

Chapter 15, "WordPress Developer Community," is an introduction to contributing to the WordPress ecosystem by working on the core, submitting plugins or themes, adding to the documentation canon, and assisting other developers. An overview of WordPress sister projects such as bbPress for forums is provided along with a brief summary of other developer resources and a glossary of WordPress-context sensitive terms.

WHAT YOU NEED TO USE THIS BOOK

You'll need at least a rudimentary understanding of HTML and some knowledge of cascading style sheets (CSS) to make use of the theme and user experience sections of the book. Experience in writing and debugging PHP code is a prerequisite for more advanced developer sections, although if you're just going to make changes based on the samples in this book, you can use the code as a template and learn on the fly. A basic knowledge of databases, especially the syntax and semantics of MySQL, is in order to make the most out of the chapter on data management as well as develop plugins that need to save data.

It's helpful to have an interactive development environment in which to view PHP code, or PHP code sprinkled through HTML pages. Choosing a set of developer tools often borders on religion and deep personal preference (and we know plenty of coders who believe that vi constitutes a development environment). Some of the more user-friendly tools will make walking through the WordPress code easier if you want to see how functions used in the examples appear in the core.

Most important, if you want to use the code samples and examples in this book, you'll need a WordPress blog in which to install them. Chapter 1 covers some basic WordPress hosting options as well as the simple mechanics of downloading the components, and installing WordPress on a desktop or test machine for debugging and closer inspection.

Finally, some people might argue that to really take advantage of WordPress you need to be able to write, but that ignores the basic beauty of the WordPress platform: it takes the power of the printing press to an individual level. This book isn't about what you say (or might say); it's about how you're going to get those ideas onto the Web and how the world will see them and interact with your blog.

CONVENTIONS

To help you get the most from the text and keep track of what's happening, we've used a number of conventions throughout the book.

Boxes with a warning icon like this one hold important, not-to-be forgotten information that is directly relevant to the surrounding text.

 The pencil icon indicates notes, tips, hints, tricks, or asides to the current discussion.

As for styles in the text:

➤ We *italicize* new terms and important words when we introduce them.

➤ We show file names, URLs, and code within the text like so: `persistence.properties`.

➤ We present code in two different ways:

```
We use a monofont type with no highlighting for most code examples.
We use bold to emphasize code that's particularly important in the present context.
```

SOURCE CODE

As you work through the examples in this book, you may choose either to type in all the code manually or to use the source code files that accompany the book. All of the source code used in this book is available for download at `http://www.wrox.com`.

 Because many books have similar titles, you may find it easiest to search by ISBN; this book's ISBN is 978-0-470-56054-9.

Once you download the code, just decompress it with your favorite compression tool. Alternately, you can go to the main Wrox code download page at `http://www.wrox.com/dynamic/books/download.aspx` to see the code available for this book and all other Wrox books.

ERRATA

We make every effort to ensure that there are no errors in the text or in the code. However, no one is perfect, and mistakes do occur. If you find an error in one of our books, like a spelling mistake or faulty piece of code, we would be very grateful for your feedback. By sending in errata you may save another reader hours of frustration and at the same time you will be helping us provide even higher quality information.

To find the errata page for this book, go to `http://www.wrox.com` and locate the title using the Search box or one of the title lists. Then, on the book details page, click the Book Errata link. On this page you can view all errata that has been submitted for this book and posted by Wrox editors. A complete book list including links to each book's errata is also available at www.wrox.com/misc-pages/booklist.shtml.

If you don't spot "your" error on the Book Errata page, go to www.wrox.com/contact/techsupport. shtml and complete the form there to send us the error you have found. We'll check the information and, if appropriate, post a message to the book's errata page and fix the problem in subsequent editions of the book.

P2P.WROX.COM

For author and peer discussion, join the P2P forums at p2p.wrox.com. The forums are a Web-based system for you to post messages relating to Wrox books and related technologies and interact with other readers and technology users. The forums offer a subscription feature to e-mail you topics of interest of your choosing when new posts are made to the forums. Wrox authors, editors, other industry experts, and your fellow readers are present on these forums.

At http://p2p.wrox.com you will find a number of different forums that will help you not only as you read this book, but also as you develop your own applications. To join the forums, just follow these steps:

1. Go to p2p.wrox.com and click the Register link.

2. Read the terms of use and click Agree.

3. Complete the required information to join as well as any optional information you wish to provide and click Submit.

4. You will receive an e-mail with information describing how to verify your account and complete the joining process.

You can read messages in the forums without joining P2P but in order to post your own messages, you must join.

Once you join, you can post new messages and respond to messages other users post. You can read messages at any time on the Web. If you would like to have new messages from a particular forum e-mailed to you, click the Subscribe to this Forum icon by the forum name in the forum listing.

For more information about how to use the Wrox P2P, be sure to read the P2P FAQs for answers to questions about how the forum software works as well as many common questions specific to P2P and Wrox books. To read the FAQs, click the FAQ link on any P2P page.

1

First Post

- ➤ Appreciating the provenance of the WordPress platform
- ➤ Choosing a suitable platform for your WordPress installation
- ➤ Downloading, installing, and performing basic configuration of WordPress
- ➤ Diagnosing and resolving common installation problems

If displaying "Hello World" on an appropriate device defines minimum competence in a programming language, generating your first post is the equivalent in the blogging world. This chapter provides a brief history of WordPress and then explores several options for hosting a WordPress installation. Common miscues and misperceptions along with their resolutions round out the chapter and put you on the edge of publishing your wit and wisdom.

Once you've installed, configured, and completed the bare-bones administration, you're ready to take advantage of the code walkthroughs and detailed component descriptions in later chapters. Of course, if you already have a functional WordPress blog, you can skip this chapter and dive head-first into the Dashboard control wonderland in Chapter 2, "Functional Overview."

WHAT IS WORDPRESS?

WordPress is one of the most popular open source blogging systems available, with global and vibrant user, developer, and support communities. Though it can be compared to TypePad, Moveable Type, Google's Blogger, and the Apache Roller project as a user-generated content workhorse, WordPress distinguishes itself with a broad array of hosting options, functional extensions (plugins), and aesthetic designs and elements (themes).

With the rise of self-publishing, low-cost web hosting and freely available core components like the MySQL database, blogging software followed the same trend as most other digital technologies, moving from high-end, high-cost products to widely available, low-cost consumer or "hobbyist" systems. WordPress isn't simply about creating a blog so that you can have a digital diary attached to your vanity URL; it has evolved into a full-fledged content management system used by individuals and enterprises alike. This section takes a brief tour through the early history of WordPress and brings you up to speed on the current release and user community.

A Short History: WordPress and Friends

WordPress started similarly to many other popular open source software packages: Some talented developers saw a need to create a powerful, simple tool based on an existing project licensed under the GPL. Michel Valdrighi's b2/cafelog system provided the starting point, and WordPress was built as a fork of that base by developers Matt Mullenweg and Mike Little. WordPress first appeared in 2003, also built on the MySQL open source database for persisting content and PHP as the development platform. Valdrighi remains a contributor to the project, which thrives and depends on a growing and interested community of users and developers.

As with other systems written in PHP, it is self-contained in the sense that installation, configuration, operation, and administration tasks are all contained in PHP modules. WordPress's popularity has been driven in part by its simplicity, with the phrase "five minute installation" making appearances in nearly every description or book about WordPress. Beyond getting to a first post, WordPress was designed to be extended.

WordPress today is supported by a handful of core developers and just under 100 key contributors. Mike Little today runs the WordPress specialty shop zed1.com and he contributes the occasional patch to the code. Matt Mullenweg's company, Automattic, continues to operate the wordpress.com hosting service as well as fund development of related content management tools: WordPress MU, a multi-user version of WordPress that is at the heart of the wordpress.com hosting system. Pronounce it "em-you" or take the rather scholarly "myu" approach if you want to impress your Greek or mathematically inclined friends. Gravatar dynamically serves images tied to e-mail addresses, providing a hosted icon with a variety of display options. Think of it as a service to make hot-linking your profile picture technically and socially acceptable.

As a content management system, the WordPress system definition doesn't stop at time-serialized posts with comments. BuddyPress is a set of themes and plugins that extends WordPress into a functional social networking platform, allowing registered users to message and interact with each other, again with all content managed within the WordPress framework. Similarly, bbPress is a PHP- and MySQL-based system designed for forums (bulletin boards) that is distinct from WordPress but is commonly integrated with it.

We cover some of these WordPress adjunct systems in more detail in Chapter 15, "The WordPress Developer Community," but they're included here to provide a sense of how WordPress has expanded beyond a basic single-user-oriented tool. At the same time, we're not endorsing or making a commercial for Automattic, but delving into the guts of WordPress without a spin of the propeller hat toward Mullenweg and Little is somewhere between incorrigible and bad community behavior.

Current State

This book is based on the WordPress 2.9 major release. Each successive release of WordPress has included improvements in the administration and control functions (Dashboard), backup, export, and import functions, and installation and upgrade features. Even if you start with a slightly down-rev version of WordPress, you'll be able to bring it up to the current release and maintain the freshness of your install. We touch on install and upgrade paths later in this chapter.

Exactly how popular and prevalent is WordPress usage? "Popular" is always a subjective metric, but statistics add some weight to those perceptions. Jason Calacanis claimed 202 million websites using WordPress in Episode 16 of "This Week in Startups" (September 2009). That includes sites using WordPress for content management, blogging, and personal rants, and has to be discounted by those of us who have multiple WordPress installations to their names, but even with that order of magnitude estimate, WordPress is immensely popular.

Here are download statistics for the core WordPress system:

➤ **2006:** 1.5 million (source: WordPress.org)

➤ **2007:** 3.8 million (source: WordPress.org)

➤ **2008:** More than 11 million (source: Matt Mullenweg's WordCamp NYC keynote)

Hosted blogs on `wordpress.com` now number over 4.6 million, with more than 35 million posts over the 2008 calendar year, reaching a run rate of about 4 million posts per month; again those statistics are courtesy of Mullenweg's WordCamp NYC keynote (available on WordCampTV for your viewing pleasure). The plugin population went from about 370 in 2006, to 1,384 in 2007, with more than 6,300 currently registered as reported on WordPress.org. The combinations of plugins and themes require scientific notation to represent in complexity, but at the same time, they're all equally simple to locate, integrate, and use. That's the result of a solid architecture and an equally solid community using it.

Today, WordPress powers CNN's blogs, the *Wall Street Journal*'s *All Things D*, and the irreverent but snowclone-driven `icanhazcheeseburger.com`. (If you looked for a backstory on "snowclone," apologies, but that's also the joy of discovering new facts in a culture of participatory media).

Where do you get started?

`wordpress.org` is the home for the current released and in-development versions of the code. Click down to `wordpress.org/extend` for a starting point in finding plugins, themes, and wish lists of ideas and features to be implemented.

`wordpress.com` has both free and paid hosting services. Over at `wordpress.org/hosting` you'll find a list of hosting providers that support WordPress and often include some additional first-time installation and configuration support in their packaging of the code for delivery as part of their hosting services.

Intersecting the Community

WordPress thrives and grows based on community contributions in addition to sheer usage. Like high school gym class, participation is the name of the game, and several semi-formal avenues along which to channel your efforts and energies are available.

WordCamp events are community-hosted, locally operated, and now happen in dozens of cities around the world. Camps that reach critical mass are listed on wordcamp.org, but you'll do just as well to search for a WordCamp event in a major city close to you. WordCamps occur nearly every weekend with bloggers, photographers, writers, editors, developers, and designers of all experience and skill levels counted among their attendees. WordCamps are a low-cost introduction to the local community and often a good opportunity to meet WordPress celebrities.

Less structured but more frequently convened than WordCamps are WordPress Meetups, comprising local users and developers in more than 40 cities. You'll need a `meetup.com` account, but once you're registered you can check on locations and timetables at `wordpress.meetup.com` to see when and where people are talking about content management.

A rich, multi-language documentation repository is hosted at `codex.wordpress.org`. The WordPress Codex, with all due respect to the term reserved for ancient handwritten manuscripts, represents the community-contributed tips and tricks for every facet of WordPress from installation to debugging. It's a wiki with fourteen administrators and well over 70,000 registered users. If you feel the urge to contribute to the WordPress documentation, register and write away in the WordPress Codex. We hope you'll find this book a cross between a companion and a travel guide to the Codex.

Finally, mailing lists (and their archives) exist for various WordPress contributors and communities. A current roster is available online at `codex.wordpress.org/Mailing_Lists`; of particular interest may be the wp-docs list for Codex contributors and the wp-hackers list for those who work on the WordPress core and steer its future directions.

WordPress and the GPL

WordPress is licensed under the Gnu Public License (GPL) version 2, contained in the `license.txt` file that you'll find in the top-level code distribution. Most people don't read the license, and simply understand that WordPress is an open source project; however, pockets of corporate legal departments still worry about the viral component of a GPL license and its implications for additional code or content that gets added to, used with, or layered on top of the original distribution. Much of this confusion stems from liberal use of the words "free" and "copyright" in contexts where they are inappropriately applied.

We're not lawyers, nor do we play them on the Internet or on television, and if you really want to understand the nuances of copyright law and what constitutes a "conveyance" of code, pick up some of Lawrence Lessig's or Cory Doctorow's work in those areas. We include this section to assuage IT departments who may be dissuaded from using WordPress as an enterprise content management system by overly zealous legal teams. Don't let this happen to you; again, if WordPress is acceptable to CNN and the *Wall Street Journal*, two companies that survive on the copyrights granted to their content, it probably fits within the legal strictures of most corporate users as well.

The core tenet of the GPL ensures that you can always get the source code for any distribution of GPL-licensed software. If a company modifies a GPL-licensed software package and then redistributes that newer version, it has to make the source code available as well. This is the "viral" nature of GPL at work; its goal is to make sure that access to the software and its derivatives is never reduced in scope. If you plan on modifying the WordPress core and then distributing that code, you'll need to make sure your changes are covered by the GPL and that the code is available in source code form. Given that WordPress is written in PHP, an interpreted language, distributing the software and distributing the source code are effectively the same thing.

Following are some common misperceptions and associated explanations about using WordPress in commercial situations.

"Free software" means we can't commercialize its use. You can charge people to use your installation of WordPress, or make money from advertisements running in your blog, or use a WordPress content

management platform as the foundation of an online store. That's how `wordpress.com` works; it also enables Google to charge advertisers for using their Linux-based services. You can find professional quality WordPress themes with non-trivial price tags, or you can pay a hosting provider hundreds or thousands of dollars a year to run your MySQL, PHP, Apache, and WordPress software stack; both involve commercialization of WordPress.

If we customize the code to handle our own {content types, security policies, obscure navigational requirements} we'll have to publish those changes. You're only required to make the source code available for software that you distribute. If you choose to make those changes inside your company, you don't have to redistribute them. On the other hand, if you've made some improvements to the Word-Press core, the entire community would benefit from them. Getting more staid employers to understand the value of community contribution and relax copyright and employee contribution rules is sometimes a bit challenging, but the fact that you had a solid starting point is proof that other employers made precisely that set of choices on behalf of the greater WordPress community.

The GPL will "infect" content that we put into WordPress. Content — including graphical elements of themes, posts, and pages managed by WordPress — is separated out from the WordPress core. It's managed by the software, but not a derivative of or part of the software. Themes, however, are a derivative of the WordPress code and therefore also fall under the GPL, requiring you to make the source code for the theme available. Note that you can still charge for the theme if you want to make it commercially available. Again, the key point here is that you make the source code available to anyone who uses the software. If you're going to charge for the use of a theme, you need to make the source code available under the GPL as well, but as pointed out previously, users installing the theme effectively get the source code.

More important than a WordPress history lesson and licensing examination are the issues of what you can do with WordPress and why you'd want to enjoy its robustness. The next section looks at WordPress as a full-fledged content management system, rather than simply a blog editing tool.

CONTENT AND CONVERSATION

Multiple linear feet of shelves in bookstores are filled with volumes that will improve your writing voice, literary style, blogging techniques, and other aspects of your content creation abilities. One of our goals for this book is define the visual, stylistic, and context management mechanisms you can build with WordPress to shape vibrant user communities around your content. That context stimulates conversation with your readers. It's not just about the words in each post, or even if you're an interesting writer. How will people find you? How will you stand out in the crowd? How do you put your own imprint on your site, and personalize it for whatever purpose: personal, enterprise, community, or commercially measured?

WordPress as a Content Management System

Blogging systems have their roots in simple content management operations: create a post, persist it in stable storage such as a filesystem or database, and display the formatted output based on some set of temporal or keyword criteria. As the richness and types of content presented in blog pages expanded, and the requirements for sorting, searching, selecting, and presenting content grew to include metadata and content taxonomies, the line between vanilla, single-user–targeted blogging software and enterprise-grade content management systems blurred.

Content management systems (CMS) handle the creation, storage, retrieval, description or annotation, and publication or display of a variety of content types. CMS also covers workflow tasks, typically from an editorial or publishing perspective, but equally including actions such as approval and marking content for additional editing or review. The WordPress Dashboard, covered in detail in Chapter 2, provides those elements of workflow management and editorial control. WordPress isn't the only open source content management system in widespread use today; the Drupal and Joomla projects are equally popular choices. Drupal and Joomla start from the perspective of managing content repositories; they handle a variety of content types, multiple authors in multiple roles, and getting the content to a consumer that requests it. WordPress is at its heart a blogging system, and the end focus is on displaying content to a reader. Although areas of functional overlap exist, you can integrate WordPress with other content management systems, a process covered in detail in Chapter 12.

WordPress has established itself as a *bona fide* content management system through its design for extensibility and the separation of content persistence from content display. Taking some liberties with the Model-View-Controller design pattern, WordPress separates the MySQL persistence layer as a data model, the theme-driven user interface and display functions, and the plugin architecture that interposes functionality into the data to presentation flow. Most important, WordPress stores content in raw form, as input by the user or an application posting through the WordPress APIs. Content is not formatted, run through templates, or laid out until the page is rendered, yielding immense power to the functions that generate the actual HTML. At the same time, the data model used by WordPress uses a rich set of tables to manage categories (taxonomies), content tags (folksonomies), author information, comments, and other pieces of cross-reference value. We explore the WordPress database schema that makes this possible in Chapter 6.

Although that design gives WordPress incredible power and flexibility as a content management system, it also requires knowledge of how those data persistence and control flows are related (it was a search for such a dissection of WordPress in functional terms that got us together to write this book).

Creating Conversation

Conversation is king; content is just something to talk about.

— Cory Doctorow

A robust CMS is measured by the utility of its content. Even the richest content types and most well-managed processes are of low return if nobody actually consumes the outputs. It's not sufficient to install blogging software, write a few posts, and hope the world shows up on your virtual doorstep; you need to create what Tim O'Reilly calls an "architecture of participation." Social networking, advertising, feeds, and taking steps to ensure your site shows up in search engine results will drive readers to your site; the design, branding, and graphic elements coupled with the quality of your content will encourage them to take the steps toward active participation.

Look at the problem from the perspective of a reader: in a world of tens of millions of blogs (many of which have a "first post" and not much else) how will you be found, heard, and echoed? Your Twitter followers should want to read your blog, and your WordPress blog can update your Twitter feed.

Conversely, your Twitter updates may appear in your WordPress blog's sidebar, marrying the ultra-short content timeline to the more thoughtful one. If you're active on Facebook, you can import blog entries into a public figure page (you're a writer, if not a more famous and self-promoting category), and Facebook readership will drive traffic back to your blog. If you cover specific, detailed, or arcane areas in your writing, Google searches for those terms should direct readers to your blog, where they'll join the conversation. We cover getting content into WordPress from social media and other content systems in Chapter 9, "Content Aggregation," and look at how your WordPress content can be more broadly distributed in Chapter 10, "Crafting a User Experience."

GETTING STARTED

Before any serious work on presentation, style, or content begins, you need a home for your blog (despite the previous discussion about WordPress and content management systems, we'll refer to your blog and the actual WordPress installation that implements it interchangeably, mostly for convenience and brevity). Factors affecting your choice include:

➤ **Cost:** Free hosting services limit your options as a developer, and frequently preclude you from generating money from advertising services. More expensive offerings may include better support, higher storage or bandwidth limits, or multiple database instances for additional applications.

➤ **Control:** What tools are provided for you to manage your MySQL database, files comprising the WordPress installation, and other content types? If you want to be able to muck around at the SQL level, or manage MySQL through a command-line interface, you should ensure your hosting provider supports those interfaces.

➤ **Complexity:** You can install the Apache web server with a PHP interpreter, MySQL, and the WordPress distribution yourself, but most hosting providers have wrapped up the installation process so that some of the rough edges are hidden from view. If you expect to need technical support on the underlying operating system platform, find a provider (including your own IT department) that provides that support in a reasonable time frame.

This section takes a quick look at some hosting options, walks through the basics of a do-it-yourself installation, and concludes with an overview of the ways in which WordPress and MySQL choose to ignore each other when installation goes into the weeds.

Hosting Options

Three broad categories of WordPress hosting exist, each with trade-offs between administrative complexity and depth of control. The easiest and most popular is to use `wordpress.com`, a free hosting service run by Automattic using WordPress MU. You can install themes and plugins through the Dashboard but you can only enable or disable the choices pre-installed for you. Further, you won't have access to the underlying MySQL databases, core code, or be able to integrate WordPress with other systems. You can redirect one of your own URLs to `wordpress.com`, but if you want full control over everything from the code to the URLs used, you're probably looking at a paid option. For our readers, the free route may be a reasonable first step, but we're assuming you're going to want to perform surgery on your installation.

You'll find a starter list of for-fee hosting providers on WordPress.org, including the paid option on `wordpress.com`. Most have the latest, or close to latest, releases of the WordPress core available as a package to be installed in conjunction with MySQL and a web server. The third hosting option is to install everything on servers that you own and operate. If your servers live in a hosting facility but you enjoy root administrative access, that's equivalent to a do-it-yourself installation.

WordPress requires a web server with PHP support, a URL rewriting facility, and an instance of MySQL. Apache is the most popular option for front-ending WordPress because it provides PHP interpretation through `mod_php` and URL rewriting in `mod_rewrite`. There is growing interest in lighttpd (Lighty) as a replacement for Apache, although the URL rewriting functionality needs a bit of hand-holding. Finally, you can use Microsoft's IIS 7.0 as a web server with its `URL_rewrite` module. The emphasis on URL rewriting stems from WordPress's support for "pretty" permalinks to blog entries, allowing you to create a URL tree organized by date, category, tag, or other metadata. Those mnemonic or readable URLs are mapped into MySQL database indices for the corresponding pages using the `.htaccess` file (in Apache parlance). It's a case of dynamic content generation, this time starting from the user path to the page in question, and relying heavily on your web server's muscle to map public neatness into internal structure. Technically, URL rewriting isn't required to install WordPress, but it's good to have because it gives you tremendous flexibility in the presentation and naming conventions used for your content's URLs. We cover permalink design and practices more in Chapter 2, but keep the requirement in mind as you select your WordPress substrate.

Up to this point we've mentioned MySQL in passing, but a brief review of MySQL requirements rounds out the hosting prerequisite list. It's worth establishing some terminology and distinguishing between the MySQL software, database instances, and WordPress instances using MySQL. When you install and configure MySQL, you have a full-fledged relational database system up and running. It doesn't have to be configured on the same machine as your web server, and some hosting providers will create horizontally scalable MySQL "farms" in parallel to their web server front ends. An *instance* of MySQL running on a server can support multiple *databases*, each with a unique name. When you install Word-Press, you'll need to know the *name* of the MySQL database reserved for your content, although this information may be auto-generated and configured for you if you're using a provider that supports WordPress and MySQL as an integrated package. WordPress creates a number of relational data *tables* in that named database for each blog that you create.

Confusion results from nomenclature and complexity. You (or your hosting provider) may run multiple MySQL instances on multiple servers, and you'll need to know where your database is hosted. Because each instance of MySQL can run multiple databases, and each database contains groups of tables, it's possible to run multiple MySQL based applications on the same hosting platform, using one MySQL instance or even one MySQL database.

If you want to have multiple WordPress blogs on the same server, you can share a single MySQL database instance for all of them provided you configure WordPress to distinguish the *MySQL database table names* within the MySQL database. It's a simple configuration option that we cover in the next section, and it highlights the distinction between multiple sets of tables in a database and multiple databases for distinct applications.

Once you've secured the necessary foundation, it's time to get the code up and running. Even if you're using a hosting provider that installs MySQL and WordPress for you, it's worth knowing how the server-side components interact in case you need to track down a problem when you're deep in plugin development.

Do It Yourself Installation

The famous, fabled, fabulous five-minute WordPress installation is a reality when everything is configured and coordinated properly. This section walks through the steps that are often hidden from view when you use a provider with packaged installs, and highlights some of the common misfires between WordPress and MySQL instances.

The installation process is quite simple (assuming that your web server and MySQL server are already running): Download the WordPress package and install it in your web server's directory tree, then navigate to your top-level URL and complete the configuration. One (compound) sentence describes it completely.

It's possible and even advisable to install a fully functioning WordPress instance on your laptop or development machine, particularly if you are going to be working on the core, developing plugins or otherwise making changes that would create embarrassing failures during testing on a public web site. MacOS X comes with an Apache web server (with PHP and URL rewriting); download MySQL from mysql.com, or use a pre-packaged configuration like MAMP (mamp.info, which includes the phpMyAdmin tool) and you'll have a self-contained development and deployment lab. For other platforms, XAMPP (www.apachefriends.org) has a neatly integrated platform stack that runs on Windows, Mac OS and Linux foundations. Having everything under one hood is a powerful option for examining failure modes, as you'll see in the next two sections.

Installing WordPress Files

If you download the WordPress code from wordpress.org, you'll get a zip (or tarball) archive that expands into a directory called "wordpress." The first part of a WordPress installation is to get the code into your web server's directory structure, and ensuring you have it in the right place is a critical step. Gloss over this part and you'll find your blog ends up with a URL like example.com/wordpress and you'll either have to start over or e-mail ugly URLs to your friends and family. If that's what you want, to distinguish your blog from other content on your web site or to isolate multiple blogs, choosing the filesystem layout is equally important.

Pick the top-level directory where you want to install WordPress. Most commonly, this is the root directory for your web server, and if you're using a hosting provider it's probably the subdirectory called public_html in the file tree. If you are using a packaged install where there's a menu asking you for the target location, make sure you pick this top-level directory (and yes, you know that it already exists, that's the point!); if you're copying files from your local machine to the web server target using an FTP client, make sure you pick the right destination. The somewhat obvious move to copy the zip file to the server then unpack it will put everything into a "wordpress" subdirectory, and if you want your blog's URL to be example.com rather than example.com/wordpress, move the files "up" one directory level before proceeding. There is a configuration option to have your WordPress installation in a subdirectory to your top-level URL, so it's not fatal if you drop WordPress into a less-than-desirable filesystem geography. We cover that at the end of this section.

Once the WordPress files are installed, your filesystem browser should show you something like Figure 1-1, with an index.php and template wp-config-sample.php file. That's the entirety of the WordPress system, which runs effectively within the web server's PHP interpreter.

At this point, if you're doing a manual installation, you'll want to create your own wp-config.php file by editing the sample provided and saving it in your top-level WordPress directory. As an alternative, you can navigate to your blog's URL, and the WordPress code will realize there's no configuration file and present you with a dialog boxes like those in Figures 1-2 and 1-3 where you can fill in the details. You'll need the MySQL database name, database username, and some idea of the WordPress database table prefix (other than the default wp_). These lower-level details are the guts of the next section on database configuration. If you are using a hosting provider with packaged installations you probably won't see this step, because the WordPress files will be extracted and the MySQL database information will be automatically inserted into a configuration file, no blogger-serviceable parts inside.

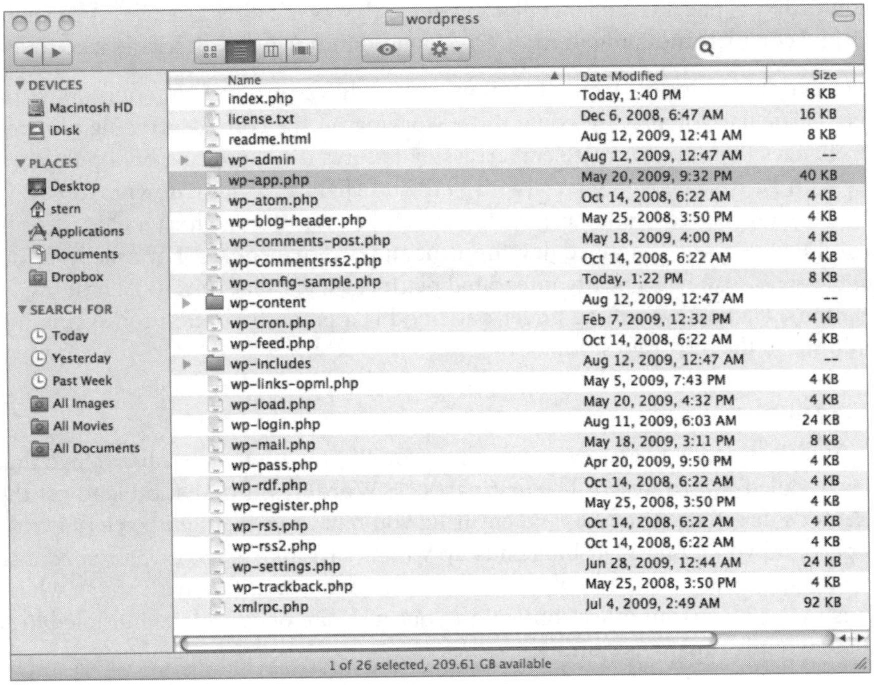

FIGURE 1-1: A clean but unconfigured WordPress installation

What do you do if you already have HTML or other content at your target URL, and you want to add WordPress to an existing site? Disposition of existing files depends on your desired first user experience upon navigating to your URL. If you want visitors to see your blog, and to use WordPress as a content management system as we've described here, your best choice is to save existing content and convert it into blog posts or pages, effectively making your previous site color commentary and context for your WordPress-driven site. Alternatively, you can install WordPress in a subdirectory, keep your existing index.html file, and direct readers to your blog through a button or link on your extant home page. Don't leave this to chance; if you have an index.html file and then install WordPress, you'll have an index.php and an index.html file side by side and users will see one or the other depending upon the Directory Index configuration of your site's web server. Actions on existing content should be informed by how much traffic that content is driving to your site: if your pages are responsible for search engine traffic, you probably don't want to disrupt the existing URLs that have been cached, and should install WordPress in a subdirectory. If you feel strongly about making WordPress the wrapper around the user experience, move the content and include URL rewriting or redirection for pages that move into the WordPress world. We'll cover migrating existing content from a variety of formats and systems into WordPress in Chapter 14.

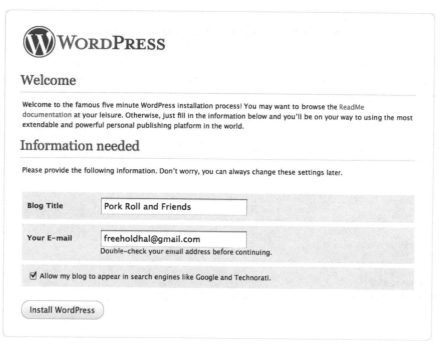

FIGURE 1-2: Basic auto-configuration dialog box

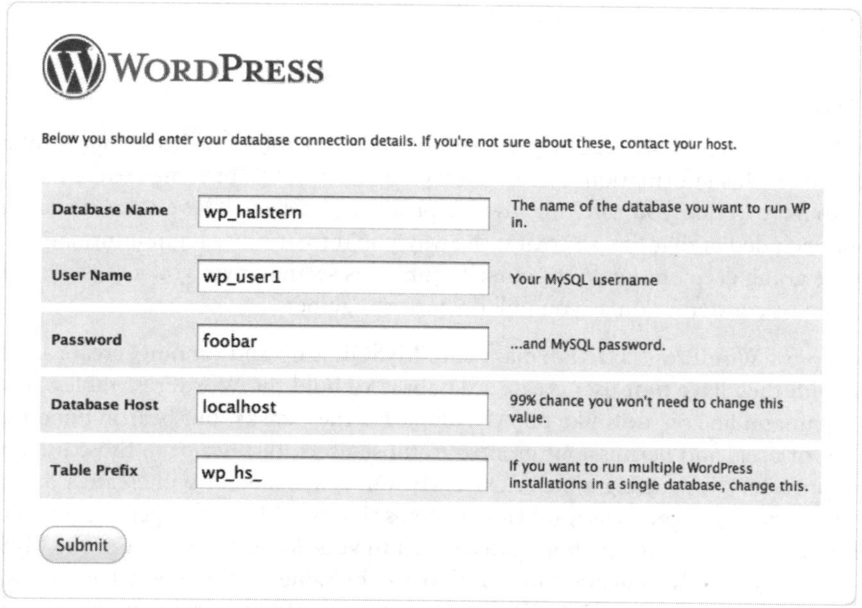

FIGURE 1-3: Database configuration dialog box

If you used a hosting provider's packaged installation, or if you manually created a `wp-config.php` file and then navigated to your top-level blog URL, WordPress should have completed creating the database tables, created an administrative user for your blog, and set an initial password. Upon a successful installation, you should see a box like Figure 1-4 that indicates your five minutes of famed installation are done.

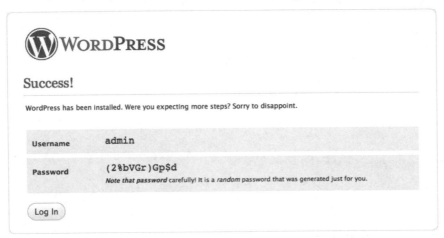

FIGURE 1-4: Administrative information at the conclusion of a clean install

The next section covers the MySQL-WordPress configuration dance in more detail, and is suitable reading even if thinking about SQL gives you hives. If you're up and running, you can skip the next section and go right into "First Time Administration."

Database Configuration

If your hosting provider spun up a MySQL database and created a user for you, check your resultant `wp-config.php` file to gather this information. It is necessary for the MySQL probing covered in this section, and it's good to have in case you run into MySQL problems later on. There's a username and password combination included in that file, so treat it the way you'd treat other login information. On the other hand, if you're going deep on the do-it-yourself route, this section gives you a sense of what's likely to create confusion or consternation as you pull the pieces together.

In theory, MySQL set up for WordPress is trivial: make sure MySQL is up and running, create a Word-Press user in MySQL, and then have that user create a database to hold the WordPress tables. You can use the MySQL command line or tools like phpMyAdmin for these tasks, but bear in mind that MySQL has its own set of users and permissions granted to those users, distinct from those used by your (or your hosting provider's) operating system. Once MySQL is installed, it will create a default table of users and grants, adding a "root" user on Unix systems that is a MySQL superuser, unrelated to the Unix root user. However, if you're attempting to connect to your MySQL instance as the MySQL root user, those connections can only be made from localhost – the same machine on which MySQL is running. If you want to learn more about MySQL permissions, the table governing grants of those permissions to users, and how MySQL users are managed, refer to the "MySQL Reference Manual" (http://dev.mysql.com/doc/) and the sections on securing the initial MySQL accounts.

No set naming conventions exist for WordPress users or databases; hosting providers will typically prepend the name of the package or your account information to distinguish users that benefit from MySQL database co-tenancy. Again, it's possible to have multiple databases, owned by the same user or different MySQL users, running in a single MySQL database server instance. In the example shown in Figure 1-3, we used wp_ as a prefix for both usernames and database names, at least providing a hint to the database administrator that these belong to a WordPress installation.

What can go wrong between WordPress and MySQL? Three primary root causes of installation failure exist: your web server can't even find the MySQL server to begin with, it connects to the database but can't log in, or it logs in successfully but can't find the named database in which to create the WordPress tables. Note that all of these conditions need to be fulfilled at installation time; there has to be some basic database structure to contain the admin user before you can log in as that admin.

Web server can't find MySQL. Either you have the hostname for the MySQL server noted incorrectly in the wp-config.php file, or the web server is looking for a local MySQL instance and can't open the socket connection to it. Here's a simple example: When you run WordPress locally on MacOS, MySQL creates the socket /tmp/mysql.sock for local connections, but the WordPress PHP code is going to look for /var/mysql/mysql.sock through the PHP engine's MySQL module. Simply symbolically link one to the other:

```
# ln -s /tmp/mysql.sock /var/mysql/mysql.sock
```

The actual filesystem path to the local MySQL socket is a function of the database configuration; when it starts up it creates the local socket. Where the PHP engine, and therefore any PHP based applications, look for this socket is PHP configuration dependent. If you want to figure out exactly where the mismatch is, a bit of heavy-handed printf() style debugging helps.

Edit wp-includes/wp-db.php, the set of functions that establish WordPress's database connection. If you're seeing the "Error establishing a database connection" message during installation, insert an echo(mysql_error()); statement where the error is detected to see the details displayed along with the generic message, as shown in Figure 1-5:

```
if (!$this->dbh) {
    echo(mysql_error());
    $this->bail(sprintf(/*WP_I18N_DB_CONN_ERROR*/"
    <h1>Error establishing a database connection</h1>
```

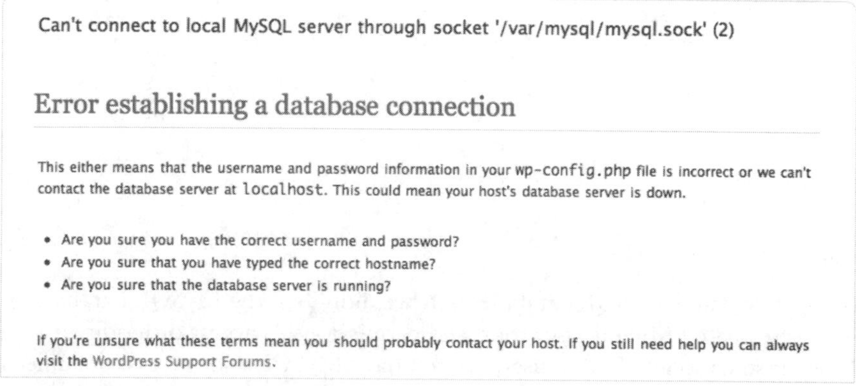

FIGURE 1-5: mysql_error() reporting a socket problem

The `mysql_error()` function is a PHP library function that spits out the error generated by the last MySQL function called.

WordPress finds MySQL but can't log in. Most of the time, the MySQL username or password are wrong, particularly when you have to copy some arbitrary username generated by a hosting provider. Double-check your username data, and verify that it is reflected properly in your `wp-config.php` file. You may also run into a password authentication issue when using MySQL 4.1 or MySQL 5.0 with some web servers' PHP implementations; they only support the older MySQL 4.0 password hashing scheme. If this is the case, use MySQL's `OLD_PASSWORD()` function to hash your WordPress user's password in the backward-compatible format; the magic SQL incantation (at the MySQL command-line prompt or within the SQL window of MAMP) to address this is:

```
SET PASSWORD FOR user@host = OLD_PASSWORD('password');
```

where `user@host` is your WordPress database username and database hostname, and `password` is the (clear text) password you provided in the configuration file.

WordPress connects to MySQL but can't select the database. Just because the web server can log in to the database server with your WordPress database user information doesn't mean that there's necessarily a database available to that user. This is another scenario best diagnosed with `mysql_error()`, inserting it in `wp-db.php` where the selection error is identified:

```
function select($db) {
    if (!@mysql_select_db($db, $this->dbh)) {
        $this->ready = false;
        echo(mysql_error());
        $this->bail(sprintf(/*WP_I18N_DB_SELECT_DB*/'
<h1>Can&#8217;t select database</h1>
        ..
```

If your attempts to complete installation result in an error box like that shown in Figure 1-6, after inserting the `mysql_error()` statement as described earlier, your MySQL database wasn't created under the appropriate database user, or the database user doesn't have privileges to use it. Double-check what MySQL believes using the command line:

```
% /usr/local/mysql/bin/mysql -u wp_user1 -p
Enter password:
Welcome to the MySQL monitor.  Commands end with; or \g.
Your MySQL connection id is 174
Server version: 5.1.37 MySQL Community Server (GPL)
mysql> show databases;
+ - - - - - - - - - +
| Database          |
+ - - - - - - - - - +
| information_schema |
| test              |
+ - - - - - - - - - +
2 rows in set (0.00 sec)
```

Once we logged in as our designated MySQL database user, we didn't see the MySQL database — in this case, it was probably created by MySQL user root, and permissions to access or modify it weren't granted to the WordPress installation's MySQL user. . If you have MySQL root access, or sufficient

MySQL user privileges to create new databases within the MySQL instance, it's easy enough to create a database once logged in on the command line:

```
mysql> create database wp_halstern;
Query OK, 1 row affected (0.00 sec)
```

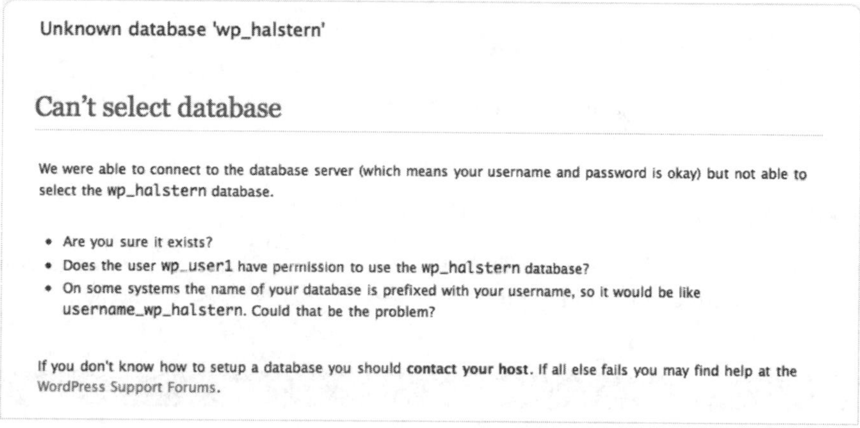

Unknown database 'wp_halstern'

Can't select database

We were able to connect to the database server (which means your username and password is okay) but not able to select the wp_halstern database.

- Are you sure it exists?
- Does the user wp_user1 have permission to use the wp_halstern database?
- On some systems the name of your database is prefixed with your username, so it would be like username_wp_halstern. Could that be the problem?

If you don't know how to setup a database you should **contact your host**. If all else fails you may find help at the WordPress Support Forums.

FIGURE 1-6: MySQL database selection error

Again, it's important to distinguish operating system users from MySQL users from WordPress users. MySQL users are defined in the database and granted privileges to create databases, muck with tables, and otherwise generate useful data. WordPress users exist within the WordPress database tables created during install; they only have privilege, context, and meaning once you're logged in to WordPress.

Once you have a clean WordPress installation, you should see a collection of tables named according to the table prefix you set in wp-config.php; again, this is easy enough to verify using the MySQL command line:

```
mysql> use wp_halstern; show tables;
Database changed
+ - - - - - - - - - - - - - +
| Tables_in_wp_halstern     |
+ - - - - - - - - - - - - - +
| wp_hs_comments            |
| wp_hs_links               |
| wp_hs_options             |
| wp_hs_postmeta            |
| wp_hs_posts               |
| wp_hs_term_relationships  |
| wp_hs_term_taxonomy       |
| wp_hs_terms               |
| wp_hs_usermeta            |
| wp_hs_users               |
+ - - - - - - - - - - - - - +
10 rows in set (0.00 sec)
```

In this example, we set the database table prefix to wp_hs_; if we later add another WordPress blog using the same database user and instance, we can simply set a different prefix and have the two blogs co-mingled in the same database table. We dig into the schema and uses of the ten basic WordPress database tables in Chapter 6. For now, once you are happily connected to MySQL, you're ready for some final clean-up and first-time blog administration.

FINISHING UP

Your MySQL database is up and running; there's a home for your content; and your web server is happily executing the WordPress core code.

First-Time Administration

Once you get the first-time admin user information shown in Figure 1-4, proceed to log in and you'll see the basic WordPress Dashboard captured in Figure 1-7.

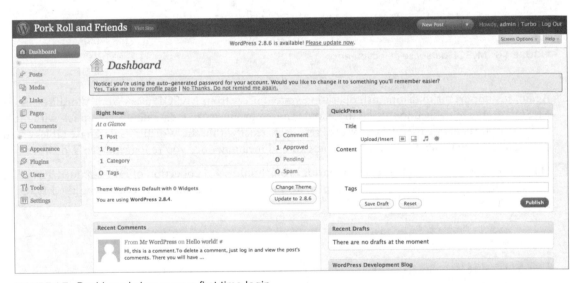

FIGURE 1-7: Dashboard view upon a first-time login

There's an admonition to change your default administrator password, which should be your first administrative step. If you're not redirected to the Dashboard through the Log In button, or if you happen to visit your blog's top-level URL first, either click the Log In link on your blog or explicitly go to the wp-admin subdirectory (example.com/wp-admin) to be presented with a login dialog box. Logging in to your blog takes you to the WordPress Dashboard, which is both amazingly simple in its power and rich in its complexity and exposed features.

What you do next with the Dashboard depends on how happy you are with the basic installation. If, as in the preceding example, you ended up with an older version of WordPress, click the Update to 2.8.6 button to do an in-place upgrade to the latest distribution. In addition to having a strong self-installation feature, WordPress includes self-update functions (in `wp-admin/includes/update.php` if you're looking for them).

WordPress gently reminds you to change the administrative password upon your first login. You can also change the name of the admin user; if you intend to do most of the editing and control as the same user but want something more descriptive, change the username details in the Dashboard while you're setting up a new administrative password.

You may also decide to change some basic configuration options, such as the database name. or the MySQL database user, although you'll only change the default of `"root@localhost"` if you have full control over the web and database servers. The configuration file also has entries for "security keys" that are used to provide stronger security for browser cookies. Security keys are discussed in more detail in Chapter 11. Editing your `wp-config.php` file effects the changes right away. Changing the database table prefix, for example, causes WordPress to instantiate a new set of tables and create a clean-slate blog. Make those edits and then go back to your top-level blog URL and you'll find yourself with new admin user information and logged in to a starter Dashboard as in Figure 1-7. Old tables aren't removed from MySQL, so you'll have to do manual cleanup.

At this point, if you want to set your blog's URL to be different from the location in which you installed WordPress, you can choose Settings and General from the Dashboard and change the URLs for both your blog's top-level address as well as the WordPress installation directory. If you dissociate your blog's URL and the WordPress directory, make sure you move the `index.php` file to the desired top-level URL, and then edit the last line to include the proper subdirectory path to WordPress.

Before creating your first post, it's also a good idea to establish a permalink structure, so that everything you write follows the naming conventions you've chosen to make it relatively easy for readers to find, share, and link to your content. As expected, it's another option in the Settings portion of the Dashboard; options for permalink naming and their impact on performance and database schema are covered in more detail in the next chapter.

Whether it's really been five minutes, or a few hours of tracking down mismatches in hostnames, usernames, and database configurations, you're now ready to publish the first post of your own writing.

First Post

A successful WordPress installation already has a first post and comment published, both assuring that all of the moving pieces are moving in unison, and giving your blog some initial content. When you're ready to add your own first words, either use the right-hand QuickPress panel in the Dashboard to post an entry, or go to Posts and click Add New to be taken to the built-in WordPress editor. Figure 1-8 shows an entry in progress in the QuickPress panel, followed by the updated Dashboard after it's been successfully posted.

If your tastes run more old-school, you can always crank out content in your favorite text editor and then copy it into the editing pane. Be careful with WYSYIWIG word processors such as Microsoft Word or OpenOffice if you want to copy into the WordPress HTML composition window, because the HTML will be riddled with additional tag and style information. Finally, a variety of standalone blog editors, such as illumnix's ecto, publish to WordPress using the Atom Publishing Protocol or XML-RPC. Options for enabling posts to be published remotely are, as you'd expect, in the Dashboard's Settings section under Writing options.

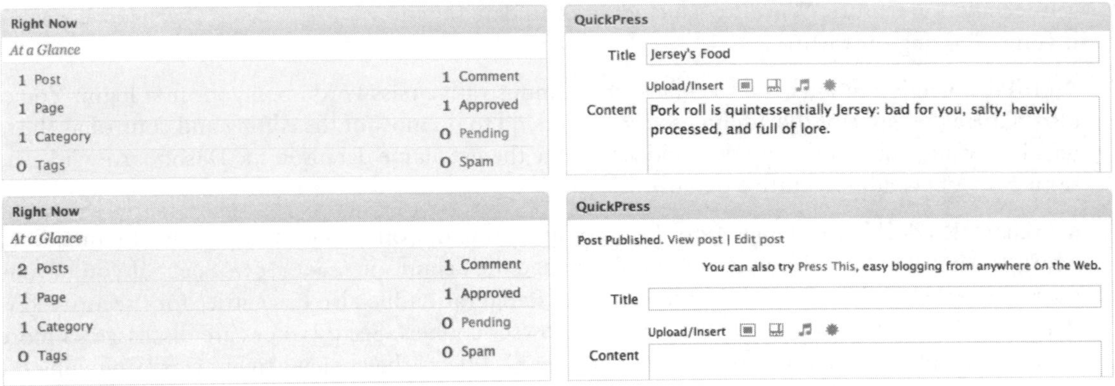

Right Now	
At a Glance	
1 Post	1 Comment
1 Page	1 Approved
1 Category	0 Pending
0 Tags	0 Spam

QuickPress

Title Jersey's Food

Upload/Insert ▣ ▦ ♫ ✳

Content Pork roll is quintessentially Jersey: bad for you, salty, heavily processed, and full of lore.

Right Now	
At a Glance	
2 Posts	1 Comment
1 Page	1 Approved
1 Category	0 Pending
0 Tags	0 Spam

QuickPress

Post Published. View post | Edit post

You can also try Press This, easy blogging from anywhere on the Web.

Title

Upload/Insert ▣ ▦ ♫ ✳

Content

FIGURE 1-8: Publishing from the QuickPress panel

Click Publish for your own hello world moment. Multiple subsystems created that editing pane, saved the content in a database, generated and saved the referential metadata, and then emitted nice-looking HTML. Most of the user-visible pieces are governed through the Dashboard, and that's what we're going to cover next in this book, so you can change, improve, or integrate those systems to suit your content management and publishing needs. From there, we're going to dive into the core of WordPress so that you can take advantage of its extensibility, friendliness in design, and function.

2

Functional Overview

WHAT'S IN THIS CHAPTER?

➤ Navigating and customizing the Dashboard

➤ Categorizing and tagging posts correctly

➤ Creating and managing users

➤ Uploading and editing media

➤ Installing and configuring themes and plugins

➤ Moderating comments

➤ Importing and exporting content

➤ Creating custom permalink structures

➤ Enabling registration and post contributions

WordPress is a powerful web site software framework that can be used to power a simple blog or customized to power much more complex web sites. By understanding how WordPress works you can begin to learn all that WordPress is capable of.

This chapter reviews how WordPress functions, how to manage and categorize your content, how to work with users and roles, how to extend WordPress with themes and plugins, and also how to configure your WordPress-powered web site to work how you want it to with various configuration settings

THE DASHBOARD

The first time you log in to WordPress, you are presented with what is called the Dashboard. The Dashboard is where you manage everything related to your web site including content, discussions, appearance, plugins, and overall web site functionality. The Dashboard has a focus on efficiency and simplicity, with most common administrator tasks just a single click away. You can find the Dashboard at `http://example.com/wp-admin`.

Dashboard Widgets

The WordPress Dashboard, shown in Figure 2-1, contains multiple widgets, or blocks, of information for quick access. These widgets provide various information and functionality for administering your WordPress web site.

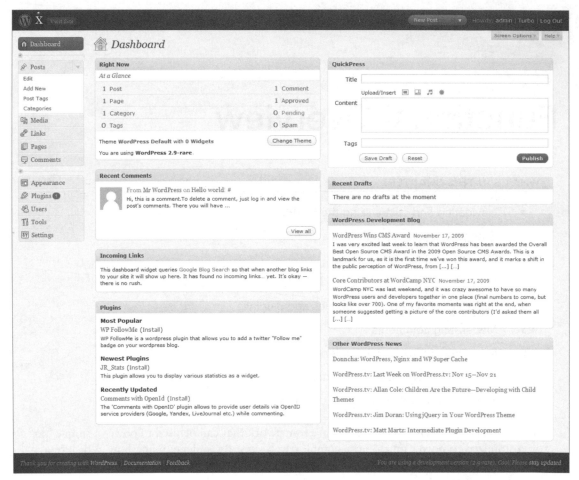

FIGURE 2-1: Default WordPress Dashboard

The Right Now widget shows top-level stats under the At a Glance title regarding your web site's content. Here, you can view how many posts, pages, drafts, comments, and even spam you currently have in your web site. Clicking any statistic takes you to the corresponding section for managing that content. Below your web site content statistics, the Right Now widget displays what theme you are currently running with total number of installed widgets. This widget count is for your sidebar widgets and not the admin dashboard widgets. Your current WordPress version is also listed. If a new version of WordPress is available, a button appears giving you the option to update.

For quick access to your drafts, check out the Recent Drafts widget. This widget shows posts that you are currently working on, but haven't been published on your web site yet. Click a recent draft to continue working on that post. Once a post has been published or deleted, it will no longer be displayed in the Recent Drafts widget. To view all recent drafts click the View All button.

Need to blog in a hurry? The QuickPress widget is the quickest way to create a new blog post. You can fill in your title and content, just as you would on a normal post. You can even upload and insert an image, or any type of media, right from QuickPress. From here you can save the post as a draft, reset all of the fields, or publish the post for the world to see!

To see who is linking to your web site, use the Incoming Links widget. This widget uses Google Blog Search (http://blogsearch.google.com/) to find incoming links to your web site. If any incoming links exist, they are displayed here in reverse chronological order, showing the most recent at the top. The Saying link takes you directly to the post that links to your web site so you can view the full context of the post. Some links may not show up in this list, so don't be alarmed if links pointed to your web site are not displayed here. For more details on incoming links and traffic, use a more advanced analytics package such as Google Analytics or the WordPress stats plugin.

The admin dashboard also contains two RSS widgets, one for the WordPress Development blog and the other for the Planet WordPress RSS feed. The WordPress Development blog contains news and information regarding the development of WordPress. This blog is where new versions of WordPress are announced, as well as beta and release candidate information. The Planet WordPress feed is a collection of WordPress-related blogs featuring news and information regarding all aspects of WordPress. These two RSS widgets can be changed to display any RSS feed you like. To change an RSS widget, hover over the title and click the Edit link that appears. Change the feed to any properly formatted RSS feed and click Save. Now you can display any RSS feed content directly on your WordPress Dashboard.

You can add additional widgets to your WordPress Dashboard from plugins. Plugins can use the Dashboard Widgets API to add any custom widget to the admin dashboard. Widgets can provide any type of custom functionality provided from a plugin. We'll discuss installing plugins and widgets in more detail later in this chapter.

Customizing the Dashboard

You can completely customize your dashboard by dragging and dropping your widgets to different positions. You can minimize any widget by hovering over the title and clicking the arrow that appears to the right of the widget title. This minimizes the widget and displays only the widget title, hiding the rest of the widget. You can also hide any widgets you don't want visible by unchecking that widget under the Screen Options tab in the header. To edit any Dashboard Widget settings, hover over the title of the widget and an Edit link appears. Click that link to view the widget's available settings.

Screen Options

The Screen Options tab shown in Figure 2-2 enables you to modify display settings on any screen of your dashboard. Each screen shows different options under the Screen Options tab. For example, clicking the Screen Options tab under Posts ➪ Edit allows you to adjust which fields are displayed. You can also adjust how many posts per page are shown.

FIGURE 2-2: Screen options tab located in the header of the admin dashboard

Under the Screen Options tab on the admin dashboard you can also adjust how many columns you want displayed, choosing between two to four columns present on your dashboard. To change this option click the Screen Options tab. Then select two, three, or four columns for your widgets to be displayed in.

Admin Menu

The WordPress Admin Menu is located on the left-hand side of the admin dashboard and features links to different administrator SubPanels. *SubPanels* are the individual admin pages in WordPress. When you hover over any SubPanel link in the menu a small arrow appears to the right of the menu item. Clicking this arrow expands that menu item to show submenu items. WordPress remembers which menus are expanded so if you log out and then log back in you will notice the exact same menus expanded as when you left. This helps hide certain Admin Menus that you don't use as often.

FIGURE 2-3: The WordPress Admin menu

The Admin Menu can also be collapsed to only show icons, giving you more space for your primary content. Just click the horizontal arrow located just below Dashboard or Comments to collapse the Admin Menu. When the Admin Menu is collapsed you can hover over any icon to show all menu options below that item. Collapsing the menu gives you a larger workable area in the admin dashboard.

CREATING AND MANAGING CONTENT

At the heart of any web site is content. Content is the primary reason web sites gain traffic and probably one of the key reasons you decided to use WordPress for your web site. WordPress makes managing content a breeze and is easily controllable by beginners and experts alike.

In this part of the chapter we cover all aspects of content in WordPress, from creating and managing posts and pages to working with the link manager. Content is one of the most important parts of your web site so it's crucial to understand how to manage your content in WordPress.

Creating Posts

Posts are content entries that typically display in reverse chronological order on your web site. These are generally considered to be blog posts, but can be used for a variety of reasons including news, events, business data, and much more. All posts are saved with a date and time stamp making the content dated material. Posts are also categorized and can be tagged to help filter posts by either category or tag.

The first step to creating a post is to click the Add New link under the Posts SubPanel. Creating a post couldn't be easier; the only actual required fields are either the post content or title. The first box on the Add New Post screen is the title of your post. Go ahead and fill in a title of "My First Post". This is one of the most important parts of your post because it describes what your post is about. It is also heavily used for search engine optimization. If you have permalinks enabled the title is also used in your post permalink or URL depending on the permalink structure set. If you leave a post title blank, the permalink will be the post ID. The current post's permalink is displayed below the post title after the initial save.

The next step in creating a post is writing your post content. The post content box, located directly below the title, is where your post content is entered. You can use either the Visual or HTML editor to create your post. To switch between the two just click the tab for which editor you would like to view. The visual editor features many word-processor-like buttons across the top of the content editor. Most of these options are standard formatting for word processing programs such as Microsoft Word. For example, clicking the B icon bolds any text you have selected or are about to write. Go ahead and enter in whatever content you like for your example post.

You can also add images or media to your post. Images are a great way to give your post visual appeal. Let's add an image to your example post. To add an image to your post, click the Add Image icon located next to the Upload/Insert text. The media overlay window appears using a lightbox effect called Thickbox. The Thickbox effect is a web site popup that "dims" the rest of the web site, putting focus on the popup. From here you can add new images, select images that have already been added to the post, and select images uploaded anywhere on your web site using WordPress. Click the Select Image button and select an image from your computer. If you are using the Flash uploader, which is the default uploader, you can select multiple images to upload in one shot. WordPress processes and uploads each image automatically.

After you have uploaded an image, you need to insert that image into your post content. Click the Insert into Post button and your image is inserted into your post. If you are using the visual editor, the image appears in your post content. You can now select the image to adjust alignment and image settings or delete the image from your post. If you are using the HTML editor, the HTML IMG tag appears linking to your newly uploaded image.

Next you'll want to select the appropriate category for your post. *Categories* help group similar posts making it easy for your readers to find additional posts under the same topic. You set the category in the Category meta box located in the right-hand column directly below the Publish box, and you can select multiple categories for a single post. If you want to add a new category, click the + Add New Category link at the bottom of the Category box and fill in your new category name. You can also view the Most Used categories by clicking the tab with the same name. In your example post, create a new category called "Examples" and assign the new post to that category.

You can also add tags to your post. Tags are keywords that describe what your post is about. They should be short and sweet, generally no more than two words per tag. The Tag meta box is located directly under the Categories box by default. Add tags to your post by entering a set of tag keywords separated by a comma. You can easily remove tags by clicking the small X next to each tag. Removing a tag will only remove that tag from your post, not your entire tag collection. As you type in a tag WordPress automatically searches for tags using the same letters, and will prompt you with them, making it quicker to find tags you have already used on previous posts. Go ahead and add a few tags to your example post now.

Once you are satisfied with your post, you'll want to publish it. To publish your example post, just click the blue Publish button. Your example post is now published and viewable on your web site. The Publish meta box also contains buttons that control the state of your post. It has three states by default: Published, Pending Review, and Draft. Published status indicates that a post is publicly viewable on your web site. Pending Review status is a post waiting to be reviewed and approved by an Editor or Administrator. Any post submitted by a Contributor is set to Pending Review. Draft status is a post that you are currently working on, but hasn't been published yet.

These posts are usually posts you are still working on writing and still need some more additional work.

You can also modify the post date by clicking the Edit button next to the date/time. To schedule a post to automatically publish at a future date and time, simply enter that date and time and click Ok. Once the publish date has been changed, the post Publish button changes to Schedule. When you click the Schedule button your new post will automatically be scheduled to be published on the date and time you have saved. This is a great feature if you are going on vacation but don't want a large lapse in fresh content on your web site. You can also set the post date in the past. This is useful if you have a large gap in your posts and want to fill in the blanks with older posts.

Finally, you can change the visibility on a post. Public posts are publicly viewable by anyone on your web site. Password-protected posts are published to everyone, but can only be viewed if you know the correct password. Private posts are only viewable by web site Editors and Administrators and not viewable by the public.

Each of the meta boxes displayed on the post add/edit screen can be dragged and dropped however you like. This can help you organize these meta boxes based on your usage, moving the boxes higher up that you use more frequently. To drag a meta box, just click the title of the box and drag to the desired new position on the page.

Managing Posts

You can manage all of your posts in WordPress under the Posts ➪ Edit SubPanel. Here you will see all of your posts listed, regardless of their current status. Notice that your example post "My First Post" is now listed at the top of the list. Multiple filter options across the top enable you to filter your posts by status, category, month, and so on. To view all posts at a Draft status, just click the Draft link at the top. You can also search all posts for specific keywords using the search box located at the top right of the Posts Edit screen.

Posts are displayed in a list view by default, but you can also display them in an excerpt view. The excerpt display shows all posts listed with an excerpt of the post content. To toggle which display is used, click the icon for either list or excerpt view located directly below the search keyword box.

Hovering over a post displays multiple options for managing that post, as shown in Figure 2-4.

FIGURE 2-4: Edit post hover action links

The Quick Edit link allows you quick access to edit the post information. The post information is loaded using AJAX, and therefore a page refresh is not necessary. Here you can quickly change the post category, edit the post title, or even change the post slug (permalink). In fact, you can change just about everything on a post except the actual post content using quick edit.

Clicking the Delete link deletes the post from WordPress. Don't get too scared of that link; WordPress confirms that you actually want to delete the post before doing so.

You'll also notice a checkbox next to each post. Checking multiple posts allows you do to a bulk edit or bulk delete on the selected posts. Using the bulk edit enables you to change the post categories, tags, author, comments, status, pings, and sticky option. This is a great time saver if you want to change the category of more than one post or delete a handful of posts.

Creating Pages

Pages in WordPress differ from posts in that they are meant for static informational content. Pages are not defined by dates, categories, or tags, but rather the content that they contain.

To create a new page, click the Add New link under the Pages SubPanel. The page title should be informative on what the page is about. Page titles are generally shorter than post titles (such as About or Contact) but can be as long as you like.

The page content box works exactly the same as a post and features all of the same formatting options. You add images and media the exact same way.

One major difference between pages and posts is the Attributes meta box located directly under the Publish box on the right-hand side. Here you can set your page hierarchy under the Parent option. This allows for pages and sub-pages to be created and assigned. For example, if you had an About page, you could create multiple sub-pages under About, such as About ⇨ Me and About ⇨ This Web site.

If your page requires additional functionality, you can assign it to a page template. Custom page templates allow you to link a WordPress page to a physical PHP template file located in your theme directory. This makes adding custom code or a completely different design to any page extremely easy. We tell you all about this feature in Chapter 8, "Theme Development."

Don't forget to set the appropriate page order for your page. Pages are ordered alphabetically by default, but you can overwrite this using the sort filter. By adding a number to the Order field and using the sort filter you can order your WordPress pages any way you like.

Managing Pages

You manage pages under the Pages ⇨ Edit SubPanel. Managing your pages in WordPress is almost identical to managing posts. You can filter what pages are displayed using the filter options across the top. You can also do a keyword search to filter pages using the search box at the top right. Pages are listed in alphabetical order, unless the sort order has been set on each post. To set the page sort order, hover over any page and click the Quick Edit link. Enter in a number for the Order field based on what order you want your pages displayed. If you want this page displayed first, set it to 0; if you want the page displayed last, set it to a really high number, such as 99. Unless you have 99 other pages, that page will always display last.

Links

WordPress has a built-in link manager system located in the Links SubPanel. Links can be created, categorized, and displayed in various ways on your web site. The links don't have to be to an external web site; they can also be internal links to your own web site.

To add a new link, navigate to Links ⇨ Add New SubPanel in your Admin Menu. Start by filling in the name of the link. The name is typically used for display purposes as the anchor text, and should be short and descriptive about what the web site is. Next fill in the Web Address, which is the fully qualified URL of the link you are creating. If you are adding an internal link, you can use the relative path. The link description is used to describe the new link. This is usually displayed when hovering over the link or just below the link, depending how your theme templates or widgets are configured.

Categorizing your link is a great way to group similar links together. You can add links to multiple link categories. Check all of the categories that you want to assign your link to. You can also create new categories by clicking the + Add New Category link.

Be sure to select the appropriate target for your link. The target determines how the new link opens when clicked. Generally a link to an external web site should open in a new window or tab, in which case you would want to select the _blank target option. Internal links should open in the same window, so the default _none option should be selected.

Once you have filled in the entire link information click the Save button to save your new link in Word-Press. Your newly created link will now show in the links list under the Links SubPanel and anywhere on your web site that displays links.

Trash

WordPress features a Trash section, which works very similar to the Recycle Bin on a Windows computer. Instead of a Delete link for your posts, pages, media, and comments, there is a "Move to Trash" link. Moving any content to the Trash does not delete that content, but instead moves it to the Trash section in WordPress. To permanently delete this content, you must visit the Trash container for that particular type of content and click the Empty Trash button located near the header. This features reduces the issue of permanently deleting content by accident as it is now a two-step process.

The Trash page is simply a filter link located with the rest of the content filters near the header of the content page. Click the Trash link to view all like content items contained in the trash section. If you hover over any content item listed you will be presented with two options: Restore and Delete permanently. Click Restore to move the content item out of the Trash section, or to erase the content completely, click the Delete permanently link. The Trash section is emptied every 30 days, so only move content to Trash if you really want to delete it.

CATEGORIZING YOUR CONTENT

Content categorization is one of the most important aspects of creating content. Properly categorized content makes it easier for visitors to read your web site. It also makes it easier for visitors to navigate your web site for additional content on the same topics.

Correctly categorizing content also allows you to aggregate that content in different places in your theme template files. For example, you could create an "Events" category that shows only posts in your Events News sidebar widget assigned to that category.

Categories versus Tags

Categories and tags are very similar, and thus the question "What's the difference?" is a very common one. Categories are a way of organizing your posts, whereas tags are a way of describing your posts.

For example, a post titled "WordCamp New Jersey Recap" might be filed under the Conference category, but tagged with keywords like WordPress, WordCamp, New Jersey, and NJ.

Another major difference between tags and categories is that categories are hierarchical. This means categories can have sub-categories, and sub-sub categories, whereas tags cannot.

Post Categories

Post categories are just that, a simple way to categorize your content. Each post you create can be assigned to multiple categories. To add your post to a category, select the appropriate category from the Categories meta box, as shown in Figure 2-5.

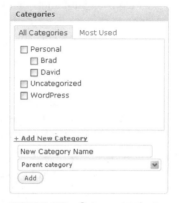

You can also view the Most Used categories by selecting that tab. To add a new category click the + Add New Category link below the Categories meta box.

Categories are managed under the Posts ⇨ Categories SubPanel. From here you can create, edit, and delete all post categories on your web site. You can also search all categories and view all posts assigned to each category. To delete or edit a category, hover over the category you want to work with. Multiple options will appear, including Edit, Quick Edit, and Delete. Clicking the Delete link deletes that category from WordPress. When deleting a category, posts filed under that category

FIGURE 2-5: Category select meta box

are not deleted, but instead are reassigned to the default Uncategorized category. A future release of WordPress will have the ability to choose which category to assign the orphaned posts to.

WordPress also provides a Category to Tag Converter and a Tag to Category Converter. These tools can be used to do exactly that, convert categories to tags and vice versa. Just click the Category to Tag Converter link, select which categories you would like to convert, and click Convert Categories to Tags. Keep in mind that if you convert a category with child categories, the children become top-level orphans.

Tagging Posts

Tags are keywords that describe your post. Think of tags as Post-it notes attached to each post, describing that post. Tags are generally limited to two words per tag, but are typically a single keyword. They differ from categories in that tags are descriptive keywords that describe your individual post. For example, a post titled "Best Cheeseburger Ever" might contain the tags ketchup, mustard, cheese, and burger, but you wouldn't have a Ketchup category unless you planned on writing more on ketchup. Tags are also used by many tag-related sites including Technorati, Delicious, and Flickr.

To add tags to your post simply enter keywords separated by a comma in the Post Tags meta box, as shown in Figure 2-6.

As you type in your tags, WordPress automatically suggests tags based on your existing tags loaded into WordPress. You can also view the most used tags by clicking the Choose from the Most Used Tags in Post Tags link.

FIGURE 2-6: Tag meta box

Tags are managed under the Posts ⇨ Post Tags SubPanel. From here you can create, edit, and delete all post tags on your web site. You can also search all tags and view all posts assigned to each tag.

Categorizing Links

WordPress also features the ability to categorize links. Categorizing links is a great way to display different groups of links across your web site. Link categories are managed under the Links ⇨ Link Categories SubPanel. By default WordPress comes with one link category called Blogroll. You can change this category name to anything you would like, but the default category will always remain.

When you add a new link the link categories are listed in the Categories meta box, as shown in Figure 2-7.

From here you can select which category the new link will be added to. You can also view the most used link categories, and create new link categories by clicking the + Add New Category link.

Deleting a category does not delete the links in that category, but instead assigns all links to the default category.

FIGURE 2-7: Category select meta box for new links

WORKING WITH MEDIA

WordPress features a robust system for managing all of your web site's media. Media refers to the images, video, audio recordings, and files uploaded to your web site using WordPress. Media that is uploaded in WordPress can easily be inserted into any post or page for display. Media can be uploaded and attached at a post/page level or directly to the Media Library.

Media Library

The WordPress Media Library is where you can add, manage, and delete all media across your entire WordPress web site. The Media Library SubPanel enables you to manage all media on your web site, whether uploaded directly in the Media Library or uploaded directly to a post or page.

Uploading Media

You can upload media to your WordPress web site by clicking the Add New link under the Media SubPanel on your Admin Menu. Click the Select Files button to upload media using the Flash uploader. If you experience issues with the Flash uploader (it doesn't work on every host) you can click the link for the Browser Uploader.

One major feature of the Flash uploader that is often overlooked is the ability to upload multiple files at a time. Simply select a group of files in the dialog box that appears and click Open. All files selected are listed showing an upload status bar while the images are uploaded to your web site. The browser uploader can upload only a single file at a time.

If you experience problems uploading media, the first thing to check is the permissions set on your uploads folder. By default WordPress folders should be set to 755 for security reasons, but some hosts require the uploads folder to be set to 777. These numbers represent the chmod access level assigned to each directory and file on your web server. If you are running WordPress on a Windows server you should give the IUSER account write permissions to the uploads folder. This allows WordPress to upload any media files directly to your web site.

WordPress does not filter by file type; therefore all file types are technically supported for uploading. This can also create a security vulnerability and should be locked down if you allow your members to upload media files. Plugins are available that can restrict the media upload to specific file types, such as only images.

Inserting Media

Media is inserted on the Post/Page Edit screen. From here you can select any media that has been uploaded across your web site and insert it directly into your post or page. You can also upload any new media that you would like for use in your post or page.

To insert media, start by clicking one of the four icons located next to the Upload/Insert text link below the post title. The icons represent image, video, sound, and media. Clicking any one of these icons brings up the Thickbox overlay to upload and insert media into your post or page. From here you will notice multiple tabs across the top of the Thickbox, but the two we are focused on are the Gallery and Media Library tabs. The Gallery tab, which only shows up after you upload an image to your post, houses all images uploaded to that particular post. The Media Library tab houses all images uploaded across your entire WordPress web site. Clicking either tab displays images in a list format.

To insert an image into your post, click the Show link located to the right of the image you want to embed. This expands the box and shows you all of the properties associated with that image. Here you can set the image title, caption, and also a short image description. You can also set the link URL for the image, so if the image should link to another web page this is where you would enter it. Be sure to select the correct alignment and size then click the Insert into Post button. Upon clicking this button the Thickbox overlay disappears and the image is embedded into the post content box. If you are using the visual editor you should see your image displayed.

WordPress also has a built in Gallery feature. This feature allows you to upload multiple images to a single post or page and display all of those images in a nicely formatted gallery. To use the gallery, start by uploading multiple images to a post. After you have a couple images uploaded, close the Thickbox overlay by clicking anywhere outside of the popup, or just click the X in the upper right hand corner. Next we'll use a shortcode in our post content to represent the gallery. A shortcode is a specific piece of code, usually wrapped in brackets, that is recognized by WordPress or a plugin. When editing a post or page you will see the actual shortcode, but when viewing the post or page on your web site the shortcode will be replaced by the functionality attached to that shortcode, in this case an image gallery. Drop this shortcode in your post content: `[gallery]` and save your post. An image gallery will now be displayed in your post! The gallery shortcode also supports different options that you can use. To specify the number of columns in your gallery (the default is 3) use this option: `[gallery columns="4"]`. You can also display a gallery from a different post by specifying the post id: `[gallery id="5"]`.

WordPress does not have a built-in video or audio player, therefore any video or audio uploaded to WordPress cannot be automatically embedded in your post or page. To embed video or sound you will need a plugin that supports the proper video format you would like to embed. Many video player plugins are available at the official WordPress.org plugin directory. A great plugin for handling embedded videos is WordTube: `http://wordpress.org/extend/plugins/wordtube/`.

Managing Media

You manage media under the Media ⇨ Library SubPanel. Here you can manage all media uploaded to your WordPress web site. Only media uploaded using WordPress will show up here, so if you used FTP to upload images to your web site they will not be displayed.

You can filter what media is displayed using the filter links located at the top of the page. You can also search your media using the provided search box at the top right.

One interesting feature of the Media Library is the Attached To column. You can upload media in one of two ways: either directly to the Media Library or directly to a post or page. If the media was uploaded directly to a post or page, this field displays the title and date of the post or page it is attached to. Clicking the post title link brings you directly to edit that particular post. If the media was uploaded using the Media Library, this field is blank.

To view all media files uploaded directly from the Media Library, click the Unattached filter. This filter displays all images that were not uploaded directly to a post/page. Also, when you are viewing Unattached images a new button appears just below called Scan for Lost Attachments. Clicking this button checks WordPress attachment records in the database for any detached images. This feature does not actually scan the directories and pull in any images found. When you hover over any unattached images found an option appears to "attach" that image. A Thickbox overlay pops up allowing you to search for a specific post or page to attach the image to.

The Media Library does not feature a bulk edit feature, but you can bulk delete media. Just select the checkbox next to each piece of media that you want to delete, or select the top checkbox to auto select them all, and select Delete from the Bulk Actions drop-down.

Edit Media

WordPress 2.9 introduced a new feature for editing media, specifically images, directly in WordPress. To edit any image you've uploaded in WordPress hover over the image and click the Edit link. Next click the "Edit image" button that appears next to the image thumbnail. This launches the new Edit Media section as shown in Figured 2-8.

Across the top of the Edit Media section are image editing buttons that perform specific editing tasks. The first button is the crop icon, which by default is not clickable. To crop the image, click anywhere on the image and drag the selection box to the desired cropping position. When the selection box exists on the image, the crop button will become active, allowing you to click it to crop the image based on your selection. Also notice the Image Crop section located in the right Edit Media sidebar menu. The selection sizing will automatically fill out as you drag the selection box around prior to cropping. This can help you specify the exact cropping dimensions needed for your image.

The next two buttons are to rotate the image clockwise or counter-clockwise. You can also flip the image horizontally or vertically. The Edit Media toolbar also features undo and redo functionality. This is handy if you make a series of edits but decide you don't like the finished product; you can simply undo the last few edits to revert back to the original. Remember changes are not saved until you click the Save button located just below your image.

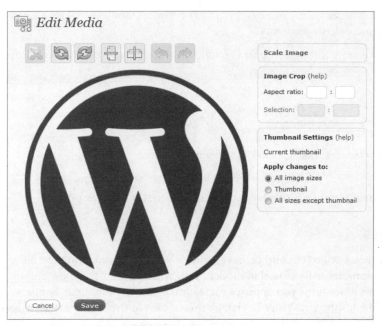

FIGURE 2-8: Edit Media in WordPress

You can easily scale the image by clicking the "Scale Image" link in the right Edit Media sidebar menu. Here you can enter new dimensions for your image. As you type in a new width or height, WordPress will dynamically fill in the appropriate dimension to maintain the aspect ratio. The Thumbnail Settings section lets you select what images the edit changes will apply to. You can apply your changes to all images sizes, just the image thumbnail, or all sizes except the image thumbnail.

COMMENTS AND DISCUSSION

Comments are a standard feature on any blog platform and WordPress is no different. WordPress features many different tools to help you maintain your web site comments and discussion. From comment moderation to comment spam, there is much to think about before opening up your web site to comments from the public.

Managing Comments

You have multiple ways to manage comments in WordPress. The most commonly used method is the Comments SubPanel. Here you can view all comments across your entire WordPress web site. Comments are listed with specific information on the commenter including name, e-mail, IP address, and more. Hovering over any comment gives you moderation options. Click Reply to reply directly to a comment from your dashboard. The comment is displayed as a public comment once added. Comments can be filtered using the links across the top. Filter comments to only show pending, approved, spam, or all comments. You can also search comments for specific keywords using the search box located at the top right.

Comments can also be managed directly from your dashboard. The Recent Comments box allows you to quickly approve, reply, edit, and delete comments.

A quick shortcut to view all comments for a given post is to click the comments icon on your Posts SubPanel, shown in Figure 2-9.

FIGURE 2-9: The comment icon displays the total number of comments on a post

Clicking the icon filters all comments and only displays comments for that particular post.

Moderating Comments

By default WordPress requires that a comment author have a previously approved comment before posting. All new comments are automatically placed in moderation, which means that new comments will not show publicly on your web site until you approve them either on the Comments SubPanel or the Recent Comments box on the dashboard. You can change this option in the Settings ➪ Discussion SubPanel.

Another popular setting is forcing all comments to be approved by an administrator. This removes the previously approved comment rule and forces all comments into moderation regardless of whether there is a previously approved comment. Disabling both of these settings will open up comments to the world, meaning a comment is displayed publicly as soon as it is posted. It's best to avoid this method because it opens up your web site to comment spam.

Handling Comment Spam

Comment spam is an ongoing problem that has been around since the beginning of comments. Comment spam is defined as any comment that is unwanted and generally promoting another web site or product. The Settings ➪ Discussion SubPanel has multiple settings that can help reduce the amount of comment spam your web site receives. For example, you can hold a comment in the moderation queue if it contains more than two links. Multiple links in a comment is a common characteristic of spam. WordPress also provides a keyword blacklist, allowing you to automatically flag a comment as spam if it contains any of the keywords you have listed. This is a good way to moderate comments that contain obscene language, competitor names, and so on.

A number of plugins can help reduce or eliminate comment spam; here are two we recommend:

➤ **Akismet:** One of only two plugins that comes pre-installed with WordPress, Akismet is an anti-spam comment plugin. Created by Automattic, Akismet scans your comments for spam as they are submitted. If a comment is determined to be spam it is automatically flagged as such and not shown on your web site. Akismet learns by combining information about spam captured on all participating web sites and then uses those spam rules to block future spam comments.

➤ **Bad Behavior:** The Bad Behavior plugin works as a gatekeeper, preventing spammers and bots from ever delivering their spam. This plugin complements other spam plugins and can run alongside Akismet without issue. Bad Behavior actually analyzes the delivery methods of comments, rather than their contents, which helps this plugin attack spam in a whole new way.

WORKING WITH USERS

WordPress comes complete with user accounts and roles for an easy and flexible way of controlling access to your WordPress web site. A default installation of WordPress comes with one user account with administrator privileges: the admin account. You can create an unlimited number of user accounts in WordPress with various web site privileges.

Creating New Users

To create a new user in WordPress, navigate to the Users ➪ Add New SubPanel. The only required fields for a new user account are username, e-mail, and password. You can also enter in the user's first and last name, web site, and a user bio. This information can be used in various places on your web site including the author template file discussed in Chapter 8, "Theme Development." Optionally you can select to have the password e-mailed directly to the new user. The default user role is Subscriber, but can be changed to any role that is appropriate for the new user.

If the Allow User Registration option is enabled under the Settings ➪ General SubPanel, visitors can create user accounts on your web site. The new user signup form is located at `http://example.com/wp-register.php`. Once a new user has registered he or she is assigned to the new user role, which by default is set to Subscriber.

Let's create a new administrator account to use on your web site. First fill in the username you would like to use. The username should be unique and hard to guess for security measures. Next, fill in the e-mail address for the new account. This should be an active e-mail account as the new user information will be e-mailed to this address. Now set a strong password for the new administrator. WordPress features a password strength indicator, so make sure your new password is indicated as a strong password. Finally set the Role to Administrator. This gives the new user full administrator privileges on your web site. Click the "Add User" button to create your new user. The user information will be e-mailed to the address you provided.

Managing Users

You can manage all users across your web site under the Users ➪ Authors & Users SubPanel. Upon accessing this page you are presented with a list of all user accounts in WordPress. Multiple filter types across the top allow you to filter by user roles. You can also search for users using the keyword search box located at the top right. Hovering over any user displays the edit and delete links. You cannot delete the account you are logged in to WordPress with; to do that you would need to log out and then back in with a different account first.

To edit any user, click the Edit link that displays when hovering over the user. The Edit User page allows you to edit all aspects of a user account except for the username. To update a username you would need to use a WordPress plugin or update the username directly in your WordPress MySQL database.

You can update all user data here including First and Last name, nickname, and what name you would like to display publicly for this user. By default the public display name is the user's username. You can also change a user's Role on the Edit User page, and update user contact info including the user's e-mail address. This address is used for all web site communication with your users. You can also add a bio to a user account. This is perfect if you are creating an About section for your authors.

The user's data can be displayed anywhere on your web site. Typically the user information is displayed on the Author bio page located in the `author.php` template file of your theme. Many themes today do not come standard with the author template file, but we'll discuss that in more detail in Chapter 8, "Theme Development."

The update password feature is located at the bottom of the Edit Users page. Here you can change any user's password. Only administrators are allowed to change another user's password for security reasons. A strength indicator tells you exactly how strong your password is. The strength indicator has four levels: Very Weak, Weak, Medium, and Strong. It's highly recommended to always have a password that is indicated by Strong for the tightest security.

User Roles and Permissions

User roles are essentially groups of permissions that define what a user can and can't do on your web site. By default WordPress comes loaded with five user roles, each with different capabilities:

➤ **Administrator:** User who has access to all administration features and functionality. The admin account created during installation is assigned the Administrator role.

➤ **Editor:** User who can create, manage, and publish posts. User can also manage other users' posts. Editor also has the ability to approve articles submitted by Contributor accounts.

➤ **Author:** User can create, manage, and publish his own posts.

➤ **Contributor:** User can create and manage his own posts, but cannot publish posts.

➤ **Subscriber:** User can comment, read comments, receive newsletters, and so on, but has no write permissions.

You can create and define additional roles with custom capabilities within WordPress. A great plugin for this job is the Role Scoper plugin (`http://wordpress.org/extend/plugins/role-scoper/`). The Role Scoper plugin allows you to easily create custom user roles with specific capabilities. This plugin also integrates with other WordPress plugins, like NextGen Gallery, for even more advanced permission handling.

User Images

WordPress comes with built-in Gravatar support. A Globally Recognized Avatar, or Gravatar for short, is an image that follows you from site to site. Whenever you comment on a blog that supports Gravatar, your image is automatically displayed next to your comment. This also holds true on your web site if you have a Gravatar-enabled theme. Gravatars are attached to a user's e-mail account, so all user images on the admin side of WordPress are displayed using a Gravatar based on the user's e-mail address.

Alternatively, you can use a plugin to allow your users to upload their own author image. The recommended plugin for this is Author Image (`http://wordpress.org/extend/plugins/sem-author-image/`). With the Author Image plugin your users can upload and change their own custom user image. You can also display the author images anywhere in your web site theme with a simple function call. Utilizing this plugin does not remove the embedded Gravatar support on the admin side of WordPress, but can replace the public user avatar.

Extending User Profiles

WordPress profiles are very basic and oftentimes you will want to add additional data fields for a user account. This is a great way to link to a user's Twitter account or Facebook profile. You can do this with the use of plugins to extend the user profile data:

➤ **Cimy User Extra Fields** (`http://wordpress.org/extend/plugins/cimy-user-extra-fields/`): This plugin allows creating custom user fields. It has form validation to verify that e-mail addresses are properly formatted, correct lengths, and so on, all defined by you. This plugin works with WordPress and WordPress MU.

➤ **Register Plus** (`http://wordpress.org/extend/plugins/register-plus/`): This plugin allows for defining and creating additional user fields. It also has functionality for Custom Logo on Registration/Login, CAPTCHA capabilities, User Moderation, and more.

EXTENDING WORDPRESS

The power of WordPress is not in the default features of WordPress, but rather the endlessly flexible framework provided for extending WordPress. Utilizing the power of themes and plugins, WordPress can be custom-tailored to fit any web site purpose.

Themes

Themes are quite simply your WordPress design. This is the entire look and feel of your web site, including fonts, colors, graphics, and content layout. Thousands of free and premium themes are available, including many free themes in the official Theme directory at WordPress.org. Themes are the quickest way to make your blog unique with your own colors, styles, and graphics. Themes come in all types as well, including standard blog themes, corporate themes, photo themes, lifestreaming themes, microblogging themes (think Twitter), and much more. Theme designers are always pushing the envelope and developing exciting new looks for WordPress.

Managing Themes

You manage themes under the Appearance ➪ Themes SubPanel on your dashboard. WordPress lists all themes currently located in your `wp-content/themes` directory in a grid format. Themes are displayed with a nice screenshot if available. The screenshot is an image file that should be included by the theme author, so if no screenshot displays the author didn't include one.

Under the screenshot you will see the theme name, a link to the author's web site, and a short description of the theme. You can view a real-time preview of the theme by clicking any theme listed or the Preview link. This pops up a Thickbox overlay showing you exactly what your current content will look like in the theme.

To activate a new theme on your web site, click the Activate Theme link located at the top right of the theme preview or below the theme description. Once a theme is activated it is live for all visitors to see, so make sure your theme is ready to go live before activating a new theme.

For reference the theme location is displayed under the theme action links. This is helpful if you have duplicated a theme to make changes, because the screenshot would still be identical. The folder displayed will help you determine which theme is which.

Themes can also come with a theme option page. Typically this is located under the Appearance Sub-Panel menu as "theme-name options." Themes can contain many different options including color and font selection, content aggregation control, image and thumbnail options, and much more. These options are created by the theme authors to work specifically with their theme template files. Deactivating a theme removes any theme option pages that are displayed.

Adding New Themes

You currently have three different ways to install a theme on your web site:

> **Auto Installer:** Themes can be auto-installed directly from the official WordPress theme directory. Click the Add New Theme link under Appearance to get started. Enter in a search term to begin searching for a theme. Feature Filter options are also available to help filter out the results. Click any theme to see a preview of that theme in action. Once found, click the Install link. WordPress automatically downloads the theme files and installs them directly to your themes folder on your web server. This method works with the majority of web hosts, but if for some reason it fails you will be prompted to enter your web server's FTP information to complete the process.

> **Zip Upload:** Zipped theme files can be installed directly from the theme installer. Click the Upload button and select the theme zip you would like to install. WordPress automatically uploads the theme to your server, unzips the theme, and places the theme in your theme directory.

> **FTP:** The final method for installing a theme is using FTP, or File Transfer Protocol. Upload all theme files directly to the `wp-content/themes` directory on your web server.

Upgrading a Theme

If you have a theme installed from the WordPress.org official theme directory and a new version becomes available, a notice appears below the theme description. The upgrade notice is triggered when a new version of a theme installed on your server has been uploaded to the theme directory. Theme updates can add new features, a better look, and also fix security vulnerabilities.

Click the View Version Details link to view theme information in a Thickbox overlay. Here you can view theme description and download stats. You can also download or preview the theme. To auto-upgrade your theme click the Upgrade Automatically link. If auto-upgrade is supported on your server, the upgrade starts immediately. If not, you will be required to enter your FTP information. This gives WordPress FTP permission to download and install the updated theme on your server. Fill in your web site's Hostname (FTP Server), Username, Password, and whether you are using FTP or FTPS (SSL). Click the Proceed button to start the upgrade process.

The updated theme is downloaded directly from WordPress.org, the new version is unpacked and installed, and the old theme is removed from your web server. Before upgrading a theme, remember to download a backup of the theme first. If there are any issues with the upgrade, you can revert to your theme backup and minimize any site downtime that might have occurred.

Using the Theme Editor

WordPress has a built-in Theme editor, which you can use to edit themes directly in your dashboard. Theme files must be writable by the web server before you can save your changes. If your theme files are not writable by the server the Save Changes button is not displayed and a message appears stating your files are not editable. You can still view all theme files, but can't make any code changes. We'll explore the logical structure of a theme and provide navigational hints for files that show up in the theme editor in Chapter 8.

All theme files are listed down the right-hand side of the editor, allowing you to view and edit any theme file you choose. There is a short description of each theme file next to the link to edit that file. For example "Search Results" is listed next to search.php, the template file that controls your search page. A bit of caution: there is no undo when using the editor, so one wrong piece of code and you could break your entire web site.

Working with Widgets

WordPress widgets are a simple way to add and arrange elements in your sidebar. Widgets aren't restricted to the sidebar and are being used in many different places including the header and footer. WordPress comes with some widgets pre-installed, but you can add other widgets by installing a plugin with widget support. You manage widgets under the Appearance ➪ Widgets SubPanel. Here you will see all installed widgets and can easily drag and drop widgets into your various sidebars. Multiple sidebars are listed in menu fashion on the right. You can expand and collapse these sidebars by clicking the arrow located to the right of the sidebar name.

Drag a widget and drop it into your sidebar. The widget is automatically saved and appears instantly in that sidebar on your public web site. All widgets have an arrow located to the right of the widget name. Clicking this arrow expands the widget and displays any widget options if they are available. Remember that not all widgets have options and some widgets may store their options under a plugins setting page rather than here. To remove a widget, click the Remove link. The widget is saved automatically and removed from your sidebar.

You can drag widgets to the Inactive Widgets box located at the bottom of the Widgets SubPanel. This box stores widgets with all of their settings intact, but the widget is not displayed on your web site. This is a great feature if you want to remove a widget from publicly displaying in your sidebar, but know you will be adding it back in eventually. To reactivate, drag the widget back to your sidebar and the widget appears exactly as it did before.

If no sidebars are listed, your current theme does not support dynamic sidebars. You can edit your theme template files and create as many sidebars as you like. This is discussed in Chapter 8, "Theme Development."

Plugins

Plugins are separate files of code that extend WordPress in any way imaginable by interacting with the WordPress API. You can add functionality to WordPress without modifying any core code files. A plugin can be as simple or as complex as needed for the job.

Currently more than 7,500 plugins are listed in the official plugin directory and even more are available across the Internet. Plugins are a key component in customizing WordPress to function exactly as you like without altering the core WordPress code. This section is where you install, configure, and manage all plugins across your web site.

A plugin can accomplish just about any functionality imaginable. Most standard CMS tasks can be accomplished via a plugin. If you are looking for a specific feature in WordPress, the first place to start is by searching the plugin directory at WordPress.org.

Managing Plugins

You manage plugins under the Plugins ➪ Installed SubPanel on your dashboard. WordPress lists all plugins currently located in your `wp-content/plugin` directory on your web server. Plugins can be activated, deactivated, and deleted from the plugin administration page. Each plugin lists the plugin name, description, and author information including the plugin site. The plugin site is typically the best resource for plugin-specific information and support.

You can filter which plugins are shown by using the filter links across the top of the page. You can also search plugins using the keyword search box at the top right. The Upgrade Available filter is a quick overview of which plugins have an upgrade available and need attention.

Adding New Plugins

To install a plugin on your web site, you can use the same three methods as you would to install a theme: the Auto Installer, Zip Upload, or FTP. Once a plugin has been uploaded to WordPress using one of these three methods, it will appear under Plugins ➪ Installed SubPanel. Here you can activate, deactivate, or delete the new plugin. Once a plugin is placed in the `wp-content/plugins` directory it automatically displays on your Plugins SubPanel.

If a plugin is removed from the plugins directory on your web server, it is automatically deactivated in WordPress. This is especially handy if a rogue plugin breaks your web site and you are locked out with error messages or the dreaded white screen of death (causing WordPress to go into an infinite loop or otherwise never finish executing some PHP code). Also, if you remove or rename the offending plugin, it will be deactivated in WordPress.

Upgrading a Plugin

WordPress comes with a built-in plugin upgrade feature. This makes upgrading your plugins easier than ever. When a plugin upgrade is available, a notice appears alerting you about the new version under the Plugins ➪ Installed SubPanel. A notice next to the Plugins SubPanel link on the Admin Menu also appears showing a number circled in red. That is the number of plugins with an upgrade available. The update notice displays links to view the new version details and to upgrade automatically. The upgrade notice is triggered when a new version of a plugin installed on your server has been uploaded to the official plugin directory at WordPress.org.

Clicking the View Version Details link opens a Thickbox overlay showing you the plugins detail page from WordPress.org. From here you can view the plugin description, installation instructions, and a changelog. The changelog features a version history showing you exactly what the new version does. This can help you determine whether the plugin features a security vulnerability fix or new features. The changelog is not a requirement for plugins, so the changelog tab may not exist on all plugins.

Clicking the Upgrade Automatically link starts the plugin upgrade process. If your web host supports automatic upgrade, the upgrade process begins immediately. The auto upgrade downloads the latest plugin zip file from WordPress.org, unpacks the plugin, deactivates the plugin, installs the latest version, and then attempts to reactivate the plugin. If everything runs smoothly your new plugin is installed and activated automatically. The automatic upgrade reactivates your plugin only if it was activated before the upgrade. Always remember to back up your plugins before upgrading. In case of an error in the plugin or on your web site you can always revert back to the backup.

If your web host doesn't support the automatic upgrade process, you are prompted to enter your FTP account information to perform the upgrade. This gives WordPress FTP permission to download and install the update plugin on your server. Fill in your web site's Hostname (FTP Server), Username, Password, and whether you are using FTP or FTPS (SSL). Click the Proceed button to start the upgrade process. From here the upgrade process is the same as the auto upgrade.

Using the Plugin Editor

Just like with themes, WordPress has a built-in plugin editor with syntax highlighting. You can view any plugin source code, but plugin files must be writable before you can save your changes. Remember there is no "undo" button on a browser. There is also no plugin revision history so one bad code edit and you could break the plugin with no way to revert back to the original code.

The editor lists all files associated with a plugin. You can choose which plugin you would like to edit from the drop-down menu in the top-right corner. A documentation lookup feature has also been added, making it easier than ever to quickly look up a function's purpose. This can help you reference the plugin's actions.

CONTENT TOOLS

WordPress comes with multiple tools to help you accomplish various tasks related to managing your content. In this section we cover import and export features, Google Gears installation, the PressThis applet, and upgrading WordPress.

Importing Content

One of the most commonly used tools is the Import feature. The WordPress Import allows you to import content from different software packages directly into WordPress. Many commonly used blogging web sites are supported including Blogger, Moveable Type and TypePad, LiveJournal, and of course WordPress.

Each import is different depending on what is needed for the import. Importing from Moveable Type and TypePad is as simple as uploading your exported content file provided by those systems. Blogger and LiveJournal, however, use an authorization process to actually pull down your content directly into WordPress.

A WordPress-to-WordPress import can be a quick and easy way to transfer to a new web server or hosting company. This is only for a content migration because settings are not transferred. This method works best when doing a complete WordPress overhaul, because you will have to perform a fresh install of plugins and themes.

You can import content from a system that is not supported by using the RSS Importer. The RSS Importer extracts posts from any valid RSS 2.0 file or feed directly into WordPress.

Using the import tools and preparing data exported from other blogging and content management systems is the heart of Chapter 14.

Exporting Content

You can export your content from WordPress using the Tools ⇨ Export SubPanel. WordPress exports an XML file, referred to as the WordPress eXtended RSS or WXR, that contains all of your posts, pages, comments, custom fields, categories, and tags. This export can also be restricted by author, allowing you to only export posts created by a specific author. Keep in mind that plugins, themes, and settings are not included in the WXR export file. This export is only for your web site's content.

The default WordPress export is very basic and has only one filter option. If you are looking for more advanced export options, look at the Advanced Export for WP & WPMU Plugin (http://wordpress.org/extend/plugins/advanced-export-for-wp-wpmu/). The Advanced Export Plugin allows you to filter the export by date range, author, category, content, and status. This is especially useful if you are exporting a very large WordPress web site. Slicing up the export file into multiple smaller files is great when working with large amounts of content. Some hosting providers may also limit an import file size, which would require this method as well.

Turbo

Turbo enables you to run your WordPress web site with Google Gears to make WordPress run even faster. Google Gears is an open source project that enables different aspects of a web site to be downloaded and run locally from your desktop. When enabled, Turbo caches images and JavaScript files to help speed load times as you navigate your WordPress web site. This can dramatically increase page load times and make administering your web site even easier.

Configuring Turbo with Google Gears is a tool that can be used by anyone accessing the Dashboard of your WordPress web site. This is not a tool your web site visitors will have access to. This helps speed up Dashboard load times for your web site administrators and contributors.

Upgrading WordPress

The upgrade section of WordPress does just that; it allows you to upgrade your WordPress installation to a newer version if available. If you are running the most current version of WordPress the upgrade section allows you to reinstall the current version. This is a great feature if you suspect a core WordPress file of being corrupt or tampered with. Reinstalling the core software would overwrite the corrupt file with the correct one.

The upgrade section also allows you to bulk-upgrade all plugins that have an upgrade available. Just select which plugins you would like to upgrade, or check the Select All option, and click the Upgrade Plugins button. WordPress will download the update for each plugin selected and install the new plugin version.

When a new version of WordPress is released, an upgrade notice appears in the header and footer of your admin dashboard. Clicking this notice brings you to the upgrade section under the Tools SubPanel, as shown in Figure 2-10.

WordPress 2.8.2 is available! Please update now.

FIGURE 2-10: Upgrade notice displayed when a new version of WordPress is released

Clicking the Please Update Now link in the header takes you to the upgrade page. From here you can either upgrade automatically or download the new version of WordPress to upgrade manually. Select Upgrade Automatically to start the upgrade process. WordPress downloads the new version directly from WordPress.org, unpacks the update, installs the latest version, and performs any upgrade procedures to finish the upgrade.

If WordPress doesn't have the proper permissions to auto upgrade you are prompted for your FTP information. Enter your Hostname (FTP Server), username, password, and connection type of FTP or FTPS (SSL).

It's very important to take a backup of your WordPress core files before upgrading to a new version. This includes all files in `wp-admin`, `wp-content`, `wp-includes`, and your root WordPress directories. A new version of WordPress may also contain new bugs, or conflict with your theme and plugins. If your web site explodes after the upgrade process you can always revert back to your latest backup files. To revert to your backup, simply upload all of the backup files you copied prior to the upgrade to your web server or hosting account.

CONFIGURING WORDPRESS

WordPress offers an entire host of settings that allow you to easily change various features and functionality on your web site. These settings can completely change how your WordPress web site functions, so it's essential to understand your options and how they work.

General Settings

The General Settings SubPanel enables you to save web site–wide preferences. You can find all settings discussed in this section under the General ⇨ Settings SubPanel.

One of the first options you will want to set is your blog title and tagline. Blog Title and Tagline are the first two options listed. The blog title is the title of your web site, and the tagline is a short description of your web site. The blog title and tag fields are generally used in the header of most themes and also all generated RSS and Atom feeds.

Make sure to enter your web site e-mail address. This is the web site administrator's e-mail, and is used for web site notices like new user notifications, new comments, and so on.

The WordPress address and Blog address settings are normally set to your web site's URL. However, it is possible to run WordPress in a different directory from your blog. This technique allows Word-Press to power your web site's root without WordPress files being installed in the root directory. For example, WordPress can run at `http://example.com` while your WordPress files are actually stored at `http://example.com/wordpress`. This helps keep your root directory clean from all WordPress-related files but still power your primary web site.

The General Settings section also allows you to change the date and time settings in WordPress. Custom date and time can also be configured using date format strings as used in PHP's date formatting functions. You can also set the starting day of the week with the Week Starts On option. The Timezone in WordPress is in UTC format. WordPress currently does not auto update for Daylight Savings Time, but plugins are available that can accomplish this for you. This feature will be added in a future release of WordPress.

Allowing user registration is a one-checkbox setting. This option enables or disables membership registration on your web site. The new user registration page is located at `http://example.com/wp-register.php` when this option is enabled. You can also set the default user role. Subscriber is the default, but you can grant all users writing permissions by setting this to Author. This would open your blog to strangers publishing any content on your web site, so a better method is discussed below.

One common technique is to allow new users to write posts and submit them for review. To do this, enable Membership and set the New User Default Role to Contributor. This gives all new users the ability to write posts and submit them to you for review, or any user with Editor-level access or above. You can publish, edit, or delete the submitted post.

Keep in mind that allowing open registration and post writing permissions is asking for a spam assault on your web site, so make sure to install a good CAPTCHA plugin for new user registrations.

Writing and Reading

The Writing and Reading SubPanels enable you to define settings for both. You can find all settings discussed in this section under the General ⇨ Writing and General ⇨ Reading SubPanels.

You can set default post and link categories under the Writing SubPanel. Changing either category makes that the default category used if one is not assigned to a post or link. Also, if a category is deleted, posts or links assigned to that category are moved to the default category set here.

Remote publishing, using the Atom Publishing Protocol or XML-RPC, can be enabled under the Writing SubPanel. This allows you to post directly to WordPress using a desktop blogging client or remote web site that uses these protocols.

WordPress allows you to create new posts by e-mail. Only three steps are involved in enabling this functionality:

1. Create a dedicated e-mail account whose sole purpose is to post to your blog.
2. Enable WordPress access to that e-mail account.
3. Configure WordPress to create posts from the e-mail in that account.

Once you have created an e-mail address to use, enter in the POP3 mail server information along with login e-mail and password. You can also select a default mail post category.

You can configure WordPress to create posts from your e-mail account in the following ways:

➤ **Manual Browser Activation:** Access `http://example.com/wp-mail.php` to connect to your e-mail account and create new posts from any new e-mails. Remember this is a manual process, so you have to access that URL every time you want to check for new posts.

➤ **Automated Browser Activation:** A different method is to automate the process. Place the following code in the `footer.php` file of your theme:

```
<iframe src="http://example.com/wp-mail.php" name="mailiframe" width="0"
height="0" frameborder="0" scrolling="no" title=""></iframe>
```

This runs the mail post script and checks for new e-mails to process. Every time your web site loads this script will be run, essentially automating the process. You can also force this to run by visiting your WordPress web site.

➤ **Cron Job Activation:** Probably the most efficient method is using a cron job. Settings up a cron job automatically runs the mail post script on a schedule. The command to execute would be:

```
wget -N http://example.com/installdir/wp-mail.php
```

If your web site's privacy settings are set to be visible by everyone, you will have the option to add update services under the Writing SubPanel. Update Services are web services that notify other web sites that you have updated your blog. These services are notified by an XML-RPC ping that is sent by WordPress to all URLs listed here. This is a great way to alert search engines and blog indexers that you have a new post that they need to come index!

A common Update Service is Ping-O-Matic. Ping-O-Matic works differently in that when you ping them, they will ping all of the other Update Services for you. So rather than pinging a hundred different services, you only have to ping one! Ping-O-Matic is owned by Automattic.

WordPress gives you options for what is displayed on your front page under the Reading SubPanel. You can display either your latest posts or a static page. To display a static home page select the static page option and choose which page will serve as your home page and posts page. The posts page now contains all of your blogs posts, and your home page displays the static page you selected. The Posts page is not required and if not set will essentially remove the blog listings page from your public web site.

Go to Settings ➪ Reading SubPanel to change the number of blog posts to display on your posts page and in your syndication feeds. By default both values are set to 10.

WordPress by default uses the UTF-8 Unicode for web page encoding, which supports a wide variety of languages. You can change this setting to any character encoding necessary. Typically this is only changed if you are importing articles written using a different character encoding. Changing this setting may change the way information is displayed on your web site.

Discussion

Blog posts are all about discussion. Reader comments are a great way to interact with your visitors and continue the discussion. The Settings ⇨ Discussion SubPanel is where all discussion settings are configured.

Enabling the Attempt to Notify Any Blogs Linked to from the Article option enables your blog to send pingbacks to other blogs. A pingback is the way WordPress notifies a blog that you have linked to one of its articles or blog posts. If the receiving blog has pingbacks enabled, it automatically posts a link to your article in the comments section of the article you linked to.

Enable Allow Link Notifications from Other Blogs to allow pingbacks and trackbacks on your web site. This feature automatically adds a link in your comments if another site sends you a pingback or trackback linking to one of your articles.

You can enable or disable comments web site–wide using the Allow People to Post Comments on New Articles option. Remember these settings can be overridden on each individual post, but the settings saved here will be the site-wide default. Updating this setting will not change any existing posts or pages.

Setting the E-mail Me Whenever options determines when an e-mail notice should be sent. E-mail notices can be sent when a new comment is posted or a comment is held for moderation. This helps alert you as the web site administer when a comment needs attention.

Media

The Media SubPanel enables you to define media options. You can find all settings discussed in this section under the General ⇨ Media SubPanel.

Prior to uploading any media to your web site you will want to make sure you define your default image sizes. WordPress has built-in image resizing functionality based on the image sizes defined under this SubPanel. When you upload a new image to your web site, WordPress automatically creates up to three different sizes of that image: thumbnail, medium, and large. The original is also saved and referred to as the full image. WordPress only resizes your image if it is larger than the image sizes defined under your Media settings, so an image that is 100×100 would not be resized to a larger medium image of 300×300.

Setting your image size dimensions is an essential step if you plan on using various image sizes throughout your theme. If you decide to change your image sizes down the road, there is no automatic way to go back and resize all of them. To do that you would need to use a third-party application or plugin to do so. The Regenerate Thumbnails plugin does an excellent job regenerating all of your WordPress thumbnails if you decide to change their sizes after the fact: `http://wordpress.org/extend/plugins/regenerate-thumbnails/`.

Image thumbnails are cropped by default. This means the image will be sliced to make a perfect square thumbnail. The advantage to this method is that the thumbnail size will be consistent throughout your entire site. The disadvantage to this method is that the image will be cropped, so you may lose parts of your image from the thumbnail. Currently there is no way to define how the thumbnail is cropped.

Privacy

The Privacy SubPanel enables you to define all WordPress privacy options. You can find all settings discussed in this section under the General ➪ Privacy SubPanel.

When you are creating a new web site it's a good practice to block all search engines from indexing your web site until after it is launched. Changing the Blog Visibility setting allows you to lock down your web site from being indexed by search engines. This is a great technique while you are in the development stages of your new web site. You don't want the search engines to index your web site when it is only half completed, but rather when it has officially launched. Setting this option to block search engines adds a `noindex, nofollow` meta tag to the header of your entire site as shown here:

```
<meta name='robots' content='noindex,nofollow' />
```

Another recommended tip to block search engines from indexing your web site is to use a `robots.txt` file. A `robots.txt` file is a method of preventing cooperating search engine spiders from accessing all or part of your web site. To block your web site from being indexed, create a new `robots.txt` file in the root of your WordPress installation. Inside the file add these lines of code and save the file:

```
User-agent: *
Disallow: /
```

The `*` indicates this rule is for all search engine spiders. `Disallow: /` tells the spiders to skip indexing anything from the root directory down. To allow search engines to index your content just remove the forward slash after Disallow.

Using these two methods pretty much guarantees your web site will not appear in search results from the major search engines until you are ready for it.

Permalinks

The Permalinks SubPanel enables you to define all WordPress permalink and URL options. You can find all settings discussed in this section under the General ➪ Permalink SubPanel. Permalinks are permanent URLs to your posts, pages, categories, archives, and so on. These links should never change and are typically used for sharing your content.

WordPress by default uses web URLs, which include a question mark followed by an ID number, to create links to your posts, pages, categories, and so on. We'll dissect post index numbers more in Chapter 6, "Data Management." WordPress offers the ability to create custom permalinks, or pretty keyword URLs, which are much more user and search-engine friendly. The permalink settings allow you to select the Default, Day and Name, Month and Name, Numeric, or define your own Custom Structure for permalinks.

When you save your permalink settings WordPress tries to modify the `.htaccess` file in your root directory. If allowed by your web server, setting `.htaccess` permissions to 644 allows WordPress to automatically update this file. If the file cannot be updated, WordPress provides the code that needs to be added to `.htaccess`. You can manually edit this file by inserting the rewrite code provided directly into the `.htaccess` file on your server.

Creating custom permalink rules gives you ultimate control over your URL structure. Using structure tags enables you to create a custom permalink rule in WordPress. As you select different Permalink

Settings the custom structure is automatically filled out with the structure tags used, showing examples of how that rule is created. Many other structure tags are also available, as described in the Table 2-1.

TABLE 2-1: Permalink Structure Tags

TAG	DESCRIPTION
%year%	The four-digit year
%monthnum%	Month of the year
%day%	Day of the month
%hour%	Hour of the day
%minute%	Minute of the hour
%second%	Second of the minute
%postname%	Sanitized post title or slug
%post_id%	Unique ID of the post
%category%	Sanitized category name
%tag%	Sanitized tag name
%author%	Author name

Custom permalink rules can also be combined with static elements. As an example you can add an extension to the end of your URL like so:

```
/%year%/%monthnum%/%day%/%postname%.html
```

This rule would produce a permalink like:

```
http://example.com/2010/06/09/this-is-my-title.html
```

Starting your permalinks with the category, tag, or postname structure tag is not recommended because there can be performance issues. Starting your permalink with one of these structure tags forces Word-Press to determine whether you are trying to view a page or post, which can slow down load times. Also be very careful when using only the postname (/%postname%) structure tag for your permalinks because you can inadvertently block access to required files such as your style sheet or wp-admin URL. It's always recommended to use some type of numeric field in your permalink, whether it is the year and month or unique post ID.

Miscellaneous

The Miscellaneous SubPanel enables you to define all additional WordPress settings that don't fit else-where. You can find all settings discussed in this section under the General ➪ Miscellaneous SubPanel.

By default all files uploaded to WordPress are stored in the `wp-content/uploads` folder. You can change this path to any directory on your web server. If you change the default uploads folder you need to also set the "Full URL path to files" setting. For example, if you want to change the uploads folder to images, the settings would be:

- ➤ Store uploads in this folder – `wp-content/images`
- ➤ Full URL path to files – `http://example.com/wp-content/images`

Also remember your uploads folder will typically need to be writable by the server for the upload process to work. If you experience difficulty uploading images, try setting the permissions on your uploads folder to 777.

WordPress stores all uploads in month and year folders like so:

```
wp-content/uploads/2010/6/image.jpg
```

This helps keep your uploads organized and much easier to maintain as your web site grows over time. Optionally you can disable this setting. By doing so all uploads will be stored directly in the uploads folder on your server. Keep in mind that over time this folder could get filled with thousands of files, making the response time to load these files slower on the server. It is recommended to keep your uploaded files organized by month and year for ease of reference and speed.

3

Code Overview

WHAT'S IN THIS CHAPTER?

➤ Where to Download WordPress

➤ Configuring `wp-config.php` and `.htaccess`

➤ Exploring the `wp-content` directories

➤ Enabling maintenance mode in WordPress

WordPress comprises groups of source code files that perform specific tasks within the system. Understanding the code, including file and folder structure, is essential to understanding how WordPress works as a whole.

After reading this chapter you will be familiar with downloading and exploring the WordPress file system. We'll discuss configuring key WordPress files including the powerful `wp-config.php` and `.htaccess` files. We'll also cover some advanced configuration options available in WordPress.

DOWNLOADING

The first step to installing WordPress on your own hosting account is to download the source files required for WordPress to run. In Chapter 1 we covered the basics of getting WordPress installed. In this section we'll dig deeper into the Core of WordPress.

Download Locations

You can download WordPress directly from WordPress.org by visiting the download page located at `http://wordpress.org/download/`.

You can also update WordPress directly from your current WordPress installation by visiting the Upgrade WordPress section under the Tools ➪ Upgrade SubPanel. Click the Download button to download the latest version of WordPress to your computer.

WordPress also features Subversion (SVN) access. Subversion is a free open source version control system. WordPress uses Subversion to manage files and directories and the changes made to them. You can download the latest WordPress source code by checking out the following URL:

```
http://core.svn.wordpress.org/trunk/
```

The SVN trunk directory contains the "bleeding edge" version of WordPress that is actively being developed. Typically this version of WordPress contains bugs, and is generally used for testing purposes. We don't recommend running a production web site using the trunk version of WordPress.

SVN is the mechanism developers use to actively develop on the WordPress core software. With SVN you can create and submit patch files for inclusion into the WordPress core. We cover this in detail in Chapter 15.

Available Formats

The default format for the WordPress software download is in a compressed zip archive named `latest.zip`. You can also download WordPress in a compressed tar archive named `latest.tar.gz`. There is no difference between the files in the archive, only the compression method used.

You can download the zip and tar archives directly from these URLs:

```
http://wordpress.org/latest.zip
```

```
http://wordpress.org/latest.tar.gz
```

These download links never change. Each new version of WordPress is automatically compressed and saved at this location when the version is tagged. When you save the archive to your computer, you should rename the file to include the WordPress version number, like `wordpress-2.9.zip`.

Release Archive

WordPress.org features a Release Archive for WordPress. The Release Archive features a list of downloadable archives for every release of WordPress since version 0.71. The archive is located here:

```
http://wordpress.org/download/release-archive/
```

Remember only the most current version of WordPress is actively maintained, so these downloads are more for reference than actual use. Another great use for these older versions of WordPress is to roll a web site back to a previous version. For example, if you upgrade a very old version of WordPress to the latest stable version and run into problems, you could easily download the old version the web site was originally running to revert to. The Release Archive also features a download for every beta and release candidate version of WordPress as well. This is great to see the overall growth of WordPress as a software platform.

EXPLORING THE CODE

The WordPress source code features many different PHP, JavaScript, and CSS code files. Each file serves a specific purpose in WordPress. The beauty of open source software is that all code is publicly available, which means you can easily explore the code to better understand how WordPress functions.

After extracting the WordPress download you will notice the set file structure for WordPress, as shown in Figure 3-1.

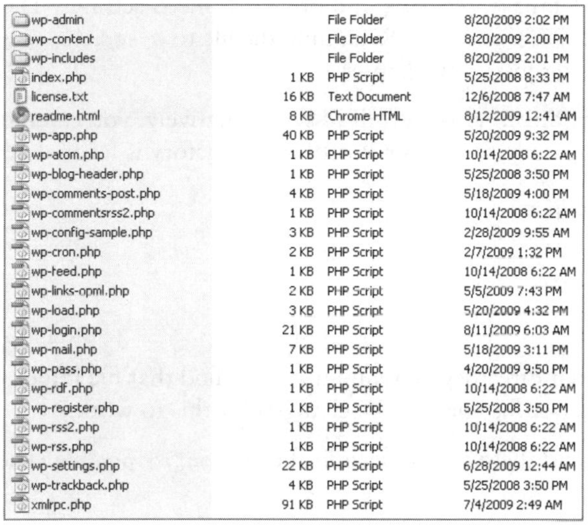

wp-admin		File Folder	8/20/2009 2:02 PM
wp-content		File Folder	8/20/2009 2:00 PM
wp-includes		File Folder	8/20/2009 2:01 PM
index.php	1 KB	PHP Script	5/25/2008 8:33 PM
license.txt	16 KB	Text Document	12/6/2008 7:47 AM
readme.html	8 KB	Chrome HTML	8/12/2009 12:41 AM
wp-app.php	40 KB	PHP Script	5/20/2009 9:32 PM
wp-atom.php	1 KB	PHP Script	10/14/2008 6:22 AM
wp-blog-header.php	1 KB	PHP Script	5/25/2008 3:50 PM
wp-comments-post.php	4 KB	PHP Script	5/18/2009 4:00 PM
wp-commentsrss2.php	1 KB	PHP Script	10/14/2008 6:22 AM
wp-config-sample.php	3 KB	PHP Script	2/28/2009 9:55 AM
wp-cron.php	2 KB	PHP Script	2/7/2009 1:32 PM
wp-feed.php	1 KB	PHP Script	10/14/2008 6:22 AM
wp-links-opml.php	2 KB	PHP Script	5/5/2009 7:43 PM
wp-load.php	3 KB	PHP Script	5/20/2009 4:32 PM
wp-login.php	21 KB	PHP Script	8/11/2009 6:03 AM
wp-mail.php	7 KB	PHP Script	5/18/2009 3:11 PM
wp-pass.php	1 KB	PHP Script	4/20/2009 9:50 PM
wp-rdf.php	1 KB	PHP Script	10/14/2008 6:22 AM
wp-register.php	1 KB	PHP Script	5/25/2008 3:50 PM
wp-rss2.php	1 KB	PHP Script	10/14/2008 6:22 AM
wp-rss.php	1 KB	PHP Script	10/14/2008 6:22 AM
wp-settings.php	22 KB	PHP Script	6/28/2009 12:44 AM
wp-trackback.php	4 KB	PHP Script	5/25/2008 3:50 PM
xmlrpc.php	91 KB	PHP Script	7/4/2009 2:49 AM

FIGURE 3-1: Default WordPress file and folder structure

WordPress comes with three directories by default: wp-admin, wp-content, and wp-includes. The wp-admin and wp-includes directories include core WordPress files that you should *never* edit. The root directory of WordPress also contains very important core files, some of which you will edit later on in this chapter. The wp-content directory holds all of your custom files including themes, plugins, media, and eventually much more. This directory is the code that controls content manipulation and presentation in WordPress.

Modifying any of the core WordPress files can result in an unstable web site. This also makes it very difficult to upgrade WordPress, because all changes made are overwritten when the updated version of WordPress is installed. *Core files* refer to all files in the wp-admin and wp-includes directories. The majority of the files in the root WordPress directory are also considered to be Core. In the next section, we'll discuss some Core files that can be modified. In general, though follow this rule: Don't hack core!

CONFIGURING KEY FILES

WordPress features specific files that can be edited for different purposes. These files can alter how WordPress functions. Always test changes in a development environment before publishing to a production server.

In this section, we'll discuss database connections, storing FTP info, enabling debugging tools, and more using wp-config.php. We'll also discuss the power of the .htaccess file, including increasing PHP memory limits and max upload sizes, creating redirects, and access restrictions.

wp-config.php file

The most important file in any WordPress installation is the `wp-config.php` file. This files stores all database connection settings, including the database name, username, and password to access your database. This file also stores additional database, security, and other advanced settings. The `wp-config.php` file is originally named `wp-config-sample.php`. Renaming the file to `wp-config.php` is one of the first steps to installing WordPress, as discussed in Chapter 1.

The `wp-config` file is typically stored in the root directory of WordPress. Alternatively, you can move the `wp-config` file outside of WordPress one directory. So if your WordPress directory is located here:

```
/public_html/my_website/wp-config.php
```

you can safely move the file here:

```
/public_html/wp-config.php
```

WordPress looks for the `wp-config` file in the root directory first, and if it can't find that file it looks up one directory. This happens automatically so no settings need to be changed for this to work.

Options in WordPress are stored as constants and these can be seen in the `wp-config.php` file. The constraints all have the same format:

```
define('OPTION_NAME', 'value');
```

`OPTION_NAME` is the name of the option constant being set. `value` is the option value and can be updated to whatever setting you would like to save for that option.

If your WordPress installation is having problems connecting to your database this is the first place to start troubleshooting. Verify that the `DB_NAME`, `DB_USER`, and `DB_PASSWORD` options are correctly set for your database server. Also verify that the `DB_HOST` name is set to the correct host for your server. Typically this is set to `localhost`, but some hosting companies require a custom value. Contact your hosting tech support or consult their online documentation for the correct host value to set here.

You can change the database character set (`charset`) by changing the `DB_CHARSET` option value. By default this is set to `utf8` (Unicode UTF-8), which supports any language, and is almost always the best option.

Since WordPress 2.2 the `DB_COLLATE` option has allowed designation of the database collation, that is, sort order of the character set. (A *character set* is a collection of symbols that represents words in a language. The collation determines the order to use when sorting the character set, usually alphabetical order). This option by default is blank and should typically stay that way. If you would like to change the database collation just add the appropriate value for your language. You should change this option before installing WordPress. Altering this value after installation could cause problems in WordPress.

WordPress security can be strengthened by setting secret keys in your `wp-config.php` file. A secret key is a hashing salt, which makes your site harder to hack by adding random elements (the salt) to the password you set. These keys aren't required for WordPress to function, but they add an extra layer of security on your web site.

To have secret keys auto-generated for you, visit the link to WordPress.org for secret key generation in your `wp-config.php` file (`https://api.wordpress.org/secret-key/1.1/`), shown in Figure 3-2.

Alternatively you can just type a bunch of random characters in place of "put your unique phrase here." The goal is to use secret keys that are 100 percent random and unique.

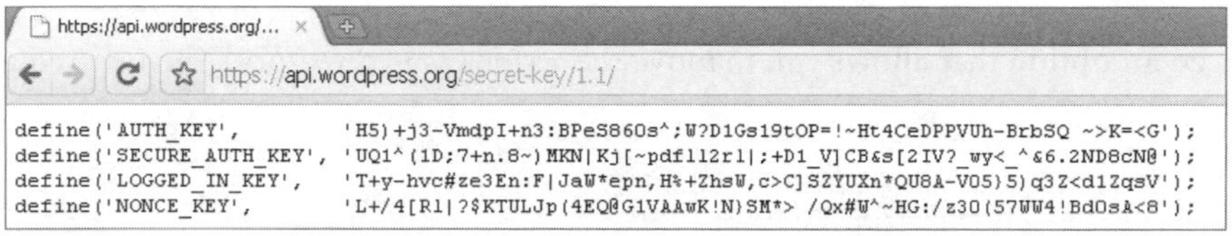

FIGURE 3-2: Randomly generated secret keys

You can add or change these keys at any time; the only thing that will happen is all current WordPress cookies will be invalidated and your users will be required to log in again.

Another security feature included in `wp-config.php` is setting your WordPress database table prefix. By default this option value is set to `wp_`. You can change this value by setting the `$table_prefix` variable value to any prefix you would like.

If a hacker is able to exploit your web site using SQL Injection, this will make it harder for him to guess your table names and quite possibly keep him from doing SQL Injection at all. Setting the table prefix to a unique value also makes it possible to run multiple WordPress installations in a single database. If you want to change the table prefix after you have installed WordPress, you can use the WP Security Scan plugin (http://wordpress.org/extend/plugins/wp-security-scan/) to do so. Make sure you make a good backup before doing this, though.

The `wp-config` file also contains the option for localizing your installation of WordPress. WordPress has the built-in capability to be used in many different languages. Setting the `WPLANG` option value sets the default language for WordPress to use. A corresponding MO file for the selected language must be installed to `wp-content/languages` for this option to work. MO (machine object) files are compressed PO (portable object) files, which contain translations for WordPress messages and text strings in a specific language. The MO and PO files are components of the GNU "gettext" subsystem that underlies the WordPress multi-language capabilities. For a full list of available MO language files visit the following resources:

➤ WordPress in Your Language Codex page: http://codex.wordpress.org/WordPress_in_Your_Language

➤ WordPress Language File Repository: http://svn.automattic.com/wordpress-i18n/

Advanced wp-config Options

You can set additional advanced options in your `wp-config` file. These options are not in the `wp-config` file by default, so you will need to manually add them to the file.

To set your WordPress address and blog address, use the following two options:

```
define('WP_SITEURL', 'http://example.com/wordpress');
define('WP_HOME', 'http://example.com/wordpress');
```

The `WP_SITEURL` option allows you to temporarily change the WordPress site URL. This does not alter the database option value for `siteurl`, but instead temporarily changes the value. If this option is removed, it reverts back to the database setting. The WP_HOME option works the exact same way, letting you temporarily change the home value for WordPress. Both values should include the full URL including http://.

Version 2.6 introduced an option that allows you to move the wp-content directory. The two required options are:

```
define( 'WP_CONTENT_DIR', $_SERVER['DOCUMENT_ROOT'] .
         '/wordpress/blog/wp-content' );
define( 'WP_CONTENT_URL', 'http://domain.com/wordpress/blog/wp-content');
```

The WP_CONTENT_DIR option value is the full local path to your wp-content directory. The WP_CONTENT_URL is the full URI of this directory. Optionally you can set the path to your plugins directory like so:

```
define( 'WP_PLUGIN_DIR', $_SERVER['DOCUMENT_ROOT'] . '/blog/wp-content/plugins' );
define( 'WP_PLUGIN_URL', 'http://example/blog/wp-content/plugins');
```

WP_PLUGIN_DIR and WP_PLUGIN_URL are options used by plugin developers to determine where your plugin folder resides. If a plugin developer is not using these constants there is a very good chance their plugin will break if you move your wp-content directory. Never move the wp-content directory on your production server without first testing in a development environment.

WordPress saves post revisions for each saved edit made to a post or page. Edits are saved by clicking either the Save or Publish button, and also by the built-in auto save feature of WordPress. Imagine if each post you create has 10 revisions. If you had 100 posts, that would be 1,000 records in your database. This can quickly increase the size of your database and may even slow down your web site because table records can take longer to fetch in larger databases. Luckily WordPress has a built-in post revisions option called WP_POST_REVISIONS. You can set this option to false to completely disable post revisions altogether, or you can specify a maximum number of revisions to keep for each post or page. Following are examples of both scenarios:

```
define('WP_POST_REVISIONS', false );
define('WP_POST_REVISIONS', 5);
```

You can also configure the auto save interval by setting the AUTOSAVE_INTERVAL option. WordPress uses AJAX when editing a post to auto-save revisions. By default this interval is 60 seconds. You can set the interval in seconds for auto save in wp-config. Set auto save to 5 minutes by using this code:

```
define('AUTOSAVE_INTERVAL', 300 );
```

Debugging errors in WordPress can be made easier using the WP_DEBUG option. Enabling WP_DEBUG shows WordPress errors on the screen, rather than suppressing those errors with a white screen. To enable WP_DEBUG just set the option value to true:

```
define('WP_DEBUG', true);
```

If this option is not defined in wp-config it defaults to false and error messages are not displayed. Remember to disable or remove this option when you are done debugging because error messages might help hackers find vulnerabilities in your web site.

Another great debugging option is SAVEQUERIES. Activating this option saves all database queries into a global array that can be displayed on your page. This can help you debug query issues, and also to see exactly what WordPress is executing on each page load. If you are working on a theme or plugin, and can't seem to get the right set of posts back, this debug option will show you exactly what WordPress is asking for out of the database. Enable this option by setting the value to true:

```
define('SAVEQUERIES', true);
```

To display the query array in your theme, add the following code to any theme template file to view:

```
If ( current_user_can('install_plugins')) {
   global $wpdb;
   print_r($wpdb->queries);
}
```

The preceding code displays the saved query array only if the logged-in user has the ability to install plugins, essentially locking it down so only site administrators will see the output. We cover themes and template files in Chapter 8, "Theme Development."

You can also enable logging directly from your wp-config file. To enable logging, first you need to create a php_error.log file and upload it to your root WordPress directory. Then simply turn on the log_errors PHP option and point to your logging file:

```
@ini_set('log_errors','On');
@ini_set('display_errors','Off');
@ini_set('error_log','/public_html/wordpress/php_error.log');
```

All errors will now be logged to this file. This will also log any errors produced by enabling the WP_DEBUG option discussed earlier. In the preceding example display_errors is set to Off, which is perfect for a production web site because you don't want error messages displayed. If you are debugging and want to view errors in real time, just set that option to On.

You can also set the memory limit WordPress is allowed to use with the WP_MEMORY_LIMIT option. If your web site hits the memory limit set for WordPress to run, you will see the error "Allowed memory size of xxxxx bytes exhausted." Increasing the memory limit fixes this problem. The memory limit is set by defining the megabytes needed:

```
define('WP_MEMORY_LIMIT', '32M');
```

Setting this option works only if you're hosting company allows it. Some hosting companies will not allow dynamically changing the memory limit and will have this value set very low. This problem is usually found on cheaper hosting companies.

This increases the memory only for WordPress and not other applications running on your server. To increase the memory limit across all of your web sites, set the php_value memory_limit variable in your php.ini file. For example, when importing large amounts of content, say months or years worth of blog posts, it's likely you'll hit this memory limit. We'll discuss importing content into WordPress in Chapter 14, "Migrating to WordPress."

One amazing feature of WordPress is the built-in localizer. WordPress displays in English by default, but can easily be set to display any language that has been translated. Setting the WPLANG option triggers WordPress to load the specified language files:

```
define ('WPLANG', 'en-GB');
```

The option value comprises the ISO-639 language code followed by the ISO-3166 country code. So en-GB would be English-Great Britain. This setting will reference your .mo and .po files for language translation.

You can also define the LANGDIR option. This option defines what directory will hold your language .mo files. By default WordPress looks in wp-content/languages for the .mo file. If you would like to move this folder just set the LANGDIR option like so:

```
define('LANGDIR', '/wp-content/bury/my/languages');
```

WordPress will now look in the new location for your .mo files.

CUSTOM_USER_TABLE and CUSTOM_USER_META_TABLE are also very powerful options. They are useful if you want to have two or more individual WordPress installs use the same user accounts. Remember to set this prior to installing WordPress.

```
define('CUSTOM_USER_TABLE', 'joined_users');
define('CUSTOM_USER_META_TABLE', 'joined_usermeta');
```

Setting these two options lets you define the name of the default WordPress user and user meta table. Doing this means both blogs share user information including usernames, passwords, author bios, and so on. This is a great way to set up a new installation of WordPress but not lose sync with your current user base.

If you would like your users to have different roles on each WordPress install, but still share user accounts, don't set the CUSTOM_USER_META_TABLE option. Everything stored in the user tables will stay the same, but everything else will be blog-specific (that is, user level, first and last name, and so on).

You can set multiple cookie options such as COOKIE_DOMAIN, COOKIEPATH, and SITECOOKIEPATH. These options are typically used in a WordPress MU (multi-user) installation utilizing subdomains for blogs. This allows you to set the primary domain so cookies can be created and validated on all subdomains in the network.

```
define('COOKIE_DOMAIN', '.domain.com');
define('COOKIEPATH', '/' );
define('SITECOOKIEPATH', '/');
```

Typically you won't need to use or change this option, but if you run into issues with cookies this is the first place to check.

Since the inclusion of the automatic installer functionality for plugins and themes, as well as the automatic upgrade process, you can set FTP settings directly in your wp-config file. This is only needed if your host is not configured to support the automatic install process. This is easily detectable because each time you try to install a plugin or theme you are asked for your FTP information.

To save your FTP information in WordPress add the following options in your wp-config file:

```
define('FTP_USER', 'username');
define('FTP_PASS', 'password');
define('FTP_HOST', 'ftp.example.com:21');
```

Just enter your FTP username, password, and host with port and you're all set! WordPress will no longer ask for your FTP information when using the automatic installer.

You can set additional FTP/SSH options for various configurations:

```
//sets the filesystem method: "direct", "ssh", "ftpext", or "ftpsockets"
define('FS_METHOD', 'ftpext');
// absolute path to root installation directory
define('FTP_BASE', '/public_html/wordpress/');
// absolute path to wp-content directory
define('FTP_CONTENT_DIR', '/public_html/wordpress/wp-content/');
// absolute path to wp-plugins directory
define('FTP_PLUGIN_DIR ', '/ public_html /wordpress/wp-content/plugins/');
// absolute path to your SSH public key
define('FTP_PUBKEY', '/home/username/.ssh/id_rsa.pub');
// absolute path to your SSH private key
define('FTP_PRIVKEY', '/home/username/.ssh/id_rsa');
```

You can also override default file permissions in WordPress using the FS_CHMOD_FILE and FS_CHMOD_DIR options:

```
define('FS_CHMOD_FILE',0644);
define('FS_CHMOD_DIR',0755);
```

The numeric single digit values represent the User, Group, and World permissions set for files and folders on your web server. To learn more about WordPress and file permissions visit: http://codex.wordpress.org/Changing_File_Permissions.

These settings can help with certain hosting companies that use restrictive permissions for all user files. This will override the server settings and should allow WordPress upgrades and auto installations to work.

The WP_CACHE option is required for some caching plugins to work. Enabling this option will include the file wp-content/advanced-cache.php. To enable this option use the following code:

```
define('WP_CACHE', true);
```

WordPress has a lot of constant options that can be set. Luckily there is a PHP function to view all constants currently set on your installation:

```
print_r(@get_defined_constants());
```

An advanced option is forcing SSL on log in to your WordPress site. This requires users to log in via the HTTPS access link and encrypts all data being transferred to and from your web site. To activate SSL on login, add the FORCE_SSL_LOGIN option like so:

```
define('FORCE_SSL_LOGIN', true);
```

You can also force all admin pages to run using SSL. This is activated with the FORCE_SSL_ADMIN option like so:

```
define('FORCE_SSL_ADMIN', true);
```

This forces all admin dashboard pages (/wp-admin) to be encrypted with SSL. Keep in mind that activating this setting slows down your admin page load times, but all data passed to and from WordPress will be encrypted using SSL. Also remember that your web site must be configured to work with SSL. The quick way to test is to visit your site using https, as in https://example.com. If the page loads, SSL is set up on your server.

.htaccess

The `.htaccess` file is used primarily for creating pretty permalinks and keyword injected URLs for your web site. WordPress by default creates ugly query-string formed URLs, usually with an ID present, like `http://example.com/?p=45` These URLs are completely functional , but aren't very friendly to search engines and site visitors. By enabling pretty permalinks WordPress creates URLs based on site content such as post and page titles, category and tag names, and dates for archives.

Enabling Permalinks

To enable permalinks visit the Settings ⇨ Permalinks SubPanel on your WordPress Dashboard, as shown in Figure 3-3. Select any permalink structure other than Default and click the Save Changes link.

Upon saving your changes, WordPress tries to create your default `.htaccess` file. If your root Word-Press directory is writable by the server, the file is created automatically. If WordPress is unable to create the `.htaccess` file, you will see instructions on how to manually create the file, as shown in Figure 3-4.

Creating a permalink structure using the month and year like:

```
/%year%/%monthnum%/%postname%/
```

creates a permalink like this:

```
http://example.com/2010/10/halloween-party
```

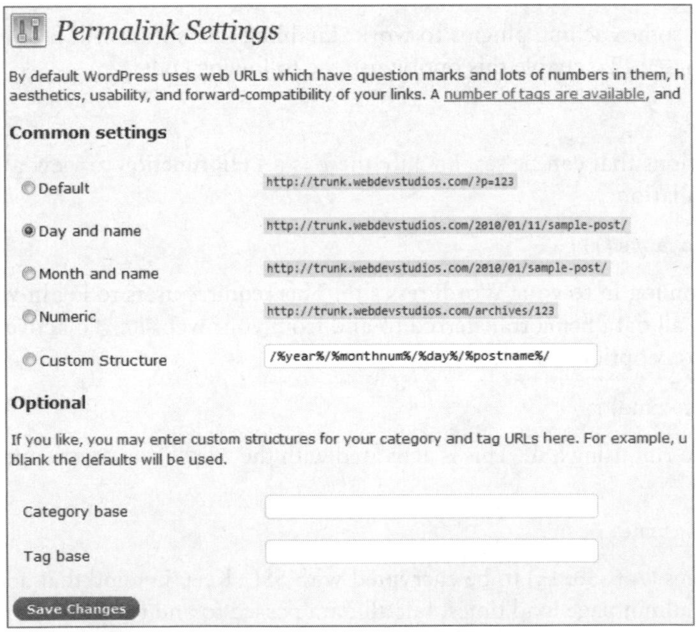

FIGURE 3-3: Enabling permalinks in WordPress

Using permalinks offers many advantages, as described in the following list:

➤ **Search Engine Optimization (SEO):** Keywords in your URL is a must for SEO. Search engines will use these keywords in their algorithm for positioning in their search results.

➤ **Forward Compatibility:** Regardless of what platform your web site uses (WordPress, Drupal, Joomla!), having a solid permalink structure can be easily replicated should you ever migrate.

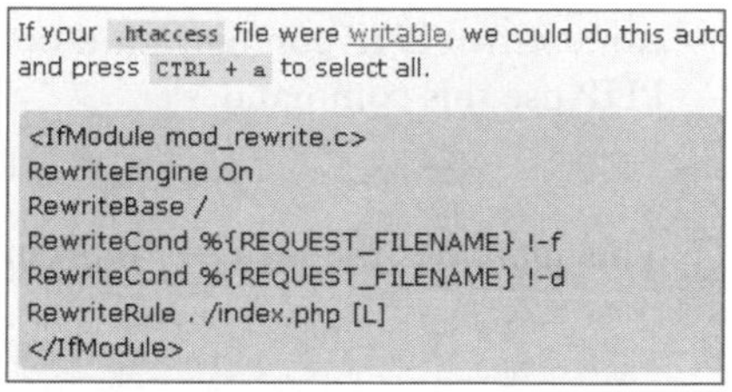

```
If your .htaccess file were writable, we could do this auto
and press CTRL + a to select all.

<IfModule mod_rewrite.c>
RewriteEngine On
RewriteBase /
RewriteCond %{REQUEST_FILENAME} !-f
RewriteCond %{REQUEST_FILENAME} !-d
RewriteRule . /index.php [L]
</IfModule>
```

FIGURE 3-4: Manual info for creating the .htaccess file

➤ **Usability:** Visitor-unfriendly ID URLs make it equally unpleasant to share a link with a friend. It's difficult to differentiate the content between your ID driven URLs.

➤ **Sharing:** In this Internet era of social networking, sharing is a natural extension of our online presence. Keywords in the URL would make finding your link extremely easy and convey an immediate context for the content.

.htaccess Rewriting Rules

The "secret sauce" behind the WordPress permalink mechanism is summarized in two rewriting rules added to the .htaccess file when you enable permalinks:

```
RewriteCond %{REQUEST_FILENAME} !-f
RewriteCond %{REQUEST_FILENAME} !-d
```

Quite simply, these rules check the URL used to access your site to see if it refers to an existing file or directory in the filesystem hierarchy. The !-f and !-d notations are negations; .htaccess is ensuring that the URL does not refer to any valid filesystem pathname. If the URL does in fact match a valid file, for example, a WordPress administrative function like wp-login.php, then the URL is left unchanged. If there's no file or directory with that name, the URL is handed to the WordPress core code to be converted into a query against the content database. We'll dig into the steps used to convert a URL string into a MySQL query in a bit more detail as a preface to our discussion of the content display loop in Chapter 5.

The .htaccess file can also manage URL redirects. If you change your About page from http://example.com/about to http://example.com/about-me, anyone who visits your original URL will hit a 404 page. A URL redirect will redirect from the old URL to the new URL so your visitors won't get lost. This also alerts search engines about the new URL so they can update their index. We'll cover rewriting rules for content that has moved or been migrated in Chapter 14.

Following is an example of a 301 permanent redirect to a static page:

```
redirect 301 /about http://example.com/about-me
```

Configuration Control Through .htaccess

The .htaccess file is very powerful and can control more than just URL structure. For instance, you can control PHP configuration options using the .htaccess file. To increase the memory allotted to PHP use this command:

```
php_value memory_limit 64M
```

This increases the memory limit in PHP to 64MB. You can also increase the max file size upload and post size:

```
php_value upload_max_filesize 20M
php_value post_max_size 20M
```

Now the maximum file size you can post from a form and upload is set to 20MB. Most hosting companies set these values to around 2MB by default, so these are settings that will be used often for larger file uploads. Not all hosting companies will allow these values to be set in your .htaccess file, and could create an error on your web site if that is the case.

The .htaccess file can also be used for security purposes. Using .htaccess allows you to restrict access to your web site by IP address, essentially locking it down from anonymous visitors. To lock down your web site by IP addresses, add the following code to your .htaccess file:

```
AuthUserFile /dev/null
AuthGroupFile /dev/null
AuthName "Access Control"
AuthType Basic
order deny,allow
deny from all
#IP address to whitelist
allow from xxx.xxx.xxx.xxx
```

Replace xxx.xxx.xxx.xxx with any IP address that you want to grant access to your web site. You can have multiple "allow from" lines so add as many IP addresses as you need. This will only allow access to your web site if you are using an IP address defined here.

A more widely used option is to lock down your wp-admin directory. This means only IP addresses you specify can access your admin dashboard URLs. This makes it much harder for anyone else to try to hack your WordPress backend. To accomplish this create a separate .htaccess file in your wp-admin directory with the preceding code.

Remember that most ISPs assign client addresses dynamically, so the IP address of the computer you are using will change on occasion. If you get locked out, just update your .htaccess file with your new IP address or delete the file altogether. This is not a good tip if you allow open registrations on your web site because you need to allow your users access to the wp-admin directory.

You can also enable error logging from the .htaccess file. The first step is to create a php-errors.log file in your WordPress root directory. Then add the following code to your .htaccess file to enable error logging:

```
php_flag display_startup_errors off
php_flag display_errors off
```

```
php_flag html_errors off
php_flag  log_errors on
php_value error_log /public_html/php-errors.log
```

This enables error logging, but suppresses any error messages from displaying. Again this is a perfect setup for a production environment because you don't want errors publicly displayed.

The .maintenance File

WordPress has a built-in maintenance mode that can be enabled by the `.maintenance` file. To test this feature simply create a new `.maintenance` file and add the following line of code:

```
<?php $upgrading = time(); ?>
```

Add this file to your WordPress root directory and your web site will instantly enter maintenance mode. This locks down your web site for all visitors and displays a generic maintenance message. The `time()` function can be replaced with any UNIX-formatted timestamp.

You can set a custom maintenance page by creating a `maintenance.php` file and placing it in your `wp-content` directory. WordPress uses this file to display during any forced maintenance periods that you set. This allows you to create a custom maintenance notice to your web site visitors.

This file is also used by the WordPress automatic upgrade process. A `.maintenance` file is created right before WordPress installs the new core files during an upgrade. This ensures there are never any error messages for your visitors during this process.

WP-CONTENT USER PLAYGROUND

The `wp-content` directory stores just about every file for customizing WordPress. This directory stores your plugins, themes, and additional files to extend WordPress in any way imaginable.

The `wp-content` directory has a single PHP file, `index.php`. The contents of this file are shown here:

```
<?php
// Silence is golden.
?>
```

So what's the point of this file? Actually this is a very important file. The `index.php` file blocks anyone from viewing a directory listing of your `wp-contents` folder. If the `index.php` file didn't exist, and your web server allowed directory listings, visiting `http://domain.com/wp-contents` would display all of the files and folders in that directory. This can help hackers gain access to key files that might help exploit your web site.

If you are manually upgrading WordPress, make sure you avoid overwriting your `wp-content` directory.

Plugins

Plugins are stored in the `wp-content/plugins` directory. A plugin can be a single file or multiple files inside of a folder. Any files inside the `/plugins` directory are scanned by WordPress to determine if the file is a properly formatted WordPress plugin. If the file is determined to be a plugin it appears under the Plugins ⇨ Installed SubPanel on your admin dashboard ready to be activated.

Remember, to automatically deactivate a plugin you can remove it from your /plugins folder. If the plugin files are missing WordPress deactivates the plugin before trying to render your web site.

We'll be revisiting plugins in Chapter 7, "Plugin Development."

Themes

Themes are stored in the wp-content/themes directory. Each theme must exist in its own subdirectory, and must consist of the proper template files for WordPress to recognize it as a usable theme. At minimum an index.php and a style.css file must exist in the theme directory, along with proper tagging to display under the Appearance ⇨ Themes SubPanel on your admin dashboard.

WordPress can store as many themes in this directory as your server allows. You can easily view a preview of any theme, or activate a new theme, under the Appearance ⇨ Themes SubPanel. We'll cover themes in much more detail in Chapter 8.

Uploads and Media Directory

WordPress stores uploaded media in the wp-content/uploads folder. This directory does not exist in a default installation of WordPress. The /uploads directory is created the first time you successfully upload a file to WordPress.

By default WordPress stores uploads in month- and year-based folders. So your uploaded image would be stored like so:

```
/wp-content/uploads/2010/06/image.png
```

You can modify the /uploads path and directory name under the Settings ⇨ Miscellaneous SubPanel in your WordPress Dashboard, shown in Figure 3-5.

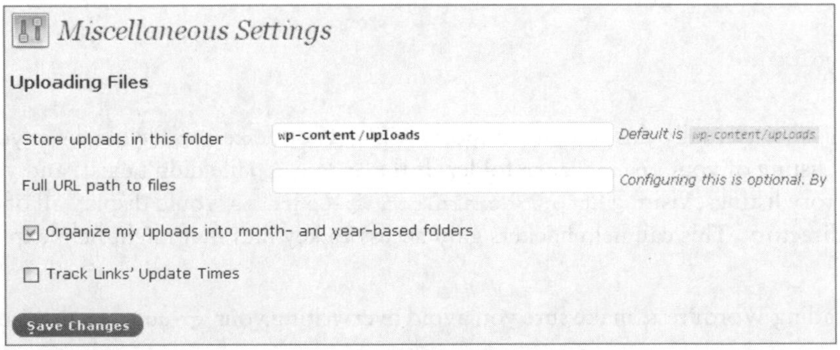

FIGURE 3-5: Changing the uploads directory

Before you can upload any images or files in WordPress you need to set the /wp-content directory to be writable. When you upload your first image, WordPress auto-creates the /uploads directory and any needed subdirectories. After you have successfully uploaded your first image, reset the `/wp-content` permissions to not be writable, typically 755. Currently there is no way to import images uploaded via FTP into the WordPress Media Library. If making the `uploads` directory writeable is not an option, there are plugins available (such as NextGen Gallery) that include this functionality.

WordPress MU stores uploaded media in a different manner. Instead of one uploads directory, WPMU creates a `blogs.dir` directory. Inside this folder are multiple subdirectories named with an ID. This ID is the blog ID the folder is attached to. For example, your first WordPress MU blog upload directory would look like this:

```
/blogs.dir/1/files/
```

This helps keep individual blog uploads separated and easier to maintain.

Upgrade Directory

The `wp-content/upgrade` directory is automatically created by WordPress when you use the automatic upgrade process. This folder is used by WordPress to store the new version of WordPress that is downloaded from WordPress.org. The compressed WordPress download is extracted in this folder prior to the upgrade. This folder should remain untouched for automatic upgrades to process successfully. If this directory is deleted, WordPress re-creates it the next time you run the auto-upgrader.

Custom Directories

Some plugins that require a lot of custom files will store those files in a directory in your `wp-content` folders.

The Super Cache plugin (`http://wordpress.org/extend/plugins/wp-super-cache/`) creates a `/wp-content/cache` directory to store all of the cached pages created for your web site. A cached page is simply a fully generated page on your web site saved as a static HTML file. Instead of generating the page each time a user clicks one of your links, the cache plugin serves up the static HTML file to the visitor. This dramatically decreases WordPress load times and increases performance because pages aren't generated on each view, but rather only when the cache is regenerated based on your settings.

The Super Cache plugin also adds two files to your `wp-content` directory: `advanced-cache.php` and `wp-cache-config.php`. These two files are required for Super Cache to function correctly. When Super Cache is activated it tries to create these two files. If it fails a notice appears alerting you of this. The files exist in the Super Cache plugin directory and can be manually moved to the `wp-content` directory.

The most popular image gallery plugin, NextGen Gallery (`http://wordpress.org/extend/plugins/nextgen-gallery/`), creates a `/wp-content/gallery` directory to store all of the images uploaded to your NextGen image galleries. Each gallery created is a subdirectory under `/gallery`. This helps keep your gallery image files very organized and easy to work with.

The WP-DB Backup plugin (`http://wordpress.org/extend/plugins/wp-db-backup/`) creates a `/wp-content/backup-b158b` folder (where `b158b` is a random string) to store local backups of your database. When you select the Save to Server option all database backup files will be stored in this directory. It's important to not delete your backups unless you are sure they are not needed anymore.

Now that we've covered the file system view of WordPress, it's time to go deeper into what the code that lives in the core actually does.

Tour of the Core

WHAT'S IN THIS CHAPTER?

➤ Exploring the WordPress Core files

➤ Searching through Core files as Reference

➤ Working with the WordPress Codex

➤ Understanding Inline Documentation

To understand how to extend WordPress properly, you must first learn how the Core of WordPress functions. This will help you learn what tools are available in the WordPress Core to make your life easier. WordPress handles most of the tedious coding and logic problems for you.

The WordPress Core is the best resource for learning how WordPress works. The beauty of open source software is you have all of the code at your disposal. If you are ever unsure how a certain aspect of WordPress functions, just start digging into the code! The answers are all there, it's just a matter of finding and understanding them.

WHAT'S IN THE CORE?

The WordPress Core is powered by a set of files that are part of the original WordPress software download. These are required "Core" files that WordPress needs to function properly. The Core files are only expected to change when you upgrade WordPress to a newer version.

The Core does not include your custom files for plugins, themes, database settings, the .htaccess file, and so on. The Core also does not include any media you have uploaded to WordPress. Basically any files added to WordPress after installation are considered outside of the Core.

The WordPress Core files are primarily PHP files, but also contain CSS, JavaScript, XML, HTML, and image files. These files control everything about WordPress including how content pages are generated to display, loading the configured theme and plugins, loading all options and settings, and much more. In short, the Core contains several major function types:

➤ *Posts and Pages*: Creating, storing, retrieving and interacting with the majority of your WordPress content. Our discussion of The Loop that controls content display and ordering in Chapter 5 relies heavily on these functions.

➤ *Metadata*: Everything from tags and categories to user-created taxonomies. We'll explore the data models used in Chapter 6.

➤ *Themes*: Supporting functions for WordPress themes. We walk through theme development and its relationship to these functions in Chapter 8.

➤ *Actions, Filters and Plugins*: Framework for extending WordPress, covered in more detail in Chapter 7.

➤ *Users and Authors:* Creating and managing access control to your site, and key to the security and enterprise use topics in Chapter 11 and Chapter 13.

➤ *Feeds, Formatting* and *Comments*: We'll refer to these as needed.

This chapter digs into these files as you explore the WordPress Core files. Think of this chapter as your guidebook to the "how" of exploring the WordPress Core; it is a field guide companion to the WordPress Codex documentation for user-contributed discussion and explanation. It's also imperative to be comfortable browsing and searching the Core to complement the functional introduction we provide here. We aren't going to provide an exhaustive list of every WordPress function, both because the list changes and evolves as the WordPress Core undergoes continuous development, and because our goal is to convey developer and deployer expertise and not summarize the Codex.

WordPress comes packaged with two Core plugins: Akismet and Hello Dolly. These two plugins exist in your plugins directory inside wp-content. Even though these two plugins are a part of the WordPress Core files, they are not considered Core functionality because they must be activated to function.

WordPress also comes packaged with two Core themes: default and classic. The default theme, nicknamed Kubrick, is the default theme on a fresh installation of WordPress. The classic theme was the original default theme since version 1.0, but was replaced by the Kubrick theme some time ago. As with the included plugins, these theme files are not considered Core functionality because they can easily be replaced with any theme that you want to use on your web site.

USING THE CORE AS A REFERENCE

To use the WordPress Core as a reference you need to understand what to expect in the Core files. Most WordPress Core files contain documentation in the form of code comments. Typically this is displayed in the header of the file and gives an overall summary of the Core file you are viewing.

All Core files, other than images, can be viewed using a text editor program. Depending on your default program settings, you may need to open up your text editor first and then open the file rather than just opening up the file directly. It's also helpful to use a text editor that has syntax highlight, meaning PHP syntax would be highlighted to help you read the code easier.

There is a full list of compatible text editors on the Codex at `http://codex.wordpress.org/Glossary #Text_editor`.

Inline Documentation

Most WordPress Core files contain inline documentation. This means each function is explained in detail directly before the function in a comment block. The following is the defined template for documenting a WordPress function:

```
/**
 * Short Description
 *
 * Long Description
 *
 * @package WordPress
 * @since version
 *
 * @param    type     $varname     Description
 * @return   type                  Description
 */
```

This is amazingly helpful in understanding how functions work. The comment includes a short and long description. It also includes the version of WordPress it was added in. This helps distinguish new functions added to WordPress when a new version is released.

Available parameters are also listed along with the parameter data type. A data type is the type of data that is required for the parameter. For example an ID parameter would likely use the `int` (integer) data type. The final piece of information is the return value. The return value data type is also listed.

All new functions added to WordPress are documented using the preceding template.

Finding Functions

Looking up a function in the Core is the quickest way to learn how a specific WordPress function works. You can see exactly what attributes are allowed to be sent to the function, as well as what the function actually does and the return values.

To start, make sure you have downloaded the latest version of WordPress locally to your computer. You will search these files as a reference for WordPress. Open up any text editor you have that can search files (I recommend TextPad for Windows and Textmate for the Mac). When searching for a function you want to eliminate calls to that function from your search. Do this by including the word *function* at the start of your search, as in "function wp_head." Not everything in WordPress is a function, but this is a good place to start. If you don't find any matches, remove *function* from the beginning of your search. Also remember to set your text editor to search all files (`*.*`), not just `.txt` files.

As an example, look at the `add_post_meta` function. This function is used to add metadata, or custom field data, to a post in WordPress. For example, we could save the current weather on every post we create in WordPress as a post metadata value. You need to know exactly what values the function expects before you can use it. Open up your text editor and search all files in WordPress for "function add_post_meta." The search should produce one result in `wp-includes/post.php`:

```
function add_post_meta($post_id, $meta_key,
    $meta_value, $unique = false) {
```

Right away you notice four variables that can be sent to this function: `$post_id`, `$meta_key`, `$meta_value`, and `$unique`. Notice the inline documentation listed directly above the function. In this case the `add_post_meta` documentation looks like this:

```
/**
 * Add meta data field to a post.
 *
 * Post meta data is called "Custom Fields"
 * on the Administration Panels.
 *
 * @since 1.5.0
 * @uses $wpdb
 * @link http://codex.wordpress.org/Function_Reference/add_post_meta
 *
 * @param int $post_id Post ID.
 * @param string $key Metadata name.
 * @param mixed $value Metadata value.
 * @param bool $unique Optional, default is false.
 *   Whether the same key should not be added.
 * @return bool False for failure. True for success.
 */
```

This is an extremely valuable block of content. The comment has a short description about what the function does, in this case "Add meta data field to a post." The comment also notes when the function was added (since version 1.5.0), what global variables are used (`$wpdb`), and a link directly to the Codex article detailing this function. *Global variables* are variables that are used throughout WordPress to store key pieces of information that can be accessed anywhere, in this case the `add_post_meta` function. For example, the `$wpdb` global variable is an instance of the WordPress Database Class containing all of the connection and context needed to talk to your database. As you'll see in Chapter 5, there are a few global variables that contain the default or current state information for WordPress, but there are also times when you'll want to create your own instances of these objects for more fine-grain or custom control of execution.

There is also information about the four variables, including the variable type and what each variable is responsible for, as well as what the expected return values will be. In this case the function will return `True` if successful, and `False` if not.

This alone is enough information to understand how this function works, but let's dig into the code for a better understanding. The first two lines look like this:

```
if ( !$meta_key )
    return false;
```

This means if the `$meta_key` value is empty, return `false` and exit the function. If the meta key value is empty, then you have no name for the meta data and therefore can't add it to the database. The next line in the function is:

```
global $wpdb;
```

This references the global database connection object. Functions and data in this class are used for all database manipulation handled in WordPress, which we'll cover in more detail in Chapter 6. So far this is pretty standard stuff. The next line actually calls another function:

```
if ( $the_post = wp_is_post_revision($post_id) )
    $post_id = $the_post;
```

The first thing you need to do is determine what exactly `wp_is_post_revision` does. To do this search your WordPress Core files for "function wp_is_post_revision." Notice the comment header above the function:

```
/**
 * Determines if the specified post is a revision.
 *
 * @package WordPress
 * @subpackage Post_Revisions
 * @since 2.6.0
 *
 * @param int|object $post Post ID or post object.
 * @return bool|int False if not a revision,
 *    ID of revision's parent otherwise.
 */
```

So now you know this function is used to determine whether a specified post is a revision. If the post is not a revision the function returns `False`; however, if it is a revision it returns the ID of the revision's parent.

Now back to the original code. You can determine that the post ID you sent to the function is verified to not be a post revision, but rather the actual published post. If the post ID is a revision the function assigns the parent ID to the `$post_id` variable and continues on. Next, the meta key value is passed through:

```
// expected_slashed ($meta_key)
$meta_key = stripslashes($meta_key);
```

`stripslashes` is a PHP function that removes any backslashes found in your string. The next line:

```
if ( $unique && $wpdb->get_var( $wpdb->prepare(
"SELECT meta_key FROM $wpdb->postmeta WHERE meta_key = %s AND post_id = %d",
$meta_key, $post_id ) ) )
    return false;
```

is a conditional statement that checks two values. The first is `$unique`, which by default is `False`. If you pass the `$unique` value as `True` when calling this function, the meta key name must be unique. If this value is `False`, you can add multiple values to the same meta key, essentially creating an array of values. If `$unique` is set to `True`, WordPress will execute a database query to determine if the meta key already exists. If the meta key exists, the function returns `false` and exits. Next up in our function the meta value is serialized and slashes are stripped if needed:

```
$meta_value = maybe_serialize( stripslashes_deep($meta_value) );
```

Serialized data is a data encoding format in PHP used to generate a storable representation of a value. For example, serializing an Array will essentially flatten the Array values into a string format making it suitable to store in the database. Finally the data is ready to be inserted into the WordPress database:

```
$wpdb->insert( $wpdb->postmeta, compact( 'post_id', 'meta_key',
'meta_value' ) );
```

This line inserts the new post metadata into the database. The next line deletes any cached `post_meta` data:

```
wp_cache_delete($post_id, 'post_meta');
```

And here's the final line of the function:

```
return true;
```

If the function makes it to the end you can assume it was successful and `true` would be returned.

After viewing this example it should be more apparent how useful the WordPress Core code can be. You learned exactly how this function works by exploring the source code. All the answers to your questions exist within the Core so it's essential to have a good understanding of how to utilize the Core to your advantage.

Exploring the Code

The WordPress Core has certain files that contain many of the most popular WordPress functions. These functions are used for all WordPress APIs and can be used in any custom plugin or theme. The following sections detail the WordPress Core files that contain key pieces of code for working with WordPress.

Functions.php

The `functions.php` file contains the main WordPress API functions. These functions are used to easily interact with WordPress using a standardized method. Plugins, themes, and the WordPress Core all use these functions.

➤ `current_time` – retrieves the current time based on specified type

➤ `add_option`, `update_option`, `get_option`: Functions to create, update, and display a saved option

➤ `force_ssl_login`: Requires SSL (https) login to WordPress

➤ `wp_nonce_ays`: Displays the "Are You Sure?" dialog box confirming the action

Formatting.php

The `formatting.php` file contains the WordPress API formatting functions. These functions format the output in many different ways:

➤ `wp_specialchars`: Converts characters into HTML entities

➤ `esc_attr`: Used to clean a string containing HTML

➤ `is_email`: Verifies an e-mail is valid

Pluggable.php

The pluggable functions file lets you override certain Core functions of WordPress. WordPress loads these functions if they are still undefined after all plugins have been loaded. Some of the more commonly used functions are listed here:

➤ `wp_mail`: Sends e-mail from WordPress

➤ `get_userdata`: Returns all user data from the specified user ID

➤ `get_currentuserinfo`: Returns user data for the currently logged-in user

➤ `wp_signon`: Authenticates a user

➤ `wp_logout`: Logs out a user, destroying the user session

➤ `wp_redirect`: Redirects to another page

➤ `get_avatar`: Returns the user's avatar

Plugin.php

The `plugin.php` file contains the WordPress Plugin API functions. This includes:

➤ `add_filter`: Hooks that the WordPress Core launches to filter content before displaying on the screen or saving in the database

➤ `add_action`: Hooks that the WordPress Core launches at specific points of execution

➤ `register_activation_hook`: Hook called when a plugin is activated

➤ `register_deactivation_hook`: Hook called when a plugin is deactivated

Post.php

The `post.php` file contains the functions used in the post process of WordPress. This includes:

➤ `wp_insert_post`: Creates a new post

➤ `get_posts`: Retrieves a list of the latest posts' matching criteria

➤ `get_pages`: Retrieves a list of pages allowing parent-child relationships

➤ `add_post_meta`: Creates metadata (custom field data) on a post

➤ `get_post_meta`: Retrieves metadata (custom field data) on a post

Category.php

The `category.php` file contains the functions used by the WordPress Category API. This includes:

➤ `get_categories`: Retrieves an array of category objects based on parameters

➤ `get_cat_ID`: Returns the category ID from its name

Many more Core functions you can be used when developing custom themes and plugins for Word-Press. Take a few minutes and explore the Core files inside `/wp-includes`. This directory contains most of the WordPress API Core function files.

To learn more about any function listed here open up the corresponding file and view the source code. Remember that each function will have inline documentation explaining how to utilize the function correctly. We'll cover the Plugin API functions in more detail in Chapter 7. The Core functions used by themes will be covered in Chapter 8.

WORDPRESS CODEX AND RESOURCES

WordPress has many different online resources that are extremely useful in learning and working with WordPress. These resources should be bookmarked for quick reference and are used by beginners and experts alike.

What Is the Codex?

The WordPress Codex is an online wiki for WordPress documentation located on WordPress.org. WordPress.org describes the Codex as an "encyclopedia of WordPress knowledge." You can visit the WordPress Codex by going to `http://codex.wordpress.org` or by clicking the Docs tab in the header of WordPress.org.

The Codex is a wiki-based web site, which means anyone can create, edit, and contribute to the articles within the Codex. The Codex is jam packed with useful knowledge covering all aspects of WordPress. From "Getting Started with WordPress" to more advanced developer topics, the Codex is an essential resource for anyone looking to learn more about WordPress.

The Codex is available in many different languages. To find a Codex version translated in your language visit the Multilingual Codex page at `http://codex.wordpress.org/Multilingual_Codex`. You can also contribute to the Codex and help expand on any language or create your own language if it is not listed.

Using the Codex

The Codex can be used in many different ways. The most common method is by searching the Codex using the search box in the header (see Figure 4-1) to easily search through the Codex for appropriate articles matching your search criteria.

FIGURE 4-1: WordPress.org Codex search

By default the Codex will only search documentation. As you can see from Figure 4-1, you can also select to search the Support Forums, WP.org Blogs, and the Bug Database. It can be useful to expand your search into these other areas if you aren't finding the answers you need in the Codex documentation.

You can also navigate through the index of articles on the Codex homepage. These articles are organized by topic and generally ordered by level of difficulty. There is also a topic toward the top for the latest version of WordPress. The articles here cover new features, compatibility tests for plugins and themes, installing, upgrading, and support for the new version.

There is also an extensive glossary of terms available for the Codex. This can help familiarize you with common words used throughout the Codex. You can view the official Codex Glossary at `http://codex.wordpress.org/Glossary`.

Another method is to use the quick index. This index allows you to look up an article by the first letter of the article's title. You can find the quick index at `http://codex.wordpress.org/Codex:Quick_index`.

A WordPress Lessons page is also featured in the Codex at `http://codex.wordpress.org/WordPress_Lessons`. This page lists out lessons on how to learn specific elements of WordPress. The lessons are organized by topic and are a great place to start if you are unsure what to read first.

Function Reference

WordPress functions are described in the Codex with an individual Function Reference page for each WordPress API function available. These pages explain in detail exactly how a WordPress function works, as shown in Figure 4-2. Bookmark this page for a quick reference on WordPress functions and their capabilities. The official Function Reference is located at `http://codex.wordpress.org/Function_Reference`.

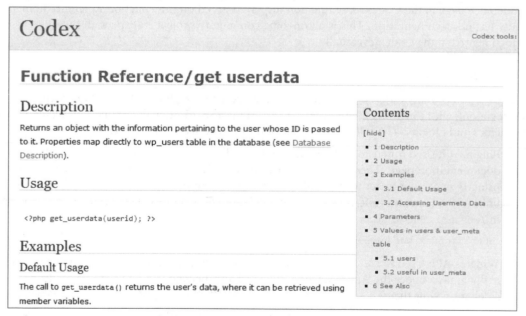

FIGURE 4-2: Function reference for get_userdata

Think of the Function Reference as an online and expanded version of a function's inline documentation. The reference has a description explaining how the function works and how it is used. The individual parameters are listed along with data types and a description of each.

The most useful section of the Function Reference is the examples toward the bottom. The examples make it very easy to see exactly how to use the function. The get_userdata example is shown here:

```php
<?php $user_info = get_userdata(1);

    echo('Username: ' . $user_info->user_login . "\n");
    echo('User level: ' . $user_info->user_level . "\n");
    echo('User ID: ' . $user_info->ID . "\n");
?>
```

This example shows how to load specific user data for user ID 1. The example output is as follows:

```
Username: admin
User Level: 10
User ID: 1
```

This is a simple example, but this along with the additional reference information can help you easily learn a new function and how to use it properly in your code.

The final Function Reference topic lists related functions. This can help identify a similar function that may accomplish that task you are working on. For example, the wp_insert_post function lists wp_update_post and wp_delete_post as related functions.

The majority of the WordPress API functions are well documented, but not all functions have a Function Reference page in the Codex. Any function displayed in red on the Function Reference homepage currently has no documentation. This is an ongoing community project so expect all functions to be fully documented in the Codex eventually.

WordPress APIs

WordPress features many different APIs that help interact with WordPress. Each API is documented in the Codex along with functions used in the API. An API is a set of predefined functions available for use in themes and plugins. The following is a list of the current WordPress APIs:

➤ **Plugin API:** Used for custom plugin development. The Codex features an extensive Plugin API documentation page. There is an introduction to Hooks, Actions, and Filters. These are the primary ways to interact with WordPress from a custom-built plugin. The Plugin API page links to the Function Reference pages for available API functions. These functions are located in /wp-includes/plugins.php.

http://codex.wordpress.org/Plugin_API

➤ **Widgets API:** Used to create and maintain widgets in your plugin. The widget will automatically appear under the Appearance ➪ Widgets SubPanel and can be used on any defined sidebar on your theme.

http://codex.wordpress.org/Widgets_API

➤ **Shortcode API:** Used for adding shortcodes in your plugin. A *shortcode* is a macro code added to a post. This allows a plugin to grab that shortcode and execute specific commands and display elements in place of it in your post. Shortcodes can also accept parameters to alter the output.

An example Core WordPress shortcode is [gallery]. Adding [gallery] to your post automatically displays all images uploaded to that post in a gallery style. When editing a post, you will see the [gallery] shortcode, but viewing it on the public side of your web site displays the actual gallery of images.

`http://codex.wordpress.org/Shortcode_API`

➤ **HTTP API:** Used for sending an HTTP request from WordPress. This API is a standardized method to grab the content of an external URL. Basically this API takes the provided URL and tests a series of PHP methods for sending the request. Depending on the hosting environment, WordPress uses the first method it deems to be configured correctly to make the HTTP request.

The current HTTP API PHP methods tested are cUrl, Streams, Fopen, FSockopen, and HTTP extension. The methods are also checked exactly in that order. You can use the Core Control plugin (`http://wordpress.org/extend/plugins/Core-control/`) to specifically choose which method is used for all HTTP requests.

Using the HTTP API you could easily interact with the Google Maps API to dynamically generate maps and plots. The HTTP API can also easily interact with the Twitter API, allowing you to post/read tweets directly from WordPress.

`http://codex.wordpress.org/HTTP_API`

➤ **Settings API:** Used for creating a settings page. This API is used for creating and managing custom options for your plugins and themes. The main advantage of using the Settings API is security. The API scrubs all of the setting data saved by the user. This means no more worrying about nonces, data validation, and cross site scripting (XSS) attacks when saving setting data. This is much easier than the old method of data validation each time you needed to save settings in a plugin.

`http://codex.wordpress.org/Settings_API`

➤ **Dashboard Widgets API:** Used for creating admin dashboard widgets. Widgets added from the API automatically contain all jQuery features that the Core admin dashboard widgets have including drag/drop, minimize, and screen options hiding.

`http://codex.wordpress.org/Dashboard_Widgets_API`

➤ **Rewrite API:** Used for creating custom rewrite rules. This API allows you to create custom rewrite rules just as you would in your `.htaccess` file. You can also create custom permalink structure tags (that is, `%postname%`), add static endpoints (that is, `/my-page/`), and even add additional feed links. The Rewrite API functions are located in `/wp-includes/rewrite.php`.

`http://codex.wordpress.org/Rewrite_API`

Remember that all WordPress APIs can be used in custom plugin and theme development. This is the primary method of extending WordPress with additional features and functionality. Utilizing the preceding APIs creates an easy and standardized way of interacting with WordPress.

Codex Controversy

As with any wiki there will always be controversy over the accuracy of the articles within it and the Codex is no different. One problem that has plagued the Codex is the freshness of the articles. WordPress is being developed at a decent pace and thus the Codex needs to keep up that pace in order to be accurate. Unfortunately that doesn't always happen, and some material is outdated. The WordPress

Codex is a community project, so you can easily create an account and start helping out! We cover contributing to WordPress in Chapter 15.

Another problem that exists within the Codex is the organization of the content. Currently there is so much information in the Codex that it can be hard and confusing to find the answers you are looking for. Again, one of our motivations for this introduction to the WordPress Core was to provide you with a map to help narrow the scope of your searches and to introduce related functional topics.

DON'T HACK CORE!

Whereas exploring the WordPress Core and using it as a reference is highly encouraged, hacking the Core is not. Hacking the Core means making any changes to the Core files of WordPress. A change could be as simple as one line of code, but a hack is a hack and doing so could cause major problems down the road.

Why Not?

Hacking the WordPress Core can make it very difficult to upgrade to the latest version of WordPress. Keeping WordPress current is an important step in overall web site security. If any security vulnerability is discovered a patch is typically released very quickly. If you can't upgrade because you have modified Core files, you are opening up your web site to these security vulnerabilities being exploited and your web site getting hacked.

Hacking Core can also lead to an unstable web site because many parts of WordPress rely on other parts to function as expected. If you make changes to those parts it could break something completely unrelated to what you have changed.

Security is another reason why you shouldn't hack Core. WordPress Core is viewed and scrutinized by security experts all over the world. By hacking Core you are relying on your own expertise to make your hacks secure. If you don't understand the many different ways a hacker can exploit your code you might end up creating a security vulnerability within the Core of WordPress.

The final reason why you should never hack Core is compassion. That is, compassion toward the developer who comes after you to maintain the web site. Most web sites will change developers over the years so there is no guarantee you will be working on a particular web site five years from now. Imagine the developer that follows you trying to determine what Core files were hacked to make the web site function. This can be a nightmare for any developer and it puts the web site owner in a bad position because most developers will refuse to work on a hacked version of WordPress. If you hack Core, you are building dependencies that will either be misunderstood or hidden, and when the WordPress Core is upgraded for this site, the hacked Core will break in silent, evil, or loud ways.

Alternatives to Hacking Core

Any feature or functionality that does not exist in WordPress can be added with a plugin. Sometimes a Core hack may be the easy answer, but in the long run it will make your life harder. We have yet to come across a feature we needed that we couldn't incorporate with a plugin. WordPress is extremely flexible, which is one of its major strengths, and therefore should never be hacked. Don't hack Core!

If you are fascinated by the WordPress Core and its intricacies, you should join the WordPress Developer Community and get involved fixing bugs and contributing to the Core build of WordPress. We'll cover this in detail in Chapter 15.

5

The Loop

WHAT'S IN THIS CHAPTER?

➤ Understanding the flow of the Loop and where it can be used

➤ Learning how the Loop determines what content to display

➤ Customizing the Loop with different granularities of data access

➤ Understanding template tags and how they work

➤ Understanding global variables and their relationship to Loop processing

➤ Working outside of the Loop

The Loop refers to how WordPress determines what content (posts and pages) to display on a page you are visiting. The Loop can display a single post or page, or a group of posts and pages that are selected and then displayed by looping through the content, thus it's called the Loop.

This is how WordPress displays blog posts by default. The Loop selects posts from the MySQL database based on a set of parameters, and those parameters are typically determined by the URL used to access your WordPress blog. For example, the homepage shows all blog posts in reverse chronological order by default. A category page, accessed via a URL like http://example.com/category/zombies, only shows blog posts assigned to that category, in this case the "zombies" list. An archive page only shows blog posts that are dated with that particular month and year. WordPress maps nearly every parameter about your posts into a selection variable, providing the basis for an equally wide number of different ways to alter the Loop output. It is very easy to customize what content is displayed and where on your web site with a thorough understanding of how the Loop translates a URL into what you see when you access that link.

This chapter discusses how the Loop works, where the Loop can be used, and the logical flow of the Loop. It also covers how to customize the Loop using the many different functions and data access methods available in WordPress. Global variables that maintain the current state are also discussed along with working outside of the Loop.

UNDERSTANDING THE LOOP

Understanding how the Loop functions will help you understand how you can control it. Controlling the Loop to display exactly the content you want will be one of your most used tools in developing WordPress-powered web sites. Because the Loop is at the heart of every WordPress theme, being able to customize the display content opens up the doors to making WordPress look and act however you want.

To understand the Loop, it helps to break down the steps WordPress takes to generate a page's content:

➤ The URL is matched against existing files and directories in the WordPress installation. If the file is there, it is loaded by the web server. WordPress doesn't actually get involved in this decision; it's up to your web server and the .htaccess file created by WordPress to decide if the URL is something handled by the web server or to be turned into a WordPress content query. This was covered in Chapter 4.

➤ If the URL is passed to WordPress, it has to determine what content to load. For example, when visiting a specific tag page like http://example.com/tag/bacon, WordPress will determine that you are viewing a tag and load the appropriate template, select the posts saved with that tag, and generate the output for the tag page.

➤ The translation of URL to content selection magic happens inside of the parse_query() method within the WP_Query object that WordPress created early on in its processing. WordPress parses the URL first into a set of query parameters that are described in the next section. All query strings from the URL are passed into WordPress to determine what content to display, even if they look like nicely formatted pathnames. If your site is using pretty permalinks, the values between slashes in those permalinks are merely parameters for query strings. For example, http://example.com/tag/bacon is the same as http://example.com?tag=bacon, which conveys a query string of "tag with a value of bacon."

➤ WordPress then converts the query specification parameters into a MySQL database query to retrieve the content. The workhorse here is the get_posts() method within the WP_Query object that we describe later in this chapter. The get_posts() method takes all of those query parameters and turns them into SQL statements, eventually invoking the SQL string on the MySQL database server and extracting the desired content. The content returned from the database is then saved in the WP_Query object to be used in the WordPress Loop and cached to speed up other references to the same posts made before another database query is executed.

➤ Once the content is retrieved, WordPress sets all of the is_ conditional tags such as is_home and is_page. These are set as part of executing the default query based on the URL parsing, and we'll discuss cases where you may need to reset these tags.

➤ WordPress picks a template from your theme based on the type of query and the number of posts returned, for example, a single post or a category only query, and the output of the query is passed to this default invocation of the Loop.

The Loop can be customized for different web site purposes. For example, a news site might use the Loop to display the latest news headlines. A business directory could use the Loop to display local businesses alphabetically by name, or always put posts about sponsoring businesses at the top of every displayed page. A photo blog might use the Loop to display the most recent photos loaded into the web site. The possibilities are endless when customizing the Loop in WordPress because it gives you complete control over what content is selected and the order in which it is rendered for display.

PUTTING THE LOOP IN CONTEXT

The Loop is the heart of a theme, which is what controls how your content is displayed. It is the functional connection between the MySQL database data and the HTML that is rendered in the visitor's browser. Basically anywhere a post or page is displayed, WordPress is going to use the Loop. This can be a single post or page, a loop of posts, or a sequence of loops with different display options.

Most WordPress themes feature a header, footer, and sidebar element. Figure 5-1 shows how the Loop is placed directly in the middle of these elements, creating your web site content area. This section of your web site is usually dynamic and will change as you navigate through it.

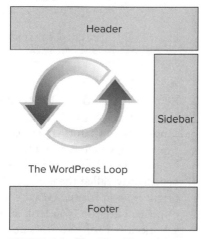

FIGURE 5-1: The WordPress Loop

The Loop by default is used in your WordPress theme template files. Custom Loops can be created anywhere in your theme template files, as Figure 5-2 shows. Custom Loops are also used in plugins and widgets. Loops can be used anywhere inside of WordPress, but different methods exist for creating custom Loops depending on where they are used, and the potential side effects of each construction will differ.

Multiple Loops can be used throughout your theme template files. Custom Loops can be created in your header, sidebars, footer, and main content areas of your web site. There is no limit to the number of Loops that can be displayed on your web site.

The following section looks at the basic flow control of the Loop, and the WordPress template functions provided to customize the way content is displayed while being handled inside of a loop. Armed with the basics, it then goes into building custom loops based on hand-tailoring those query parameters.

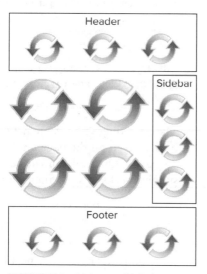

FIGURE 5-2: Using multiple Loops

FLOW OF THE LOOP

The Loop uses some standard programming conditional statements to determine what and how to display. The first statement in the Loop is an `if` statement, checking whether any posts exist, because you might not have any posts with the specified category or tag. If content exists, the `while` statement is used to initiate the Loop and cycle through all posts or pages that need to be displayed. Finally, the_post() function is called to build the post data, making it accessible to other WordPress functions. Once the post data has been built, Loop content can be displayed in whatever format you like.

Following is a minimal Loop example. This example features the only required elements for the Loop to function properly:

```php
<?php
if (have_posts()) :
    while (have_posts()) :
        the_post();
        //loop content (template tags, html, etc)
    endwhile;
endif;
?>
```

Remember that this is PHP code, so it needs to be surrounded in `<?php` and `?>` tags. This is the Loop in its simplest form. If you're wondering how the output from the database query got handed to this simple Loop when there are no variables passed as parameters, the answer lies in the global variable `$wp_query`, which is an instance of `WP_Query` that is referenced by the functions in the simple Loop. It is in effect the "default query" for the Loop. Note that by the time this default Loop is called, WordPress has already called the `get_posts()` method within the default query object to build the list of appropriate content for the URL being viewed, and the Loop in this case is charged with displaying that list of posts. Later on, you look at how to hand-structure queries to exercise fine-grain control over post selection, but for now it's safe to assume that the database heavy lifting has been done, and the results are stored in `$wp_query`, when the Loop is invoked.

Some very minimal requirements exist for the Loop to work in WordPress. Let's break down this example to look at the different parts of the Loop:

```php
if (have_posts()) :
```

This line checks if any posts or pages are going to be displayed on the current page you are viewing. If posts or pages exist the next line will execute:

```php
while (have_posts()) :
```

The preceding `while` statement starts the Loop, essentially looping through all posts and pages to be displayed on the page until there are no more. The Loop will continue while content exists to be displayed. Once all content has been displayed the `while` loop will end. The `have_posts()` function simply checks to see if the list of posts being processed is exhausted, or had no entries to begin with.

```php
the_post();
```

Next, the `the_post()` function is called to load all of the post data. This function must be called inside your loop for the post data to be set correctly. Calling `the_post()` in turn calls the `setup_postdata()` function to set up the per-post metadata such as the author and tags of the content you are displaying in the Loop, as well as the content of the post itself. This data is assigned to a global variable each time through the Loop iteration. Specifically calling `the_post()` has the side effect of setting up the global `$post` variable used by most of the template tags described later on, and then advances to the next post in the list.

Setting up the post data also applies the appropriate filters to the raw content that comes out of the WordPress database. WordPress stores user-edited content exactly as entered, so if a user adds a shortcode, for example, to add a Google AdSense item at the end of a post, the shortcode is stored in the database content. When the post setup is done, the plugin that converts that shortcode to a chunk of JavaScript is called, along with other registered plugins that modify the raw post content. We'll look at the plugin mechanics in Chapter 7, but for now, it's important to note the distinction between the raw post data in the WordPress query object and the filtered content that is eventually rendered.

```
//loop content
```

This is where all Loop template tags are placed and any additional code you want displayed inside the Loop. We cover this in more detail further along in this chapter.

```
endwhile;
endif;
```

The `endwhile` and `endif` calls end the Loop. Any code placed after these two lines will show at the bottom of your page, after all posts have been displayed. You could also place an `else` clause to display a message if there is no content to display in the Loop.

The Loop is usually surrounded by HTML tags in your theme template files. The following code shows how the Loop is structured in the default Kubrick theme that comes with WordPress:

```
<div id="content" class="narrowcolumn" role="main">

<?php if (have_posts()) : ?>

<?php while (have_posts()) : the_post(); ?>

<div <?php post_class() ?> id="post-<?php the_ID(); ?>">
<h2><a href="<?php the_permalink() ?>" rel="bookmark" title="Permanent Link to
<?php the_title_attribute(); ?>"><?php the_title(); ?></a></h2>
<small><?php the_time('F jS, Y') ?> <!-- by <?php the_author() ?> --></small>

<div class="entry">
    <?php the_content('Read the rest of this entry &raquo;'); ?>
</div>

<p class="postmetadata"><?php the_tags('Tags: ', ', ', '<br />'); ?> Posted in
<?php the_category(', ') ?> | <?php edit_post_link('Edit', '', ' | '); ?>
<?php comments_popup_link('No Comments &#187;', '1 Comment &#187;',
'% Comments &#187;');
?></p>
</div>

<?php endwhile; ?>

<div class="navigation">
<div class="alignleft"><?php next_posts_link('&laquo; Older Entries') ?></div>
<div class="alignright"><?php previous_posts_link('Newer Entries &raquo;') ?>
</div>
</div>

<?php else : ?>
```

```
<h2 class="center">Not Found</h2>
<p class="center">Sorry, but you are looking for something that isn't here.</p>
<?php get_search_form(); ?>

<?php endif; ?>


</div>
```

Notice how the minimal Loop elements exist, but are surrounded by HTML tags. This is how a normal theme template file will be structured to utilize the Loop. The HTML elements can certainly change, but the Loop elements stay the same. Customizing the style in which content is displayed and choosing post metadata to include in the page composition is done through template tags.

TEMPLATE TAGS

PHP functions used in your WordPress theme templates to display Loop content are called *template tags*. These tags are used to display specific pieces of data about your web site and content. This allows you to customize how and where content is displayed on your web site.

For example, the `the_title()` template tag displays the title of your post or page inside the Loop. The major benefit of using template tags is that you don't need to know PHP code to use them.

Many different template tags are available in WordPress. Some template tags must be inside the Loop, whereas other tags can be used anywhere in your theme template files. Note that in this context, template tags refer to the WordPress functions used to extract post data for display; template files are the theme elements that control how content for a particular content type is displayed. Put another way, template files contain Loops comprising template tags. For an updated list of template tags available in WordPress visit `http://codex.wordpress.org/Template_Tags`.

Commonly Used Template Tags

There is no shortage of template tags, but typically you will use only a handful of tags in your Loops. Following are the most commonly used template tags available in the Loop. These template tags will return and display the post data listed.

- ➤ `the_permalink()`: Returns the URL of your post.
- ➤ `the_title()`: Returns the title of the post.
- ➤ `the_ID()`: Returns the unique ID of your post.
- ➤ `the_content()`: Returns the full content of your post.
- ➤ `the_excerpt()`: Returns just an excerpt of your post. If the Excerpt field is filled out on the Post edit screen, that will be used. If not WordPress will auto-generate a short excerpt from your post content.

➤ `the_time()`: Returns the date/time your post was published.

➤ `the_author()`: Returns the author of the post.

➤ `the_tags()`: Returns the tags attached to the post.

➤ `the_category()`: Returns the categories assigned to the post.

➤ `edit_post_link()`: Displays an "edit" link that is shown only if you are logged in and allowed to edit the post.

➤ `comments_popup_link()`: Displays a link to the comments form of your post.

To learn how template tags work, just place any template tag inside the Loop and view the results. The following example views the values of a couple different template tags:

```php
<?php
if (have_posts()) :
   while (have_posts()) :
      the_post();
      ?>
      <a href="<?php the_permalink(); ?>"><?php the_title(); ?></a>
      <br>
      <?php
      the_content();
   endwhile;
endif;
?>
```

As you can see your post titles are displayed with links to the permalink for each post. The content of the post is displayed directly below the post title.

Tag Parameters

Most template tags have parameters that can be added to modify the value returned. For example, the `the_content()` template tag has three parameters. The first parameter allows you to set the "more" link text like so:

```php
<?php the_content('Read more', False); ?>
```

Your post content will be displayed as normal, but when the `<!--more-->` tag is found in your post, WordPress will automatically add the text "Read more," which would link to the entire blog post. The second parameter determines whether to display the teaser paragraph again when viewing the full post. The default value is `False` so the teaser will be displayed in both places.

The More tag in WordPress allows you to display a defined teaser from the full post on your web site. For example, you could display the first paragraph of a post on your homepage, and only show the full blog post when a visitor clicks the link to view the full post. To accomplish this you can place `<!--more-->` in your content in HTML view where you want this break to happen. In the visual editor there is a button to insert a More tag.

You can also send multiple parameters to any tag that supports it. For example, the template tag `the_title()` accepts three parameters: `$before`, `$after`, and `$echo`. The following code sets the `the_title()` tag's `$before` and `$after` parameters to wrap the post title with h1 tags:

```php
<?php the_title('<h1>', '</h1>'); ?>
```

You can also view the actual function in the WordPress source code. The post template functions are located in `wp-includes/post-template.php`. Doing a quick search for "function the_title()" will lead you to the exact function for the `the_title()` tag. You can also use the Codex for a detailed description of the template tag you are working with, in this case `http://codex.wordpress.org/Template_Tags/the_title`.

CUSTOMIZING THE LOOP

In our opening discussion of Loop flow of control, we mentioned that the main workhorse for data selection is the `get_posts()` method of the `WP_Query` object. In most cases, if you want to build a custom Loop, you'll build your own `WP_Query` object and reference it explicitly. Alternatively, you can use the lower-level `query_posts()` and `get_posts()` functions (not to be confused with the methods within the `WP_query` object of the same name) to manipulate the output of the default query that was passed into your Loop. Both `query_posts` and `get_posts` use the `WP_Query` class to retrieve content. We'll look at the lower level approaches and discuss how and where you should — and shouldn't — use them, but we'll start with a discussion of how you build a custom query object.

Using the WP_Query Object

Once WordPress is handed a URL to parse by the web server, it goes to work disassembling the tokens in that URL and converting them into parameters for a database query. Here's a bit more detail on what happens when manipulating your own `WP_Query`.

`WP_Query` is a class defined in WordPress that makes it easy to create your own custom Loops. Both `query_posts` and `get_posts` use the `WP_Query` class to retrieve the WordPress content. When you're using `query_posts()` the global variable `$wp_query` is used as an instance of `WP_Query`, making `$wp_query` the default data store for several operations. Custom Loops can be used anywhere in your theme template files to display different types of content; they must build on separate instances of a `WP_Query` variable.

When you create a new `WP_Query` object, it's instantiated with some default functions for building queries, executing the query to get posts, and parsing parameters out of a URL. However, you can use these built-in object methods to construct your own parameter strings, creating custom loops that extract whatever particular content you need for that point in your Loop.

The following is an example of a custom Loop displaying the five most recent posts on your web site:

```php
<?php
$myPosts = new WP_Query();
$myPosts->query('posts_per_page=5');
while ($myPosts->have_posts()) : $myPosts->the_post();
?>
  <!-- do something -->
<?php endwhile; ?>
```

Rather than using the simpler `have_posts()` and `the_post()` calls that we saw in the basic Loop, this custom loop calls the methods of the newly created WP_Query object `myPosts`. The explicit invocation shown here and the default `have_posts()` call are functionally equivalent; `have_posts()` for example is merely calling `$wp_query->have_posts()` using the global query variable for the default query, that is, the one generated from parsing the URL handed to WordPress by the web server.

Going into your default Loop from the URL used to invoke WordPress, there's an additional step that takes the URL and parses it into an appropriate query string using the `parse_query()` method of the query object. When you build your own custom Loop, you explicitly set the parameters you want to control the query. Here's a bit more detail on what happens inside the query function:

➤ Calling `$myPosts->query()` converts the parameters into a SQL statement via the function `$myPosts->get_posts()`, which then executes the query against the MySQL database and extracts the content you've requested.

➤ Equally important, the query call sets up the conditional tags such as `is_home()` and `is_single()` that are dependent upon the type of page displayed and the quantity of content for that page.

➤ The array of posts returned by the query is cached by WordPress so that future references to the same query won't generate additional database traffic.

The key to building a powerful custom Loop is to map your content selection criteria into the right set of query parameters.

Building A Custom Query

Parameters are used to define what content will be returned in your Loop, whether a custom Loop or altering the primary Loop. When creating Loops it's essential to understand what parameters are available to help define what content will be displayed. You can use many different, sometimes confusing, parameters in creating your custom Loop to alter the output of your content.

Multiple parameters can also be set per query by separating the parameter name and values with an ampersand. For a detailed list of available parameters, visit `http://codex.wordpress.org/Template_Tags/query_posts#Parameters`.

Following are some of the more commonly used parameters.

Post Parameters

The most obvious, and sometimes most used parameters, select the number and types of posts to be displayed:

➤ `p=2`: Loads an individual post by ID.

➤ `name=my-slug`: Loads post based on post slug (permalink tail).

➤ `post_status=pending`: Loads posts by post status. For example, if you choose to only see drafts, use `post_status=draft` .

➤ `caller_get_posts=1`: Excludes sticky posts from being returned first. A "sticky post" is one that always sorts to the head of the list of posts, independent of the other parameters set for the query. You can have multiple sticky posts, making them useful for news announcements, highlighting changes, or otherwise grabbing reader attention, and this parameter lets you drop them from their priority slot at the head of the list.

➤ `post_type=page`: Loads posts based on type. If you only want to look at pages, not posts, `post_type=page` will retrieve them.

➤ `posts_per_page=5`: Number of posts to load per page. This is the default.

➤ `offset=1`: Number of posts to skip before loading.

Page Parameters

Pages have parameters similar to those for posts to control their selection:

➤ `page_id=5`: Loads an individual page by ID. Like post ids and user ids, page ids can be found in the dashboard by hovering over a page, and looking at the URL displayed at the bottom on your browser.

➤ `pagename=Contact`: Loads a page by name, in this case the "Contact" page.

➤ `pagename=parent/child`: Loads a child page by slug, or hierarchy of slugs (that is, its path).

Category, Tag, and Author Parameters

Posts can also be sorted by the category into which they were placed, tags applied to the post, or author information:

➤ `cat=3,4,5`: Load posts based on category ID.

➤ `category_name=About Us`: Loads posts based on category name. Note that if a post belongs to more than one category, it will show up in selections for each of those categories.

➤ `tag=writing`: Loads posts based on tag name.

➤ `tag_id=34`: Loads posts based on tag ID.

➤ `author=1`: Loads posts based on author ID.

➤ `author_name=Brad`: Loads posts based on author's name.

Time, Date, Ordering, and Custom Parameters

Parameters to select content based on their chronology are a key part of building an archive of posts, or providing a view into content through a calendar on your blog's homepage. You can also change the sort parameter and the sort order. If you're building an online index, and want to show an alphabetical post listing, you'll set the parameters for querying posts by month and author, but order the results by title.

➤ `monthnum=6`: Loads posts created in June.

➤ `day=9`: Loads posts created on the 9th day of the month.

➤ `year=2009`: Loads posts created in 2009.

➤ `orderby=title`: Field to order posts by.

➤ order=ASC: Defines ascending or descending order of `orderby`.

➤ meta_key=color: Loads posts by custom field name. Refer to the custom taxonomy and data discussion in Chapter 6 to see how custom fields are added to posts.

➤ meta_value=blue: Loads posts by custom field value. Must be used in conjunction with the meta_key parameter above.

Putting It Together

Let's look at some examples using parameters. The following examples use the `$myPosts->query()` function from the `$myPosts` custom query object created in the example to select the content displayed in your custom Loop.

Display post based on post ID:

```
$myPosts->query('p=1');
```

Display the five latest posts, skipping the first post:

```
$myPosts->query('posts_per_page=5&offset=1');
```

Display all posts from today:

```
$today = getdate(); // get todays date
$myPosts->query('year=' .$today["year"] .'&monthnum=' .$today["mon"] .'&day='
.$today["mday"] ); // display all posts from the current date
```

Display all posts from October 31st, 2009:

```
$myPosts->query('monthnum=10&day=31&year=2009');
```

Display all posts from category ID 5 with the bacon tag:

```
$myPosts->query('cat=5&tag=bacon');
```

Display all posts with the bacon tag, excluding posts in category ID 5:

```
$myPosts->query('cat=-5&tag=bacon');
```

Display all posts with the tag writing OR reading:

```
$myPosts->query('tag=writing,reading');
```

Display all posts with the tags writing AND reading AND tv:

```
$myPosts->query('tag=writing+reading+tv);
```

Display all posts with a custom field named color with a value of blue:

```
$myPosts->query('meta_key=color&meta_value=blue');
```

Adding Paging To A Loop

If your custom Loop requires paging (navigation links), you will need to take a few extra steps. Paging is currently designed to work only with the `$wp_query` global variable; that is, it works within the default Loop and requires some sleight of hand to make it work in custom loops. You need to trick WordPress into thinking your custom query is actually $wp_query for paging to work.

```php
<?php
$temp = $wp_query;
$wp_query= null;
$wp_query = new WP_Query();
$wp_query->query('posts_per_page=5&paged='.$paged);
while ($wp_query->have_posts()) : $wp_query->the_post();
?>
        <h2>
        <a href="<?php the_permalink() ?>"><?php the_title(); ?></a>
        </h2>
        <?php the_excerpt(); ?>
<?php endwhile; ?>
```

First you have to store the original $wp_query variable into the temporary variable $temp. Next you set $wp_query to null to completely flush it clean. This is one of the few times it's acceptable to overwrite a global variable value in WordPress. Now set your new WP_Query object into the $wp_query variable and execute it by calling the object's query() function to select posts for your custom Loop. Notice the $paged variable added to the end of the query. This stores the current page so WordPress knows how to display the navigation links. Now display your navigation links for paging:

```html
<div class="navigation">
  <div class="alignleft"><?php previous_posts_link('&laquo; Previous') ?></div>
  <div class="alignright"><?php next_posts_link('More &raquo;') ?></div>
</div>
```

Finally, you need to reset $wp_query back to its original value:

```php
<?php
$wp_query = null;
$wp_query = $temp;
?>
```

Now your custom Loop will contain proper pagination based on the content returned.

Using query_posts()

There's a tremendous amount of customization that can be done by specifying the appropriate set of parameters for your Loop. While using the WP_Query object is the most general purpose mechanism for extracting posts and pages from the WordPress database, there are other lower-level methods that you'll encounter.

The query_posts() function is used to easily modify the content returned for the default WordPress Loop. Specifically, you can modify the content returned in $wp_query after the default database query has executed, fine-tune the query parameters and re-execute the query using query_posts(). The downside to calling query_posts() in this fashion is that the previously cached results from the default query are discarded, so you're incurring a database performance hit to use this shortcut. The query_posts() function should be placed directly above the start of the Loop:

```php
query_posts('posts_per_page=5&paged='.$paged);
if (have_posts()) :
   while (have_posts()) : the_post();
```

```
            //loop content (template tags, html, etc)
        endwhile;
    endif;
```

This example tells WordPress to display only five posts.

Explicitly calling `query_posts()` overwrites the original post content extracted for the Loop. This means any content you were expecting to be returned before using `query_posts()` will not be returned. For example, if the URL passed to WordPress is for a category page at www.example.com/category/zombie/, none of the "zombie" category posts will be in the post list after `query_posts()` has been called unless one is in the five most recent posts. You explicitly overwrite the query parameters established by the URL parsing and default processing when you pass the query string to `query_posts()`.

To avoid losing your original Loop content you can save the parsed query parameters by using the $query_string global variable:

```
global $query_string; // initialize the global query_string variable
query_posts($query_string . "&orderby=title&order=ASC"); // keep original Loop
                                         //content and change the sort order
```

In the preceding example you would still see all of your zombie category posts, but they would be ordered alphabetically by ascending title. This technique is used to modify the original Loop content without losing that content.

You can also pack all of your `query_posts()` parameters in an array, making it easier to manage. Following is an example of how to retrieve only the sticky post set in WordPress using an array to store the parameter values:

```
$args = array(
'posts_per_page' => 1,
'post__in'  => get_option('sticky_posts')
);
query_posts($args);
```

If no sticky post is found, the latest post will be returned instead. The `query_posts` function is used to modify the main page Loop only. It is not intended to create additional custom Loops. If you want a make a slight change to the default query, for example adding posts of a specific category or tag to every displayed page, then the `query_posts()` approach is a shortcut. However, it's not without side effects or cautions:

➤ `query_posts()` modifies the global variable $wp_query and has other side effects, it should not be called more than once, and shouldn't be used inside the Loop. The example shows the call to `query_posts()` before post processing has started, when the extra parameters are added to the query string but before the Loop has begun to step through the returned post list. Calling `query_posts()` more than once, or inside the Loop itself, can result in your main Loop being incorrect and displaying unintended content.

➤ `query_posts()` unsets the global $wp_query object, and in doing so, may invalidate the values of conditional tags like `is_page()` or `is_home()`. Going through the entire WP_Query object instantiation sets all of the conditional tags appropriately. For example, you may find with the shortcut that you have added content to a selection that the default query found contained only one post, and therefore `is_single()` is no longer valid.

➤ Calling `query_posts()` executes another database query, invalidating all of the cached results from the first, default query. You at least double the number of database queries executed and are incurring a performance hit for each trip back to MySQL; on the other hand the default query has already been run by the time you get to the default Loop, so there's little chance to work around it if you're building an entirely custom main Loop.

Using get_posts()

Like `query_posts()`, there's an alternative, simpler access function called `get_posts()` that retrieves raw post data. You'll see `get_posts()` used in administration pages to generate a list of pages of a particular type, or it may be used within a plugin to grab all raw data for a set of posts, examine it for patterns such as common terms, tags, or external links, with the intent of discarding the content after a quick digestion. It's not intended for user-facing content display, because it turns off much of query processing and filtering that is done within the more general `WP_Query` approach.

What `get_posts()` lacks, specifically, is the ability to set up all of the global data needed to make template tags reflect the current post data. One main issue is that not all template tags are available to `get_posts()` by default. To fix this deficiency you need to call the `setup_postdata()` function to populate the template tags for use in your Loop. The following example shows how to retrieve a single random post using `get_posts()`:

```php
<?php

$randompost = get_posts('numberposts=1&orderby=rand');
foreach($randompost as $post) :
    setup_postdata($post);
?>
<h1><a href="<?php the_permalink(); ?>"><?php the_title(); ?></a></h1>
<?php the_content(); ?>
<?php endforeach; ?>
```

You'll notice another major difference using `get_posts()` — the value returned is an array. The `foreach` loop code is used to cycle through the array values. This example returns only one post, but if more than one were returned this would cycle through each. Then the `setup_postdata()` function is called to populate the data for your template tags.

Remember that you can also set up your `get_posts()` parameters using an array:

```php
<?php
$args = array(
'numberposts' => 1,
'orderby'  => rand
);

$randompost = get_posts($args);
```

Although you may see older code using `get_posts()` or `query_posts()` constructions, `WP_Query` is the preferred approach and should be the heart of custom loop syntax. However, there are times when you'll want the quick-and-dirty access provided by `get_posts()` to generate additional context or data for further customization of your Loop or in a plugin.

Resetting a Query

From time to time you may run into problems with page-level conditional tags being used after a custom Loop has been created. Conditional tags allow you to run different code on different pages in WordPress, for example, using the conditional tag `is_home()` to determine if you are viewing the main blog page. This problem is caused, as indicated in the "Using query_posts()" section, by potentially changing the output of a database query after setting the conditional tags based on its original set of values. To fix this issue you need to call a function called `wp_reset_query()`. This function will properly restore the original query, including the conditional tags set up early in the URL parsing process.

As an example, look at the following code:

```php
<?php query_posts('showposts=5'); ?>
<?php if (have_posts()) : while (have_posts()) : the_post(); ?>
<a href="<?php the_permalink() ?>"><?php the_title() ?></a><br />
<?php endwhile; endif; ?>

<?php
if(is_home() && !is_paged()):
wp_list_bookmarks('title_li=&categorize=0');
endif;
?>
```

Executing this code will return the latest five posts followed by the links saved in your WordPress link manager. The problem you will run into is that the `is_home()` conditional tag will not be interpreted correctly, meaning your links will show on every page, not just the homepage. To fix this issue you need to include `wp_reset_query()` directly below your Loop:

```php
<?php query_posts('posts_per_page=5'); ?>
<?php if (have_posts()) : while (have_posts()) : the_post(); ?>
<a href="<?php the_permalink() ?>"><?php the_title() ?></a><br />
<?php endwhile; endif; ?>
<?php wp_reset_query(); ?>

<?php
if(is_home() && !is_paged()):
wp_list_bookmarks('title_li=&categorize=0');
endif;
?>
```

Now that you have properly restored your Loop's instance of the `WP_Query` object, the conditional tag `is_home()` will be followed and your links will now display only on the homepage of your web site. It's a good practice to add `wp_reset_query` after using `query_posts()` in your Loop to ensure you do not run into problems down the road.

More Than One Loop

The Loop can be used multiple times throughout your theme and plugins. This makes it easy to display different types of content in multiple places throughout your WordPress web site. Maybe you want to display your most recent blog posts below each page on your web site. You can achieve this by creating more complex Loops that make multiple passes through the list of posts, or generate multiple post arrays over which to loop.

Nested Loops

Nested Loops can be created inside your theme templates using a combination of the main Loop and separate WP_Query instances. For example, you can create a nested Loop to display related posts based on post tags. The following is an example of creating a nested Loop inside the main Loop to display related posts based on tags:

```php
<?php
if (have_posts()) :
   while (have_posts()) :
        the_post();

        //loop content (template tags, html, etc)
        ?>
        <h1><a href="<?php the_permalink(); ?>" title="<?php the_title_
attribute();
?>"><?php the_title(); ?></a></h1>
        <?php
        the_content();

        //load current post tags
        $tags = wp_get_post_terms(get_the_ID());
        if ($tags) {
          echo 'Related Posts';
          $first_tag = $tags[0]->term_id;
          $args=array(
            'tag__in' => array($first_tag),
            'post__not_in' => array($post->ID),
            'posts_per_page'=>5,
            'caller_get_posts'=>1
          );
          $relatedPosts = new WP_Query($args);
          if( $relatedPosts->have_posts() ) {
            //loop through related posts based on the tag
            while ($relatedPosts->have_posts()) : $relatedPosts->the_post(); ?>
              <p><a href="<?php the_permalink() ?>"
title="<?php the_title_attribute(); ?>"><?php the_title(); ?></a></p>
              <?php
            endwhile;
          }
        }
   endwhile;
endif;
?>
```

This code will display all of your posts as normal. Inside the main Loop you check if any other posts contain the same tag as your main post. If so you display the latest five posts that match as related posts. If no posts match, the related posts section will not be displayed.

Multi-Pass Loops

The `rewind_posts()` function is used to reset the post query and loop counter, allowing you to do another Loop. Place this function call directly after you finish your first Loop. Here's an example that processes the main Loop content twice:

```php
<?php while (have_posts()) : the_post(); ?>
  <!-- content. -->
<?php endwhile; ?>

<?php rewind_posts(); ?>

<?php while (have_posts()) : the_post(); ?>
  <!-- content -->
<?php endwhile; ?>
```

GLOBAL VARIABLES

A *global variable* is a variable that has a defined value that can be accessed anywhere within the Word-Press execution environment. These variables store all types of information about the Loop content, author, and users, and specific information about the WordPress installation such as how to connect to the MySQL database. Global variables should only be used to retrieve data, meaning you should never write data to these variables directly. Overwriting the global variable values could cause unexpected results in WordPress because significant parts of core and extended functionality depend on these values being set within one context and remaining consistent for the duration of a query, page load, or single post handling. Assigning values to global variables almost always has unintended side effects, and they're almost always not what the user or blog author wanted. However, we discuss the globals here to shed more light on how post data can be manipulated, and you may see code snippets that utilize these functions for post processing outside of the Loop.

Post Data

You saw how the key first step in the Loop is calling `the_post()`. Once invoked, you will have access to all of the data in WordPress specific to the post being displayed. This data is stored in the global `$post` variable. The `$post` variable stores the post data of the last post displayed on the page. So if your Loop displays ten posts, the `$post` variable will store post data for the tenth post displayed.

The following examples show how you can reference the `$post` global variable and display the post title and content. You can also display all of the array values using the `print_r` PHP function.

```php
<?php
global $post;
echo $post->post_title;  //view the posts title
echo $post->post_content;  //view the post content
print_r($post);  //view all data stored in the $post array
?>
```

Accessing the content through the global $post variable is accessing the unfiltered content. This means any plugins that would normally alter the output of the content will not affect the global content value. For example, if you had the built-in [gallery] shortcode in your post to display all images uploaded on the post, retrieving the post content as shown would return [gallery] instead of the actual image gallery.

Remember that WordPress provides template tags that can be called anywhere to retrieve these values as well, and in most cases, template tags are going to be the preferred mechanism for getting at these bits. For example, if you need to get the permalink of your post you can use the following method:

```php
<?php
global $post;
echo get_permalink($post->ID);  //displays the current posts permalink
?>
```

This is covered in more detail in the "Working Outside the Loop" section of this chapter.

Author Data

$authordata is a global variable that stores information about the author of the post being displayed. You can use this global variable to display the author's name:

```php
<?php
global $authordata;
echo 'Author: ' .$authordata->display_name;
?>
```

The $authordata variable is created when setup_postdata() is called during the_post() function call in the Loop. This means the $authordata global variable will not be created until the Loop has run for the first time. Another problem with this method is the global values do not get passed through hook Filters, meaning any plugin you install to override this functionality would not be ran.

The preferred method for accessing the author metadata, like that for getting post data, is using the available WordPress template tags. For example, to display the author's display name you would use this code:

```php
<?php
echo 'Author: ' .get_the_author_meta('display_name');
?>
```

The get_the_author_meta() and the_author_meta() functions are available for retrieving all metadata related to the author of the content. If this template tag is used inside the Loop there is no need to pass the user ID parameter. If used outside of the Loop the user ID is required to determine what author metadata to retrieve.

User Data

The $current_user global variable stores information on the currently logged-in user. This is the account that you are currently logged in to WordPress with. Following is an example showing how to display the logged-in user's display name:

```php
<?php
global $current_user;
echo $current_user->display_name;
?>
```

This is a useful technique if you want to display a welcome message to your users. Remember that the display name will default to the user's username. To display a welcome message to any user that is logged in you could use this code:

```php
<?php
global $current_user;
If ($current_user->display_name) {
    echo 'Welcome ' .$current_user->display_name;
}
?>
```

Environmental Data

WordPress also has global variables created for browser detection. The following is an example showing how you can detect the user's browser version in WordPress using global variables:

```php
<?php
global $is_lynx, $is_gecko, $is_IE, $is_opera, $is_NS4,
$is_safari, $is_chrome, $is_iphone;

If ($is_lynx) {
    echo "You are using Lynx";
}Elseif ($is_gecko) {
    echo "You are using Firefox";
}Elseif ($is_IE) {
    echo "You are using Internet Explorer";
}Elseif ($is_opera) {
    echo "You are using Opera";
}Elseif ($is_NS4) {
    echo "You are using Netscape";
}Elseif ($is_safari) {
    echo "You are using Safari";
}Elseif ($is_chrome) {
    echo "You are using Chrome";
}Elseif ($is_iphone) {
    echo "You are using an iPhone";
}
?>
```

This is extremely useful when designing a web site that needs to include browser specific tasks or functionality. As always it's best to stick with web standards and degrade gracefully for lesser browsers, but in some circumstances this can be very beneficial. For example you can use the `$is_iphone` variable to load a custom stylesheet for iPhone web users.

WordPress also stores what type of web server the web site is hosted on using the `$is_IIS` and `$is_apache` global variables. Here's an example:

```php
<?php
global $is_apache, $is_IIS;
If ($is_apache) {
    echo 'web server is running Apache';
}Elseif ($is_IIS) {
    echo 'web server is running IIS';
}
?>
```

Depending what web server a web site is using, code can produce different results than expected. As a developer, you need to consider that your plugins and themes may be running on WordPress installations on different web servers; you might also need to check what the user is running in order to accomplish specific tasks.

Global Variables or Template Tags?

Generally speaking, template tags should be used whenever they can be. There will be certain instances where a template tag will not be available. In this case global variables can be substituted to access the information you need. Also, global variables are great for retrieving unfiltered data, meaning the values will bypass any plugin altering that would normally be used against the content, giving you the original value to work with. Once your code has accessed or processed the original value, you can still cause the plugin filters to run using the following code:

```php
<?php apply_filters('the_content', $post->post_content);?>
```

While we're including this in a discussion of working outside of the Loop, you can access these global variables inside the loop, but again we'll repeat the caveat to treat globals as read-only, as changing their values will have possibly negative side effects.

WORKING OUTSIDE THE LOOP

There are times when you'll want to access generic post information, or manipulate some information about the currently displayed post outside of the Loop. WordPress provides some functions to operate on sets of posts for even finer-grain control over post display.

Along with access to global variables, there are a set of Wordpress functions to return generic information that's not specific to a single post, or the post currently displayed. Following is a list of frequently used outside the Loop functions:

- ➤ `wp_list_pages()`: Displays a list of pages as links
- ➤ `wp_list_categories()`: Displays a list of categories as links
- ➤ `wp_list_bookmarks()`: Displays links saved in the Links SubPanel
- ➤ `wp_tag_cloud()`: Displays a tag cloud from all tags
- ➤ `get_permalink()`: Returns the permalink of a post
- ➤ `next_posts_link()`: Link to display previous posts
- ➤ `previous_posts_link()`: Link to display next posts

You already saw how you could create navigational links using `next_posts_link()` and `previous_posts_link()` in the custom Loop example. Let's explore some of these functions in action to get a real feel for how they work.

Most menus in a WordPress theme are generated using the `wp_list_pages()` function. This function will return your pages in a list format, so it's important to wrap the function call with `<ul>` tags as shown here:

```
<ul>
    <?php wp_list_pages('title_li='); ?>
</ul>
```

The preceding code would generate a list of pages from WordPress with links. Notice you set the parameter `title_li` to nothing, which eliminates the default title displayed for your pages. The function would generate your menu list like so:

```
<ul>
    <li class="page_item page-item-1">
        <a href="http://example.com/about/" title="About">About</a>
    </li>
    <li class="page_item page-item-2">
        <a href="http://example.com/order/" title="Order">Order</a>
    </li>
    <li class="page_item page-item-3">
        <a href="http://example.com/contact/" title="Contact">Contact</a>
    </li>
</ul>
```

You could also use the newer `wp_page_menu()` function to generate a page menu. There are several advantages to this newer menu function. The first is a new `show_home` parameter allowing a Home link to automatically be added to the list of pages. You also don't have to remove the title using `title_li` as we did in the preceding code. This function also wraps a custom `<div>` around your menu, the class of which you can set. An example of this function follows:

```
<?php wp_page_menu('show_home=1&menu_class=my-menu&sort_column=menu_order'); ?>
```

Another common function for generating menus is `wp_list_categories()`. This function lists your categories, and subcategories, in a list as well. Look at an example:

```
<ul>
    <?php wp_list_categories('title_li=&depth=4&orderby=name&exclude=8,16,34'); ?>
</ul>
```

This code will generate a list of categories with links. Just as before you are setting your title to nothing, rather than the default "Categories" title. You are also setting the depth to 4. The depth parameter controls how many levels in the hierarchy of categories to be included in the list. The categories will be ordered by their name. You are also excluding three categories (8, 16, and 34) based on their IDs.

`next_posts_link()` and `previous_posts_link()` are typically used directly after your Loop has completed. These two functions will generate the previous and next links for viewing more posts on your web site. Notice that the `next_posts_link()` function actually returns your previous posts. The reason for this is that WordPress assumes your posts are displaying in reverse chronological order, meaning the next page of posts would actually be posts from earlier in the timeline.

Now imagine you'd like to load a single post outside of the Loop. To do this you use the `get_post()` function to load your post data. The following example loads the post data for post ID 178:

```php
<?php
$my_id = 178;
$myPost = get_post($my_id);
echo 'Post Title: ' .$myPost->post_title .'<br>';
echo 'Post Content: ' .$myPost->post_content .'<br>';
?>
```

The `get_post()` function only has one required parameter: the post ID you want to load. You must pass a variable containing an integer for the ID. Passing a literal integer (for example, 5) will cause a fatal error. The second optional parameter is how you would like the results returned: either an object, an associative array, or a numeric array. By default an object is returned. To return an associative array you could run this code:

```php
<?php
$my_id = 178;
$myPost = get_post($my_id, ARRAY_A);
echo 'Post Title: ' .$myPost['post_title'] .'<br>';
echo 'Post Content: ' .$myPost['post_content'] .'<br>';
print_r($myPost);
?>
```

No matter how you return the results, though, this invocation of `get_post()` returns the raw content from the WordPress database. Filters and processing normally done within the loop won't be applied to the returned content. The solution is to use the `setup_postdata()` function in conjunction with `get_post()` to set up your global post data and template tags for use with your post:

```php
<?php
$my_id = 178;
$myPost=get_post($my_id);
setup_postdata($myPost);
the_title();
the_content();
?>
```

The `get_post()` function uses the internal WordPress object cache. This means if the post you are loading is already in the cache you will save on running an unneeded database query. It's easy to see how useful this function can be to quickly and efficiently load a single post outside of the Loop.

Some functions that can be used inside the Loop can also be used outside of the Loop. For example, you can use the `the_author_meta()` function to retrieve specific author meta:

```
The email address for user id 1 is <?php the_author_meta('user_email',1); ?>
```

Remember that when calling the `the_author_meta()` function outside of the Loop you have to specify the author's ID that you want to load metadata for. If you call this function inside the Loop you do not need to specify this ID, because it will load the author data for the current post.

WordPress also features specific functions for retrieving individual data about a post outside of the Loop. For example, you can use the `get_the_title()` function to retrieve a post's title based on post ID like so:

```php
<?php
echo 'Title: ' .get_the_title(178);
?>
```

You can also use a function to retrieve post metadata (custom fields) from an individual post. To do this you use the `get_post_meta()` function as shown here:

```php
<?php
echo 'Color: ' .get_post_meta(178, 'color', true);
?>
```

The `get_post_meta()` function accepts three parameters: post ID, key, and single. The post ID is the ID of the post you want to load metadata for. The key is the name of the meta value you want to load. The third optional value determines whether the results are returned as an array or whether the function will return a single result. By default this is set to False so an array would be returned. As you can see, you set this value to True so only a single color is returned.

We've covered the basic mechanics of WordPress content selection and display, and provided a guide to the WordPress core to help you locate the code used to implement these functions. The real power of WordPress is in its extensibility through plugins and themes. We are first going to look at the WordPress data model in more detail in Chapter 6, showing how the various data items saved for all content, users and metadata relate to each other, using that as the basis for a full-fledged plugin construction discussion in Chapter 7. Along with plugins, themes are the other primary avenue for extending and customizing WordPress, and we re-apply some of the Loop constructs with a deeper look at templates and content presentation in Chapter 8.

Data Management

WHAT'S IN THIS CHAPTER?

➤ Understanding the WordPress Database

➤ Learning about Database Table Relationships

➤ Working with the WordPress Database Class

➤ Debugging Custom Queries

➤ Creating Custom Taxonomies

Almost every web site on the Internet today is connected to a database that stores information about that web site. WordPress is no different and is powered by a MySQL database backend. This database stores all of the data for your web site, including your content, users, links, meta-data, settings, and more. This chapter covers how data is stored, what data is stored, and how to work with that data in WordPress to help you build amazing web sites.

DATABASE SCHEMA

The default installation of WordPress contains 11 database tables. WordPress prides itself on being very lightweight and the database is the starting point for this. The database structure is designed to be very minimal yet allow for endless flexibility when developing and designing for WordPress. To start understanding the database schema it helps to view a database diagram.

Figure 6-1 shows an overview of the WordPress database structure and the relationships between the tables created during a standard WordPress installation. Keep in mind that plugins and themes have the ability to create custom tables so your WordPress database may contain more tables than just the default WordPress tables.

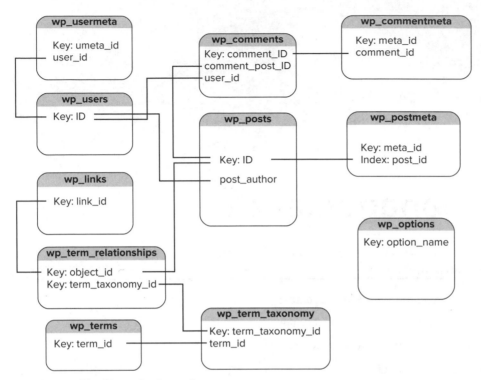

FIGURE 6-1: WordPress database diagram

When a new major release of WordPress is launched, a few database changes are usually made. These changes are usually very minor, such as changing a table field data type or removing a field that is no longer in use. Backward compatibility is a major concern for the WordPress community so any changes made to the database are highly scrutinized and will rarely affect active plugins and themes. The Codex features a very thorough database changelog you can reference when a new version of WordPress is released: http://codex.wordpress.org/Database_Description#Changelog.

Table Structure

The table structure in WordPress is very consistent. Each table in your database contains a unique ID field, which is the primary key of the table. Each table also contains one or more indexes on fields, which improves the speed of data retrieval when executing queries against the data. As we saw in Chapter 5, each trip through the Loop in a theme is going to generate at least one, and perhaps several queries, to extract posts, pages and their related metadata or comments.

The most important field in every table is the unique ID field. This field is not always named ID, but is an auto-incrementing field used to give each record in the table a unique identifier. For example, when you first install WordPress a default post is created titled "Hello world!" Because this is the first post created in the wp_posts table, the ID for this post is 1. Each post is given a unique ID that can be used to load post-specific information and also be used as the joining field against other tables in the database.

There is one caveat to this, and that is post revisions and attachments. Each post revision and attachment is saved as a new record in the wp_posts table. So each post revision and attachment gets its own unique ID, which means your published post IDs may not be sequential. For example, your first post may have an ID of 1, whereas your second post may have an ID of 15. It all depends on how many post revisions and attachments have been created between each post.

TABLE DETAILS

Currently, 11 database tables have been created for WordPress. Following is a list of those tables and details on what data they store:

➤ **wp_comments:** Contains all comments within WordPress. Individual comments are linked back to posts through a post ID.

➤ **wp_commentsmeta:** Contains all metadata for comments.

➤ **wp_links:** Contains all links added via the Link Manager section.

➤ **wp_options:** Stores all web site options defined under the Settings SubPanel. Also stores plugin options, active plugins and themes, and more.

➤ **wp_postmeta:** Contains all post metadata (custom fields).

➤ **wp_posts:** Contains all posts, pages, media records, and revisions. Under most circumstances, this is the largest table in the database.

➤ **wp_terms:** Contains all taxonomy terms defined for your web site.

➤ **wp_term_relationships:** Joins taxonomy terms with content (that is, posts, links, and so on).

➤ **wp_term_taxonomy:** Defines what taxonomy each term is assigned to.

➤ **wp_users:** Contains all users created in your web site (login, password, e-mail).

➤ **wp_usermeta:** Contains metadata for users (first/last name, nickname, user level, and so on).

As you can see, each table has a specific purpose within WordPress. Let's break down some of the more common tables and look at some examples of working with each.

To retrieve all of your web site content you'll be accessing the wp_posts table. This table stores all of your posts, pages, attachments, and revisions. Attachment records are stored in this table, but the actual attachments are not. They are physically stored on your hosting server as a standard file. The following SQL query is an example of how to extract all of your posts from the database, and is the short form of what happens in the default WordPress Loop:

```
SELECT * FROM wp_posts
WHERE post_type = 'post'
ORDER BY post_date DESC
```

This query selects all records from wp_posts with a post_type of 'post'. The post_type field designates what type of content you are viewing. To return all pages, just change that value to 'page'. You are also ordering your table records by post_date descending, so your posts will be displayed in reverse chronological order. Below we'll discuss querying data and what tools are available to help you do so.

Let's explore some of the more useful fields in the `wp_posts` table. You already know your ID field contains your post's unique ID. The `post_author` field is the unique ID of the author of the post. You can use this to retrieve author-specific data from the `wp_users` table. The `post_date` is the date the post was created. The `post_content` field stores the main content of your post or page and `post_title` is the title of that content.

One very important field is the `post_status` field. Currently seven different post statuses are defined in WordPress:

➤ **publish:** A published post or page

➤ **inherit:** A post revision

➤ **pending:** Post that is pending review by an Administrator or Editor

➤ **private:** A private post

➤ **future:** A post scheduled to publish at a future date and time

➤ **draft:** A post still being created and is a draft

➤ **trash:** Content is in the trash bin and can still be recovered

Post status comes into play when contributor roles are used to limit a post creator's ability to post or edit existing content. We discuss the use of roles in Chapter 11 and their impact on content management workflow in Chapter 12.

The `post_type` is also stored in this table. This value is what distinguishes different types of content in WordPress: posts, pages, revisions, and attachments. Since the release of WordPress 2.9 custom post types can be created, which opens the door to endless possibilities when defining custom post types.

The `wp_users` table contains data for your registered member accounts. Again you see the ID field indicating the unique identifier for user records. The `user_login` is the username of the user. This is the value the user must enter when logging in to WordPress. The `user_pass` field contains the phpass-encrypted user password. The registered user's e-mail is stored in the `user_email` field. The `user_url` field contains the member's web site and the user registration date is saved in `user_registered`.

Let's explore the `wp_comments` table next. This table stores all of the comments, pingbacks, and trackbacks for your web site.

Viewing the comment records you'll notice the ID field is named `comment_ID`. Even though this field is not named ID, it is still the unique identifier for this record in the table. The `comment_post_ID` is the unique ID of the post the comment was added to. Remember by default you don't have to be logged in to make comments in WordPress. For this reason you'll see similar fields as in your users table.

The `comment_author` field stores the name of the commenter. If the comment is a pingback or trackback it will contain the name of the post that sent the ping. The `comment_author_email` contains the commenter's e-mail address and his or her web site is stored in `comment_author_url`. Another important field is the `comment_date`, which is the date the comment was created. This field is used to display your post comments in the correct order.

WordPress Database Class

WordPress features an object class with method functions for working with the database directly. This database class is called `wpdb` and is located in `wp-includes/wp-db.php`. Any time you are querying the WordPress database in PHP code you should use the wpdb class. The main reason for using this class is to allow WordPress to execute your queries in the safest way possible.

Simple Database Queries

When using the `wpdb` class, you must first define `$wpdb` as a global variable before it will be available for use. To do so just drop this line of code directly preceding any `$wpdb` function call:

```
global $wpdb;
```

One of the most important functions in the `wpdb` class is the `prepare` function. This function is used for escaping variables passed to your SQL queries. This is a critical step in preventing SQL injection attacks on your web site. All queries should be passed through the `prepare` function before being executed. Here's an example:

```php
<?php
$field_key = "address";
$field_value ="123 Elm St";
$wpdb->query( $wpdb->prepare("INSERT INTO $wpdb->my_custom_table
    ( id, field_key, field_value ) VALUES ( %d, %s, %s )",1,
        $field_key, $field_value) );

?>
```

This example adds data into a non-default, custom table in WordPress that you would have previously created. When using `prepare`, make sure to replace any variables in your query with `%s` for strings and `%d` for integers. Then list the variables as parameters for the `prepare` function in the exact same order. In the preceding example, `%d` represents 1, `%s` represents `$field_key`, and the second `%s` represents `$field_value`. The `prepare` function is used on all queries from here on out.

Notice this example uses `$wpdb->my_custom_table` to reference the table in WordPress. This translates to `wp_my_custom_table` if `wp_` is the table prefix. This is the proper way to determine the correct table prefix when working with tables in the WordPress database.

The `wpdb` query method is used to execute a simple query. This function is primarily used for INSERT, UPDATE, and DELETE statements. Despite its name, it's not only for SQL SELECT queries, but will execute a variety of SQL statements against the database. Here's a basic query function example:

```php
<?php
$wpdb->query( $wpdb->prepare(" DELETE FROM $wpdb->my_custom_table WHERE id = '1'
    AND field_key = 'address' " ) );

?>
```

As you can see you execute your query using the `wpdb` class `query` function to delete the field "address" with an ID of 1. Although the `query` function allows you to execute any SQL query on the WordPress database, other database object class functions are more appropriate for SELECT queries. For instance, the get_var function is used for retrieving a single variable from the database:

```php
<?php
$comment_count = $wpdb->get_var($wpdb->prepare("SELECT COUNT(*)
    FROM $wpdb->comments;"));
echo '<p>Total comments: ' . $comment_count . '</p>';
?>
```

This example retrieves a count of all comments in WordPress and displays the total number. Although only one scalar variable is returned, the entire result set of the query is cached. It's best to try and limit the result set returned from your queries using a WHERE clause to only retrieve the records you actually need. In this example, all comment record rows are returned, even though you display the total count of comments. This would obviously be a big memory hit on larger web sites.

Complex Database Operations

To retrieve an entire table row you'll want to use the get_row function. The get_row function can return the row data as an object, an associative array, or a numerically indexed array. By default the row is returned as an object, in this case an instance of the per-post data. Here's an example:

```php
<?php
$thepost = $wpdb->get_row( $wpdb->prepare( "SELECT *
    FROM $wpdb->posts WHERE ID = 1" ) );
echo $thepost->post_title;
?>
```

This retrieves the entire row data for post ID 1 and displays the post title. The properties of $thepost object are the column names from the table you queried, which is wp_posts in this case. To retrieve the results as an array you can send in an additional parameter to the get_row function:

```php
<?php
$thepost = $wpdb->get_row( $wpdb->prepare( "SELECT *
    FROM $wpdb->posts WHERE ID = 1" ), ARRAY_A );
print_r ($thepost);
?>
```

By using the ARRAY_A parameter in get_row your post data is returned as an associative array. Alternatively, you could use the ARRAY_N parameter to return your post data in a numerically indexed array.

Standard SELECT queries should use the get_results function for retrieving multiple rows of data from the database. The following function returns the SQL result data as an array:

```php
<?php
$liveposts = $wpdb->get_results( $wpdb->prepare("SELECT ID, post_title
    FROM $wpdb->posts WHERE post_status = 'publish'") );

foreach ($liveposts as $livepost) {
    echo '<p>' .$livepost->post_title. '</p>';
}
?>
```

The preceding example is querying all published posts in WordPress and displaying the post titles. The query results are returned and stored as an array in `$liveposts`, which you can then loop through to display your query values.

The WordPress database class also features specific functions for UPDATE and INSERT statements. These two functions eliminate the need for custom SQL queries, because WordPress will create them for you based on the values passed into the function. Let's explore how the `insert` function is structured:

```
$wpdb->insert( $table, $data );
```

The `$table` variable is the name of the table you want to insert a value into. The `$data` variable is an array of field names and data to be inserted into those field names. So, for example, if you want to insert data into a custom table, you would execute this:

```php
<?php
$newvalueone = 'Hello World!';
$newvaluetwo = 'This is my data';
$wpdb->insert( $wpdb->my_custom_table, array( 'field_one' => $newvalueone,
    'field_two' => $newvaluetwo ) );

?>
```

The first thing you do is set two variables to store the data you want to insert. Next you execute the `insert` function, passing in both variables through an array. Notice how you set `field_one` and `field_two` as the two fields you are inserting. You can pass any field available in the table you are inserting with data to insert into that field.

The `update` function works very similarly to the `insert` function, except you also need to set the WHERE clause variable so WordPress knows which records to update:

```
$wpdb->update( $table, $data, $where );
```

The `$where` variable is an array of field names and data for the SQL WHERE clause. This is normally set to the unique ID of the field you are updating, but can also contain other field names from the table.

```php
<?php
$newtitle = 'My updated post title';
$newcontent = 'My new content';
$my_id = 1;
$wpdb->update( $wpdb->posts, array( 'post_title' => $newtitle,
    'post_content' => $newcontent ), array( 'ID' => $my_id ) );
?>
```

First you set your updated title and content variables. You also set a variable `$my_id` that contains the ID of the post you want to update. Next you execute the `update` function. Notice that the third parameter you send is an array containing your WHERE clause values, in this case the post ID. The preceding query updates the title and content for post ID 1. Remember, you can send multiple values through the WHERE parameter when updating a table record.

The `insert` and `update` functions shown do not need to be wrapped with the `prepare` function. Both of these functions actually use the `prepare` function after concatenating the query from the values passed to the functions. This is a much easier method than manually creating your `insert` and `update` queries in WordPress.

Dealing With Errors

Any time you are working with queries it's nice to see error messages. By default, if a custom query fails nothing is returned, so it's hard to determine what is wrong with your query. The `wpdb` class provides functions for displaying MySQL errors to the page. Here's an example of using these functions:

```php
<?php
$wpdb->show_errors();
$liveposts = $wpdb->get_results( $wpdb->prepare("SELECT ID, post_title
    FROM $wpdb->posts_FAKE WHERE post_status = 'publish'") );
$wpdb->print_error();
?>
```

The `show_errors` function must be called directly before you execute a query. The `print_error` function must be called directly after you execute a query. If there are any errors in your SQL statement the error messages are displayed. You can also call the `$wpdb->hide_errors()` function to hide all MySQL errors, or call the `$wpdb->flush()` function to delete the cached query results.

The database class contains additional variables that store information about WordPress queries. Following is a list of some of the more common variables:

```php
print_r($wpdb->num_queries); // total number of queries ran
print_r($wpdb->num_rows ); // total number of rows returned by the last query
print_r($wpdb->last_result ); // most recent query results
print_r($wpdb->last_query ); // most recent query executed
print_r($wpdb->col_info ); // column information for the most recent query
```

Another very powerful database variable is the `$queries` variable. This stores all of the queries run by WordPress. To enable this variable you must first set the constant value SAVEQUERIES to TRUE in your `wp-config.php` file. This tells WordPress to store all of the queries executed on each page load in the `$queries` variable. First drop this line of code in your `wp-config.php` file:

```php
define('SAVEQUERIES', true);
```

Now all queries will be stored in the `$queries` variable. You can display all of the query information like so:

```php
print_r($wpdb->queries); // stores all queries executed during page load
```

This is especially handy when troubleshooting slow load times. If a plugin is executing an obscene number of queries, that can dramatically slow down load times in WordPress. Remember to disable the SAVEQUERIES constant option when you are finished viewing queries because storing all queries can also slow down load times.

The database query class is a major asset when working with the WordPress database directly, as you may be when developing a plugin or building a more complex Loop. All of the previously mentioned database class functions use specific escaping techniques to verify that your queries are executed in the safest manner possible. To borrow from Randall Munroe's **xkcd** joke, you don't want a user hand-crafting an input item that contains DROP TABLES as a malicious SQL injection, resulting in the loss of your WordPress database tables. The query preparation and escaping functions ensure that inputs don't become SQL functions, no matter how craftily they're set up. It is essential that you follow these methods for querying data to ensure your web site is the most efficient and uses the safest techniques possible.

DIRECT DATABASE MANIPULATION

There may be times when you want to work with the WordPress database data directly. This can include accessing custom database tables created by a plugin or theme. To do this you'll need to use SQL to query the data from the MySQL database. Remember the WordPress APIs provide access to all of the WordPress tables and only very occasionally will you need to access the tables directly. All example queries in this chapter use the wp_ prefix for tables, but your database tables may use a different prefix as defined in your wp-config.php file when installing WordPress.

One of the most common methods for working with a WordPress database directly is by using php-MyAdmin, shown in Figure 6-2. phpMyAdmin is a free software tool provided by most hosting companies for administering MySQL databases through a web interface. Most of the examples in this section involve direct interaction with MySQL, and you'll need to use an SQL command line for their execution. Figure 6-2 shows the default database view using phpMyAdmin.

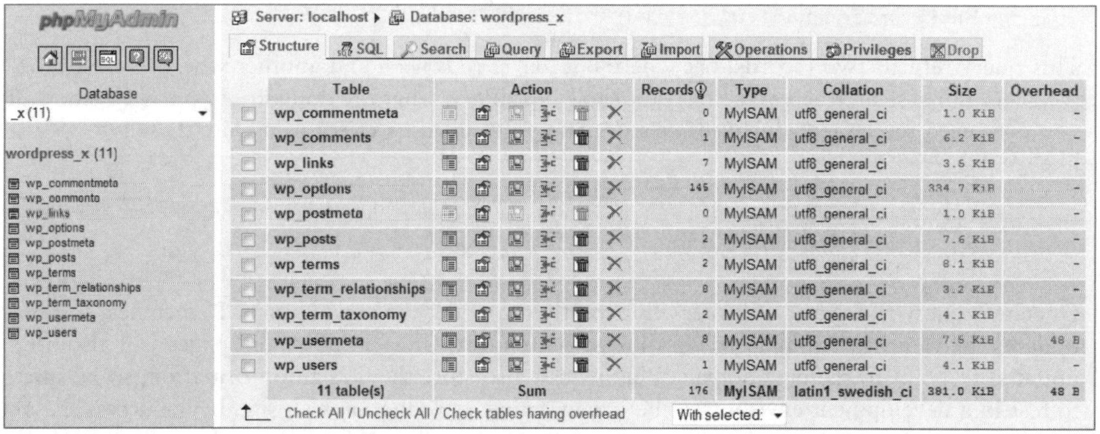

FIGURE 6-2: phpMyAdmin viewing a WordPress database

To run SQL statements in phpMyAdmin simply click the SQL tab across the top. Here you can execute any queries against your WordPress database. I always recommend creating your query directly in phpMyAdmin first before moving it over to your PHP scripts. The reasoning behind this is that debugging SQL statements is much faster directly in phpMyAdmin than it is using PHP code in WordPress. Once you have perfected your query, you can use it in your PHP code and you can be confident the results will be as expected. In the examples that follow we'll be using raw SQL queries. Remember if you want to run these queries in a theme or plugin you'll need to wrap the queries in the WordPress database class.

One of the most commonly accessed tables is the wp_posts table. Remember that this table stores all posts, pages, revisions, and even attachment records. The different types of content are defined by the `post_type` field. This field by default can contain four different post types: post, page, attachment, or revision. WordPress 2.9 introduced the ability for developers to define custom post types. This means additional `post_type` values may exist in this field. To view all post revisions in your database you can run this query:

```
SELECT * FROM wp_posts
WHERE post_type = 'revision'
```

This returns all records in `wp_posts` that are of a revision `post_type`. You can modify the preceding query to view all post attachments that have been uploaded to WordPress:

```
SELECT guid, wp_posts.* FROM wp_posts
WHERE post_type = 'attachment'
```

This example places the field `guid` as the first value to be returned in the query. The `guid` field contains the full URL of the attachment file on the server.

The `wp_options` table contains all of the settings saved for your WordPress installation. Options saved in this table are saved with an `option_name` and `option_value`. Therefore, the actual field name you call will always be those two names, rather than a specific field based on the option value. Following are two extremely important records in this table:

```
SELECT * FROM wp_options
WHERE option_name IN ('siteurl','home')
```

This query returns two records, one where `option_name` is `home` and another where `option_name` is `siteurl`. These are the two settings that tell WordPress what the domain of your web site is. If you ever need to change your web site's domain you can run a query to update these two values like so:

```
UPDATE wp_options
SET option_value = 'http://yournewdomain.com'
WHERE option_name IN ('siteurl','home')
```

Once this query runs your web site will instantly run under the new domain. Remember, this only updates the web site's domain in WordPress. Attachment URLs in posts and pages will also need updated to point to the new domain. Plugins can also store the domain information, so be sure to test in a development environment before updating a production web site. If you access the old domain you will be redirected to the new one. If you were logged in, your cookies and session will be invalidated and you will have to log in again. This is a great technique if you built a new web site under a subdomain (for example, `new.domain.com`) and are updating the URLs to push the web site live.

The `wp_options` table contains other very important fields. To view all active plugins on your web site, you can view the `active_plugins` `option_name` like so:

```
SELECT *
FROM wp_options
WHERE option_name = 'active_plugins'
```

The options table also stores all options defined by plugins. Most plugins activated in WordPress will have some type of settings page. These settings are saved in `wp_options` so the plugins can retrieve these settings as needed. For example, the Akismet plugin stores an option named `akismet_spam_count` that stores the total number of spam comments. You can view this option by running the following query:

```
SELECT * FROM wp_options
WHERE option_name = 'akismet_spam_count'
```

The `wp_users` table contains all of the users you currently have set up in WordPress. If you allow open registration on your web site new users will be created in this table as they join your site. The `wp_users` table stores very important user information including username, password, e-mail, web site URL, and date registered. Say you want to export all of your users' e-mail addresses. You can easily do so by running the following query:

```
SELECT DISTINCT user_email
FROM wp_users
```

Now you can easily export all of the e-mail addresses loaded into WordPress! Another common query used in `wp_users` is to reset a user's password. You can do this in a couple different ways, but if you are absolutely locked out of WordPress you can always reset the password directly in the database. To do so you need to update the `user_pass` field from the MySQL command line:

```
UPDATE wp_users
SET user_pass = MD5('Hall0w33n')
WHERE user_login ='admin'
LIMIT 1;
```

Running this query resets the admin password to Hall0w33n. Notice how you wrap the new password in `MD5()`. This converts the password to an MD5 hash. Since WordPress 2.5, passwords are now salted and hashed using the phpass encryption library rather than MD5. Not to worry, though, because WordPress is built to detect MD5 hash passwords and convert them to phpass encryption instead. So the preceding query will successfully reset your password in WordPress.

The `wp_comments` table stores all comments submitted to your web site. This table contains the comment, author, e-mail, web site URL, IP address, and more. Here's an example query for displaying comments:

```
SELECT wc.* FROM wp_posts wp
INNER JOIN wp_comments wc ON wp.ID = wc.comment_post_ID
WHERE wp.ID = '1554'
```

This query returns all comments for post ID 1554. Another important field in `wp_comments` is the `user_id` field. If a user is logged in to your web site and posts a comment, this field will contain his or her user ID. As an example, the following displays all comments left by the user admin:

```
SELECT wc.* FROM wp_comments wc
INNER JOIN wp_users wu ON wc.user_id = wu.ID
WHERE wu.user_login = 'admin'
```

In the database diagram in Figure 6-1 the arrows show the relationships between each table. This is incredibly useful when writing custom queries to retrieve data directly from the database. For example, to retrieve all comments for a particular post you could run this query:

```
SELECT * FROM wp_comments
INNER JOIN wp_posts ON wp_comments.comment_post_id = wp_posts.ID
WHERE wp_posts.ID = '1'
```

This query returns all comments for post ID 1. Notice how you join the `wp_comments.comment_post_ID` field on the `wp_posts.ID` field. The SQL `JOIN` is necessary because there is an N:1 relationship between comments and posts; each post may have many comments but comments only apply to one post. These two fields are shown in the diagram as the joining fields for these tables. As another example, look at how to join the `wp_users` and `wp_usermeta` tables together:w

```
SELECT * FROM wp_users
INNER JOIN wp_usermeta ON wp_users.ID = wp_usermeta.user_id
WHERE wp_users.ID = '1'
```

As you can see in the database diagram, the `wp_users.ID` field was joined on the `wp_usermeta.user_id` field. The preceding query retrieves all of the user information, including user metadata, for user ID 1, which is the default admin account. Again the database diagram makes it extremely easy to determine how tables are joined by index value inside the WordPress database, and how logical INNER JOIN operations can build result sets of related table rows

If you are interested in learning more about SQL you can read some amazing tutorials at http://www.w3schools.com/sql/default.asp.

WORDPRESS TAXONOMY

Taxonomy is defined as a way to group similar items together. This basically adds a relational dimension to your web site's content. In the case of WordPress you use categories and tags to group your posts together. By grouping these posts together you are defining the taxonomy of those posts. Taxonomy can be hierarchical (that is, categories and subcategories) but it is not required as with the case of tags.

Default Taxonomies

WordPress comes loaded with three taxonomies by default: categories, tags, and link categories:

- ➤ **Category:** A bucket for grouping similar posts together
- ➤ **Tag:** A label attached to a post
- ➤ **Link Category:** A bucket for grouping similar links together

Categories are hierarchical and defined when creating a post. Tags do not use hierarchy and are also defined when creating a post. Link categories are used when grouping similar links together using the WordPress link manager. All three out-of-the-box taxonomies are available for use in a default installation of WordPress.

Each category or tag you create is a term of that taxonomy. For example, a category named Music is a term of the category taxonomy. A tag named Ketchup is a term of the tag taxonomy. Understanding taxonomy and terms will help you when defining your own custom taxonomies in WordPress.

Understanding how you can classify your content using a solid taxonomy structure will make structuring web site content in WordPress much easier from the start. Developing a solid taxonomy framework enables easy and accurate information access throughout your web site.

Taxonomy Table Structure

WordPress features three database tables that store all taxonomy information: `wp_terms`, `wp_term_relationships`, and `wp_term_taxonomy`. This taxonomy schema, which was added in WordPress 2.3, makes the taxonomy functionality extremely flexible in WordPress. This means you can create and define any type of custom taxonomy to use on your web site.

The `wp_terms` table stores all of your taxonomy terms. This can be categories, tags, link categories, and any custom taxonomy terms you have defined. The `wp_term_taxonomy` table defines what taxonomy each term belongs to. For example, all of your tag IDs will be listed in this table with a taxonomy value of `post_tag`. If you created a custom taxonomy the taxonomy value would be the name of your custom taxonomy. The `wp_term_relationships` table is the cross-reference table that joins taxonomy terms with your content. For example, when you assign a tag to your post, a new record is created here joining your post ID and the term ID together.

Understanding Taxonomy Relationships

To really understand the relationship between the taxonomy tables it's best to look at a database diagram of the taxonomy table structure, shown in Figure 6-3.

As you can see, the three taxonomy tables are joined together by unique IDs. The following is a query to display all posts along with all taxonomy terms assigned to those posts:

```
SELECT wt.name, wp.post_title, wp.post_date FROM wp_terms wt
INNER JOIN wp_term_taxonomy wtt ON wt.term_id  = wtt.term_id
INNER JOIN wp_term_relationships wtr ON wtt.
    term_taxonomy_id = wtr.term_taxonomy_id
INNER JOIN wp_posts wp ON wtr.object_id = wp.ID
WHERE wp.post_type = 'post'
```

Notice how you are joining on the table fields as depicted in Figure 6-3. The preceding example only returns three fields: the taxonomy term, post title, and post date. This query example returns all posts in your WordPress database along with all taxonomy terms attached to those posts.

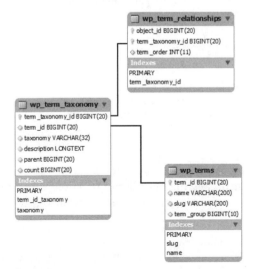

FIGURE 6-3: WordPress taxonomy table structure

BUILDING YOUR OWN TAXONOMIES

Creating your own custom taxonomies has many benefits. Imagine running a food blogging web site. When creating new posts you'll want to label a certain recipe as Asian, but you also may want to label the individual ingredients, heat factor, prep time, and so on. Building custom taxonomies allows you the freedom to define these different methods of categorizing your content and really expands WordPress from blogging software into a full-fledged content management system (CMS).

Custom Taxonomy Overview

Since the revamp of the taxonomy schema in WordPress 2.3, you now have the ability to define custom taxonomies for your content. WordPress makes it easier than ever to create custom taxonomies, as well as integrate your new taxonomies into WordPress.

WordPress 2.8 added the feature to automatically display a meta box to the post edit screen for adding taxonomy terms directly to your posts. WordPress will also create a menu item to access the new taxonomy admin panel for administering your taxonomy terms. Currently this works only on posts, but pages and links will be added in a future release. This also does not work if you are using hierarchy in your custom taxonomy.

Building Custom Taxonomies

Now it's time to build your first custom taxonomy! As an example you are going to create a simple taxonomy for defining ingredients. Imagine you are a food blogger who likes to post recipes online. You are going to set up a custom taxonomy to define each type of ingredient in the recipes you post.

The first thing you are going to do is define your new taxonomy using the `register_taxonomy` WordPress function. This function allows you to customize how your new taxonomy will work and look. The following code would work in a custom plugin, but for this example you'll use the `functions.php` file in your theme folder. Open up `functions.php` in your theme and add the following code:

```php
<?php
add_action( 'init', 'define_ingredient_taxonomy', 0 );

function define_ingredient_taxonomy() {
    register_taxonomy( 'ingredients', 'post', array( 'hierarchical' => false,
        'label' => 'Ingredients', 'query_var' => true, 'rewrite' => true ) );
}
?>
```

The first thing you do is call the `init` hook, which tells WordPress to execute your `define_ingredient_taxonomy` function during initialization. Your function then calls the WordPress function `register_taxonomy`. This function is used to create your custom taxonomy based on what values you send.

Let's break down the parameters you are sending to the `register_taxonomy` function. The first parameter is the taxonomy name, in this case `'ingredients'`. This is the name that will define this taxonomy in the database. The second parameter is the object type. For this example, you will use `'post'`, but you can also create custom taxonomies for pages and links as well. The third and final parameter is for arguments, meaning you actually send multiple values to this parameter.

Four arguments can be sent to the argument parameter. The first is `hierarchical`, which defines whether or not your custom taxonomy will contain hierarchy. In the preceding example you set this to `false`, so your taxonomy will function just like tags. The next argument, `label`, is used to set the name of your taxonomy for use in admin pages within WordPress. The `query_var` argument is used to set whether custom query posts should be allowed against this taxonomy. You see an example of this feature later in the chapter.

The final argument is for `rewrite`, which you set to `true`. This tells WordPress whether or not you want a pretty permalink when viewing your custom taxonomy. By setting this to `true` you can access your custom taxonomy posts like example.com/ingredients/bacon rather than the ugly method of example.com/?ingredients=bacon.

FIGURE 6-4: Custom taxonomy menu option

Now that you have created your custom taxonomy for ingredients, take a look at what WordPress has done with your new taxonomy. The first thing you will notice on your admin dashboard is a new link under the Posts menu for your taxonomy labeled ingredients, as shown in Figure 6-4.

Clicking this new menu item brings you to the custom taxonomy admin panel for ingredients, shown in Figure 6-5. This admin panel works exactly as the post tags admin panel does. Here you can create new taxonomy terms, edit and delete existing terms, find how many posts are assigned to each, and also search taxonomy terms.

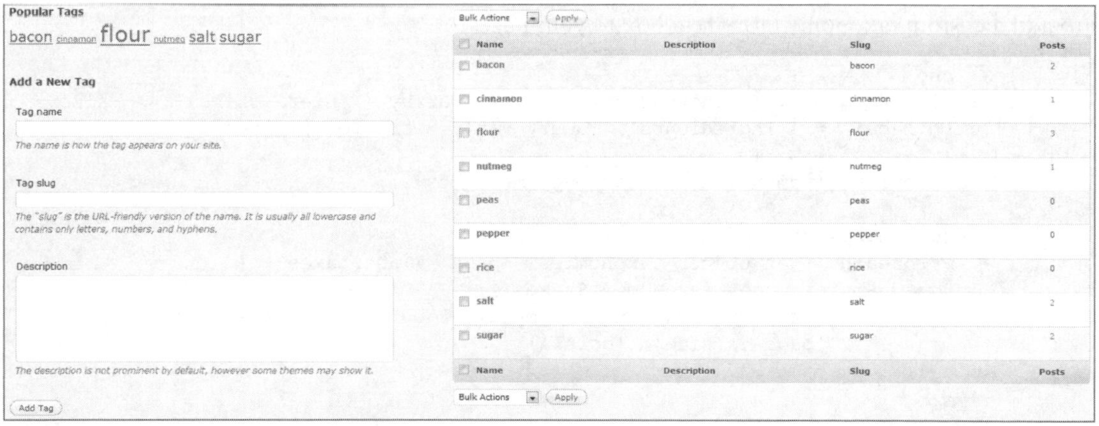

FIGURE 6-5: Custom taxonomy admin panel

The final new item added for your custom taxonomy is a meta box on the post edit screen, shown in Figure 6-6. To view this, click Add New Post. The meta box should appear on the right-hand side of your screen, and look very similar to the Post Tags meta box. Here you can easily add and delete new ingredients on your posts.

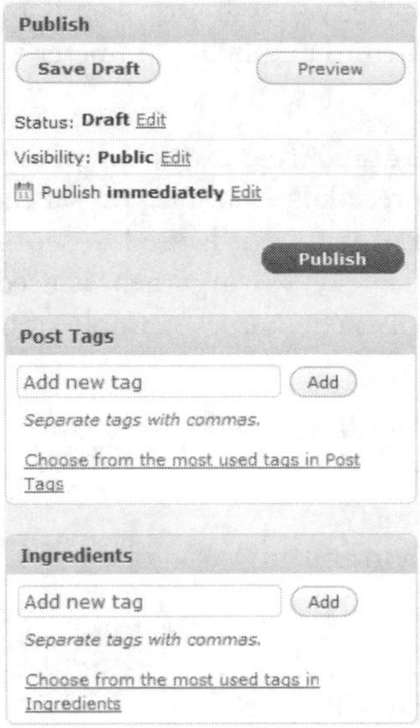

FIGURE 6-6: Custom taxonomy
meta box

Remember that these features will not display if you are using hierarchy in your custom taxonomy. Also, this only works on posts, but pages and links will be added in a future release.

Starting with WordPress 2.9 you have access to the meta box functions. This means you can add post-specific meta boxes to other areas of WordPress, such as pages. Following is an example showing how to add a custom taxonomy term meta box to your pages:

```php
<?php
register_taxonomy( 'ingredients', 'page', array ( 'hierarchical' => false,
    'label' => 'Ingredients', 'query_var' => true, 'rewrite' => true ) );

add_action( 'admin_menu', 'tax_page_meta_box' );

function tax_page_meta_box() {
    foreach ( get_object_taxonomies( 'page' ) as $taxes ) {
        $mytax = get_taxonomy( $taxes );
        add_meta_box( "tag-ings", $mytax->label, 'post_tags_meta_box',
            'page', 'side', 'core' );
    }
}

?>
```

First you define your new custom taxonomy name: ingredients. You also set your taxonomy type to page. Currently hierarchy taxonomies are not supported using this method, so make sure you set hierarchical to false. Next you use the admin_menu hook to call your function, tax_page_meta_box. Finally, the add_meta_box function is called to add the meta box to your page screen. This example is a little more complex, but it shows the power of custom taxonomies and how you can use that power for more than just your posts.

Using Your Custom Taxonomy

Now that you've created your custom taxonomy you need to know how to use it on your web site. As always, WordPress features some very easy-to-use functions for working with your custom taxonomy. The following shows how you can display a tag cloud showing your custom taxonomy terms:

```php
<?php wp_tag_cloud( array( 'taxonomy' => 'ingredients', 'number' => 5 ) ); ?>
```

The `wp_tag_cloud` function can accept a lot of different arguments, but in this example you're only using two: `taxonomy` and `number`. First, you set your taxonomy to `ingredients`; this tells WordPress to only return taxonomy terms defined under the custom taxonomy you created for ingredients. Next you define the number of terms you want to display, which in this example is 5. Calling this function in your theme sidebar displays a nice tag cloud that shows the five taxonomy terms with the most posts assigned to them.

You can also use `query_posts` to display posts for a specific taxonomy term. Say you want to create a custom loop to only display recipes that use nutmeg:

```php
<?php query_posts( array( 'ingredients' => 'nutmeg', 'showposts' => 15 ) ); ?>
```

That's it! The two `query_posts` arguments you send are the taxonomy name, `ingredients` in this case, and the number of posts to display. Remember that you can pass more `query_posts` arguments to further define what posts are displayed and in what order.

You can also easily display custom taxonomy terms assigned to each post. To do this you'll be using the `get_the_term_list` WordPress function. This function works very similarly to `get_the_tag_list`, but is for building a custom taxonomy term list instead.

```php
<?php echo get_the_term_list( $post->ID, 'ingredients',
    'Ingredients Used: ', ', ', '' ); ?>
```

The preceding code displays all custom taxonomy terms assigned to the post you are viewing. This code does need to be in The Loop in your theme template file to work correctly. To execute the function you send in the post ID, custom taxonomy name, and the title you want displayed next to the terms. Remember, you can always visit the function reference to learn more about this function and what parameters are allowed: http://codex.wordpress.org/Function_Reference/get_the_term_list.

The `get_terms` function can also be used to retrieve an array of your custom taxonomy values. In the following example you retrieve all of the terms for your `ingredients` taxonomy and loop through the values displaying the term name:

```php
<?php
$terms = get_terms('ingredients');
foreach ($terms as $term) {
    echo '<p>' .$term->name. '</p>';
}
?>
```

Keep in mind that you need to make sure the taxonomy is defined before you start working with custom taxonomy values. If any of the preceding examples return blank, that means they are being executed before your `register_taxonomy` function is being called to define your custom taxonomy.

Defining custom taxonomies in WordPress is a very powerful way to organize your web site content. Using the preceding methods can help transform your web site into a content management system using the power of WordPress.

7

Plugin Development

WHAT'S IN THIS CHAPTER?

- ➤ Creating plugin files
- ➤ Using WordPress filter and action hooks
- ➤ How to properly use the Settings API
- ➤ Create a widget and Dashboard Widget
- ➤ Create custom shortcodes
- ➤ Data validation and plugin security
- ➤ Support language translation
- ➤ Publish a plugin to the official Plugin Directory

One of the main reasons WordPress is such a popular software platform is the ease with which it can be extended. Plugins are the primary reason for this and allow almost endless possibilities in extending WordPress. This chapter discusses everything you need to know to create amazing plugins in WordPress.

We're going to look at plugins from both a functional and structural perspective. Starting with the packaging of plugin files, we'll dig into the API hooks that connect your custom plugin code to the WordPress core and show how to integrate a plugin into various parts of the WordPress editing, management and display processes. Finally, we show how to publish a plugin for others to use. At the end of this chapter you build a WordPress plugin from the ground up. You'll utilize many of the features discussed in this chapter and learn the proper way to extend WordPress through a custom plugin.

PLUGIN PACKAGING

When developing plugins in WordPress it's best to follow a standard plugin packaging template, that is, certain functional and descriptive components that will exist in all plugins you create for

WordPress. This chapter discusses the requirements for a plugin, as well as recommended additions such as software license and internationalization. While the actual code implementation of the plugin is the exciting part of the process, consider the plugin packaging like elementary grammar rules for a new language: necessary for making yourself understood.

Create a Plugin File

The first step in creating a WordPress plugin is to create a new PHP file for your plugin code. The plugin filename should be descriptive of your plugin so it's easy to identify your plugin in the `plugins` directory. It should also be unique because all WordPress plugins exist in the same folder. If your plugin filename is too generic you run the risk of another plugin having the same filename, which would be an obvious problem.

A plugin can also exist in a folder containing all of the necessary files the plugin needs to run. A folder should always be used if your plugin requires more than one file because it helps keep the user's plugin folder organized. It's also a good idea to create an `/images` folder inside your plugin folder to store any custom images your plugin might use, such as a custom menu icon.

Creating the Plugin Header

A requirement for all WordPress plugins is a valid plugin header. The plugin header must be defined at the very top of your main PHP file as a PHP comment. It does not need to exist in every file for your plugin, only the main PHP file. This header tells WordPress that your PHP file is in fact a legitimate WordPress plugin and should be processed as such. Following is an example of a standard plugin header:

```php
<?php
/*
Plugin Name: My Awesome Plugin
Plugin URI: http://example.com/wordpress-plugins/my-plugin
Description: This is a brief description of my plugin
Version: 1.0
Author: Brad Williams
Author URI: http://example.com
*/
?>
```

The only required line in the plugin header is the `Plugin Name`. The rest of the information is optional but highly recommended. The information listed in your plugin header is

FIGURE 7-1: Example plugin listing

used on the Manage Plugins section of WordPress. For example, you can see what the header looks like in WordPress in Figure 7-1.

You can see how important the plugin header information is, including all optional data. The information should be accurate and provide good links to your web site and the plugin URI for additional information and support regarding your plugin.

Plugin License

When developing a plugin you plan on releasing to the public, it's customary to include the software license that the plugin is released under just below your plugin header. This is not a requirement for the plugin to function, but is a good idea to clearly state what software license your plugin uses. A license comment block will also state there is no warranty, which makes sure you are not liable should someone decide your plugin destroyed his or her site. Following is a standard GPL license, under which most WordPress plugins are released:

```php
<?php
/*  Copyright YEAR  PLUGIN_AUTHOR_NAME  (email : PLUGIN AUTHOR EMAIL)

    This program is free software; you can redistribute it and/or modify
    it under the terms of the GNU General Public License as published by
    the Free Software Foundation; either version 2 of the License, or
    (at your option) any later version.

    This program is distributed in the hope that it will be useful,
    but WITHOUT ANY WARRANTY; without even the implied warranty of
    MERCHANTABILITY or FITNESS FOR A PARTICULAR PURPOSE.  See the
    GNU General Public License for more details.

    You should have received a copy of the GNU General Public License
    along with this program; if not, write to the Free Software
    Foundation, Inc., 51 Franklin St, Fifth Floor, Boston, MA  02110-1301  USA
*/
?>
```

To use this license in your plugin fill in the year, plugin author name, and plugin author e-mail in the preceding comment. By doing so your plugin will be licensed under the GPL. For more information on GPL licensing visit http://www.gnu.org/licenses/licenses.html.

Activate and Deactivate Functions

You'll want to utilize some important functions when creating plugins. The first of these is called the register_activation_hook function. This function is executed when your plugin is activated in the WordPress Plugins SubPanel. The function accepts two parameters: the path to the main plugin file and the function to execute when the plugin is activated.

In most of the code examples in this chapter, we're going to use "gmp" as a function and variable prefix, as well as a descriptive name for our plugin . It's just an example short name, but one that you're going to see in a lot of code. The following example executes the function gmp_install when the plugin is activated:

```php
<?php
register_activation_hook(__FILE__,'gmp_install');

function gmp_install() {
    //do something
}
?>
```

This is an extremely useful function if you need to execute any actions when your plugin is activated. For example, you may want to check the current WordPress version to verify your plugin is compatible. You may also want to create some default option settings or create a custom database table to store your plugin data.

One important check you should always do when your plugin is activated is verify that the version of WordPress the user is running is compatible with your plugin. This ensures any functions, hooks, and so on that your plugin uses are available in WordPress.

```
register_activation_hook(__FILE__,'gmp_install');

function gmp_install() {
    global $wp_version;
        If (version_compare($wp_version, "2.9", "<")) {
            deactivate_plugins(basename(__FILE__)); // Deactivate our plugin
            wp_die("This plugin requires WordPress version 2.9 or higher.");
        }
    }
```

The preceding function uses the global variable `$wp_version`, which stores the current version of WordPress running, and verifies it is not running a version lower than 2.9. You do the version comparison using the `version_compare` PHP function. If the WordPress version is lower than 2.9 you automatically deactivate your plugin and display an error message to the users that they need to upgrade.

There is also a function that executes when a plugin is deactivated called the `register_deactivation_hook` function. This function is executed when your plugin is deactivated in the WordPress Plugins SubPanel. This function accepts the same two arguments as the `register_activation_hook` function. Following is an example using the deactivation function:

```
<?php
register_deactivation_hook(__FILE__,'gmp_uninstall');

function gmp_uninstall() {
    //do something
}
?>
```

Internationalization

Internationalization, sometimes shortened to "i18n" in the WordPress Codex, is the process of making your plugin or theme ready for translation, or localized. In WordPress this means marking strings that should be translated. Localization is the process of translating the text displayed by the theme or plugin into different languages. This isn't a requirement but internationalization should be used on any plugin you plan on distributing. This opens up your plugin to the widest possible audience.

WordPress features two functions to make a string translatable. The first function is the `__()` function. That isn't a typo; the function is two underscores as shown here:

```
<?php $howdy = __('Howdy Neighbor!','gmp-plugin'); ?>
```

The first parameter you pass is the string that you want to be translatable. This string is what will be displayed to the browser if the text is not translated into a different language. The second parameter is the text domain. In the case of themes and plugins the domain should be a unique identifier, which is used to distinguish between all loaded translations.

If your code should echo the translatable string to the browser you'll want to use the _e() function as shown here:

```php
<?php _e('Howdy Neighbor!','gmp-plugin'); ?>
```

This function works exactly the same as __(); the only difference is that the value is echoed to the browser. These translation functions are used throughout this chapter in the example code.

Placeholders need special consideration when internationalizing your plugins and themes. As an example, look at an error message you want to make translatable:

```
Error Code 6980: Email is a required field
```

The obvious, but incorrect, way to attempt to split a string into translatable parts is to separate the field name, error number and descriptive string::

```php
<?php
$error_number = 6980;
$error_field = "Email";
$error = __('Error Code ','gmp-plugin') .$error_number. ': '
.$error_field .__(' is a required field','gmp-plugin');
echo $error;
?>
```

This is actually the wrong way to include dynamic values in your translatable string because your translatable string is cut into two parts. These two parts may not work independently in another language. This could also seriously confuse the translator viewing a bunch of cryptic phrases that mean nothing when separated. The proper way is shown here:

```php
<?php
$error_number = 6980;
$error_field = "Email";
printf(__('Error Code %1$d: %2$s is a required field','gmp-plugin'),
$error_number, $error_field);
?>
```

As you can see this uses the PHP printf function, which outputs the formatted string. Your two variables are passed to printf and inserted into the string in the designated spots. In this example a developer translating your plugin messages into another language would see the line as "Error Code %1$d: %2$s is a required field" and know it's possible to move around the error number and field values to make sense in the target language. Splitting the strings leads to split translations and possibly unintentionally funny translated grammar. Alternatively you could use the PHP sprintf function if you want to store the error message value in a variable prior to displaying it.

Plurals also need special consideration when defining your translatable strings. Say you need to translate a string like:

```php
<?php
$count = 1;
printf(__('You have %d new message','gmp-plugin'), $count);
?>
```

This works great if you have one new message, but what if you have more than one new message? Luckily, WordPress contains a function you can use to handle this problem called __ngettext. The following code shows it in action:

```php
<?php
$count = 34;
printf(__ngettext('You have %d new message', 'You have %d new messages',
$count,'gmp-plugin'), $count);
?>
```

This function accepts four parameters: the singular version, the plural version, the actual number, and the domain text for your plugin. The _ngettext function uses the number parameter ($count in the example) to determine whether the singular or plural string should be returned.

WordPress also features a translation function you can use to add comments to your translatable strings. This is helpful if you have a string set up for translation that might have multiple meanings. To do this you use the _c function as shown in the following code:

```php
<?php
echo _c('Editor|user role','gmp-plugin');
echo _c('Editor|rich-text editor','gmp-plugin');
?>
```

As you can see you use _c just as you would __, except you add a pipe to the end of your translatable text with your comment directly after. Everything after, and including, the pipe will be ignored and not displayed. This allows you to add custom comment messages that the translator can read to explain the context of your text to be translated.

Now that you've prepared your plugin for translation you must load the localization file to do the translation. To do so you execute the load_plugin_textdomain function as shown here:

```php
<?php
add_action('init', 'gmp_init');

function gmp_init() {
    load_plugin_textdomain('gmp-plugin', false,
        plugin_basename(dirname(__FILE__).'/localization'));
}
?>
```

The first parameter you pass is the domain text name that you've used to identify all of your translatable strings. The second parameter is the path relative to the ABSPATH variable; however, this parameter is now deprecated in favor of the third parameter. The final parameter is the path to your translation files from the /plugins directory. To store these files you should create a folder inside your plugin directory called /localization . You use the plugin_basename and dirname functions to retrieve the path to your localization folder.

You can learn more about the process of creating translation files in the WordPress Codex at http://codex.wordpress.org/I18n_for_WordPress_Developers.

Directory Constants

When creating WordPress plugins you will often need to reference files and folders throughout the WordPress installation. Since WordPress 2.6, users have had the ability to move this directory anywhere they want. Because of this you should never use hardcoded paths in a plugin. WordPress has defined a set of PHP constants to store the path to the wp-content and plugins directories. You can use these constants in your plugins to verify that any paths you are referencing are correct regardless of where the actual directory might exist on the server:

➤ WP_CONTENT_URL: Full URL to wp-content

➤ WP_CONTENT_DIR: The server path to the wp-content directory

➤ WP_PLUGIN_URL: Full URL to the plugins directory

➤ WP_PLUGIN_DIR: The server path to the plugins directory

➤ WP_LANG_DIR: The server path to the language directory

These constants were added in WordPress 2.6, so any version older than that will not have these set. However, if you want to maintain backward compatibility you can create these constants with just a few lines of code:

```php
<?php
// pre-2.6 compatibility
if ( !defined( 'WP_CONTENT_URL' ) )
    define( 'WP_CONTENT_URL', get_option( 'siteurl' ) . '/wp-content' );
if ( !defined( 'WP_CONTENT_DIR' ) )
    define( 'WP_CONTENT_DIR', ABSPATH . 'wp-content' );
if ( !defined( 'WP_PLUGIN_URL' ) )
    define( 'WP_PLUGIN_URL', WP_CONTENT_URL. '/plugins' );
if ( !defined( 'WP_PLUGIN_DIR' ) )
    define( 'WP_PLUGIN_DIR', WP_CONTENT_DIR . '/plugins' );
if ( !defined( 'WP LANG_DIR') )
    define( 'WP_LANG_DIR', WP_CONTENT_DIR . '/languages' );
?>
```

Notice how you are verifying that the constant has not been defined before setting it. If the constant already exists you don't want to overwrite its value. By placing this code in your plugin you can be certain that your plugin will work with these constants regardless of the user's WordPress version.

KNOW YOUR HOOKS: ACTIONS AND FILTERS

One of the most important features for extending WordPress is called a *hook*. Hooks are simply a standardized way of "hooking" into WordPress. Using hooks you can execute functions at specific times in the WordPress process, allowing you to alter how WordPress functions and the expected output. Hooks are the primary way plugins interact with your content in WordPress. Up to this point we've focused on the structure and format of plugins, but now we're actually going to make a plugin do something.

A hook is simply a PHP function call with various parameters that can be sent. Following is an example showing a properly formatted Action hook call:

```php
<?php add_action( $tag, $function_to_add, $priority, $accepted_args ); ?>
```

Actions and Filters

Two types of hooks can be used: Actions and Filters. Action hooks are triggered by events in Word-Press. For example, an Action hook is triggered when a new post is published. Filter hooks are used to modify WordPress content before saving it to the database or displaying it to the screen. For example, a Filter hook is available for the content of the post or page. This means you can alter that content after it is retrieved from the database, but before it is displayed in your browser.

Look at an example of a Filter hook in action. Remember that Filter hooks modify content, so this example modifies the post content:

```php
<?php add_filter('the_content', 'my_function'); ?>
```

The `add_filter` function is used to execute a Filter action. You are using the Filter called `the_content`, which is the Filter for your post content. This tells WordPress that every time the content is displayed it needs to pass through your custom function called `my_function`. The `add_filter` function can accept four parameters:

➤ *filter_action* (string): The filter to use.

➤ *custom_filter_function* (string): The custom function to pass the filter through.

➤ *priority* (integer): The priority in which this filter should run.

➤ *accepted args* (integer): The number of arguments the function accepts.

Here's an example of the `the_content` Filter in action:

```php
<?php
function profanity_filter($content) {
    $profanities = array("sissy","dummy");
    $content=str_ireplace($profanities,'[censored]',$content);
    return $content;
}

add_filter('the_content', 'profanity_filter');
?>
```

The `profanity_filter` function will replace the words "sissy" and "dummy" with [censored] automatically on all posts and pages on your web site. We are using the `str_ireplace` PHP function to handle the replace. This function will replace some characters in a string with other characters in a string. The `str_ireplace` function is also case-insensitive. Because you are using a Filter hook the content isn't actually modified in the database; instead it's modified during processing of `the_post()`, before being displayed, when this filter is invoked. The content in the database is not affected so the words "sissy" and "dummy" will still exist in your content, and if you ever disable or change the plugin those words will appear in the displayed text. Filter hooks always receive data, in this case the `$content` variable is passed to your function and contains your post content. Also notice the last line of your function returns the `$content` variable. Remember that you must always return the content you are modifying or else it returns empty and therefore displays nothing.

Now that you've seen the Filter hook in action, take a look at the Action hook and what it can do. The Action hook is triggered by events in WordPress. WordPress doesn't require any return values from your Action hook function; the WordPress Core just notifies your code that a specific event has taken place. The Action hook is structured exactly like a Filter hook, as you can see in the following code:

```php
<?php add_action('hook_name', 'your_function_name'
[,priority] [,accepted_args] ); ?>
```

The `add_action` function accepts four parameters just like the `add_filter` function. Here you can set the hook name you want to hook into, the custom function name you are going to execute when the event is triggered, and the priority and the number of accepted args. Here's a real example using an Action hook:

```php
<?php
function email_new_comment() {
    wp_mail('me@example.com', __('New blog comment', 'gmp-plugin') ,
__('There is a new comment on your website: http://example.com','gmp-plugin'));
}

add_action('comment_post', 'email_new_comment');
?>
```

Notice you are using the `comment_post` Action hook. This Action is triggered whenever a new comment is posted in WordPress. As you can see the `email_new_comment` function will send an e-mail anytime a new comment is created. Also notice you are not sending in any variables to your function, or returning any values out of your function. Action filters don't require this, but if needed you can pass values into your function.

Popular Filter Hooks

More than 1,000 different hooks are available in WordPress, which is a bit overwhelming at first. Luckily, a handful of them are used much more often than the rest. This section explores some of the more commonly used hooks in WordPress.

Some of the more common Filter hooks are:

➤ `the_content`: Applied to the content of the post or page before displaying.

➤ `the_content_rss`: Applied to the content of post or page for RSS inclusion.

➤ `the_title`: Applied to the post or page title before displaying.

➤ `comment_text`: Applied to the comment text before displaying.

➤ `wp_title`: Applied to the page `<title>` before displaying.

➤ `get_categories`: Applied to the category list generated by `get_categories`.

➤ `the_permalink`: Applied to the permalink URL.

Let's look at some of the more popular Filter hooks in WordPress, starting with a more practical example than our profanity filter using `the_content` Filter hook. This hook allows you to alter the content for posts and pages prior to it being displayed in the browser. By using this hook you can add your custom content either before, in the middle, or after the content:

```php
<?php
function SubscribeFooter($content) {
        if(is_single()) {
                $content.= '<h3>' .__('Enjoyed this article?', 'gmp-plugin')
                        . '</h3>';
                $content.= '<p>' .__('Subscribe to our
```

```
         <a href="http://example.com/feed">RSS feed</a>!', 'gmp-plugin'). '</p>';
                }
                return $content;
    }

    add_filter ('the_content', 'SubscribeFooter');
    ?>
```

In this example you are adding your subscribe text to the bottom of your content. Notice you are also using the `is_single` conditional tag to verify that your subscribe text is added only on a single post page. The `$content` variable stores all of the post or page content, so by appending your subscribe text you are adding it to the bottom of your content. This is the ideal way to add content to the bottom of all posts because you aren't actually modifying the post. In the future if you decide to change this message you can change it in one place, rather than updating every post in your web site.

Another powerful Filter hook is `the_title`. This hook is used for changing the post or page title prior to being displayed. Here's an example using this Filter:

```
<?php
function custom_title($title) {
    $title .= ' - ' .__('By Example.com', 'gmp-plugin');
    return $title;
}

add_filter('the_title', 'custom_title');
?>
```

This example adds " - By Example.com" to all of your post and page titles. Remember, this doesn't actually modify the title in the database, but instead modifies the display of the title to the end user.

The `default_content` Filter hook is useful for setting the default content for your post and pages. This is helpful if you have a set format for all of your posts and can save valuable writing time:

```
<?php
function my_default_content($content) {
    $content = __('For more great content please subscribe to my RSS feed',
                'gmp-plugin');
    return $content;
}

add_filter('default_content', 'my_default_content');
?>
```

Filter hooks are exceptionally powerful for inserting your own processing into a variety of points in the Loop processing of each post. Realizing the full power of the WordPress plugin system means also using action hooks to fire your own code in response to events within the WordPress core.

Popular Action Hooks

Some of the more common Action hooks are:

➤ `publish_post`: Triggered when a new post is published.

➤ `create_category`: Triggered when a new category is created.

➤ `switch_theme`: Triggered when you switch themes.

➤ `admin_head`: Triggered in the `<head>` section of the admin dashboard.

➤ `wp_head`: Triggered in the `<head>` section of your theme.

➤ `wp_footer`: Triggered in the footer section of your theme usually directly before the `</body>` tag.

➤ `init`: Triggered after WordPress has finished loading, but before any headers are sent. Good place to intercept $_GET and $_POST HTML requests

➤ `admin_init`: Same as `init` but only runs on admin dashboard pages.

➤ `user_register`: Triggered when a new user is created.

➤ `comment_post`: Triggered when a new comment is created.

One of the most commonly used Action hooks is the `wp_head` hook. Using the `wp_head` hook you can insert any custom code into the `<head>` section of the WordPress theme. Here's an example:

```php
<?php
function custom_css() {
 ?>
    <style type="text/css">
    a {
        font-size: 14px;
        color: #000000;
        text-decoration: none;
    }
    a:hover {
        font-size: 14px;
        color: #FF0000;
        text-decoration: underline;
    }
    </style>
<?php
}

add_action('wp_head', 'custom_css');
?>
```

This code will drop anything inside your `custom_css` function into the header of the WordPress theme, in this case your custom CSS script.

The `wp_footer` hook is also a very commonly used Action hook. Using this hook you can insert any custom code in the footer of the WordPress theme. This is a great method for adding analytic tracking code to your web site:

```
function site_analytics()  {
?>
    <script type="text/javascript">
    var gaJsHost = (("https:" == document.location.protocol) ?
      "https://ssl." : "http://www.");
    document.write(unescape("%3Cscript src='" + gaJsHost +
      'google-analytics.com/ga.js' type='text/javascript'%3E%3C/script%3E"));
    </script>
```

```
    <script type="text/javascript">
    var pageTracker = _gat._getTracker("UA-XXXXXX-XX");
    pageTracker._trackPageview();
    </script>
<?php
}

add_action('wp_footer', 'site_analytics');
```

In the preceding example you can see how you can easily insert your Google Analytics tracking code to the footer of every page on your web site, something we discuss more in Chapter 11.

The `admin_head` Action hook is very similar to the `wp_head` hook, but rather than hooking into the theme header, it hooks into the admin dashboard header. This is useful if your plugin requires custom CSS on the admin dashboard, or any other custom header code.

The `user_register` Action hook is executed when a new user is created in WordPress. This user can be created by an admin or by the new user. This is a useful hook if you want to set some default values for a new user or to e-mail your new members thanking them for joining your web site.

Hooks are probably one of the most under-documented features in WordPress. It can be a real challenge finding the correct hooks to use for the job. The first resource to use is always the Codex. Here you can find the Filter Reference (`http://codex.wordpress.org/Plugin_API/Filter_Reference`) and Action Reference (`http://codex.wordpress.org/Plugin_API/Action_Reference`) sections helpful in tracking down appropriate hooks.

Another highly recommended reference is the Plugin Directory (`http://wordpress.org/extend/plugins/`) on WordPress.org. Sometimes the best way to figure something out is to see how other developers accomplished a similar task. Find a plugin in the directory that is similar in functionality to what you want to build. Most likely the plugin author will have already dug up the correct hooks for WordPress that you will be using. It never hurts to learn by example, and published plugins are the perfect examples in this case!

PLUGIN SETTINGS

Most plugins feature a settings page. This helps users configure the plugin to act in different ways without actually modifying the code behind the plugin by saving various option settings. The first step in this process is saving and retrieving options in WordPress.

Saving Plugin Options

Chances are when building a plugin you will need to save some options for your plugin. WordPress features some very easy-to-use functions to save, edit, and delete options. Two functions are available for creating options: `add_option` and `update_option`. Both functions create options, but `update_option` also updates the option if it already exists. Here's an example of adding a new option:

```
<?php add_option('gmp_display_mode', 'Christmas Tree'); ?>
```

The first parameter you send to the `add_option` function is the name of your option. This is a required field and must be unique from all other options saved in WordPress, including from other plugins.

The second parameter is the option value. This is also a required field and can be a string, an array, an object, or a serialized value. You can also use `update_option` to create new options. This function checks whether the option exists first, and if not creates it. If, however, the option already exists it updates the value with the new option value you are sending in. You call the `update_option` function exactly as you did when adding an option like so:

```php
<?php update_option('gmp_display_mode', 'Christmas Tree'); ?>
```

Generally the `update_option` function is used for both adding and updating options in plugins. It's much easier to stay consistent with one function call for both rather than calls to different functions for adding and updating your plugin options.

Retrieving an option value is just as easy. To retrieve any option use the `get_option` function as shown here:

```php
<?php echo get_option('gmp_display_mode'); ?>
```

The only required field for `get_option` is the name of the option you want to retrieve. If the option exists it is returned to display or stored in a variable. If the option doesn't exist the function returns FALSE.

Options can be deleted as easily as they are created. To delete an option use the `delete_option` function. The only parameter is the option name that you want to delete:

```php
<?php delete_option('gmp_display_mode'); ?>
```

A good rule of thumb is to start all of your option names with the same prefix, like `gmp_` in the preceding examples. This is useful for a couple of reasons: uniqueness and readability. Using a prefix will help validate the uniqueness of your option names. If you have a number of options, it is a smart idea to store them in an array (see the next section). This also makes it much easier to follow your code logic when there is a set naming convention used on variables, functions, and so on.

Options in WordPress are not reserved for just plugins. Themes can also create options to store specific theme data. Many of the themes available today offer a settings page, enabling you to customize the theme through settings rather than code.

Array of Options

Every option you create in WordPress adds a new record to the `wp_options` database table. Because of this it's a smart idea to store your options in an array, thus creating fewer records in the database and fewer `update_option` calls you need to make.

```php
<?php
$gmp_options_arr=array(
    "gmp_display_mode"=>'Christmas Tree',
    "gmp_default_browser"=>'Chrome',
    "gmp_favorite_book"=>'Professional WordPress',
    );

update_option('gmp_plugin_options', $gmp_options_arr);
?>
```

In this code you are creating an array to store your plugin option values. So rather than call `update_option` three times, and save three records in the database, you only need to call it once and save your array to the option named `gmp_plugin_options`. This is a small example but imagine a collection of plugins that store 50 options to the database's `options` table. That would really start to clutter up your options table and would most likely slow down your web site load speeds due to the repeated database query options to fetch or set those options individually.

To retrieve the array of options you use the same `get_option` function as before:

```php
<?php
$gmp_options_arr = get_option('gmp_plugin_options');

$gmp_display_mode = $gmp_options_arr["gmp_display_mode"];
$gmp_default_browser = $gmp_options_arr["gmp_default_browser"];
$gmp_favorite_book = $gmp_options_arr["gmp_favorite_book"];
?>
```

The next section discusses how to create a menu for your plugin settings page.

Create a Menu and Submenus

WordPress features two different ways to create a custom menu for your plugin. The first thing you'll want to decide is where to locate your options page. The options page link can be located in its own top-level menu (My Plugin Settings), or as a submenu item of an existing menu (Settings ➪ My Plugin Settings). This section explores both methods and how to configure each.

Creating a Top-Level Menu

The first method you'll explore is creating a new top-level menu. Using a top-level menu is useful if your plugin has multiple setting pages that need to be separate. To create your own top-level menu you'll use the `add_menu_page` function as shown here:

```php
<?php add_menu_page(page_title, menu_title, capability,
handle, function, icon_url); ?>
```

Here's a breakdown of the parameters allowed:

➤ `page_title`: Text used for the HTML title (between `<title>` tags)

➤ `menu_title`: Text used for the menu name in the Dashboard

➤ `capability`: Minimum user capability required to see menu (or user level)

➤ `handle/file`: PHP file that handles display (`__FILE__` is recommended, as that is the path to the plugin file)

➤ `function`: Displays page content for the menu settings page

➤ `icon_url`: Path to custom icon for menu (default: `images/generic.png`)

You can also create submenu items for your new menu. You use the `add_submenu_page` function to create additional submenu items:

```php
add_submenu_page(parent, page_title, menu_title, capability required, file/handle,
[function]);
```

Create a custom menu for a plugin with multiple submenu items as shown in Figure 7-2.

FIGURE 7-2:
Custom top-level menu

```php
<?php
// create custom plugin settings menu
add_action('admin_menu', 'gmp_create_menu');

function gmp_create_menu() {

    //create new top-level menu
    add_menu_page('GMP Plugin Settings', 'GMP Settings',
'administrator', __FILE__, 'gmp_settings_page',
plugins_url('/images/wordpress.png', __FILE__));

    //create three sub-menus: email, template, and general
    add_submenu_page( __FILE__, 'Email Settings Page', 'Email',
'administrator', __FILE__.'_email_settings', 'gmp_settings_email');
    add_submenu_page( __FILE__, 'Template Settings Page', 'Template',
'administrator', __FILE__.'_template_settings', 'gmp_settings_template');
    add_submenu_page( __FILE__, 'General Settings Page', 'General',
'administrator', __FILE__.'_general_settings', 'gmp_settings_general');
}
?>
```

First you call the `admin_menu` Action hook. This hook is triggered after the basic admin panel menu structure is in place. Once triggered you execute your custom function `gmp_create_menu` to build your menu.

To create your menu you call the `add_menu_page` function. The first two parameters set your page title and menu title. You also set the capability level to `administrator`, so only an admin will see this new menu. Next you set the handle/file to `__FILE__`, which is the unique local path to your plugin file. Your custom menu function name is next, in this case `gmp_settings_page`. Remember that you haven't created this function yet so when viewing the settings page you will get a PHP warning. Finally, you set the custom icon location to display the WordPress logo.

Now that you've created your top-level menu you need to create your submenu items. In this example you are creating three submenu items: Email, Template, and General. To do this you use the `add_submenu_page` function.

The first parameter you send is the handle/file of the top-level menu you want this to fall under. Remember you set this to `__FILE__`, which is the unique local path to your plugin file. Next you set the page title and menu title just like before. You also set the access level for viewing to `administrator`. You also have to create a unique handle for your submenu items; in this example you concatenate the value using `__FILE__` and `_email_settings` (where `email` is the submenu item). The final value is the custom function to build the settings page for each submenu.

Adding To An Existing Menu

Next you'll explore how to add a submenu item to an existing menu in WordPress. Most plugins only have one options page and therefore do not require an entirely separate top-level menu. To accomplish this you can add a plugin option page to any existing menu in WordPress. Add a menu to the Setting menu:

```php
<?php
add_options_page('GMP Settings Page', 'GMP Settings',
'administrator', __FILE__, 'gmp_settings_page');
?>
```

WordPress features multiple functions to make adding submenus extremely easy. To add your GMP Settings submenu you use the `add_options_page` function. The first parameter is the page title followed by the submenu display name. Like your other menus you set the access level to `administrator`. Next you set the unique menu handle to `__FILE__`. Finally, you call your custom `gmp_settings_page` function to build your options page. The preceding example adds your custom submenu item GMP Settings at the bottom of the settings menu.

Following is a list of the available submenu functions in WordPress. Each function can be used exactly as the preceding example; just swap out the function name called with one of the functions listed here:

- ➤ `add_dashboard_page`: Adds menu items to the Dashboard menu
- ➤ `add_posts_page`: Adds menu items to the Posts menu
- ➤ `add_media_page`: Adds a menu item to the Media menu
- ➤ `add_links_page`: Adds a menu item to the Links menu
- ➤ `add_pages_page`: Adds a menu item to the Pages menu
- ➤ `add_comments_page`: Adds a menu item to the Comments menu
- ➤ `add_theme_page`: Adds a menu item to the Appearance menu
- ➤ `add_users_page`: Adds a menu item to the Users page (or Profile based on role)
- ➤ `add_management_page`: Adds a menu item to the Tools menu
- ➤ `add_options_page`: Adds a menu item to the Settings menu

Now that you've created your menu and submenu items you need to create an options page to display your plugin configuration.

Create an Options Page

WordPress 2.7 introduced a new Settings API that you will be using for all of the option methods you use in this section. The Settings API is a powerful set of functions to help make saving options in WordPress easy and secure. One of the major benefits of the Settings API is that WordPress handles the security checks, meaning you don't need to include a nonce in your form.

The first option page method you'll explore is creating a unique option page for your top-level menu. Remember that when using the `add_menu_page` and `add_submenu_page` functions you defined your menu item function name to display your options page. To create an options page you need to create this function to display your options. First set up your plugin menu:

```php
<?php
// create custom plugin settings menu
add_action('admin_menu', 'gmp_create_menu');

function gmp_create_menu() {
```

```php
    //create new top-level menu
    add_menu_page('GMP Plugin Settings', 'GMP Settings', 'administrator',
__FILE__, 'gmp_settings_page', plugins_url('/images/wordpress.png', __FILE__));

    //call register settings function
    add_action( 'admin_init', 'gmp_register_settings' );
}
?>
```

Notice you've added a new Action hook for admin_init to execute your gmp_register_settings function as shown in the following code:

```php
<?php
function gmp_register_settings() {
    //register our settings
    register_setting( 'gmp-settings-group', 'gmp_option_name' );
    register_setting( 'gmp-settings-group', 'gmp_option_email' );
    register_setting( 'gmp-settings-group', 'gmp_option_url' );
}
?>
```

Using the Setting API's register_setting function you define the three options you are going to offer on your plugin options page. The first parameter is the options group name. This required field needs to be a group name to identify all options in this set. The second parameter is the actual option name and must be unique. Now that you've registered your options you need to build your options page. To do so you'll create the gmp_settings_page function as called from your menu:

```php
<?php
function gmp_settings_page() {
?>
<div class="wrap">
<h2><?php _e('GMP Plugin Options', 'gmp-plugin') ?></h2>

<form method="post" action="options.php">
    <?php settings_fields( 'gmp-settings-group' ); ?>
    <table class="form-table">
        <tr valign="top">
        <th scope="row"><?php _e('Name', 'gmp-plugin') ?></th>
        <td><input type="text" name="gmp_option_name"
        value="<?php echo get_option('gmp_option_name'); ?>" /></td>
        </tr>

        <tr valign="top">
        <th scope="row"><?php _e('Email', 'gmp-plugin') ?></th>
        <td><input type="text" name="gmp_option_email"
        value="<?php echo get_option('gmp_option_email'); ?>" /></td>
        </tr>


        <tr valign="top">
        <th scope="row"><?php _e('URL', 'gmp-plugin') ?></th>
        <td><input type="text" name="gmp_option_url"
        value="<?php echo get_option('gmp_option_url'); ?>" /></td>
        </tr>
    </table>
```

```
            <p class="submit">
        <input type="submit" class="button-primary"
            value="<?php _e('Save Changes', 'gmp-plugin') ?>" />
        </p>

    </form>
    </div>
    <?php } ?>
```

As you can see this looks like a standard form with a couple noticeable differences. The `<form>` tag must be set to post to `options.php`. Inside your form you need to define your settings group, which you set to `gmp-settings-group` when you registered your settings. This establishes the link between your options and their values. You do so with this line of code:

```php
<?php settings_fields( 'gmp-settings-group' ); ?>
```

Next you build the table to display your form options. Notice the name of the form field needs to be exactly the same as the option names you registered. You also use the `get_option` function to retrieve the value of your plugin option. The Settings API will store all option values in `wp_options` so you can retrieve your option values anywhere inside of WordPress using `get_option`:

```php
<input type="text" name="gmp_option_email"
value="<?php echo get_option('gmp_option_email'); ?>" />
```

After you have displayed all of your form fields you need to display a Submit button to post the form and save your options. That's it! You have just created a very basic plugin options page using the Settings API in WordPress. Listing 7-1 shows the entire code to build an options page.

LISTING 7-1: Building the Options Page

```php
<?php
//execute our settings section function

// create custom plugin settings menu
add_action('admin_menu', 'gmp_create_menu');

function gmp_create_menu() {

    //create new top-level menu
    add_menu_page('GMP Plugin Settings', 'GMP Settings', 'administrator'
, __FILE__, 'gmp_settings_page', plugins_url('/images/wordpress.png', __FILE__));

    //call register settings function
    add_action( 'admin_init', 'gmp_register_settings' );
}

function gmp_register_settings() {
    //register our settings
    register_setting( 'gmp-settings-group', 'gmp_option_name' );
    register_setting( 'gmp-settings-group', 'gmp_option_email' );
    register_setting( 'gmp-settings-group', 'gmp_option_url' );
}
```

```php
function gmp_settings_page() {
?>
<div class="wrap">
<h2><?php _e('GMP Plugin Options', 'gmp-plugin') ?></h2>

<form method="post" action="options.php">
    <?php settings_fields( 'gmp-settings-group' ); ?>
    <table class="form-table">
        <tr valign="top">
        <th scope="row"><?php _e('Name', 'gmp-plugin') ?></th>
        <td><input type="text" name="gmp_option_name"
        value="<?php echo get_option('gmp_option_name'); ?>" /></td>
        </tr>

        <tr valign="top">
        <th scope="row"><?php _e('Email', 'gmp-plugin') ?></th>
        <td><input type="text" name="gmp_option_email"
        value="<?php echo get_option('gmp_option_email'); ?>" /></td>
        </tr>

        <tr valign="top">
        <th scope="row"><?php _e('URL', 'gmp-plugin') ?></th>
        <td><input type="text" name="gmp_option_url"
        value="<?php echo get_option('gmp_option_url'); ?>" /></td>
        </tr>
    </table>

    <p class="submit">
    <input type="submit" class="button-primary"
    value="<?php _e('Save Changes', 'gmp-plugin') ?>" />
    </p>

</form>
</div>
<?php } ?>
```

The second option page method is adding your plugin settings to an existing Settings page in WordPress as shown in Figure 7-3. You will also be using the WordPress Settings API functions to hook into these pages and add your plugin settings. Remember that the Settings API was added in version 2.7, so any older installations will not have these functions available for use. First you'll start with creating a new settings section using the add_settings_section function.

Now look over at the code to create your custom settings section. In the following example you are going to add a new settings section at the bottom of the Settings ➪ Reading Settings page. This section will contain options for your plugin.

```php
<?php
//execute our settings section function
add_action('admin_init', 'gmp_settings_init');

function gmp_settings_init() {
    //create the new setting section on the Settings > Reading page
    add_settings_section('gmp_setting_section', 'GMP Plugin Settings',
    'gmp_setting_section', 'reading');
```

```
      // register the individual setting options
      add_settings_field('gmp_setting_enable_id',
'Enable GMP Plugin?',
'gmp_setting_enabled', 'reading', 'gmp_setting_section');
      add_settings_field('gmp_saved_setting_name_id',
'Your Name',
'gmp_setting_name', 'reading', 'gmp_setting_section');

      // register our setting to store our array of values
      register_setting('reading','gmp_setting_values');
    }
    ?>
```

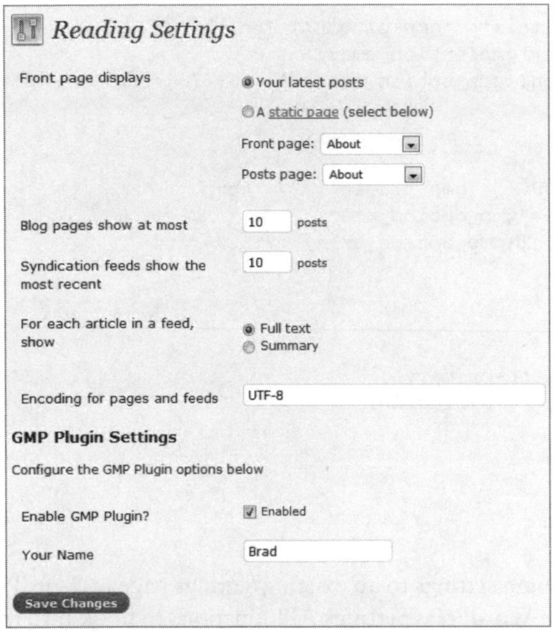

FIGURE 7-3: Custom settings section

First you use the `admin_init` Action hook to load your custom function `gmp_settings_init` before any admin page is rendered. Next you call the `add_settings_section` function to create your new section:

```
<?php add_settings_field('gmp_setting_enable_id', 'Enable GMP Plugin?',
'gmp_setting_enabled', 'reading', 'gmp_setting_section'); ?>
```

The first parameter passed is a unique ID for the section. The second parameter is the display name output on the page. Next you pass in the callback function name to display the actual section itself. The final parameter sets what settings page to add your section to. The accepted values are `general`, `writing`, `reading`, `discussion`, `media`, `privacy`, `permalink`, and `misc`.

```php
<?php
add_settings_field('gmp_setting_ enable_id', 'Enable GMP Plugin?',
'gmp_setting_enabled', 'reading', 'gmp_setting_section');
add_settings_field('gmp_saved_setting_name_id', 'Your Name',
'gmp_setting_name', 'reading', 'gmp_setting_section');
?>
```

Now that you've registered your custom settings section you need to register your individual setting options. To do this you'll be using the `add_settings_field` function. The first parameter you are passing is a unique ID for the field. Next you pass in the title of the field, which is displayed directly to the left of the option field. The third parameter is the callback function name, which you'll use to display your option field. The fourth parameter is the settings page where the field should be displayed. The final parameter is the name of the section you are adding the field to, which in this example is the `gmp_setting_section` you created with the `add_setting_section` function call.

```php
<?php
register_setting('reading','gmp_setting_values');
?>
```

Next you need to register your setting field. In this example you are going to register two different settings: one for an enable/disable checkbox and one for the user's name. Even though you have two setting fields you are going to store both values in an array, so you only need to register one setting called `gmp_setting_values`. The first parameter you pass is the option group. In this example you are saving your options in the reading group with the rest of the reading options. The second parameter is the option name. The option name should be unique and is used to retrieve the value of the option. A third optional value can be passed that is a custom function name used to sanitize the option values.

Now that you've registered your setting section you need to create your custom functions to display it. The first function you'll create is the `gmp_setting_section` you called in when you created your setting section:

```php
<?php
function gmp_setting_section() {
    echo '<p>Configure the GMP Plugin options below</p>';
}
?>
```

This is where you can set the subheading for your settings section. This section is great for plugin instructions, configuration information, and more. Next you need to create the function to display your first settings field, Enabled:

```php
<?php
function gmp_setting_enabled() {
    //load our options array
    $gmp_options = get_option('gmp_setting_values');

    // if the option exists the checkbox needs to be checked
    If ($gmp_options['enabled']) {
        $checked = ' checked="checked" ';
    }
```

```
    //display the checkbox form field
    echo '<input '.$checked.' name="gmp_setting_values[enabled]" type="checkbox" />
Enabled';

}?>
```

This is the callback function you defined when you used the `add_settings_field` function. The first step is to load the options array if it exists. Because this option is a checkbox you know that if it is set, the checkbox should be checked. Next you display the actual setting field that will be used in the setting section. Your field input name needs to be the same setting name you registered previously. Because you are saving your options as an array you need to define the array name value; in this example `gmp_setting_values[enabled]`. This is how the Settings API knows what option to save and where. Now your Enabled checkbox field will display at the bottom of the Settings ➪ Reading page. Now you need to create the function for your second setting field:

```php
<?php
function gmp_setting_name() {
    //load the option array
    $gmp_options = get_option('gmp_setting_values');

    //load the proper array option value
    $name = $gmp_options['name'];

    //display the text form field
    echo '<input type="text" name="gmp_setting_values[name]"
    value="'.esc_attr($name).'" />';
}?>
```

Just like with your checkbox option, the first thing to do is load the current option value. Next you display your input text field with the same name as defined above in the `register_setting` function. That's it! You have successfully created your custom settings section and added it to the Settings ➪ Reading SubPanel. Listing 7-2 shows the full code.

LISTING 7-2: Custom Settings Section

Available for
download on
Wrox.com

```php
<?php
//execute our settings section function
add_action('admin_init', 'gmp_settings_init');

function gmp_settings_init() {
    //create the new setting section on the Settings > Reading page
    add_settings_section('gmp_setting_section', 'GMP Plugin Settings',
    'gmp_setting_section', 'reading');

    // register the individual setting options
    add_settings_field('gmp_setting_enable_id', 'Enable GMP Plugin?',
    'gmp_setting_enabled', 'reading', 'gmp_setting_section');
    add_settings_field('gmp_saved_setting_name_id', 'Your Name',
    'gmp_setting_name', 'reading', 'gmp_setting_section');
```

```
        // register our setting to store our array of values
        register_setting('reading','gmp_setting_values');
    }

    // settings section
    function gmp_setting_section() {
        echo '<p>Configure the GMP plugin options below</p>';
    }

    // create the enabled checkbox option to save the checkbox value
    function gmp_setting_enabled() {
        // if the option exists the checkbox needs to be checked
        $gmp_options = get_option('gmp_setting_values');
If ($gmp_options['enabled']) {
            $checked = ' checked="checked" ';
        }
        //display the checkbox form field
        echo '<input '.$checked.' name="gmp_setting_values[enabled]" type="checkbox" />
Enabled';

    }

    // create the text field setting to save the name
    function gmp_setting_name() {
        //load the option value
        $gmp_options = get_option('gmp_setting_values');
        $name = $gmp_options['name'];

        //display the text form field
        echo '<input type="text" name="gmp_setting_values[name]"
        value="'.esc_attr($name).'"
 />';
    }
    ?>
```

WORDPRESS INTEGRATION

Integrating your plugin into WordPress is an essential step for users to interact with your plugin in the admin dashboard. WordPress features many different areas where your plugin can be integrated including a meta box, sidebar, and dashboard widgets, and custom shortcodes.

Create a Meta Box

WordPress features multiple meta boxes on the add new post, page, and link screens. These meta boxes are used for adding additional information to your posts and pages.

Meta boxes can be created in a plugin using the add_meta_box function in WordPress. This function accepts six parameters as shown here:

```
<?php add_meta_box( $id, $title, $callback, $page, $context, $priority ); ?>
```

Each parameter helps define where and how your meta box is displayed.

➤ `$id`: The CSS ID attribute for the meta box

➤ `$title`: The title displayed in the header of the meta box

➤ `$callback`: The custom function name to display your meta box information

➤ `$page`: The page you want your meta box to display on (`'post'`, `'page'`, or `'link'`)

➤ `$context`: The part of the page where the meta box should be displayed (`'normal'`, `'advanced'`, or `'side'`)

➤ `$priority`: The priority within the context where the meta box should display (`'high'`, `'core'`, `'default'`, or `'low'`)

Now that you understand the `add_meta_box` function you can build your first custom meta box in WordPress:

```php
<?php
add_action('admin_init','gmp_meta_box_init');

// meta box functions for adding the meta box and saving the data
function gmp_meta_box_init() {
    // create our custom meta box
    add_meta_box('gmp-meta',__('Product Information',
'gmp-plugin'), 'gmp_meta_box','post','side','default');

    // hook to save our meta box data when the post is saved
    add_action('save_post','gmp_save_meta_box');
}
?>
```

The first step to adding your own meta box is to use the `admin_init` Action hook to execute your custom function `gmp_meta_box_init`. In this function you will call the `add_meta_box` function to create your custom meta box for Product Information. You also use the Action hook `save_post` to execute your custom function for saving your meta box data. This function is covered in detail a little later.

You set the CSS ID attribute to `gmp-meta` for your meta box. The second parameter is the title, which you set to Product Information. The next parameter is your custom function `gmp_meta_box`, which will display the HTML for your meta box. Next you define your meta box to display on the post page and in the sidebar. Finally, you set the priority to `default`. Now create your custom `gmp_meta_box` function to display your meta box fields:

```php
function gmp_meta_box($post,$box) {
    // retrieve our custom meta box values
    $featured = get_post_meta($post->ID,'_gmp_type',true);
    $gmp_price = get_post_meta($post->ID,'_gmp_price',true);

    // custom meta box form elements
    echo '<p>' .__('Price','gmp-plugin'). ': <input type="text"
        name="gmp_price" value="'.esc_attr($gmp_price).'" size="5" /></p>
        <p>' .__('Type','gmp-plugin'). ': <select name="gmp_product_type"
        id="gmp_product_type">
```

```
            <option value="0" '.(is_null($featured) || $featured == '0' ?
            'selected="selected" ' : '').'>Normal</option>
            <option value="1" '.($featured == '1' ? 'selected="selected" ' : '').'>
            Special</option>
            <option value="2" '.($featured == '2' ? 'selected="selected" ' : '').'>
            Featured</option>
            <option value="3" '.($featured == '3' ? 'selected="selected" ' : '').'>
            Clearance</option>
        </select></p>';
    }
```

The first step in your custom function is to retrieve the saved values for your meta box. If you are creating a new post there won't be any saved values yet. Next you display the form elements in your meta box. Notice you don't need any <form> tags or a submit button. Remember, you added a hook to save your meta box form data when the post is saved. The custom function you just created will generate your custom meta box as shown in Figure 7-4.

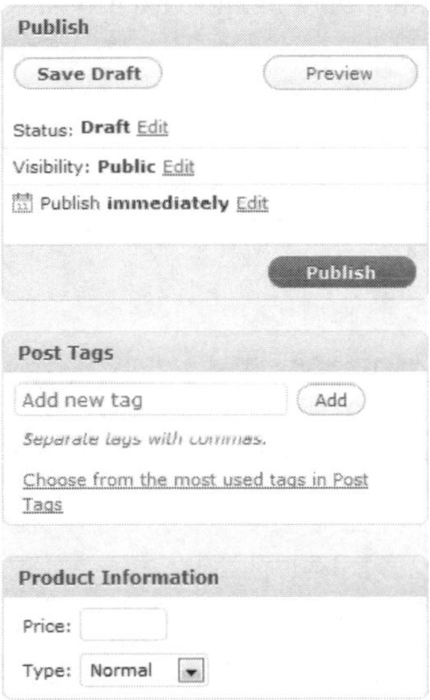

FIGURE 7-4: Custom meta box

Now that you have your meta box and form elements you need to save that data when your post is saved. To do so you'll create a custom function gmp_save_meta_box that is trigged by the save_post Action hook:

```
<?php
function gmp_save_meta_box($post_id,$post) {
    // if post is a revision skip saving our meta box data
    if($post->post_type == 'revision') { return; }

    // process form data if $_POST is set
    if(isset($_POST['gmp_product_type'])) {
        // save the meta box data as post meta using the post ID as a unique prefix
        update_post_meta($post_id,'_gmp_type', esc_attr($_POST['gmp_product_type']));
```

```
                    update_post_meta($post_id,'_gmp_price', esc_attr($_POST['gmp_price']));
            }
    }
    ?>
```

The `save_post` Action hook runs for active posts and revisions, but in this example you only want to save your post data for active posts. To do so you check the post type and if this post is a revision you exit the function. If the post is active and your form elements have been set you save the form data. You use `update_post_meta` to save your meta box data as a custom field against your post.

As you can see, you send in the post ID as the first parameter to `update_post_meta`. This tells Word-Press what post the meta data will be attached to. Next you pass in the name of the meta key you are updating. Notice the meta key name is prefixed with an underscore. This prevents these values from being listed in the custom fields meta box on the post edit screen. Since you've provided a UI to edit these values, you don't need them in the custom fields box. The final parameter you send is the new value for the meta key.

You now have a fully functional custom meta box that saves individual data against each post. Listing 7-3 shows the full custom meta box code.

LISTING 7-3: Custom Meta Box

```php
<?php
add_action('admin_init','gmp_meta_box_init');

// meta box functions for adding the meta box and saving the data
function gmp_meta_box_init() {
    // create our custom meta box
    add_meta_box('gmp-meta',__('Product Information',
    'gmp-plugin'), 'gmp_meta_box','post','side','default');

    // hook to save our meta box data when the post is saved
    add_action('save_post','gmp_save_meta_box');
}

function gmp_meta_box($post,$box) {
    // retrieve our custom meta box values
    $featured = get_post_meta($post->ID,'_gmp_type',true);
    $gmp_price = get_post_meta($post->ID,'_gmp_price',true);

    // custom meta box form elements
    echo '<p>' .__('Price','gmp-plugin'). ': <input type="text"
    name="gmp_price" value="'.esc_attr($gmp_price).'" size="5"></p>
        <p>' .__('Type','gmp-plugin'). ': <select name="gmp_product_type"
        id="gmp_product_type">
           <option value="0" '.(is_null($featured) || $featured == '0' ?
           'selected="selected" ' : '').'>Normal</option>
           <option value="1" '.($featured == '1' ? 'selected="selected" ' : '').'>
            Special</option>
           <option value="2" '.($featured == '2' ? 'selected="selected" ' : '').'>
```

```
            Featured</option>
            <option value="3" '.($featured == '3' ? 'selected="selected" ' : '').'>
            Clearance</option>
        </select></p>';
}

function gmp_save_meta_box($post_id,$post) {
    // if post is a revision skip saving our meta box data
    if($post->post_type == 'revision') { return; }
    // process form data if $_POST is set
    if(isset($_POST['gmp_product_type'])) {
        // save the meta box data as post meta using the post ID as a unique prefix
        update_post_meta($post_id,'_gmp_type',
        esc_attr($_POST['gmp_product_type']));
        update_post_meta($post_id,'_gmp_price', esc_attr($_POST['gmp_price']));
    }
}
?>
```

Now that you've saved your meta box data you'll probably want to display it somewhere. You can easily display your saved meta box data in your theme using the get_post_meta function inside the Loop like so:

```
<?php
$gmp_type = get_post_meta($post->ID,'_gmp_type',true);
$gmp_price = get_post_meta($post->ID,'_gmp_price',true);
echo '<p>PRICE: '.esc_html($gmp_price).'</p>';
echo '<p>TYPE: '.esc_html($gmp_type).'</p>';
?>
```

Adding a custom meta box is a great way to extend the data on posts and pages and is very intuitive for users as well.

Shortcodes

WordPress features a Shortcode API that can be used to easily create shortcode functionality in your plugins. Shortcodes are basically text macro codes that can be inserted into a post or page. When being displayed these shortcodes are replaced by some other type of content. Look at a simple example using the Shortcode API:

```
<?php
function siteURL() {
    return 'http://example.com';
}

add_shortcode('mysite', 'siteURL');
?>
```

Now any time you use the [mysite] shortcode in your content it will be replaced with http://example.com when displayed in the browser. As you can see this is a very powerful feature in WordPress, which many plugins out there currently take advantage of, often inserting small pieces of JavaScript to place a button or advertisement in the specific spot in a post.

Shortcodes can also be configured to accept attributes. This is very useful for passing arguments to your custom functions, thereby altering the output of the shortcode based on those arguments. Modify your shortcode function to accept a site parameter:

```php
<?php
function siteURL($atts, $content = null) {
    extract(shortcode_atts(array(
        "site" => 'http://example.com' // set attribute default
    ), $atts));
    If ($site == "blog1") {
        return 'http://blog1.example.com/';
    }Elseif ($site == "blog2") {
        return 'http://blog2.example.com/';
    }
}

add_shortcode('mysite', 'siteURL');
?>
```

This code creates the same shortcode as before, but now you are defining an attribute called site. With this attribute you can specify which site URL you want to display. To display the URL for blog1 you would use the shortcode [mysite site=blog1]. Alternatively you can also easily display the URL for blog2 like so: [mysite site=blog2]. Shortcodes can also accept multiple attributes from the array set in your shortcode function.

Create a Widget

Widgets are a common feature included in many WordPress plugins. By creating a widget with your plugin you can easily give users a way to add your plugin information to their sidebar or other widgetized areas.

To understand how widgets work it's helpful to view an overview of the widget class in WordPress. The widget class features built-in functions for building a widget, each with a specific purpose as shown in the following code:

```php
<?php
class My_Widget extends WP_Widget {
    function My_Widget() {
        // process the widget
    }

    function form($instance) {
        // widget form in admin dashboard
    }

    function update($new_instance, $old_instance) {
        // save widget options
    }

    function widget($args, $instance) {
        // display the widget
    }
}
?>
```

The first step in creating your own widget is to use the appropriate hook to initialize your widget. This hook is called `widgets_init` and is triggered right after the default WordPress widgets have been registered:

```
add_action( 'widgets_init', 'gmp_register_widgets' );

function gmp_register_widgets() {
    register_widget( 'gmp_widget' );
}
```

Calling the Action hook `widgets_init` executes the function `gmp_register_widgets` as shown in the preceding code. Here you register your widget called `gmp_widget`. You could also register multiple widgets in this function if needed.

The revamped Widget API released with WordPress 2.8 makes creating a widget much easier than before. To begin you have to extend the preexisting `WP_Widget` class by creating a new class with a unique name as shown here:

```
class gmp_widget extends WP_Widget {
```

Next you'll add your first function, which should be the same name as your unique class name. This is referred to as the *constructor*:

```
function gmp_widget() {
        $widget_ops = array('classname' => 'gmp_widget',
'description' => __('Example widget that displays a user\'s bio.','gmp-plugin') );
        $this->WP_Widget('gmp_widget_bio',
__('Bio Widget','gmp-plugin'), $widget_ops);
    }
```

In your `gmp_widget` function you define your classname for your widget. The classname is the CSS class that will be added to the `li` tag of the widget when it's displayed. You also set the description for your widget. This is displayed on the Widget dashboard below the widget name. These options are then passed to `WP_Widget`. You also pass the CSS ID name (`gmp_widget_bio`) and the widget name (Bio Widget).

Next you need to create the function to build your widget settings form. Widget settings are located on the widget admin page upon expanding any widget listed on a sidebar. The widget class makes this process very easy, as shown in the following code:

```
function form($instance) {
        $defaults = array( 'title' => __('My Bio','gmp-plugin'), 'name' => '',
'bio' => '' );
        $instance = wp_parse_args( (array) $instance, $defaults );
        $title = strip_tags($instance['title']);
        $name = strip_tags($instance['name']);
        $bio = strip_tags($instance['bio']);
        ?>
        <p><?php _e('Title','gmp-plugin') ?>: <input class="widefat"
name="<?php echo $this->get_field_name('title'); ?>" type="text"
value="<?php echo esc_attr($title); ?>" /></p>
        <p><?php _e('Name','gmp-plugin') ?>: <input class="widefat"
name="<?php echo $this->get_field_name('name'); ?>" type="text"
value="<?php echo esc_attr($name); ?>" /></p>
```

```
                 <p><?php _e('Bio','gmp-plugin') ?>: <textarea class="widefat"
name="<?php echo $this->get_field_name('bio'); ?>"
<?php echo esc_attr($bio); ?></textarea></p>
        <?php
    }
```

The first thing you do is define your default widget values. If the user doesn't fill in the settings you can default these values to whatever you like. In this case you're only setting the default title to My Bio. Next you pull in the instance values, which are your widget settings. If the widget was just added to a sidebar there are no settings saved so these values will be empty. Finally, you display the three form fields for your widget settings: title, name, and bio. The first two values are using text input boxes and the bio value is using a textarea box. Notice you don't need <form> tags or a submit button; the widget class will handle this for you. Remember to use the appropriate escaping functions when displaying your data, in this case esc_attr for your field values.

Next you need to save your widget settings using the update() widget class function:

```
function update($new_instance, $old_instance) {
    $instance = $old_instance;
    $instance['title'] = strip_tags($new_instance['title']);
    $instance['name'] = strip_tags($new_instance['name']);
    $instance['bio'] = strip_tags($new_instance['bio']);

    return $instance;
}
```

This function is pretty straightforward. You'll notice you don't need to save the settings yourself, the widget class does it for you. You pass in the $new_instance values for each of your setting fields. You're also using strip_tags to strip out any HTML that might be entered. If you want to accept HTML values you'd use esc_html instead.

The final function in your gmp_widget class handles displaying your widget:

```
function widget($args, $instance) {
    extract($args);

    echo $before_widget;

    $title = apply_filters('widget_title', $instance['title'] );
    $name = empty($instance['name']) ? ' ' :
    apply_filters('widget_name', $instance['name']);
    $bio = empty($instance['bio']) ? ' ' :
    apply_filters('widget_bio', $instance['bio']);

    if ( !empty( $title ) ) { echo $before_title . $title . $after_title; };
    echo '<p>' .__('Name','gmp-plugin') .': ' . $name . '</p>';
    echo '<p>' .__('Bio','gmp-plugin') .': ' . $bio . '</p>';
    echo $after_widget;
}
```

The first thing you do is extract the $args parameter. This variable stores some global theme values such as $before_widget and $after_widget. These variables can be used by theme developers to customize what code will wrap your widget, for example, a custom <div> tag. After extracting the $args parameter, you display the $before_widget variable. The $before_title and $after_title are also set in this variable. This is useful for passing custom HTML tags to wrap the widget title in. You also apply filters to your three setting values, allowing plugin authors or theme developers to use these Filter hooks to modify your widget display if necessary.

Next you display your widget values. The title is displayed first, and wrapped by `$before_title` and `$after_title`. Next you echo out the name and bio values. Finally, you display the `$after_widget` value.

That's it! You've just created a custom widget for your plugin using the widget class in WordPress. Remember, using the new widget class you can add multiple copies of the same widget to the sidebar or additional sidebars. Listing 7-4 shows the completed widget code.

LISTING 7-4: Custom Widget

```php
<?php
// use widgets_init Action hook to execute custom function
add_action( 'widgets_init', 'gmp_register_widgets' );

 //register our widget
function gmp_register_widgets() {
    register_widget( 'gmp_widget' );
}
//gmp_widget class
class gmp_widget extends WP_Widget {

    //process our new widget
    function gmp_widget() {
        $widget_ops = array('classname' => 'gmp_widget',
'description' => __('Example widget that displays a user\'s bio.','gmp-plugin') );
        $this->WP_Widget('gmp_widget_bio',
__('Bio Widget','gmp-plugin'), $widget_ops);
    }

     //build our widget settings form
    function form($instance) {
        $defaults = array( 'title' => __('My Bio','gmp-plugin'),
'name' => '', 'bio' => '' );
        $instance = wp_parse_args( (array) $instance, $defaults );
        $title = strip_tags($instance['title']);
        $name = strip_tags($instance['name']);
        $bio = strip_tags($instance['bio']);
        ?>
            <p><?php _e('Title','gmp-plugin') ?>:
<input class="widefat" name="<?php echo $this->get_field_name('title'); ?>"
type="text" value="<?php echo esc_attr($title); ?>" /></p>
            <p><?php _e('Name','gmp-plugin') ?>:
<input class="widefat" name="<?php echo $this->get_field_name('name'); ?>"
type="text" value="<?php echo esc_attr($name); ?>" /></p>
            <p><?php _e('Bio','gmp-plugin') ?>:
<textarea class="widefat" name="<?php echo $this->get_field_name('bio'); ?>" >
<?php echo esc_attr($bio); ?></textarea></p>
```

continues

```php
        <?php
    }

    //save our widget settings
    function update($new_instance, $old_instance) {
        $instance = $old_instance;
        $instance['title'] = strip_tags($new_instance['title']);
        $instance['name'] = strip_tags($new_instance['name']);
        $instance['bio'] = strip_tags($new_instance['bio']);

        return $instance;
    }

    //display our widget
    function widget($args, $instance) {
        extract($args);

        echo $before_widget;

        $title = apply_filters('widget_title', $instance['title'] );
        $name = empty($instance['name']) ? ' ' : apply_filters('widget_name',
        $instance['name']);
        $bio = empty($instance['bio']) ? ' ' :
        apply_filters('widget_bio', $instance['bio']);

        if ( !empty( $title ) ) { echo $before_title . $title . $after_title; };
        echo '<p>' .__('Name','gmp-plugin') .': ' . $name . '</p>';
        echo '<p>' .__('Bio','gmp-plugin') .': ' . $bio . '</p>';
        echo $after_widget;
    }
}
?>
```

Create a Dashboard Widget

WordPress 2.7 introduced Dashboard Widgets, which are the widgets displayed on the main Dashboard of your WordPress installation. Along with these new widgets came the Dashboard Widgets API, which allows you to create any custom Dashboard Widget that you would like.

To create a custom Dashboard Widget you'll be using the `wp_add_dashboard_widget` function as shown here:

```php
<?php
add_action('wp_dashboard_setup', 'gmp_add_dashboard_widget' );

// call function to create our dashboard widget
function gmp_add_dashboard_widget() {
    wp_add_dashboard_widget('gmp_dashboard_widget',
__('GMP Dashboard Widget','gmp-plugin'), 'gmp_create_dashboard_widget');
}
```

```
// function to display our dashboard widget content
function gmp_create_dashboard_widget() {
    _e('Hello World! This is my Dashboard Widget','gmp-plugin');
}
?>
```

First you call the `wp_dashboard_setup` Action hook to execute the function to build your custom Dashboard Widget. This hook is triggered after all of the default Dashboard Widgets have been built. Next you execute the `wp_add_dashboard_widget` function to create your Dashboard Widget. The first parameter is the widget ID slug. This is used for the CSS classname and the key in the array of widgets. The next parameter is the display name for your widget. The final parameter you send is your custom function name to display your widget contents. An optional fourth parameter can be sent for a control callback function. This function would be used to process any form elements that might exist in your Dashboard Widget.

FIGURE 7-5: Example dashboard widget

After executing the `wp_add_dashboard_widget` function your custom function is called to display your widget contents. In this example you display a simple string, with internationalization support, of course. The result is a custom Dashboard Widget as shown in Figure 7-5.

Creating Custom Tables

WordPress contains a variety of tables in which to store your plugin data. However, you might find that your plugin needs a custom table or two to store plugin data. This can be useful for more complex plugins such as an e-commerce plugin which would need to store order history, product and inventory data, and other data that is accessed using database SQL semantics rather than the simple key and value pairing of the options table.

The first step in creating a custom database table is to create an installation function. You will execute this function when the plugin is activated to create your new table.

```
<?php
register_activation_hook(__FILE__,'gmp_install');

function gmp_install() {

}
?>
```

Now that you have an installation function you need to define your custom table name. Remember that the table prefix can be custom defined by the user in `wp-config.php` so you need to incorporate this table prefix for your custom table name. To get the table prefix you use the global `$wpdb->prefix` value like so:

```
global $wpdb;
$table_name = $wpdb->prefix . "gmp_data";
```

This code would store your table named wp_gmp_data in the $table_name variable.

Now it's time to build your SQL query for creating your new table. You'll create your query in a variable called $sql before executing it. You also need to include the upgrade.php file prior to executing your query like so:

```
$sql = "CREATE TABLE " . $table_name . " (
    id mediumint(9) NOT NULL AUTO_INCREMENT,
    time bigint(11) DEFAULT '0' NOT NULL,
    name tinytext NOT NULL,
    text text NOT NULL,
    url VARCHAR(55) NOT NULL,
    UNIQUE KEY id (id)
);";

require_once(ABSPATH . 'wp-admin/includes/upgrade.php');
dbDelta($sql);
```

After this executes your new table has been created in the database. The dbDelta() function will verify the table you are creating doesn't exist first, so you don't have to worry about checking if a table exists before creating it. It's also a good idea to save the version number for your database table structure. This can help down the road if you upgrade your plugin and need to change the table structure. You can check what table version the users have installed for your plugin and determine if they need to upgrade:

```
add_option("gmp_db_version", "1.0");
```

Look at the full function in action:

```
register_activation_hook(__FILE__,'gmp_install');

function gmp_install() {
    global $wpdb;
    //define the custom table name
    $table_name = $wpdb->prefix . "gmp_data";

    //set the table structure version
    $gmp_db_version = "1.0";

    //verify the table doesn't already exist
    if($wpdb->get_var("SHOW TABLES LIKE '$table_name'") != $table_name) {

        //build our query to create our new table
        $sql = "CREATE TABLE " . $table_name . " (
            id mediumint(9) NOT NULL AUTO_INCREMENT,
            time bigint(11) DEFAULT '0' NOT NULL,
            name tinytext NOT NULL,
            text text NOT NULL,
            url VARCHAR(55) NOT NULL,
            UNIQUE KEY id (id)
        );";
```

```
require_once(ABSPATH . 'wp-admin/includes/upgrade.php');
//execute the query creating our table
dbDelta($sql);

//save the table structure version number
add_option("gmp_db_version", $gmp_db_version);

        }
    }
```

If you want to upgrade your table structure for a new version of your plugin you can just compare the table structure version numbers:

```
$installed_ver = get_option( "gmp_db_version" );

if( $installed_ver != $gmp_db_version ) {

    //update database table here

    //update table version
    update_option( "gmp_db_version", $gmp_db_version );
}
```

Before creating a custom table for your plugin, you should consider whether this is the best method. It's generally a good idea to avoid creating custom tables unless there is no alternative. Remember that you can easily store options in WordPress using the options API. You can also utilize the wp_*meta tables for storing extended data about posts, pages, comments, and users.

To work with a custom table once you've created it you'll need to use the WordPress database class, as shown in Chapter 6.

Uninstall Your Plugin

A nice feature to include with your plugin is an uninstall feature. WordPress features two ways to register the uninstaller for your plugin: the uninstall.php method and the uninstall hook. Both methods are executed when a deactivated plugin is deleted in WordPress.

The first method you'll look at is the uninstall.php uninstaller method. This is the preferred method for uninstalling a plugin. The first step to using this method is to create an uninstall.php file. This file must exist in the root directory of your plugin, and if it does it will execute in preference to the uninstall hook.

```
<?php
// If uninstall/delete not called from WordPress then exit
if( ! defined( 'ABSPATH' ) && ! defined( 'WP_UNINSTALL_PLUGIN' ) )
    exit ();

// Delete option from options table
delete_option( 'gmp_options_arr' );

//remove any additional options and custom tables
global $wpdb;

$table_name = $wpdb->prefix . "gmp_data";
```

```
//build our query to delete our custom table

$sql = "DROP TABLE " . $table_name . ";";
//execute the query deleting the table
$wpdb->query($sql);

require_once(ABSPATH .'wp-admin/includes/upgrade.php');
dbDelta($sql);
?>
```

The first thing your `uninstall.php` file should check is that `ABSPATH` and `WP_UNINSTALL_PLUGIN` constants have been defined, meaning they were actually called from WordPress. This is a security measure to ensure this file is not executed except during the uninstall process of your plugin. The next step is to remove any options and custom tables your plugin created. In a perfect uninstall scenario there would be no trace of your plugin left over in the database once it has been uninstalled. The preceding example uses `delete_option` to delete the option array. It also runs a `DROP` SQL query to delete the custom plugin table. Remember that once this function runs, all custom plugin data saved will be destroyed.

The second method for uninstalling a plugin is using the uninstall hook. When a plugin is deleted, and `uninstall.php` does not exist but the uninstall hook does exist, the plugin will be run one last time to execute the uninstall hook. After the hook has been called your plugin will be deleted. Here's the uninstall hook in action:

```
<?php
if ( function_exists('register_uninstall_hook') )
    register_uninstall_hook(__FILE__, 'gmp_uninstall_hook');

function gmp_uninstall_hook()
{
    delete_option('gmp_options_arr');

    //remove any additional options and custom tables
    global $wpdb;

    $table_name = $wpdb->prefix . "gmp_data";

    //build our query to delete our custom table
    $sql = "DROP TABLE " . $table_name . ";";

    //execute the query deleting the table
    $wpdb->query($sql);

    require_once(ABSPATH .'wp-admin/includes/upgrade.php');
    dbDelta($sql);

}
?>
```

First you want to verify that the `register_uninstall_hook` function exists. Because the uninstall hook function was added in WordPress 2.7 it won't exist on older versions of WordPress. Next you call your custom uninstall function to properly uninstall your plugin options. If you do include uninstall functionality in your plugin, such as removing custom tables and options, make sure to warn the users that all plugin data will be deleted if they delete the plugin.

The difference between this method and the `register_deactivation_hook` is that the `register_uninstall_hook` is executed when a deactivated plugin is deleted. The `register_deactivation_hook` is executed when the plugin is deactivated, which means the user may want to activate the plugin again eventually. You wouldn't want to delete all of the plugin settings if the user is planning on using your plugin again.

PLUGIN SECURITY

One of the most important steps in creating a plugin is making sure it is secure from hacks and exploits. If a plugin contains security holes it opens up the entire WordPress web site for malicious hackers to wreak havoc. WordPress features some built-in security tools that you can utilize to make sure your plugins are as secure as can be.

Nonces

Nonces, which in WordPress stands for **number used once**, are used in requests (saving options, form posts, Ajax requests, actions) to stop unauthorized access by generating a secret key. This secret key is generated prior to generating a request (that is, form post). The key is then passed in the request to your script and verified to be the same key before anything else is processed. Up until this point we've used different WordPress APIs to save form data, which handles nonce creation and checking automatically. Now you're going to learn how to manually create and check nonces. Look at an example using a nonce in a form:

```
<form method="post">
    <?php
    if ( function_exists('wp_nonce_field') ) wp_nonce_field('gmp_nonce_check');
    ?>

    Enter your name: <input type="text" name="text">

    <input type="submit" name="submit" value="Save Options">
</form>
```

When creating a form nonce, the function `wp_nonce_field` must be called inside of your `<form>` tags. The only parameter you send into the function is the unique name for your nonce, in this case `gmp_nonce_check`. Also notice how you are verifying that the `wp_nonce_field` function exists before trying to call it for backward compatibility. When the function is called it will generate a unique secret key that will be passed with your form data. After your form is posted the first thing you need to do is check your nonce secret key using the `check_admin_referer` function like so:

```
function gmp_update_options()
{
    if ( isset($_POST['submit']) ) {
        check_admin_referer('gmp_nonce_check');
        //do stuff
    }
}
```

Verifying that the nonce is valid is as simple as calling the `check_admin_referer` function and passing it your unique nonce name. If the nonce secret key does not match the secret key created on your form

WordPress will stop processing the page and issue an error message. This primarily protects it from cross-site scripting attacks, or XSS.

Nonces can also be used on links that perform actions. To create a URL nonce you use the `wp_nonce_url` function. This can be used in conjunction with multiple querystrings in your URL like so:

```php
<?php
$link = 'my-url.php?action=delete&ID=15';
?>
<a href="<?php echo wp_nonce_url($link, 'gmp_nonce_url_check'); ?>">
```

The `wp_nonce_url` function accepts two parameters: the URL to add the nonce to and the unique nonce name you are creating. The preceding code would generate a link that looks like this:

```
http://example.com/wp-admin/my-url.php?action=delete&ID=15&_wpnonce=e9d6673015
```

Notice how the `_wpnonce` querystring is appended to the link. This is the secret key value that was generated for your URL nonce. If your URL has no querystrings the `wp_nonce_url` function will add the nonce value as the only querystring being passed. If your URL contains querystrings that nonce value will be added to the end of the URL. You can verify the nonce is correct just like you did with your form using the `check_admin_referer` function:

```php
function gmp_update_options()
{
    if ( isset($_GET['action']) ) {
        check_admin_referer('gmp_nonce_url_check');
        //do stuff
    }
}
```

This function verifies that your action querystring is set before checking your nonce value. Once the nonce has been validated the script will continue. Remember that if the nonce is not validated the page execution will stop, preventing any type of hack attempt.

Data Validation

Any data that comes from somewhere external to your code (such as user input) needs to be scrubbed to verify it's free from illegal characters. Data validation is essential to proper plugin security. Improperly validated data can lead to SQL Injection hacks, exploits, errors, and much more.

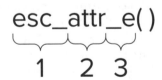

FIGURE 7-6: Escaping API breakdown

WordPress features a set of escaping functions that you can use to verify that your data is scrubbed properly prior to being displayed or inserted into the database. These escaping functions follow a set naming standard, which makes it easy to identify what they are escaping. Figure 7-6 shows the escaping function naming template.

➤ `esc_`: The prefix for the escaping functions.

➤ `attr`: The escaping context (`attr`, `html`, `js`, `sql`, `url`, and `url_raw`).

➤ `_e`: The optional translation suffix. Available suffixes are `__` and `_e`.

The `esc_html` function is used for scrubbing data that contains HTML. This function encodes special characters into their HTML entities. These characters include &, <, >, ", and '.

```php
<?php esc_html($text); ?>
```

The `esc_attr` function is used for escaping HTML attributes. This function should be used whenever you need to display data inside an HTML element.

```html
<input type="text" name="first_name" value="<?php echo esc_attr($text); ?>">
```

WordPress also features a function for validating URLs called `esc_url`. This function should be used to scrub the URL for illegal characters. Even though the `href` is technically an HTML attribute, you should use the `esc_url` function like so:

```html
<a href="<?php echo esc_url($url); ?>">
```

The `esc_js` function escapes text strings in JavaScript.

```html
<script>
    var bwar='<?php echo esc_js($text); ?>';
</script>
```

The `esc_sql` function escapes data for use in a MySQL query. This function is really just a shortcut for `$wpdb->escape()`.

```php
<?php esc_sql($sql); ?>
```

The optional translation suffix (`__` or `_e`) is used for translating the escaped data. The `_e` suffix will echo the escaped translated text, whereas `__` only returns the escaped translated value.

```php
<?php
//escapes, translates, and displays the text
esc_html_e($text);

//escapes, translates, but does NOT display
$text = esc_html__($text);
?>
```

The escaping API functions were added in WordPress 2.8. When using these functions you'll want to make sure you detect the user's version of WordPress to confirm your plugin is compatible with the installation. If the user is using an older version of WordPress these functions will not exist.

If the data you are validating is supposed to be an integer, use the `intval` PHP function to verify that. The `intval` function will return the integer value of a variable. If the variable is a string, and therefore not an integer, it will return 0.

```php
$variable = 12345;
$variable = intval($variable);
```

Remember that all data external to your plugin code is suspect until proven valid. Always validate your data before displaying to the browser or inserting into the database to help keep your plugins secure from hacks and exploits.

CREATING A PLUGIN EXAMPLE

Now that you've seen the many different options WordPress provides for use in your plugins, you can put that knowledge to work! In this example you will utilize many of the features covered in this chapter. At the end of this section the entire plugin source code will be available.

The example plugin you are going to build is called Post Products. The goal of this plugin is to create an easy way to add product data to posts. This plugin will include the following features:

➤ settings page using the Settings API

➤ widget for displaying newest products using the `Widget` class

➤ post meta box for adding product data to posts

➤ Shortcode support to easily display product data in a post

The first step in creating your plugin is to create your plugin files. For this plugin you'll have two files: `post-products.php` and `uninstall.php`. Because your plugin contains two files you'll need to save these files in a separate folder for your plugin named `post-products`. Next you need to set up your plugin header and license.

To start you'll be working in `post-products.php`. First you want to define your plugin header as shown here:

```
<?php
/*
Plugin Name: Post Products
Plugin URI: http://webdevstudios.com/support/wordpress-plugins/
Description: Easily add product data to posts.
Version: 1.0
Author: Brad Williams
Author URI: http://webdevstudios.com
*/

/*  Copyright 2010  Brad Williams  (email : brad@webdevstudios.com)

    This program is free software; you can redistribute it and/or modify
    it under the terms of the GNU General Public License as published by
    the Free Software Foundation; either version 2 of the License, or
    (at your option) any later version.

    This program is distributed in the hope that it will be useful,
    but WITHOUT ANY WARRANTY; without even the implied warranty of
    MERCHANTABILITY or FITNESS FOR A PARTICULAR PURPOSE.  See the
    GNU General Public License for more details.

    You should have received a copy of the GNU General Public License
    along with this program; if not, write to the Free Software
    Foundation, Inc., 51 Franklin St, Fifth Floor, Boston, MA  02110-1301  USA
*/
```

As you can see you created the appropriate plugin header for your new plugin. Because you will be releasing this plugin you'll want to include the GPL software license below your plugin header.

Next you are going to register all of the Action hooks needed for your plugin to work. It's generally a good idea to group all hook calls together. This helps other developers follow the logic of the plugin.

```
// Call function when plugin is activated
register_activation_hook(__FILE__,'pp_install');

// Action hook to initialize the plugin
add_action('admin_init', 'pp_init');

// Action hook to register our option settings
add_action( 'admin_init', 'pp_register_settings' );

// Action hook to add the post products menu item
add_action('admin_menu', 'pp_menu');

// Action hook to save the meta box data when the post is saved
add_action('save_post','pp_save_meta_box');

// Action hook to create the post products shortcode
add_shortcode('pp', 'pp_shortcode');

// Action hook to create plugin widget
add_action( 'widgets_init', 'pp_register_widgets' );
```

First you call the `register_activation_hook` function to set up your default plugin settings. Next you call the `admin_init` hook to initialize your plugin, register your settings, and create your plugin submenu item. You'll be creating the functions for each Action hook next.

The first function you are going to create is `pp_install`, which is run when your plugin is activated:

```
function pp_install() {
    //setup our default option values
    $pp_options_arr=array(
        "currency_sign"=>'$'
        );

    //save our default option values
    update_option('pp_options', $pp_options_arr);
}
```

The `pp_install` function is used to create your default option values. In this case, you want to set the default currency sign to the dollar sign. After you've created your options array you'll save the value using the `update_option` function. The next function you'll create is `pp_menu` as shown in the following code:

```
//create the post products sub-menu
function pp_menu() {
    add_options_page(__('Post Products Settings Page','pp-plugin'),
    __('Post Products Settings','pp-plugin'), 'administrator',
    __FILE__, 'pp_settings_page');
}
```

As you can see this function is used to create your submenu item. Using the `add_options_page` function your Post Products Settings submenu item will be located at the bottom of the Settings menu in your

Dashboard. You also set this menu item to only be viewable by an administrator. The next function you'll create is the pp_init:

```
//create post meta box
function pp_init() {
    // create our custom meta box
    add_meta_box('pp-meta',__('Post Product Information','pp-plugin'),
    'pp_meta_box','post','side','default');
}
```

This function is used to create your Post Meta Box. You give your Meta Box a title of "Post Product Information." You also set the Meta Box to display in the side just below the Post Tags Meta Box on a default installation of WordPress. Next you're going to set up the plugin shortcode:

```
//create shortcode
function pp_shortcode($atts, $content = null) {
    global $post;
    extract(shortcode_atts(array(
        "show" => ''
    ), $atts));

    //load options array
    $pp_options = get_option('pp_options');

    If ($show == 'sku') {
        $pp_show = get_post_meta($post->ID,'pp_sku',true);
    }elseif ($show == 'price') {
        $pp_show = $pp_options['currency_sign'].
                    get_post_meta($post->ID,'pp_price',true);
    }elseif ($show == 'weight') {
        $pp_show = get_post_meta($post->ID,'pp_weight',true);
    }elseif ($show == 'color') {
        $pp_show = get_post_meta($post->ID,'pp_color',true);
    }elseif ($show == 'inventory') {
        $pp_show = get_post_meta($post->ID,'pp_inventory',true);
    }

    return $pp_show;
}
```

The first thing you do it initialize the global variable $post. This will bring in the $post->ID value for the post in which you are using the shortcode. Next you extract the shortcode attributes that you've defined, in this case show. Next you load your options array. The plugin settings are covered later in this section. Finally, you check what attribute value is being sent to the shortcode to determine what value to show. Using the shortcode like [pp show=price] would display the price of the product. Next up is creating the Post Meta Box as shown here:

```
//build post product meta box
function pp_meta_box($post,$box) {
    // retrieve our custom meta box values
    $pp_sku = get_post_meta($post->ID,'pp_sku',true);
    $pp_price = get_post_meta($post->ID,'pp_price',true);
```

```
        $pp_weight = get_post_meta($post->ID,'pp_weight',true);
        $pp_color = get_post_meta($post->ID,'pp_color',true);
        $pp_inventory = get_post_meta($post->ID,'pp_inventory',true);

        // display meta box form
        echo '<table>';
        echo '<tr>';
        echo '<td>' .__('Sku', 'pp-plugin'). ':</td><td><input type="text"
name="pp_sku" value="'.esc_attr($pp_sku).'" size="10" /></td>';
        echo '</tr><tr>';
        echo '<td>' .__('Price', 'pp-plugin'). ':</td><td><input type="text"
name="pp_price" value="'.esc_attr($pp_price).'" size="5" /></td>';
        echo '</tr><tr>';
        echo '<td>' .__('Weight', 'pp-plugin'). ':</td><td><input type="text"
name="pp_weight" value="'.esc_attr($pp_weight).'" size="5" /></td>';
        echo '</tr><tr>';
        echo '<td>' .__('Color', 'pp-plugin'). ':</td><td><input type="text"
name="pp_color" value="'.esc_attr($pp_color).'" size="5" /></td>';
        echo '</tr><tr>';
        echo '<td>Inventory:</td><td><select name="pp_inventory" id="pp_inventory">
            <option value="' .__('In Stock', 'pp-plugin'). '"
'.(is_null($pp_inventory) || $pp_inventory == __('In Stock', 'pp-plugin') ?
'selected="selected" ' : '').'>' .__('In Stock', 'pp-plugin'). '</option>
            <option value="' .__('Backordered', 'pp-plugin'). '"
'.($pp_inventory == __('Backordered', 'pp-plugin') ? 'selected="selected" '
: '').'>' .__('Backordered', 'pp-plugin'). '</option>
            <option value="' .__('Out of Stock', 'pp-plugin'). '"
'.($pp_inventory == __('Out of Stock', 'pp-plugin') ?
'selected="selected" ' : '').'>' .__('Out of Stock', 'pp-plugin'). '</option>
            <option value="' .__('Discontinued', 'pp-plugin'). '"
'.($pp_inventory == __('Discontinued', 'pp-plugin') ?
'selected="selected" ' : '').'>' .__('Discontinued', 'pp-plugin'). '</option>
          </select></td>';
        echo '</tr>';

        //display the meta box shortcode legend section
        echo '<tr><td colspan="2"><hr></td></tr>';
        echo '<tr><td colspan="2"><strong>'
.__('Shortcode Legend', 'pp-plugin') .'</strong></td></tr>';
        echo '<tr><td>' .__('Sku', 'pp-plugin') .':</td><td>[pp show=sku]</td></tr>';
        echo '<tr><td>' .__('Price', 'pp-plugin')
.':</td><td>[pp show=price]</td></tr>';
        echo '<tr><td>' .__('Weight', 'pp-plugin')
.':</td><td>[pp show=weight]</td></tr>';
        echo '<tr><td>' .__('Color', 'pp-plugin')
.':</td><td>[pp show=color]</td></tr>';
        echo '<tr><td>' .__('Inventory', 'pp-plugin')
.':</td><td>[pp show=inventory]</td></tr>';
        echo '</table>';
}
```

Your Post Product plugin saves five different product values on every post: sku, price, weight, color, and inventory. As you can see the first step is to load these five custom field values. Next you display the Meta Box form and fill in the current values if any exist. Below the Meta Box form you display a simple shortcode legend to show the user what shortcode options are available. Once completed your custom Meta Box will look like Figure 7-7.

FIGURE 7-7: Post product meta box

Now that you've created your custom Meta Box you need to save the data entered in the form as shown in the following code:

```
//save meta box data
function pp_save_meta_box($post_id,$post) {
    // if post is a revision skip saving our meta box data
    if($post->post_type == 'revision') { return; }

    // process form data if $_POST is set
    if(isset($_POST['pp_sku']) && $_POST['pp_sku'] != '') {

        // save the meta box data as post meta using the post ID as a unique prefix
        update_post_meta($post_id,'pp_sku', esc_attr($_POST['pp_sku']));
        update_post_meta($post_id,'pp_price', esc_attr($_POST['pp_price']));
        update_post_meta($post_id,'pp_weight', esc_attr($_POST['pp_weight']));
        update_post_meta($post_id,'pp_color', esc_attr($_POST['pp_color']));
        update_post_meta($post_id,'pp_inventory',esc_attr($_POST['pp_inventory']));

    }
}
```

First you verify that the post being saved is not a revision. Next you check that the post field pp_sku exists and is not blank. The only required field is the product sku, so if this field is blank the post will *not* be treated as a product and product data will not be saved. After you have verified that a sku exists you save your custom product fields as post meta for the post you are creating. Next up you are going to create your latest products widget:

```
//register our widget
function pp_register_widgets() {
    register_widget( 'pp_widget' );
}

//pp_widget class
class pp_widget extends WP_Widget {
```

First you have to register your widget as `pp_widget`. Next you extend the `Widget` class as `pp_widget`. Now you need to create the four widget functions needed to build your widget:

```php
        //process our new widget
    function pp_widget() {
        $widget_ops = array('classname' => 'pp_widget',
'description' => __('Display Post Products','pp-plugin') );
        $this->WP_Widget('pp_widget', __('Post Products Widget','pp-plugin'),
$widget_ops);
    }
```

The first function you create is the `pp_widget` function, also known as the constructor. Here you set the widget title, description, and class name for your custom widget.

```php
        //build our widget settings form
    function form($instance) {
        $defaults = array( 'title' => __('Products','pp-plugin'),
'number_products' => '' );
        $instance = wp_parse_args( (array) $instance, $defaults );
        $title = strip_tags($instance['title']);
        $number_products = strip_tags($instance['number_products']);
        ?>
<p>
    <?php _e('Title', 'pp-plugin') ?>:
    <input class="widefat" name="<?php echo $this->get_field_name('title'); ?>"
    type="text" value="<?php echo esc_attr($title); ?>" />
</p>
<p>
    <?php _e('Number of Products', 'pp-plugin') ?>:
    <input name="<?php echo $this->get_field_name('number_products'); ?>"
    type="text" value="<?php echo esc_attr($number_products); ?>" size="2"
maxlength="2" />
</p>
        <?php
    }
```

The second function you define is the `form` function. This builds the form for saving your widget settings. You are saving two settings in your widget: the widget title and the number of products to display. First you define the setting defaults if no settings have been saved. Next you load in the saved values for your two settings. Finally, you display both setting form fields with the setting values if they exist.

```php
        //save our widget settings
    function update($new_instance, $old_instance) {
        $instance = $old_instance;
        $instance['title'] = strip_tags(esc_attr($new_instance['title']));
        $instance['number_products'] = intval($new_instance['number_products']);

        return $instance;
    }
```

The next function you create is the `update` function. This function saves your widget settings. Notice how you utilize the `strip_tags` and `esc_attr` functions to sanitize your widget title. You also use the PHP `intval` function to verify the number of products value is an integer.

```php
        //display our widget
        function widget($args, $instance) {
            global $post;
            extract($args);

            echo $before_widget;
            $title = apply_filters('widget_title', $instance['title'] );
            $number_products = empty($instance['number_products']) ?
' ' : apply_filters('widget_number_products', $instance['number_products']);


            if ( !empty( $title ) ) { echo $before_title . $title . $after_title; };

            $dispProducts = new WP_Query();
            $dispProducts->query('meta_key=pp_sku&showposts='.$number_products);
            while ($dispProducts->have_posts()) : $dispProducts->the_post();

                //load options array
                $pp_options = get_option('pp_options');

                //load custom meta values
                $pp_price = get_post_meta($post->ID,'pp_price',true);
                $pp_inventory = get_post_meta($post->ID,'pp_inventory',true);
                ?><p><a href="<?php the_permalink() ?>" rel="bookmark"
title="<?php the_title_attribute(); ?> Product Information">
<?php the_title(); ?></a></p><?php
                echo '<p>' .__('Price', 'pp-plugin'). ': '
.$pp_options['currency_sign'].$pp_price .'</p>';

                //check if Show Inventory option is enabled
                If ($pp_options['show_inventory']) {
                    echo '<p>' .__('Stock', 'pp-plugin'). ': ' .$pp_inventory .'</p>';
                }
                echo '<hr />';

            endwhile;

            echo $after_widget;
        }
    }
```

The final function defined is the `widget` function. This function displays your widget on the public side of your web site. First you initialize the global `$post` variable and extract the `$args` for the widget. Next you display the `$before_widget` variable. This variable can be set by theme and plugin developers to display specified content before and after the plugin. Next you retrieve your two setting values. If the `$title` value is not empty you use it, but if it is you'll use the default title you defined earlier.

To display the products in your widget you are creating a custom Loop using `WP_Query`, as discussed in Chapter 5. Remember, because this is not your main Loop you'll want to use `WP_Query` to create your custom Loop instead of `query_posts`. To define your custom Loop you pass in two parameters: one for the post meta value and one for number of products to display. The first value (`meta_key=pp_sku`) tells your custom Loop to only return posts that have this custom meta value set. The second value, `showposts`, determines how many post products to display. This number is pulled from the widget options value set by the user.

Next you load your option values and the custom meta values you will be displaying in your widget. Finally you display your post product values in the widget. If the option Show Inventory is enabled the inventory value will be displayed. After successfully creating the Post Products widget it should look like Figure 7-8.

FIGURE 7-8: Post Products widget

The final part to your custom plugin is creating the plugin settings page:

```php
function pp_register_settings() {
    //register our array of settings
    register_setting( 'pp-settings-group', 'pp_options' );
}

function pp_settings_page() {
    //load our options array
    $pp_options = get_option('pp_options');

    // if the show inventory option exists the checkbox needs to be checked
    If ($pp_options['show_inventory']) {
        $checked = ' checked="checked" ';
    }

    $pp_currency = $pp_options['currency_sign'];
    ?>
    <div class="wrap">
    <h2><?php _e('Post Products Options', 'pp-plugin') ?></h2>

    <form method="post" action="options.php">
        <?php settings_fields( 'pp-settings-group' ); ?>
        <table class="form-table">
          <tr valign="top">
          <th scope="row"><?php _e('Show Product Inventory', 'pp-plugin') ?></th>
          <td><input type="checkbox" name="pp_options[show_inventory]"
          <?php echo $checked; ?> /></td>
          </tr>
```

```
            <tr valign="top">
            <th scope="row"><?php _e('Currency Sign', 'pp-plugin') ?></th>
            <td><input type="text" name="pp_options[currency_sign]" value="
<?php echo $pp_currency; ?>" size="1" maxlength="1" /></td>
            </tr>
        </table>

        <p class="submit">
        <input type="submit" class="button-primary" value="
<?php _e('Save Changes', 'pp-plugin') ?>" />
        </p>

    </form>
    </div>
<?php
}
?>
```

The first function is used to register your plugin settings. In this example you are saving all of your setting values in an array so you need only one setting to be registered: `pp_options`. Next you create the function to display your settings page called `pp_settings_page`.

First you load your plugin options array value. Next you check if the show inventory option should be CHECKED. You also load in the current currency value into a variable for display. Next you display your settings page form with both option form fields listed. Notice you are using the `settings_fields` function to link your settings form to your registered setting you defined. You also set the name for your form fields to your options array name with the unique option name in brackets like `pp_options['show_inventory']`. This is the proper way to save your setting options in an array using the Settings API. When the form is submitted WordPress will use the Settings API to sanitize the form values and save them in the database.

The final step to your Post Products plugin is to create your `uninstall.php` file:

```
<?php
// If uninstall/delete not called from WordPress then exit
if( ! defined( 'ABSPATH' ) && ! defined( 'WP_UNINSTALL_PLUGIN' ) )
    exit ();

// Delete options array from options table
delete_option( 'pp_options' );
?>
```

The first thing you check is that ABSPATH and WP_UNINSTALL_PLUGIN constants exist. This means they were called from WordPress and adds a layer of security on the uninstaller. After you have verified the request is valid you delete your single option value from the database. You could also define other uninstall functionality here if needed such as removing every product post meta value you saved in the database.

That's it! You just successfully built an entire plugin that includes many of the features covered in this chapter. This is a fairly basic plugin but should give you the examples and tools needed to expand upon. Listing 7-5 shows the plugin source code in its entirety.

LISTING 7-5: Complete Plugin Source Code

```php
<?php
/*
Plugin Name: Post Products
Plugin URI: http://webdevstudios.com/support/wordpress-plugins/
Description: Easily add product data to posts.
Version: 1.0
Author: Brad Williams
Author URI: http://webdevstudios.com
*/

/*  Copyright 2010  Brad Williams  (email : brad@webdevstudios.com)

    This program is free software; you can redistribute it and/or modify
    it under the terms of the GNU General Public License as published by
    the Free Software Foundation; either version 2 of the License, or
    (at your option) any later version.

    This program is distributed in the hope that it will be useful,
    but WITHOUT ANY WARRANTY; without even the implied warranty of
    MERCHANTABILITY or FITNESS FOR A PARTICULAR PURPOSE.  See the
    GNU General Public License for more details.

    You should have received a copy of the GNU General Public License
    along with this program; if not, write to the Free Software
    Foundation, Inc., 51 Franklin St, Fifth Floor, Boston, MA  02110-1301  USA
*/

// Call function when plugin is activated
register_activation_hook(__FILE__,'pp_install');

// Action hook to initialize the plugin
add_action('admin_init', 'pp_init');

// Action hook to register our option settings
add_action( 'admin_init', 'pp_register_settings' );

// Action hook to add the post products menu item
add_action('admin_menu', 'pp_menu');

// Action hook to save the meta box data when the post is saved
add_action('save_post','pp_save_meta_box');

// Action hook to create the post products shortcode
add_shortcode('pp', 'pp_shortcode');

// Action hook to create plugin widget
add_action( 'widgets_init', 'pp_register_widgets' );
```

continues

LISTING 7-5 *(continued)*

```php
function pp_install() {
    //setup our default option values
    $pp_options_arr=array(
        "currency_sign"=>'$'
        );

    //save our default option values
    update_option('pp_options', $pp_options_arr);
}

//create the post products sub-menu
function pp_menu() {
    add_options_page(__('Post Products Settings Page','pp-plugin'),
__('Post Products Settings','pp-plugin'), 'administrator', __FILE__,
'pp_settings_page');
}

//create post meta box
function pp_init() {
    // create our custom meta box
    add_meta_box('pp-meta',__('Post Product Information','pp-plugin'),
 'pp_meta_box','post','side','default');
}

//create shortcode
function pp_shortcode($atts, $content = null) {
    global $post;
    extract(shortcode_atts(array(
        "show" => ''
    ), $atts));

    //load options array
    $pp_options = get_option('pp_options');

    If ($show == 'sku') {
        $pp_show = get_post_meta($post->ID,'pp_sku',true);
    }elseif ($show == 'price') {
        $pp_show = $pp_options['currency_sign'].
        get_post_meta($post->ID,'pp_price',true);
    }elseif ($show == 'weight') {
        $pp_show = get_post_meta($post->ID,'pp_weight',true);
    }elseif ($show == 'color') {
        $pp_show = get_post_meta($post->ID,'pp_color',true);
    }elseif ($show == 'inventory') {
        $pp_show = get_post_meta($post->ID,'pp_inventory',true);
    }

    return $pp_show;
}

//build post product meta box
function pp_meta_box($post,$box) {
```

```
    // retrieve our custom meta box values
    $pp_sku = get_post_meta($post->ID,'pp_sku',true);
    $pp_price = get_post_meta($post->ID,'pp_price',true);
    $pp_weight = get_post_meta($post->ID,'pp_weight',true);
    $pp_color = get_post_meta($post->ID,'pp_color',true);
    $pp_inventory = get_post_meta($post->ID,'pp_inventory',true);


    // display meta box form
    echo '<table>';
    echo '<tr>';
    echo '<td>' .__('Sku', 'pp-plugin').
':</td><td><input type="text" name="pp_sku" value="'.esc_attr($pp_sku).
'" size="10"></td>';
    echo '</tr><tr>';
    echo '<td>' .__('Price', 'pp-plugin').
':</td><td><input type="text" name="pp_price" value="'.esc_attr($pp_price).
'" size="5"></td>';
    echo '</tr><tr>';
    echo '<td>' .__('Weight', 'pp-plugin').
':</td><td><input type="text" name="pp_weight" value="'.esc_attr($pp_weight).'"
size="5"></td>';
    echo '</tr><tr>';
    echo '<td>' .__('Color', 'pp-plugin').
':</td><td><input type="text" name="pp_color" value="'.esc_attr($pp_color).
'" size="5"></td>';
    echo '</tr><tr>';
    echo '<td>Inventory:</td><td><select name="pp_inventory" id="pp_inventory">
         <option value="' .__('In Stock', 'pp-plugin').
'" '.(is_null($pp_inventory) || $pp_inventory == __('In Stock', 'pp-plugin') ?
'selected="selected" ' : '').'>' .__('In Stock', 'pp-plugin'). '</option>
         <option value="' .__('Backordered', 'pp-plugin'). '"
'.($pp_inventory == __('Backordered', 'pp-plugin') ?
'selected="selected" ' : '').'>' .__('Backordered', 'pp-plugin'). '</option>
         <option value="' .__('Out of Stock', 'pp-plugin').
'" '.($pp_inventory == __('Out of Stock', 'pp-plugin') ?
'selected="selected" ' : '').'>' .__('Out of Stock', 'pp-plugin'). '</option>
         <option value="' .__('Discontinued', 'pp-plug
in').
'" '.($pp_inventory == __('Discontinued', 'pp-plugin') ?
'selected="selected" ' : '').'>' .__('Discontinued', 'pp-plugin'). '</option>
       </select></td>';
    echo '</tr>';


    //display the meta box shortcode legend section
    echo '<tr><td colspan="2"><hr></td></tr>';
    echo '<tr><td colspan="2"><strong>' .__('Shortcode Legend', 'pp-plugin')
.'</strong></td></tr>';
    echo '<tr><td>' .__('Sku', 'pp-plugin') .':</td><td>[pp show=sku]</td></tr>';
    echo '<tr><td>' .__('Price', 'pp-plugin')
.':</td><td>[pp show=price]</td></tr>';
    echo '<tr><td>' .__('Weight', 'pp-plugin')
.':</td><td>[pp show=weight]</td></tr>';
    echo '<tr><td>' .__('Color', 'pp-plugin')
```

continues

LISTING 7-5 *(continued)*

```
 .':</td><td>[pp show=color]</td></tr>';
    echo '<tr><td>' .__('Inventory', 'pp-plugin')
 .':</td><td>[pp show=inventory]</td></tr>';
    echo '</table>';
}

//save meta box data
function pp_save_meta_box($post_id,$post) {
    // if post is a revision skip saving our meta box data
    if($post->post_type == 'revision') { return; }

    // process form data if $_POST is set
    if(isset($_POST['pp_sku']) && $_POST['pp_sku'] != '') {

        // save the meta box data as post meta using the post ID as a unique prefix
        update_post_meta($post_id,'pp_sku', esc_attr($_POST['pp_sku']));
        update_post_meta($post_id,'pp_price', esc_attr($_POST['pp_price']));
        update_post_meta($post_id,'pp_weight', esc_attr($_POST['pp_weight']));
        update_post_meta($post_id,'pp_color', esc_attr($_POST['pp_color']));
        update_post_meta($post_id,'pp_inventory',esc_attr($_POST['pp_inventory']));

    }
}

//register our widget
function pp_register_widgets() {
    register_widget( 'pp_widget' );
}

//pp_widget class
class pp_widget extends WP_Widget {

    //process our new widget
    function pp_widget() {
        $widget_ops = array('classname' => 'pp_widget', 'description' =>
__('Display Post Products','pp-plugin') );
        $this->WP_Widget('pp_widget', __('Post Products Widget','pp-plugin'),
$widget_ops);
    }

    //build our widget settings form
    function form($instance) {
        $defaults = array( 'title' => __('Products','pp-plugin'), 'number_products'
 => '' );
        $instance = wp_parse_args( (array) $instance, $defaults );
        $title = strip_tags($instance['title']);
        $number_products = strip_tags($instance['number_products']);
        ?>
            <p><?php _e('Title', 'pp-plugin') ?>: <input class="widefat"
name="<?php echo $this->get_field_name('title'); ?>" type="text" value="<?php echo
esc_attr($title); ?>" /></p>
            <p><?php _e('Number of Products', 'pp-plugin') ?>: <input
name="<?php echo $this->get_field_name('number_products'); ?>"
```

```php
type="text" value="<?php echo esc_attr($number_products); ?>"
size="2" maxlength="2" /></p>
        <?php
    }

    //save our widget settings
    function update($new_instance, $old_instance) {
        $instance = $old_instance;
        $instance['title'] = strip_tags(esc_attr($new_instance['title']));
        $instance['number_products'] = intval($new_instance['number_products']);

        return $instance;
    }

    //display our widget
    function widget($args, $instance) {
        global $post;
        extract($args);

        echo $before_widget;
        $title = apply_filters('widget_title', $instance['title'] );
        $number_products = empty($instance['number_products']) ?
' ' : apply_filters('widget_number_products', $instance['number_products']);

        if ( !empty( $title ) ) { echo $before_title . $title . $after_title; };

        $dispProducts = new WP_Query();
        $dispProducts->query('meta_key=pp_sku&showposts='.$number_products);
        while ($dispProducts->have_posts()) : $dispProducts->the_post();

            //load options array
            $pp_options = get_option('pp_options');

            //load custom meta values
            $pp_price = get_post_meta($post->ID,'pp_price',true);
            $pp_inventory = get_post_meta($post->ID,'pp_inventory',true);

            ?><p><a href="<?php the_permalink() ?>" rel="bookmark"
title="<?php the_title_attribute(); ?> Product Information">
<?php the_title(); ?></a></p><?php
            echo '<p>' .__('Price', 'pp-plugin'). ': '
.$pp_options['currency_sign'].$pp_price .'</p>';

            //check if Show Inventory option is enabled
            If ($pp_options['show_inventory']) {
                echo '<p>' .__('Stock', 'pp-plugin'). ': ' .$pp_inventory .'</p>';
            }
            echo '<hr>';

        endwhile;

        echo $after_widget;
    }
}
```

continues

LISTING 7-5 *(continued)*

```php
function pp_register_settings() {
    //register our array of settings
    register_setting( 'pp-settings-group', 'pp_options' );
}

function pp_settings_page() {
    //load our options array
    $pp_options = get_option('pp_options');

    // if the show inventory option exists the checkbox needs to be checked
    If ($pp_options['show_inventory']) {
        $checked = ' checked="checked" ';
    }

    $pp_currency = $pp_options['currency_sign'];
    ?>
    <div class="wrap">
    <h2><?php _e('Post Products Options', 'pp-plugin') ?></h2>

    <form method="post" action="options.php">
        <?php settings_fields( 'pp-settings-group' ); ?>
        <table class="form-table">
            <tr valign="top">
            <th scope="row"><?php _e('Show Product Inventory', 'pp-plugin') ?></th>
            <td><input type="checkbox" name="pp_options[show_inventory]"
<?php echo $checked; ?> /></td>
            </tr>

            <tr valign="top">
            <th scope="row"><?php _e('Currency Sign', 'pp-plugin') ?></th>
            <td><input type="text" name="pp_options[currency_sign]"
value="<?php echo $pp_currency; ?>" size="1" maxlength="1" /></td>
            </tr>
        </table>

        <p class="submit">
        <input type="submit" class="button-primary"
value="<?php _e('Save Changes', 'pp-plugin') ?>" />
        </p>

    </form>
    </div>
<?php
}
?>
```

PUBLISH TO THE PLUGIN DIRECTORY

Now it's time to release your plugin to the world! Releasing your plugin is not a requirement, but it is the best way to get your plugin publicized and have other WordPress users download and install it. Remember that the Plugin Directory is directly hooked to every installation of WordPress, so if your plugin exists in the directory then anyone running WordPress can easily download and install it.

Restrictions

A few restrictions exist to submitting your plugin to the Plugin Directory:

➤ Plugin must be GPLv2 compatible

➤ Plugin must not do anything illegal or morally offensive

➤ Must use the Subversion (SVN) repository to host your plugin

➤ Plugin must not embed external links on the user's site (like a "powered by" link) without asking the plugin user's permission

Make sure to follow these guidelines or your plugin will be removed from the Plugin Directory.

Submit Your Plugin

The first step is to create an account on WordPress.org if you don't already have one. To register a new account visit the registration page at `http://wordpress.org/extend/plugins/register.php`. This WordPress.org account is used in the Plugin Directory as well as the support forums.

After you have registered your account and signed in it's time to submit your plugin for inclusion in the Plugin Directory on WordPress.org. To submit your plugin visit the Add Your Plugin page located at `http://wordpress.org/extend/plugins/add/`.

The first required field is the Plugin Name. The plugin name should be the exact name you want to use for your plugin. Keep in mind the plugin name will be used as the URL in the directory. For example, if you submit a plugin named "WP Brad," the URL to your plugin in the Plugin Directory will be `http://wordpress.org/extend/plugins/wp-brad/`. As you can see the name you insert here is very important and cannot be changed.

The second required field is the Plugin Description. This field should contain a detailed description about your plugin. Remember that the description is really the only information used to decide whether or not to allow your plugin in the directory. Clearly state the plugin functionality, the purpose of the plugin, and installation instructions for the plugin.

The final field is the Plugin URL. This is not a required field, but it's a good idea to include a download link to your plugin. This allows the reviewer of your plugin to request the ability to download and look at your plugin if needed. Again this is not a required field but you are strongly encouraged to fill it in.

After you have filled out all of the information click the Send Post button to submit your plugin request. The Plugin Directory states "Within some vaguely defined amount of time, someone will approve your request." This doesn't really tell us much, but most plugins are approved within a day or so. Once your plugin has been approved it does not mean you are done. The next step is to upload your plugin to the Subversion Repository that has been created for it.

Create a readme.txt File

One required file to submit your plugin to the Plugin Directory is a readme.txt file. This file is used to fill in all of the plugin information on the Plugin detail page in the Directory. WordPress has developed the "readme file standard," which details exactly how your readme.txt file should be defined. Here's an example readme.txt file:

```
=== Plugin Name ===
Contributors: williamsba1, messenlehner, wds-scott
Donate link: http://example.com/donate
Tags: admin, post, images, page, widget
Requires at least: 2.8
Tested up to: 2.9
Stable tag: 1.1.0.0

Short description of the plugin with 150 chars max.  No markup here.

== Description ==

This is the long description.  No limit, and you can use Markdown

Additional plugin features

*    Feature 1
*    Feature 2
*    Feature 3

For support visit the [Support Forum](http://example.com/forum/ " Support Forum")

== Installation ==

1. Upload `plugin-directory` to the `/wp-content/plugins/` directory
2. Activate the plugin through the 'Plugins' SubPanel in WordPress
3. Place `<?php gmp_custom_function(); ?>` in your theme templates

== Frequently Asked Questions ==

= A question that someone might have =

An answer to that question.

= Does this plugin work with WordPress MU? =

Absolutely!  This plugin has been tested and
verified to work on the most current version of WordPress MU
```

```
== Screenshots ==

1. Screenshot of plugin settings page
2. Screenshot of plugin in action

== Changelog ==

= 1.1 =
* New feature details
* Bug fix details

= 1.0 =
* First official release
```

WordPress.org also features a `readme.txt` validator so you can verify you have a properly formatted `readme.txt` file before submitting to the Subversion directory. You can access the validator at `http://wordpress.org/extend/plugins/about/validator/`. Let's break down the individual `readme.txt` sections:

```
=== Plugin Name ===
Contributors: williamsba1, messenlehner, wds-scott
Donate link: http://example.com/donate
Tags: admin, post, images, page, widget
Requires at least: 2.8
Tested up to: 2.9
Stable tag: 1.1.0.0

Short description of the plugin with 150 chars max.  No markup here.
```

The Plugin Name section is one of the most important parts of your `readme.txt` file. The first line lists the contributors to the plugin. This is a comma-separated list of WordPress.org usernames that helped contribute to the plugin. The donate link should be a URL to either a donate link or a web page that explains how users can donate to the plugin author. This is a great place for a Paypal donation link. Tags are a comma-separated list of tags describing your plugin.

The "Requires at least" field is the minimal version of WordPress required to run the plugin. If your plugin won't run on anything prior to 2.7, then 2.7 would be the "Requires at least" value. Likewise, "Tested up to" is the latest version the plugin has been tested on. This will typically be the latest stable version of WordPress. The Stable tag is also a very important field and should be the current version of the plugin. This value should always match the version number listed in the plugin header. Last is a short description of the plugin, which should be no more than 150 characters and cannot contain any markup.

```
== Description ==

This is the long description.  No limit, and you can use Markdown

Additional plugin features

*    Feature 1
*    Feature 2
*    Feature 3

For support visit the [Support Forum](http://example.com/forum/ " Support Forum")
```

The Description section features a detailed description of your plugin. This is the default information displayed on the plugin detail page in the Plugin Directory. There is no limit to the length of the description. You can also use unordered lists, shown in the preceding example, and ordered lists in your description. Links can also be inserted.

```
== Installation ==

1. Upload `plugin-directory` to the `/wp-content/plugins/` directory
2. Activate the plugin through the 'Plugins' SubPanel in WordPress
3. Place `<?php gmp_custom_function(); ?>` in your theme templates
```

The Installation section details the steps involved to install a plugin. If your plugin has very specific installation requirements make sure they are listed here in detail. It's also a good idea to list the function name and shortcode that can be used with the plugin.

```
== Frequently Asked Questions ==

= A question that someone might have =

An answer to that question.

= Does this plugin work with WordPress MU? =

Absolutely!  This plugin has been tested and
verified to work on the most current version of WordPress MU
```

The FAQ section is the perfect place to list frequently asked questions, of course! This helps answer commonly asked questions and can eliminate many support requests. You can list multiple questions with answers as this example shows.

```
== Screenshots ==

1. Screenshot of plugin settings page
2. Screenshot of plugin in action
```

The Screenshots section is used to add individual screenshots of your plugin to the plugin detail page. This is actually a two-step process. The first step is to list out each screenshot description in an ordered list. The next step is to place image files in your trunk directory (which is discussed in more detail next). These images filenames must match the listing number. For instance, the screenshot of your settings page should be named screenshot-1.png. The screenshot of your plugin in action should be named screenshot-2.png. The file types accepted are png, jpg, jpeg, and gif.

```
== Changelog ==

= 1.1 =
* New feature details
* Bug fix details

= 1.0 =
* First official release
```

The final section is the Changelog. This section is important for listing out what each plugin version release has added or fixed. This is a very helpful section for anyone looking to upgrade to the latest version. It's always nice to know exactly what is being added and fixed to determine how critical the plugin update is. A new item should be added for each version you release to the Plugin Directory, regardless of how minor that update may be.

The `readme.txt` file can also accept arbitrary sections in the same format as the rest. This is useful for more complicated plugins that need to provide additional information. Arbitrary sections will be displayed below the built-in sections described previously.

Setup SVN

The Plugin Directory uses Subversion (SVN) for handling plugins. To publish your plugin to the directory you'll need to set up and configure an SVN client. In this example you are going to use TortoiseSVN for Windows. TortoiseSVN is a free gui client interface for SVN. For a list of additional SVN clients for different platforms visit `http://subversion.tigris.org/`.

First you'll need to download the appropriate installer located at `http://tortoisesvn.net/downloads`. After installing TortoiseSVN you'll be required to reboot your computer. The next step is to create a new directory on your computer to store your plugin files. I recommend making a folder to store all of your plugins in such as `c:\projects\wordpress-plugins`. This makes it much easier going forward if you create and release multiple plugins to WordPress.org.

Next navigate to your new `wordpress-plugins` directory and create a new directory for your plugin. Right-click this new folder to pull up a context menu. You'll notice the new TortoiseSVN options listed: SVN Checkout and ToirtoiseSVN. Select SVN Checkout and a dialog box appears as shown in Figure 7-9.

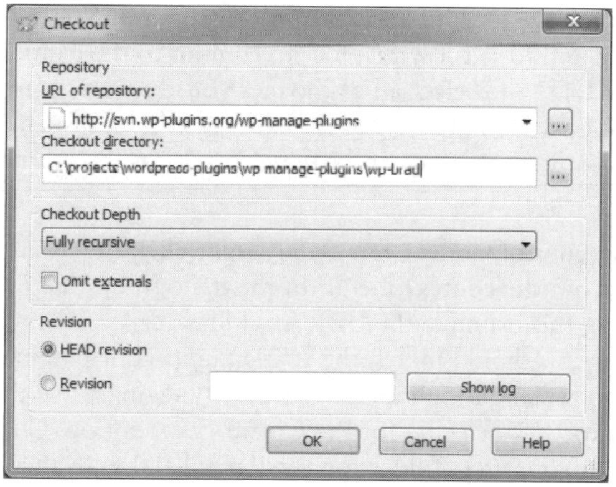

FIGURE 7-9: SVN Checkout dialog

The URL of the repository was provided to you in the e-mail you received when your plugin was approved. This URL should be the same as the plugin URL so in this example the URL would be `http://svn.wp-plugins.org/wp-brad`. The Checkout directory is the local folder in which to store your plugin. In this case you will use new folder you created at `c:\projects\wordpress-plugins\wp-brad`. Make sure Checkout Depth is set to Fully Recursive. Also verify that the Revision is set to HEAD Revision. Finally, click the OK button. TortoiseSVN will connect to the SVN Repository for your plugin and if all goes well will create three new directories in your folder called `branches`, `tags`, and `trunk`. These three folders each serve a specific purpose for SVN:

➤ **Branches:** Every time a new major version is released it gets a branch. This allows for bug fixes without releasing new functionality from `trunk`

➤ **Tags:** Every time a new version is released you'll make a new tag for it.

➤ **Trunk:** Main development area. The next major release of code lives here.

Now that you've connected to your plugin's SVN Repository you need to move your plugin files to the `trunk` directory. Remember to also place your `readme.txt` file and any screenshots, includes, and so on in the `trunk` directory for your plugin. Remember, you're just staging the plugin files to publish to the plugin directory. We'll cover publishing the files to WordPress.org in the next section.

Once you've verified all of the plugin files are in `trunk` you are ready to publish your plugin to the Plugin Directory!

Publish to the Plugin Directory

Publishing your plugin to the Plugin Directory is a two-step process. First you need to SVN Commit the `trunk` folder to your SVN Repository. Second you need to tag your plugin release. Once both steps have been completed your new plugin will appear in the Plugin Directory within about 15 minutes.

To commit your plugin trunk simply right-click the `trunk` folder and select SVN Commit. You'll be presented with a dialog box to enter a log message and to select which files to commit to the trunk. Fill in a brief log message, such as "Adding WP-Brad 1.1," and select all of the files you want to commit. TortoiseSVN will automatically select all files that have changed so you probably won't need to change this. Next, click OK and you will be prompted to enter a username and password. This is the username and password you created on WordPress.org.

Next you need to tag your plugin version. To tag your plugin version simply right-click the `trunk` directory and select TortoiseSVN ⇨ Branch/tag from the context menu. In the dialog box that appears fill in the path to your tag directory. Using this example the URL would be `http://svn.wp-plugins.org/wp-brad/tags/1.1.0.0`. This tag version should match the stable tag in your plugin's `readme.txt` file, in your case version 1.1.0.0. Also type in a log message such as "tagging version 1.1.0.0" and verify "HEAD revision in the repository" is selected for the Create Copy option. Click OK and your plugin will create a new directory in your `tags` folder for version 1.1.0.0 with the appropriate plugin files.

That's it! If everything worked successfully your plugin should appear in the Plugin Directory within about 15 minutes. Once your plugin is successfully published you'll want to verify all of the information is correct. One way to verify that your plugin was published successfully is to visit the Subversion URL, which for this example would be `http://svn.wp-plugins.org/wp-brad/`. Here you can ensure the `trunk` and `tag` directories were uploaded successfully. After 15 minutes you can also verify your plugin by visiting the official Plugin Directory page at `http://www.wordpress.org/extend/plugins/wp-brad`.

If you need to make any changes to your `readme.txt` file simply edit it locally in your `trunk` folder, right-click the file, and click SVN Commit.

Releasing a New Version

A great feature about WordPress plugins is that you can easily release updates for your plugins in the Plugin Directory. When a new plugin version is released, a notice is displayed on any WordPress site that currently has that plugin uploaded to its server, whether or not it is activated. The user can use the automatic upgrade process to easily upgrade the plugin to the latest version. This is especially important if there are security patches in your plugin to help keep WordPress secure.

To release a new plugin version, make sure you copy the updated plugin files to the `/trunk` directory you set up earlier. This folder should contain all files for the updated plugin version. Once you have verified that all of the updates plugin files exist, simply right-click the `trunk` directory and select SVN Commit. Remember to type in a brief message such as "Committing version 1.2." TortoiseSVN should have already selected all of the files that have changed, but if not, select all of the files you want to publish and click OK.

The final step is to tag your new version. To tag your new release right-click the `trunk` directory and select TortoiseSVN ➪ Branch/tag. For this example the URL would be `http://svn.wp-plugins .org/wp-brad/tags/1.2.0.0`. Remember to write a brief log entry such as "Tagging version 1.2" and click OK. That's it! Your new plugin version will be published in the Plugin Directory within 15 minutes. After the new version has been released your plugin will appear at the top of the Recently Updated Plugins list on WordPress.org.

The WordPress Plugin Directory is a great source for inspiration and reference when building custom plugins. Don't be scared to look at another plugin source code for reference. Find a plugin that functions similarly to what you want and see how the plugin author structured the code or used hooks to interpose his or her plugin ideas in the WordPress core processing.

Plugins are only half of the WordPress extensibility story, giving you the power to add custom functions and event-driving processing to your site. If you want to change the look and feel of your site, change the way in which WordPress displays posts, or provide slots for those widgets you created, you'll extend want to WordPress through theme development.

8

Theme Development

WHAT'S IN THIS CHAPTER?

➤   Understanding the various files and templates that constitute a theme

➤   Modifying an existing theme to meet your own needs

➤   Creating a new theme based on the Sandbox theme framework

Content is king, right? That is certainly true. Nothing is going to drive visitors to your site, and keep them coming back, except for your content. Even if you have the best content on the Internet for your topic, you have to present it to the reader, the browser, and to the search engines so that your content can be consumed.

That's where themes come in. Themes control the presentation layer of your site. That includes both the user experience and how it is offered to the consumer as well as the logic that determines which type of page, and therefore which type of loop, is to be used.

This chapter reviews how to install a theme on your web site and then takes you through the various aspects of a theme and how they apply to the presentation of your content. We will be focusing on using the wonderful Sandbox theme framework. By the end of this chapter you will have an understanding on theme functionality and establish a solid foundation for you to build your own custom themes from scratch for use in your own projects.

WHY USE A THEME?

Your web site theme is essentially the face of your web site. It is what makes the first impression on your visitor. Even though none of us are shallow enough to judge a book simply by its cover, if your web site has valuable content but your theme makes the content hard to read, hard to find, generally inaccessible in any way, or is slow to load, not to mention downright ugly, you have probably lost that visitor. Based on first impressions, you may never have had that visitor to lose.

The theme accomplishes many things for your web site. Generally people think of the theme as the appearance of your site. It is the look and feel that gives your web site that certain style or flair. It is the x-factor that gives your site a personality and makes your site stand out from the crowd. Your theme is all that; a picture really is worth a thousand words.

But this is simply the graphical aspect of your site; your theme is so much more than the cohesive marketing and branding facade. Your theme encompasses the entire user experience and more. Your theme controls what content gets rendered, including any error conditions. Your theme converts your content and look and feel into the raw HTML that is delivered to the browser through its various templates.

In general, that is what this chapter is about: using your theme to structure and control the content delivery and the overall personality of your web site. Your theme also has other functions including user experience and search engine optimization, which are addressed in later chapters.

INSTALLING A THEME

Your web site is up and running, but out of the box it uses the boring old Kubrik default theme (sorry everyone, it is boring, and may be one of the reasons developers see WordPress as only a blog engine). How do you make WordPress use a new theme? First, you either have to find one you like or make one. Countless WordPress theme resources are available, and they all vary in quality. It is best to try some out and see how they work with your content and if they match the personality and branding you want your site to convey.

You have two simple ways to activate a new theme on your web site. There is the traditional FTP installation, and as of WordPress 2.8 there is a new integrated theme browser and installer. The Theme Browser is limited in that it allows you to install themes only from the sanctioned WordPress Theme Directory on WordPress.org. This is not inherently bad, because plenty of solid, good-looking themes are in the Theme Directory and they are all GPL licensed and free (two of the requirements for being listed in the Directory). However, the Directory is a limited market; heaps of other sites offer valuable WordPress themes, still of varying quality, both for free and for premiums. In order to install these non-Directory themes you will have to use the FTP method.

FTP Installation

File Transfer Protocol, or FTP, is the old standby for transferring files from your local workstation to the server. If your host supports it, you should use a secure form of transfer, such as SFTP or SCP, to move the files, but the concepts here are similar.

Download the theme package that you would like to try to your local computer and unzip it to a local directory. If you have shell access on your server, you can unzip on the server to save in transfer time. FTP or copy the files into your themes directory of your site. Your themes folder is located in /example.com/wp-content/themes/.

Once your theme files are on the server, log in to your site's WordPress Control Panel. Select Appearance, select your theme to preview it, and then activate it. Your web site is now using the new theme.

Theme Installer

WordPress 2.8 introduced a new Theme Installer. In your WordPress Control Panel under Appearance you will see a new menu item titled Add New Themes.

This new Control Panel item allows the site administrator (or anyone else with proper permissions) to search and filter the online WordPress Theme Directory. All themes in the Directory are subject to certain conditions in order to be listed; most notably, they must be licensed to be GPL compatible.

This new Theme Installer is pretty slick. You simply work the filters and search terms to browse the Directory until you find one you like. Click Install for the screenshot preview and then click Install again to actually install it.

On a development system running Microsoft Vista and WAMP, this just works, which is a little disconcerting. It is a permissions issue in your webroot. Although this raises some concerns about what else could so easily be installed on the site, in this case, it is just a development machine, and the convenience of being able to test drive new themes outweighs the concerns.

Trying the Theme Installer on a production server for a WordPress site running on Ubuntu Linux may yield different results. After selecting an appropriate obnoxious theme to try out, the Theme Installer asked for FTP credentials to put the files on the server, In this case because the file security permissions on the production server are properly set for production and not to allow this sort of thing. Again, there is some concern about the actual security implications of giving out FTP credentials that are required to proceed. This is similar to how the WordPress core updates and plugin updates work. See Chapter 11 on securing your WordPress installation for information about directory permissions.

In short, the Theme Installer is really slick and convenient for development to test out new themes, but due to possible security implications, carefully consider its use in a production environment. The balance of convenience and security is often a difficult choice.

WHAT IS A THEME?

What actually makes up a theme? You have an idea of what themes do, but how do they do it and what's really involved? As previously mentioned, a theme does several things, including structuring your content and providing the personality of your web site. This is done through a combination of files and file types. You will notice a mix of PHP files and CSS files in the theme. A good WordPress theme keeps the style, which is CSS, separate from the structure and logic, which make up the PHP files. Although there are always reasons for breaking the rules, striving to keep these separate will improve the maintainability and efficiency of your theme. Each theme has variations on these files and each theme's files are different.

Template Files

Template files are the meat of your theme. Template files are PHP code files that control what content gets shown to your visitor. These files also render the HTML to the browser to control how your content is shown. WordPress actually decides which template file to use based on the content requested.

Certain template files are used for different tasks. At first glance the quantity of template files in a theme can be daunting. Although each theme is different, some have only a couple of files, while others can be very complex. After you learn the different files involved in a theme, we will review the Template Hierarchy which is the mechanism WordPress uses to determine which templates to use when.

This Template Hierarchy, covered later in this chapter and the numerous types of template files available can be overwhelming when you are starting out on theme design, but you will develop an appreciation for the power of this setup. This flexibility allows for a huge amount of control over your site and what is delivered to the browser, which is the beauty of WordPress and definitely one of its strongest traits.

CSS

WordPress themes truly strive to separate content from style. A theme developer can ignore these guidelines and create a poorly divided theme, but a good theme developer does this well.

A theme must have at least one cascading style sheet. The primary style sheet for the theme must be named `style.css`. In addition, the first few lines of this style sheet file must adhere to certain guidelines. These specific requirements are covered later in this chapter in the section on the stylesheet. WordPress uses this information to determine which themes are available to the WordPress site and to make them show up in the Appearance Control Panel.

The style sheet is just what it sounds like. It is where you put all your CSS styles. How you structure it, or what you do with it, is entirely up to the theme developer. CSS development is both an art and a science and a whole topic worthy of its own discussion. We are not going to cover the intricacies of CSS in this book, but Wrox has a number of excellent CSS titles that can assist you on this topic.

Images and Assets

The theme probably includes some image files and other creative assets, possibly Adobe Flash files. These assets are used in your theme to give your web site a special look and feel; the look you want. How these files are structured in your theme is up to you; generally they are placed in a subfolder of the theme's main directory, such as `img/`, `images/`, or `assets/`. One of the nice things about themes being compartmentalized and packaged like they are is that the images can be referenced with relative paths from your CSS file.

In addition, these creative assets can be referenced from your template files using built-in WordPress functions such as `bloginfo('stylesheet_directory')`. This keeps the theme very portable, if done properly.

Plugins

As covered in Chapter 7, plugins contribute advanced functionality to a web site. Some themes require specific plugins because the functionality is part of the theme's personality, or they are needed to achieve a certain purpose in the theme. These plugins may be packaged with theme or may require separate downloads. All plugins reside in the plugin folder.

CREATING YOUR OWN THEME

Now you know how to install and activate a theme on your site as well as what the different aspects of the theme are. It's time to take the next step and make your own theme. You can start a theme from scratch, but why not stand on the shoulders of giants and start with a theme that is similar to the look you want? Or, if you cannot find one, start with a theme framework where most of the heavy lifting is done for you. There is no sense in reinventing the wheel, especially when you can use the power of open source software and start from working code.

Starting from a Working Theme

Sometimes it is easiest to find a theme close to what you have in mind and modify it. At the minimum, you can add your own logo. Of course you have to pay special attention to the licensing on the theme. Conveniently, themes in the `wordpress.org` Theme Directory are all GPL themes, so you can modify and use them however you desire.

Things to consider when starting from a working theme include:

➤ Licensing on the original theme

➤ Code quality

➤ How much modification will be required

➤ Source artwork for the creative assets

You will want to make sure that you are permitted to change the source theme you are starting with. You will also want to review the code quality of the theme, because you will be the one making the modifications going forward. Does the theme accomplish the same presentation goals as your site, template-wise; does it convey your data the way you want it conveyed? There is no point in starting with a theme that you have to completely retool. Does the theme have enough CSS hooks for you to style? Was search engine optimization (SEO) a consideration when the theme was developed? How much modification will be needed to meet your requirements and will you be happy with the end result? Finally, does the theme come with source art, like the original Photoshop document, for you to modify? If not, do you need it, or will you be able to re-create any assets you must have?

You have many considerations when developing a new or modified theme for either yourself or a client. The convenience of modifying a pre-built theme is quite a temptation to get a site up and running and out the door quickly. In practice, many sites have been built this way, where a client could select a stock template with a few minor modifications needed to quickly launch a new site. The catch is when a site goes beyond these simple modifications and you are stuck with modifying a poorly built theme. For that reason, even if a client likes a particular theme preview, you may find it easier in the long run to rebuild a similar theme from scratch with the Sandbox theme as a starting point.

Starting with the Sandbox Theme

Building a theme using a theme framework provides many advantages, especially for development teams. Because all of our deployed themes use this framework, we already have an idea of how the parts of the theme work. In addition, we have a common CSS vocabulary — rather than reading each theme's style sheet, we can expect certain styles to be available because at the core is a theme framework. Finally, using a theme framework takes most of the heavy lifting out of the theme development process because many common problems and browser incompatibilities have already been addressed.

For example, the Sandbox theme framework has pre-built examples for several different web site styles. One-column, two-column (with the sidebar on the left or right), and three-column examples are shipped with the framework. All of these variants have been tried and tested in the current browsers and are known to work. This is extremely convenient when you need to start a site quickly. It should be noted that once you resize the sidebar widths in the CSS, you will have to tweak the entire CSS layout to accommodate different browsers' rendering quirks (Internet Explorer will always cause you problems) but with a little arithmetic, it's not too difficult to work out.

The Sandbox framework is very well thought out and loaded with CSS hooks for the body HTML element, each post, and each comment. For example, with a default Sandbox template, the body tag of each HTML document is multi-classed with a wide range of details. Using the Firebug add-on for Firefox, available online at http://getfirebug.com/, consider this inspection of a single-post page shown in Figure 8-1.

 If you are not using Firebug for development of the front end of your web site, you are really missing out. Firebug has proven to be the most valuable web developer's tool in recent memory.

```
Inspect   Edit | body.wordpress ‹ html
Console   HTML   CSS   Script   DOM   Net                                    Options ⋆
⊟ <html lang="en-US" xmlns="http://www.w3.org/1999/xhtml" dir="ltr">
   ⊞ <head profile="http://gmpg.org/xfn/11">
   ⊟ <body class="wordpress y2009 m06 d22 h21 single postid-3 s-y2009 s-m06 s-d22 s-h21 s-category-
      uncategorized s-author-ddamstra loggedin">
      ⊟ <div id="wrapper" class="hfeed">
         ⊞ <div id="header">
         ⊞ <div id="access">
         ⊟ <div id="container">
            ⊟ <div id="content">
               ⊞ <div id="nav-above" class="navigation">
               ⊞ <div id="post-3" class="hentry p1 post publish author-david category-uncategorized
                  untagged y2009 m06 d22 h21">
               ⊞ <div id="nav-below" class="navigation">
               ⊞ <div id="comments">
```

FIGURE 8-1: Firebug inspection of stock Sandbox theme CSS classes

The body tag is classed with year, month, day, and hour of the post, as well as the category, tags, and author. If the post were tagged with multiple keywords or in multiple categories, they would each be listed. Similar functionality has recently been added to the WordPress core and will work just as well, and in fact, many framework-type themes are emulating this behavior because it is so powerful to the front end developer. We feel this stands as a further testament on why Sandbox is a great theme to begin your theme build.

This same multi-classed CSS also applies to the posts on a loop page and the comments. The vast array of CSS hooks allows for easy CSS styling and opens up a ton of possibilities. Posts could be styled by the time of day they were posted or change colors every month to give your site an "edition" feel.

Additionally, Sandbox is chock-full of microformat support. Microformats are part of the semantic web, where markup enhances the content by following certain conventions. Search engines and some browsers respect these conventions and augment the user experience with the additional structured content. You will see microformats in the author information and a few other spots throughout the Sandbox theme.

 In the Sandbox theme, each post is classed with the CSS class hentry. *Hentry is part of the Atom microformat specification.*

You will find that with the stock Sandbox installation your theme is very minimal and plain. That is entirely by design. Sandbox is intended to be a minimal theme, but is entirely functional. Some people find this type of theme very appealing; after all, beauty is in the eye of the beholder. For development, this is advantageous because you are not bringing any cobwebs with you. With Sandbox you are building up entirely from a solid CSS foundation.

Sandbox is widget compatible with dynamic sidebars. It does, however, have only the two traditional sidebars built in, whereas some newer theme frameworks have multiple widget-ready zones — *sidebars* seems a misnomer when they are placed in different locations on the page.

The Sandbox theme does have its flaws. The minimal CSS is both a blessing and a burden. The default appearance looks basic and unfinished. No matter what, you will have to add some styling, which is expected. But with some theme frameworks, the default styles are at least presentable.

The Sandbox theme also does not include CSS reset style sheet. This leaves browsers to render unstyled elements in their own different styles, which can lead to box model rendering problems. The simple fix is to use a reset style sheet at the beginning of the theme style sheet or refer to other reset style sheets such as Eric Meyers' which is available online at http://meyerweb.com/eric/tools/css/reset/.

If you are developing several themes for various clients, like we are, we recommend keeping a modified Sandbox theme in your toolbox. Our modified Sandbox theme is the starting point for all internally developed themes. This "Better Sandbox" theme addresses the preceding issues, including delineating some base typography to build on and resetting elements to improve browser rendering. Our foundation theme also includes many common styles that are used across sites but are lacking in the stock Sandbox. These additional styles include classes like success and error for appropriate messages and extend the development team's common vocabulary.

Several newer theme frameworks have built on the Sandbox ideas. These are discussed later in this chapter. You should try these other frameworks and make a decision for yourself. In our opinion, Sandbox continues to be an excellent theme foundation to start with and it is what we continue to use daily. The balance between learning a theme framework on top of the WordPress framework and being able to dive right in on the PHP fits our needs nicely.

CREATING YOUR OWN THEME: GETTING STARTED

Creating your own theme can be as simple or as complicated as you want it to be. Sometimes, you merely want to change a logo or a color and it is a basic process. Often, you are creating a theme from scratch to meet a certain need or condition, or solely to obtain a specific design look and feel. Whatever your motivations are, this section discusses the basics for getting a new theme and site design up quickly using the Sandbox theme as a foundation.

Essential File: Style.css

The `style.css` file is what WordPress uses to reference your theme, and this file is required for your theme to work. In practice, you could create a new theme with only a style sheet and `index.php` template file, though the index file can be empty. Using the power of WordPress's theme hierarchy, WordPress automatically substitutes missing templates if your new theme does not have them. More on that later, but understand that is what allows you to get started creating your own theme.

In practice, a `style.css` file is all you need to create a new theme. See the section on child themes later in the chapter.

When creating your own `styles.css` for your new theme, the first few lines are absolutely critical. These lines provide information to WordPress to use in the theme Control Panel and further reference your theme in the core. Your first few lines should read as follows (substitute your information, of course):

```
/*
THEME NAME: MyTheme
THEME URI: http://www.mirmillo.com/mytheme/
DESCRIPTION: Theme for my new site.  Based on Sandbox.
VERSION: 1.0
AUTHOR: David Damstra (and friends)
AUTHOR URI: http://mirmillo.com/author/ddamstra
TAGS: sandbox, microformats, hcard, hatom, xoxo, widgets, blank slate,
starter theme, minimalist, developer
*/
```

The information here is pretty self-explanatory. There is an additional optional field for theme hierarchy, covered later in the chapter. Make sure your theme name is unique to your installation. If you intend to release your theme for public use, either for free or for a premium, you should try to come up with a unique name to reduce naming collision in the directory and other installations. In addition, if you are deriving your theme from another theme, license permitting of course, you should uphold the license and copyright information from the original theme. Once you have addressed this required information for WordPress, the remainder of the file is traditional CSS and subject to the rules and structure imposed as such.

Not all development shops use the child theme functionality that is covered later. In some cases, the workflow fits better if a new theme is created by copying and renaming the foundation theme to a new folder and revising the `style.css` to reflect the new project. This technique has pros and cons, but it works well for some teams because the foundation theme does not change often enough to warrant more complex methodologies. Plus, when you have a theme in production, you do not want a change to the parent theme to cause a cascading rendering issue in your successfully deployed site. Creating a copy and making a working theme in this new directory removes the dependency on future browser rendering testing, which is a time- and human-intensive procedure — that is, no one has automated this procedure yet. In the event that there is a substantial change to the parent theme, changes can be ported to the derivative themes on a case-by-case basis and tested as needed. Making a copy of the foundation theme also presents the advantage of creating a hand-crafted CSS file by modifying the actual theme files rather than overriding the styles and carrying that additional byte baggage.

The next step in your CSS file is to determine the layout of your web site. Sandbox provides several example layouts for the common web site arrangements, so generally the next line in the CSS is usually pulling in this structure, like so:

```
/* Two-column with sidebar on left from the /examples/ folder  */
@import url('examples/2c-1.css');
```

This line of code imports the two-column with the sidebar on the left-hand side example layout from the Sandbox examples. Because we are starting with a full copy of the stock Sandbox theme, we have access to the pre-built examples. Notice the relative path reference to the `2c-1.css` file. The example layouts are excellent ways to get your site layout established and then modify them to match your specific design as needed. Of course, you do not have to start with the example layouts and could build your own structure from scratch. If you intend to use one of the CSS grid layouts that are currently in fashion, this may be the way to go. You can mix and match different CSS frameworks to fit your needs.

For example, as previously mentioned the Sandbox theme is a very minimal theme and does not address typography or some common use classes. In some themes we have tried various stock typography CSS frameworks to get up and going quickly. For example:

```
/* blue trip typography */
@import url('bluetrip/screen.css');
```

In this example theme we imported the nice Blue Trip Typography CSS from `bluetrip.org`. We stripped out all the styles except the typography classes to reduce conflicts. The downside to importing these style sheets and using pre-built classes is that your sheets may contain extraneous rules that you will never use, or do not know they exist, and that extra baggage is carried down to the browser in added load time. There certainly is a trade-off in using some pre-fabricated CSS versus handcrafting it all yourself for your specific needs. This is a choice you have to make as a developer.

Moving forward, CSS rules are written out in the `style.css` file to turn your minimal layout into the professionally designed theme you are creating. CSS coding is outside the scope of this book and if done well, is an art and skill. Again, Wrox has several great books on working with CSS.

Showing Your Content: Index.php

When creating your theme, you often have a chicken-and-egg problem. Maybe you are lucky and you know exactly what content is going to be published on your WordPress site, and exactly how it's going to be structured. Maybe you even know exactly how the final theme is going to look, or you've had a professional designer create some mockups for you. But odds are, your site is going to grow organically and to see how the design, and therefore the style sheet, is going to play out, you need to have some content to display.

You can use certain stock content files to import into your site and work through all the styles or you can start building your site.

The index.php file is the default template of your site. WordPress has a built-in decision engine that decides which type of information your visitor is requesting and then determines if there is a template file available for that information type. This hierarchy is covered later in the chapter, but the index.php template is the default, or template of last resort. If WordPress does not determine that there is a more specific template to use, index.php is it.

Usually the index.php file contains your standard loop. This is a traditional blog format where the posts are displayed in reverse chronological order. For example, this is the loop from the Sandbox:

```php
<?php while ( have_posts() ) : the_post() ?>
    <div id="post-<?php the_ID() ?>" class="<?php sandbox_post_class() ?>">
        <h2 class="entry-title">
            <a href="<?php the_permalink() ?>"
                    title="<?php printf( __('Permalink to %s','sandbox'),
             the_title_attribute('echo=0') ) ?>" rel="bookmark">
                    <?php the_title() ?>
            </a>
        </h2>
        <div class="entry-date">
            <abbr class="published" title="<?php the_time('Y-m-d\TH:i:sO') ?>">
              <?php unset($previousday); printf( __( '%1$s &#8211; %2$s', 'sandbox' ),
                the_date( '', '', '', false ), get_the_time() ) ?>
            </abbr>
        </div>
        <div class="entry-content">
            <?php the_content( __( 'Read More <span class="meta-nav">&raquo;</span>',
             'sandbox' ) ) ?>
            <?php wp_link_pages('before=<div class="page-link">'
             . __( 'Pages:', 'sandbox' ) . '&after=</div>') ?>
        </div>
        <div class="entry-meta">
            <span class="author vcard">
                <?php printf( __( 'By %s', 'sandbox' ), '<a class="url fn n" href="' .
                get_author_link( false, $authordata->ID, $authordata->user_nicename ) .
                '" title="' . sprintf( __( 'View all posts by %s', 'sandbox' ),
                $authordata->display_name ) . '">' . get_the_author() . '</a>' ) ?>
            </span>
            <span class="meta-sep">|</span>
            <span class="cat-links">
                <?php printf( __( 'Posted in %s', 'sandbox' ),
                 get_the_category_list(', ') ) ?>
            </span>
            <span class="meta-sep">|</span>
            <?php the_tags( __( '<span class="tag-links">Tagged ', 'sandbox' ), ", ",
             "</span>\n\t\t\t\t\t<span class=\"meta-sep\">|</span>\n" ) ?>
            <?php edit_post_link( __( 'Edit', 'sandbox' ),
                 "\t\t\t\t\t<span class=\"edit-link\">",
             "</span>\n\t\t\t\t\t<span class=\"meta-sep\">|</span>\n" ) ?>
            <span class="comments-link">
                <?php comments_popup_link( __( 'Comments (0)', 'sandbox' ), __(
                 'Comments (1)', 'sandbox' ), __( 'Comments (%)', 'sandbox' ) ) ?>
            </span>
        </div>
    </div><!-- .post -->
```

```
                    <?php comments_template() ?>
               <?php endwhile; ?>
```

As covered in Chapter 5, the loop is really the heart of WordPress. It is the most important concept to grasp because it is how your content is read out to be published. The Sandbox main loop is a traditional loop but includes all the semantic HTML, microformats, and CSS hooks that make the Sandbox theme a great foundation.

There certainly is a ton of stuff going on in that code snippet, but if you break it apart into the discrete sections and cross reference it with the rendered HTML, it will all come together quite quickly. Realize, also, that this loop uses many Sandbox-specific functions to simplify the coding, even if it appears to complicate the template. Theme functions are covered later in this chapter.

Showing Your Content in Different Ways: Index.php

The index.php file is really the most important template file in your theme. Although you cannot have an active theme in WordPress without styles.css — because that is how WordPress knows you have the theme available — index.php does the heavy lifting.

In the early days of WordPress, the index template was the only template. The whole theme was just this one file, and it was really just the loop. That worked fine for WordPress when you used it as a traditional blog and this bloggy look is probably why WordPress is still derided as a blog engine.

We hope you are reading this book because you know WordPress can be so much more, or if you did not know, you are realizing it now. Your index template is very important; we cannot stress that enough. It is the template of last resort that WordPress will use when it cannot find a more specific one to use (see "Template Hierarchy," later in the chapter.)

Nevertheless, your index file does not have to be a single loop showing your most recent posts. That is very traditional, and may work well for your site, but you can branch out. Your index file can be structured in so many different ways, it is truly limitless. It could contain multiple different loops from different tags or categories, or it could contain no loops at all. The index template could function as your error page, where you have more specific templates for every other piece of content in your site.

CREATING YOUR OWN THEME: DRY

As just discussed, these are the basics; WordPress requires a style.css file with properly formatted header information and it is required to have an index.php template. Now you want to expand your theme to use more template files and capitalize on the robust theme engine found in WordPress.

A good developer knows that you do not want to repeat code in multiple places; it is a bad design and gives your code one of those nasty smells. (You knew that right?) The code smell is called Don't Repeat Yourself (DRY) and is in fact one of the easiest smells to get a whiff of, and avoid. When you find yourself tempted to cut and paste a code block from one template to another, that should be your first whiff. Here is your opportunity to break out your templates into reusable parts. There are three obvious places where you can do this because you will reuse these components on nearly all pages on your site to give it that cohesive look and feel and structure. The header, the footer, and the sidebar information is essentially the same on all pages. We also show you how to tweak these included files with additional logic to handle design exceptions.

Header.php

We think this file is a misnamed, but it is the standard name of this file that WordPress looks for. The header.php file includes everything at the top of your rendered page, up to the content area. The reason we think this is confusing is because a properly formatted HTML document includes its own <head> information, which has its own special requirements. This header.php template file includes the HTML head, but it also includes the start of the HTML document and usually includes the site logo and navigation, assuming you are using an across-the-top horizontal navigation scheme. It can also include any additional elements at the top of your page, such as secondary navigation or a search area.

Because this file includes so much more than the HTML header, we tend to take the printing term and call this area the *nameplate*, as in the nameplate of a newspaper or magazine. However, we do stick with tradition and leave the filename header.php in order to remain compatible with the built-in functionality of WordPress.

When creating your header template file there is a very important WordPress function that must be included: wp_head(). This is a hook for WordPress to queue in certain functionality into your site and is used by plugins. For some reason this function is not included in early Sandbox templates, so check that it is included.

```
<!DOCTYPE html     PUBLIC "-//W3C//DTD XHTML 1.0 Strict//EN"
"http://www.w3.org/TR/xhtml1/DTD/xhtml1-strict.dtd">
<html xmlns="http://www.w3.org/1999/xhtml" <?php language_attributes() ?>>
<head profile="http://gmpg.org/xfn/11">
    <title>
        <?php wp_title( '-', true, 'right' );
         echo wp_specialchars( get_bloginfo('name'), 1 ) ?>
    </title>
    <meta http-equiv="content-type" content="<?php bloginfo('html_type') ?>;
     charset=<?php bloginfo('charset') ?>" />
    <link rel="stylesheet" type="text/css" href="<?php bloginfo('stylesheet_url')
     ? >" />
    <?php wp_head(); ?>
```

The wp_head() function is dropped in your HTML <head> node and is critical to the long-term compatibility and functionality of your theme.

Now that you have broken out the nameplate section of your pages into the separate header.php template, you need to adjust your index.php file to include it. You could use the traditional PHP include or require family of functions, but the WordPress core functionality has a handy function to get around the theme paths. At the top of your index.php (and subsequent template files discussed later) simply add the following code:

```
<?php
    get_header()
?>
```

This function automatically includes the filename header.php from the current theme's directory into the current file for rendering. This function does not have any additional functionality over a PHP include besides determining the correct include path for you, but we find it much more readable when working on a theme.

Optionally, you could split out additional components from your `header.php` file and include them back in with PHP `includes`. Occasionally, if a site has a particularly long or complex global navigation, we break it out for inclusion. In practice, working on smaller files is easier for editing, because each template file has a specific function and reduces the complexity of debugging.

> *In a past life, one of the authors was called in to work on a web application where the entire application was created in a single file and the functionality was handled by triggering specific functions. Although the functions were nicely broken out, any time the application had to be debugged, the error messages were nearly meaningless. Although the line number would change (and skyrocket into the multiple thousands) they all occurred in* index.php *and inevitably the whole application had to be traced to determine what happened.*
>
> *Imagine how much easier it would be to troubleshoot a problem on the application if the error message indicated that the error took place in a 100-line navigation file, rather than a 10,000-line complete application file.*
>
> *Everyone writes bad code in their careers, and certainly we are no exceptions, though none of us wrote this atrocity. What we are saying is do yourself a favor and break code into smaller, manageable files whenever possible.*

Footer.php

In the same vein as the `header.php` file, everything below your content area should be separated out into a footer file. The nature of footer files has changed recently. Historically they have been the copyright and contact information but in recent years, this real estate has been expanded to include additional navigation options and information relevant to your site. What you put in your footer is up to you, but because it remains by and large the same on every page, it is a prime candidate for breaking out into a separate include.

Again, make sure you incorporate the `wp_foot()` function into your footer template. This function allows WordPress to inject any necessary information from your active plugins and, as a rule, will include your `</body></html>` closing tags.

Similar to the way your header template is included, WordPress offers the same functionality for your footer information. At the bottom of your template files add the following code:

```
<?php
    get_footer()
?>
```

Sidebar.php

Another candidate for breaking out is the sidebar, which is everything to the right or left of your content. This could be the navigation of your site, if you have elected a vertical navigation scheme, as well as the less important, or supporting information on your site.

The Sandbox theme includes both a right and left sidebar in the same `sidebar.php` file and hides any unused sidebars with CSS. This certainly is not optimized for your final site, but when using the example layouts it is an easy way to get something up and going quickly, although we all know proof of concept usually becomes proof of production.

You have some considerations to take for sidebars. You have to decide first how many you are going to have. Second, you have to decide if they are going to be static sidebars, widgetized sidebars, or some hybrid. Finally, you have to determine how the HTML is structured so that you can make the CSS put the sidebars in the correct spots. Then you have to test in your target browsers and in all likelihood start over. Such is the life of the web developer.

As mentioned, the Sandbox theme's stock sidebars are both included in the same file and are fully widgetized. This enables you to sketch up a site with relative ease and use the WordPress Control Panel to place widgets as needed.

In your template files place the following code to include the `sidebar.php` file:

```php
<?php get_sidebar(); ?>
```

Sometimes having both sidebars in the same file does not pan out in the design, or more likely, the CSS. Or, you have broken out the sidebars into individuals files for each sidebar location. For whatever reason, you can create two sidebar files for the traditional left and right places. For example

```php
<?php
    get_sidebar('right');
?>
```

gets the file named `sidebar-right.php`, as indicated in the parameter of the function call and includes it in the appropriate place.

More advanced theme frameworks have multiple sidebars that break from the common notion that a sidebar is vertical space on the left and right of your content. Some of these theme frameworks have what are essentially sidebars above, below and even in middle of the post loops. Having multiple widgetized areas like this transfers some power to the site administrator who can now place WordPress widgets all over the layout of the page.

An important consideration when working with sidebars is keeping the balance between what portions are widgetized — meaning they can be controlled and managed by the content creator in the Control Panel — and what portions are hard-coded in PHP into the template file. Widgets can be very powerful, especially with some of the plugins that are available. But there are also cases where PHP code in the template file will get the job done and the content does not need to be updated by the administrator or is using built in WordPress functionality to keep itself updated. Keeping this balance right is a developer decision.

Deviations from the Norm: Conditional Tags

You have been a good developer and broken out all your repeating code snippets into their own templates or inclusion files. Good job, but the marketing director just called, and even though the site is almost done, and he signed off on the design, he forgot to tell you that all the pages and posts in the Ponies category are supposed to have a pretty rainbow in the nameplate next to the site's logo.

Personal taste aside, this sucks, because you just made all the `header.php` files the same, and now only a handful of them need some special consideration.

As with all things open source, you have many ways to handle this situation. You could probably handle such a simple example with some well-crafted CSS and the Sandbox theme alone. Alternatively, you could create a whole category template file (discussed later) to style just this category. But because you're only dealing with a tiny element, it seems like overkill to create a whole new template file.

But wait, all is not lost. WordPress developers have had to deal with marketing directors before and knew this type of situation would come up eventually, which is why they included Conditional Tags. WordPress has many Conditional Tags built in, and covering each one is outside the scope of this book, not to mention particularly boring. But rest assured, these Conditional Tags exist, and can address specific needs such as what type of page is being viewed, or the meta information about the content on the page.

To appease the marketing director, you might include something like this in the `header.php` file:

```
<div id="nameplate">
    <h1 id="blog-title">
        <span>
            <a href="<?php bloginfo('home') ?>/" title="<?php echo
              wp_specialchars( get_bloginfo('name'), 1 ) ?>" rel="home">
                <img id="logo" src="<?php bloginfo('template_directory');
                 ?>/img/logo_black.png" alt="My Stables Website " />
                 <?php bloginfo('name') ?>
            </a>
        </span>
    </h1>
    <?php
    if (is_category('Ponies')) { ?>
        // overlay a pretty rainbow on the logo for the ponies category
        <img id="raibow" src="<?php bloginfo('template_directory');?>
         /img/rainbow.png" alt="OMG! Ponies! " />
    <?php } ?>
    <span id="blog-description"><?php bloginfo('description') ?></span>
</div>
```

Now, any time the category of the content of the current page is in the Ponies category, your header also includes the `rainbow.png`. With PNG's alpha transparency, it actually turns out pretty nice. This example only works for the category pages and not for the individual single posts pages in the "Ponies" category.

CREATING YOUR OWN THEME: CONTENT DISPLAY

A good theme enhances the content on your site. Not only is it visually appealing, suitable for the nature of the site, and brand appropriate, but the theme should also structure the content properly. WordPress has a variety of different templates and functionality to meet the needs of every site type. Uncovering the best combination of template files to include in order to achieve the optimal organization of your content is the challenge here. Not all themes need to have every template file type, and most do not; it is best to mix and match templates to meet your needs.

Customizing Your Homepage: home.php

Homepage — who uses that term anymore? It sounds so 1990s, but we do not know what else to call this. In this section we are talking about the first page on your site when a visitor goes to your root

URL. Apache users know that the index page of your site, the homepage if you will, is called "index." It is usually called "default" on a Microsoft IIS server. The WordPress Control Panel refers to this as the front page, we can run with it for consistency's sake.

A theme should always have an index.php file because after all else, index.php is the template of last resort. What if want your front page to have a special layout, perhaps one that features something about your site — product pages, for example? You do not want to mess with your index.php layout because you do not want reinvent your whole theme just to accommodate this one special layout.

Plugins and other tricks are available to handle this scenario; in fact, you can even use the WordPress control panel to set a static front page. But the easiest way is to use the built-in template hierarchy and set a special front page by using a home.php template.

Creating a special layout, and therefore template file, for your front page is useful when your front page is unique. By and large, creating a unique front page is a marketing tool. Some reasons for creating a unique front page include:

➤ Featuring or showcasing a product or service

➤ Featuring or showcasing other portions of your web site

➤ Driving traffic to a certain portion of your site

➤ Explanatory steps of the processes involved with your product

➤ Delineating tiered levels of service that you provide

Take a look at the basic example in Figure 8-2, where the front page is showcasing products or services that the web site is marketing. These products would have their own supporting pages or posts in your site. Your front page has a nice image showcase front and center with links to the individual pages. You'll use jQuery to enhance this showcase and rotate through the images. Alternatively, you could use a different JavaScript toolkit or Adobe Flash, but jQuery is already included with WordPress and, frankly, it rocks, so you will use that. The bottom portion of the layout will include a recent news section.

If you cannot tell already, this is going to involve multiple loops. We will use the first loop to create the content for the showcase. This loop will pull posts from a specific category. That way, the site admin can add and remove content from the showcase as needed, without visiting the code at all. Of course there will be certain design restrictions, such as image size and format and possibly certain conventions that must be followed in the post, but the ability to change this information in the WordPress Control Panel is a very powerful tool.

The showcase loop could look something like this:

```
<div id="showcase">
    <?php
    $my_query = new WP_Query("category_name=Showcase&showposts=3&orderby=rand");
    while ($my_query->have_posts()) : $my_query->the_post();
        echo '<div id="showcase-'.$post->ID.'" class="slide" title="' .
            $post->post_title .'">';
        echo '<div class="showcase-post-content">'. $post->post_content .'</div>';
        echo '</div>';
    endwhile;
    ?>
</div>
```

This could would create an HTML rendering as shown in Figure 8-2.

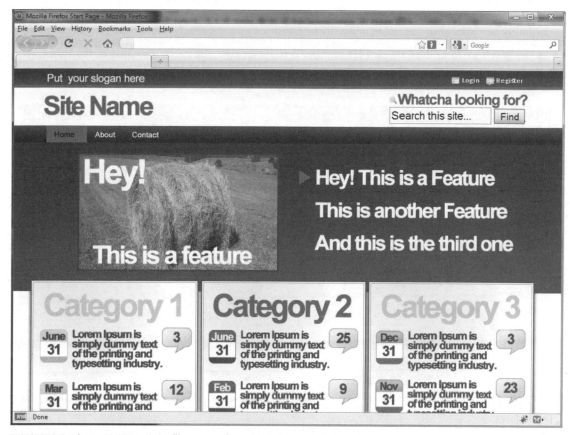

FIGURE 8-2: A special template file can make your front page look unique.

Take a look at what is happening here. The whole showcase loop is wrapped in a <div> with an id of "showcase." This is for the jQuery to hook onto later. In the PHP code, you are creating a custom query for the loop. The query is looking for posts in the Showcase category, which you would have previously set up in the WordPress Control Panel. It is only pulling three posts from the category and returning them in random order. The loop then proceeds to create three <div> elements, each with a unique ID, again for jQuery and CSS hooks. The content of the posts would contain a properly sized image for the showcase to work. Finally, countless jQuery plugins are available that can turn this now unwieldy block of content on your page into a very elegant slideshow.

The bottom section could be a traditional loop similar to the index.php template stock loop. But, you do not want the showcase posts to also show up in the current news area, because that would look goofy and unprofessional. So you would want to exclude the Showcase category from the second loop. Like this:

```php
<?php
    query_posts("cat=-3&paged=$paged&showposts=3");
?>
<div id="recentNews">
    <?php while (have_posts() ) : the_post() ?>
    // output posts
```

Here we are creating a new query for the recent news section using the `query_posts()` function. In this example, the query is excluding category 3 (`cat=-3`), which is the category ID for the `Showcase` category and grabbing three posts in paginated format. To exactly match the preceding mockup, it would probably be easier (but not more efficient) to run three queries, one for each category content box.

The easiest way to find a category ID number is to hover over the category name in the Edit Category Control Panel and look in the status bar at the bottom of the browser window, as shown in Figure 8-3.

FIGURE 8-3: Hover over the category name in the Control Panel to see the category ID in the status bar.

Sandbox does not come with this template built in because when using this template you are already on your way to creating a custom theme. Also, this is not the only way to get this functionality. As of WordPress 2.1, you can control what is shown on your front page and set it to any static page you have created and then create a special page template to accomplish the previously described design decisions. This is one of those choices you have to make as a developer and balance the needs of your client with the ease of maintenance for your developers.

Show Your Older Posts by Date: Archive.php

Eventually, if you are diligent, your site will have older content. And if you are really industrious you will be able to do those fun "one year ago on my site I told you about X" posts. Eventually you may have copious amounts of content, and so much that it is not feasible or appealing to show it all on the front page. That is, if content is being generated on a regular schedule, there will come a point in time where you will want to refer to something that is clearly not going to be still on the front page or in the recent posts lists; this is the time when you need to delve into the vault of past content.

This is where the `archive.php` template steps in. You have many ways to present your older content. Harking back to WordPress's blogging origins, the most obvious method is to continue in reverse chronological order of your posts.

If you do not have an archive template, WordPress simply uses your index template to show the older posts. The Sandbox theme has an interesting take on the `archive.php` template and is very flexible in the date-based format. Consider this code from the Sandbox `archive.php` template:

```php
<?php if ( is_day() ) : ?>
    <h2 class="page-title">
        <?php printf( __( 'Daily Archives: <span>%s</span>', 'sandbox' ),
        get_the_time(get_option('date_format')) ) ?>
    </h2>
<?php elseif ( is_month() ) : ?>
    <h2 class="page-title">
        <?php printf( __( 'Monthly Archives: <span>%s</span>', 'sandbox' ),
        get_the_time('F Y') ) ?>
    </h2>
<?php elseif ( is_year() ) : ?>
    <h2 class="page-title">
        <?php printf( __( 'Yearly Archives: <span>%s</span>', 'sandbox' ),
        get_the_time('Y') ) ?>
    </h2>
<?php elseif ( isset($_GET['paged']) && !empty($_GET['paged']) ) : ?>
    <h2 class="page-title"><?php _e( 'Blog Archives', 'sandbox' ) ?></h2>
<?php endif; ?>
```

This code block shows how the Sandbox theme archive template displays a unique header depending on whether the visitor is looking at the archived posts for a day, a month, a whole year, or traversing by conventional pagination.

Except for the fact that WordPress is inherently date based, the archive template is not all that important. Although having the date information is useful when determining how recent certain information is, in reality, do you ever go back and look for posts published in May of 2007? More likely you are looking for posts on a certain topic or filed in a particular category or topic.

Showing Only One Category: Category.php

Enter the category template. The `category.php` template creates a loop of posts from only a specific category. The category template is invoked when a visitor hits a specific URL with the category name in it. This could be something like `http://example.com/category/ponies`. In the `category.php` template, WordPress has already determined that your visitor is looking for posts in the particular category requests, so the default loop automatically makes this query for you, no special interaction required.

When you use this template you can generically display category posts and information, which is the way the Sandbox theme is set up. For example, the Sandbox theme places a header and category explanation information pulled from the category description, if it is available:

```php
<h2 class="page-title">
    <?php _e( 'Category Archives:', 'sandbox' ) ?> <span><?php single_cat_title() ?>
    </span>
</h2>
<?php
```

```
$categorydesc = category_description();
    if ( !empty($categorydesc) ) {
        echo apply_filters( 'archive_meta', '<div class="archive-meta">' .
        $categorydesc . '</div>' );
    }
?>
```

This covers the default category case, which is a nice default fallback template to have. But what if you want to make each category template have a unique look, for example, a color scheme or an icon?

Let's go back to the marketing director and the Ponies category. Instead of using conditional tags, we can make a specific category template. Following the template hierarchy, WordPress will look to see if there exists a category template that is specific to the category requested in the URL. If you have not noticed yet, WordPress works from most specific to least specific until it finds the proper template. WordPress will select the most specific template for the type of information requested and work toward the more generic templates until it defaults to the index.php template.

For the marketing director, we can make a category-3.php template because the Ponies category has an ID of 3.

There is a little bit of chicken-and-egg problem when you want to create a category template for a specific category. In order to name the template file correctly you must create the category first to get the category ID.

These specific category templates work exactly the same as the generic category templates and pull the posts for that category automatically. Although technically, it works the other way around, WordPress already knows which posts it is going to show you, it is just determining how to show them to you. What you are gaining with using a specific category template is the flexibility to style each category individually.

You have probably noticed by now that with WordPress there is always more than one way to do something. In this simplest case, with the marketing director, you can solve his problem with conditional tags, category-specific templates, or if you are using the stock Sandbox theme, you can most likely meet his requirements by using CSS because Sandbox has rich CSS hooks.

But the extensibility of this feature is the killer aspect. Just knowing that WordPress has the feature built in will save you one day, as it has us.

Show Posts of a Specific Tag: Tag.php

The tag.php template functions nearly identically to the category.php template. It is invoked when a visitor requests a specific tag. This template is only beneficial if you are actively tagging the content on your site. Most likely, you are assigning categories to content, because that is a natural human organization structure, but tagging is not as clear cut, and often feels like an additional step.

Nevertheless, if you are diligent in tagging content, a tag template is a nice addition to your layouts and can be beneficial to cross-pollinate posts with related content. When this template is called, the loop automatically filled with posts of a particular tag for rendering. For a more in-depth look at how the loop actually works, refer to Chapter 5.

Likewise, you can create a template for a specific tag. The difference here is that the template filename uses the tag slug rather than the ID. If you wanted a special template for the Ponies tag, you would use

TO SHOW POST LIST <?WHILE (HAVE POST); THE_POST(); ?>
         <? THE_CONTENT ('READ THE REST OF THIS ENTRY'); ?>
      <? END WHILE ?>

TO SHOW EXCERPT REPLACE "THE_CONTENT" W/ THE_EXCERPT

the slug of the tag, to create a new template titled `tag-ponies.php`. You will need to verify the tag's slug on the Manage Tags Control Panel.

Using the category and tag templates may not be the way you envisioned your content being viewed, especially if you are using WordPress more as a content management system. However, simply including these templates is free functionality delivered from the WordPress core. These templates enable your visitors to explore your content in different ways and perhaps add a little stickiness to your site because your content is viewed in new and interesting ways. Categories and tags group related content and using these templates creates an organic presentation for discovery of your site.

Do not brush these off as simply reverse chronological listings of related content, like an archives page. Envision creative ways to present your data; because you have visitors who are interested in at least some of your content, why not expose them to related items?

How to Show a Single Post: single.php

You have set the bait with a great post headline, something witty and engaging. After the nibble you set the hook with your excerpt of the post, and now you caught the visitor. He has clicked through to read the rest of the article.

The `single.php` template view is most likely the landing page on your site when a visitor arrives via a search engine. Assuming you have great content, the search engine will rank the explanatory page of your site higher than the index page, which only lists the excerpt. Therefore, it is best to invest some time in this template because it is a very commonly viewed template. Enhancing this template with related posts and other teaser content only increases the possibility of enticing a visitor to further explore your site, bookmark it, subscribe to your feeds, or best of all, link back to you. All of these events increase your search engine respectability.

You can display the full content of a single post with the `single.php` template file. WordPress has decided that the visitor has requested the full content of a single post, therefore this template does not need to contain a loop, but simply a call to the `the_post()` function to get the data from the database.

If you have a very long post, you can break it up among several pages by using the built in WordPress functionality or special plugins. Internet users have very mixed feelings on this. Though general guidelines and studies have shown certain line lengths and content lengths improve readability, some vocal visitors detest the load time wait when paginating. This is a design choice based on your content type and site design.

Adding links that are related to this post is a great way to entice visitors to explore your site more. Several plugins add related content to the bottom of a single post page or scan your content for keywords and links. In practice, you will have to try these out and see how they work with your site.

Alternatively, the poor man's solution is to add a simple category or tag loop to grab some related-topic posts to the bottom of the page. It could be something as simple as this:

```
<h2>Other posts in this category</h2>
<ul id="related">
    <?php
    $category = get_the_category();
    $my_query = new WP_Query("category_name=".$category[0]->name."
        &showposts=5&orderby=rand");
    while ($my_query->have_posts()) : $my_query->the_post();
```

```
        echo '<li><a href="'. $post->permalink.'">"' . $post->post_title ."'</a>
                </li>';
    endwhile;
    ?>
</ul>
```

Here we are taking five random posts from the first category of the current post. It's not the most sophisticated method, but it is a simple way to show some related content links on the single post view. Another option would be to show additional posts by the same author:

```
<h2>Other posts by this author</h2>
<ul id="related">
    <?php
    $author = get_the_author_meta('id');
    $my_query = new WP_Query("author=".$author&showposts=5&orderby=rand");
    while ($my_query->have_posts()) : $my_query->the_post();

echo '<li><a href="'. $post->permalink.'">"' . $post->post_title ."'</a>
            </li>';
    endwhile;
    ?>
</ul>
```

Display a Page: Page.php

When you're using WordPress as a content management system you have to make some decisions such as whether to use pages or posts. This is like cats or dogs — people have strong feelings about each.

When working with a client, we generally create hybrid designs that use both pages and posts. Posts are used for temporal-based items, like news and promotions, whereas pages are used for static information that does not change very often, such as products or services. Product pages are then augmented with related posts. This gives the client the benefit of using the posts facets of the web site to drive traffic to the static product pages.

The most difficult part of the hybrid pages and posts layout is creating a meaningful navigation. Your site's global navigation is a very important aspect of your site if you intend to have any stickiness with your visitors. Visitors should be able to explore your content organically and experimentally through related posts and pages, but there should also be a strategy to your content organization and this is the function of your global navigation. On occasion, we have lucked out on the structure of a site and have been able to create two tiers of navigation, one for the page content and one for the post content. But more often than not, the two content types essentially need to be intertwined and the navigation must be hand coded.

That is not to say that you cannot still use WordPress hooks to get the content you want. In circumstances such as this, it can be very handy to use parent pages to organize your content. Consider this header template:

```
<div id="menu1">
    <ul>
        <li class="first"><a href="/">Home</a></li>
        <?php wp_list_pages('&exclude_tree=56&sort_column=menu_order&title_li=
            &depth=0'); ?>
```

```
                <li class="page_item last"><a href="/related-sites/">Related Sites</a>
                </li>
        </ul>
    </div>
    <div id="header">
        <h1 id="blog-title">
            <span>
                <a href="<?php bloginfo('home') ?>/" title="
                <?php echo wp_specialchars( get_bloginfo('name'), 1 ) ?>" rel="home">
                    <img id="logo" src="<?php bloginfo('template_directory');?>
                    /img/logo_black.png" alt="David's Rocking WordPress Site" />
                    <?php bloginfo('name') ?>
                </a>
            </span>
        </h1>
    </div><!-- #header -->
    <div id="menu2">
        <ul>
            <?php //sandbox_globalnav();
              wp_list_pages('&child_of=56&sort_column=menu_order&title_li=');
            ?>
        </ul>
    </div><!-- #menu -->
```

This lays out where there is a "super-menu" above the logo, div #menu1, then the site logo, then the regular navigation. The logo is the meat with two different menu slices of bread.

Notice in #menu1 that there are two additional hand-coded menu items, the first and the last. However, the bulk of the menu utilizes the WordPress function to list pages. Here this function is grabbing all the pages of the site, except those whose parent page is page ID 56.

 The easiest way to find a page ID number is to hover over the page name in the Edit Control Panel and look in the status bar at the bottom of the browser window.

This unordered list of pages is being returned in menu_order, which is the way they are ordered in the Control Panel. A recommended plugin for page order management is the drag-and-drop page ordering plugin called Page Mash. It has a fantastic AJAX interface that allows you to visually move pages around into different orders and parents. This plugin is essential for managing pages and greatly assists a novice user or a non-developer site administrator in visually structuring their pages. As long as you keep the sort_column=menu_order parameter set and use the built-in WordPress functionality, this plugin accentuates the content management aspect of the site and keeps the control in the hands of the end user.

Finally, this unordered list is not descending into the child pages of these pages. This will keep the menu all in one row so there are no flyout or drop-down menus.

For #menu2 we are commenting out the default Sandbox global navigation, which constructs a list of all pages in the site. That is not what we want, so away it goes and we replace it with another variation of wp_list_pages(). However, this time we are only grabbing the child pages of page ID 56 and again sorting by menu order. Also, this time we are grabbing the grandchildren pages, so there can be flyout or drop-down menus.

You might be wondering what happens to page 56. It is being excluded in the top menu, and skipped over in the second menu. That is exactly right. Page 56 is essentially being used as a container for the second menu items. It is entirely about structuring your content. However, just because a page is not directly listed in your navigation does not stop a visitor from accidentally or curiously stumbling across it.

You have a couple ways to handle this. You could create generic content for this page and that might suffice. Alternatively, you could use a page template to create a special use case for this page ID. Page templates are covered more in depth later in this chapter, but two ideas for a page template for page 56 are:

➤ Create a special loop that displays the children and grandchildren pages, essentially providing a limited scope site map.

➤ Create a PHP redirect to a more appropriate page of the site.

Other than special navigation consideration, the `page.php` template works essentially the same as the single post template. There is no loop — unless you have created a special page template, but technically that is a different template file — only the call to `the_post()`. Yes, this is the same function as in `single.php`. WordPress considers the posts and pages to be fundamentally the same type of content and `the_post()` gathers the content from the database.

Display an Image from Your Gallery: Image.php

To be honest, we do not think we have ever used this template file in a production web site. First introduced with WordPress 2.5, this is the newest template file. Many themes do not even have this template. In essence this template works very similarly to `single.php`, so much so that `single.php` is the next default if this template does not exist in your theme.

The intention of the `image.php` template is to provide a special template strictly for viewing your media gallery. A gallery can contain many different types of media, that is, it is not limited to images. This template will be called for any media item, unless there is a more specific match, and usually includes a description of the media and comment functionality. A great use of this template file would be for a portfolio site, such as a photography studio or another artistic collection. Again, this template functions nearly identically to the single post template, with slight variation to render an image rather than a paragraph.

Similarl templates types can be used with different media types besides images. You could create templates for video, audio, or applications; however, we imagine these would be very specific use cases and in the wild you would rarely see or need these templates unless you were creating a specific niche web site.

Template Hierarchy

With all these template files to choose from, how does WordPress decide which one to use? The WordPress core is pretty smart in this regard. Based on the URL, WordPress determines what type of content is being requested and can make a starting determination. Then WordPress works out the specificity of the template to be used, using the most specific template that matches the criteria first, and falling back to more general templates until it finds a match. This system works well, in that it is fault tolerant by always cascading back to index.php, but extremely powerful because as the developer you can make custom templates for very specific situations if needed.

This is best illustrated with the flowchart in Figure 8-4, adapted from the WordPress Codex.

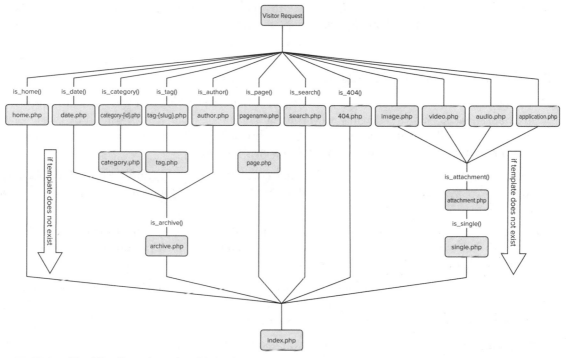

FIGURE 8-4: The WordPress template hierarchy

As you can see, there is a nice decision tree happening here, and the flexibility is very powerful. Not all themes have or need all template files. But certain more customized or special use case themes can capitalize on this hierarchy and create a unique application of WordPress.

On some sites we have built there have been occasions where categories, tags, pages, and even authors have had the same or similar taxonomies. For example, on a corporate news site, you may have a page about a department, a department category for news about that department, and some information may be tagged by the department name. In cases like these, the WordPress template decision tree can get confused and make unintended choices. You can work around this in several of ways: either by carefully crafting your taxonomy, by ensuring each slug is sufficiently unique to avoid collisions, or by enforcing your desired behavior via the .htaccess file. The crux of the issue here is how WordPress handles permalinks, which boils down to pattern matching on the slug metadata.

CREATING YOUR OWN THEME: ADDITIONAL FILES

It is tough to sort out the various template files into which ones are critical, essential, or just nice to have. Each theme's template file collection will be different and tailored to match the content or design goals of the author. The truly critical and essential templates have already been covered. In some circles, many of the following templates would fall into the categories we've already discussed, so you will have to make your own decisions here. Do not think that because these templates are being covered later, they are any less important than any other template. Consider each template type a tool, and how you use the tools is what truly matters.

Handle 404 Errors: 404.php

A 404 page is a fact of life. Eventually your visitors will find something that went stale. In contrast to a traditional web site, WordPress really helps you out in avoiding them because usually all the navigation items are dynamically created by content that actually exists. But it is still possible that your visitor will find a link that is no longer around, so your 404 page comes up.

The Sandbox theme provides a really good practice with the stock 404 template by including a search box. This way, visitors who stumble across this page have an opportunity to find what they are looking for.

Other good practices include showing a list of possibly related content, in the form of "I couldn't find what you asked for, but maybe one of these posts would interest you." You do not want a 404 page to be a dead end; always offer something else to view and a way out.

At our shop we trigger a developer e-mail or Twitter warning to let you know someone got an oopsy. Especially if there is a referrer in the HTTP headers, you can track down where the broken link originated from. At the least you know something went wrong and can do some research.

Also, your 404 page should be funny. Humor is good medicine and it is nice to disarm visitors who might be upset that what they were looking for is not there. It is good practice to expose errors to your developers but show something useful and meaningful to your site visitor. Think about the Twitter fail whale. Clearly, at times, Twitter has had scalability issues and the fail whale was seen more often than not. But by keeping the error message lighthearted, the Twitter fail whale has quickly emerged as an Internet icon and garnered its own cult following.

Though not strictly a template file, another error to hide from your visitors is a database connection error. The default database connection error is ugly and exposes a little too much information to your visitor, who hopefully is a good guy and not going to use that information against your web site.

WordPress introduced a new function in version 2.5 and later back-ported it to previous versions where if the database connection fails, WordPress looks for a `db-error.php` file in your `wp-content` directory.

 This file resides outside of your theme directory. Because there is no database connection, WordPress does not know what theme to display.

You can put whatever code and CSS in the db-error.php template you want, except dynamic data or WordPress functions, because they will not work without the database. This is another situation where we place a stock db-error.php in all of our WordPress sites, with a generic, but friendly error message and then notify the development team that an error has occurred.

Here is a sample db-error.php file:

```php
<?php
//error_reporting('E_ERROR');
mail('developers@mysite.com','WP SQL Connection Issue on '.$_SERVER['HTTP_HOST'],
'This is an automated message from the wordpress custom db error message file.');
?>
<html>
<head>
<title>Temporarily Unavailable</title>
<style>
body { background-color: #000; }
#wrapper
{
    width: 600px;
    height: 300px;
    margin: 2em auto 0;
    border: 4px solid #666;
    background-color: #fff;
    padding: 0 2em;
}
p { font-size: larger; }
</style>
</head>
<body>
<div id="wrapper">
    <center>
    <!-- /* This is the generic database error page that will be shown when a fatal
 db connection issue arises */ -->
    <h1><?php echo $_SERVER['HTTP_HOST']; ?> is Temporarily Unavailable</h1>
    <p>The webmaster has been alerted. Please try again later.</p>
    </center>
</div>
</body>
</html>
```

In the rare occurrence that WordPress cannot connect to the MySQL database, rather than showing an ugly database error, site visitors get a friendlier error message and our developers receive an e-mail. This also informs the visitors that no further action is required on their part, besides checking back later, because the error occurred on the web hosting server and not on their side. This acknowledgment removes confusion and uncertainty on the visitor's side. The caveat to this is that when things go really wrong, beyond just a hiccup, the developers can get flooded with e-mails.

Attachment.php

Attachment.php is related to special media files on your web site. If you review the template hierarchy, you will see special templates for images, video, audio files, or application files. These template file selections are based on the first part of the MIME type of the file, and you could possibly have other specific templates if you required them and the MIME type was unique. However, if you do not include specific template files, WordPress uses `attachment.php`.

Just like the media-specific templates, this template functions very similarly to the single post template and in practice is not used very often. For this template to be of much use, your site would have to be heavily media-centric, and in that respect, your theme will be profoundly modified to support this direction. In our opinion, this is not a very important template file, except for the unique edge cases where you need these media file templates.

Author.php

Sometimes your site has multiple authors, such as our development team site at work. In cases like these, a visitor may want to find additional articles posted by the same individual. The `author.php` template file shows only posts written by a specific author.

The author template behaves just like a category or tag loop. One nice feature of the Sandbox theme is that this template also includes any author information that the author chose to submit in the admin Control Panel.

```
<h2 class="page-title author">
    <?php printf( __( 'Author Archives: <span class="vcard">%s</span>',
'sandbox' ),
    "<a class='url fn n' href='$authordata->user_url'
    title='$authordata->display_name'
    rel='me'>$authordata->display_name</a>" ) ?>
</h2>
<?php
    $authordesc = $authordata->user_description;
    if ( !empty($authordesc) ) {
        echo apply_filters( 'archive_meta', '<div class="archive-meta">' .
        $authordesc . '</div>' );
    }
?>
```

Here you see the author name in the `<h2>` linking to the URL that is listed on the profile page in the Control Panel. Also, if the author submitted some biographical data, that information is published here. We think this functionality could be enhanced if the profile page had a rich text editor for the biographical information, and possibly some expanded custom fields.

In production sites, we have used these fields to create a multi-business partner site where each author was in effect a company. We have also created a Rolodex-type site using this method.

Comments.php

The comments template is one of the more complex templates and breaks the separation of content from presentation rule some. This template file handles both the comment loop, including trackbacks and pings, and the input form for a visitor to submit the comment in both logged-in and logged-out cases. Although these tasks are functionally related, sorting through this template file is a lot of if . . . else conditionals that make it difficult to theme. The Sandbox comments template is particularly complex, and the WordPress core has made some changes that could simplify this, so it is worth revisiting your comment functionality and make changes to your template to make things easier.

Your theme may not even include comments, especially if you are using WordPress as a CMS, but if it does, you can include the comments functionality templates in your other templates with the following code:

```
<?php comments_template(); ?>
```

Countless variations on the comments theme exist for the look and feel; way too many to discuss the merits of any in particular. One thing to consider when working on this template file is to bear in mind the threaded comments functionality introduced in WordPress 2.7. See the WordPress Codex for more information about using wp_list_comments().

It should also be noted that in WordPress 2.7 the comments loop was simplified to look more like a traditional post loop in the code. The Sandbox theme has not been updated to reflect this new vernacular including wp_list_comments(), have_comments(), and comment pagination.

As mentioned, the comments template can be confusing and is a whole subtheme unto itself because there is so much going on. Recently there have been some partial theme web sites popping up that simply sell comments themes, for example http://commentbits.com/. Not a whole site theme, but just the special templates for comments with a few variations. This could be a simple way to get a stylized comment subsystem up and running quickly. It is probably too early to decide if partial WordPress themes are here to stay or just a fad.

Add Functionality to Your Templates: Functions.php

The functions.php template is not a display template, so it is not like the other templates we have covered, but it is a very important file even though it does not directly display content on your web site. Chiefly, the functions.php file is where the special sauce that makes your theme tick goes. It is the place where you can put what has traditionally been called "library code." If in your templates you find repeating code or need some special functionality, this is where it can go. WordPress automatically includes this file during execution so the functions are available in all of your template files.

So far in the examples, you have probably seen all the funny sandbox_post_class() and other Sandbox references and scratched your head. Here is where we will clear that up. The Sandbox theme comes with a whole slew of functions that provide all the semantic CSS hooks, microformat code snippets, and other functionality that makes Sandbox a great starting spot.

The stock functions.php theme is very well commented. Each function and logic block of a function has a one line comment explaining what it does. This makes functions.php easy to modify and extend. However, the majority of these functions will not need to be modified in your production site, unless you have very specific needs. Most of them simply add to the template files to create a hook-rich HTML template for your CSS styling skills.

For example, the function sandbox_post_class() creates the CSS classes for each post in your templates that show posts. In truth, these posts may actually be over-classed, meaning that more classes are assigned to the post than you could ever possibly use. And, that is not optimized for a high-traffic web site, because you are sending HTML that you are not using. But let's face it; your web site is not experiencing the same high traffic volumes as the big guys, so it is probably not worth optimizing these functions too much because the plentiful CSS hooks offer a great convenience for styling.

What we really like about this function is that it provides classes for nearly all the metadata about your post. Consider this HTML code:

```
<div class="hentry p1 post publish author-david category-generic
category-othercategory tag-awesome tag-verycool y2009 m06 d22 h21" id="post-3">
```

This is the encapsulating `div` for a singular post, either in the loop or on the `single.php` display. This post is multi-classed with a wealth of information. The `hentry` class is in there for Atom feed compliance.

In a loop, each post is assigned an incrementing number; for example, this example is classed `p1`, meaning it is the first post in the loop. This is not related to the actual WordPress post ID, but is strictly ordinal in the display. You could use this class to create a gradient down the page of gradually fading color, as the ordinal post class increases.

The `post` class is your generic hook for all posts. This is where you can assign the base attributes to a post. The next class is for the status of the post. In the preceding example this post is `published`.

Each post is also classed with the originating author of the post. This class is prefaced with the term `author-` to avoid conflicts with other CSS classes. You could use this class in a multi-author blog to include a profile picture with each post.

The next set of classes is one class for each category the post is in. Again, these classes use a namespacing `category-` prefix for each one to avoid collisions. These classes could be effectively used to assign icons or special coloring to different categories for instant recognition, similar to the way Slashdot has icons for the different post categories.

Similarly, the next set is classes for each tag assigned to the post. Again, these classes use collision-resistant prefixing. Both the category classes and the tag classes use the slugs from their respective subsystems. They also will always be sorted in the WordPress returned sort, so cascading your CSS becomes very important when you are styling multiple categories or tags. That is, watch the order that they appear in the HTML and compare that to the order, inheritance, and specificity in your `styles.css`.

These next classes we think are really cool, though we have yet to have a client come forward where we can really use them to their fullest potential. These classes are for the year, month, day, and hour of the post. The previous example was written June 2, 2009, sometime after 9:00 PM, local time. You can use these classes to give various months and years different styles in a sort of magazine edition feel. What we would really like to do is have different styles based on the time of day each post is made, but no one has stepped up.

Some other potential classes that you do not see in the previous example including private and password-protected posts, have the CSS class `protected` assigned. Also, every other post has an `alt` class assigned for you to zebra stripe, or alternate the background colors of your posts if desired.

Finally, if you have not been able to get the styles assigned that you need through these classes, each post is also assigned an ID. This post-id is the actual WordPress post ID from the Control Panel. But really, what is missing from these CSS hooks? Possibly the local weather from when you were publishing the post, but with a little ingenuity and a web service, these could even be included in your CSS classes. We will leave this as an exercise for the reader.

The Sandbox theme includes a similar function to to assign classes to the body tag of each page. In addition, many other helper functions can help with cleaning up the user experience or overriding the default WordPress behavior of certain features.

When modifying the Sandbox functions you have to make a choice. Sometimes, if you are making minimal changes to the file, you can just modify the file directly, accepting that this will break any upgradeability of the theme. Alternatively, you can include your own custom_functions.php from the functions.php file and make all your own custom changes here. The caveat is that if you overwrite the functions.php file, either through a theme update or other user error, you have to remember to put the include back in that file before your head gets too bloody from beating it against the wall wondering why your custom functions are not running. In practice, we have successfully used both of these scenarios.

The most likely function in the Sandbox theme to be overridden or rewritten is the sandbox_ globalnav() function. In the default Sandbox theme, this function is used to create a nice unordered list of the pages in your site, devoid of whitespace, wrapped inside a div with an ID of menu. This is a great start but may not cover all the various needs of your client and so it will probably be rewritten. Depending on the scope of changes, there are a couple of paths we have chosen in the past.

One, we have modified this function directly, because the changes required were not severe. Two, we have commented out this function call entirely and rewritten it to meet the needs of the site. Three, we have commented out this function call altogether in the header.php file and started over on global navigation from scratch directly in the header template. As it reads over and over in the Sandbox comments and support documents, the Sandbox theme is a playground and is meant as a starting point to build your own wondrous theme, so do not take the functions set forth as the best way of doing something. It is merely a means to an end.

Some of the more advanced themes and the premium theme frameworks include their own control panels to modify theme settings. These other theme frameworks are covered later in this chapter. However, the theme control panel code resides in the functions.php file.

For example, the Thematic theme framework functions.php is a list of includes of other function files. This logically breaks up and separates the different facets of the theme framework and keeps the files manageable. This theme also includes a basic control panel to control some of the theme settings.

To create your own theme control panel, you have to register your theme control panel functions with WordPress. In addition, you have to create the HTML form for your control panel within your functions.php file. This is one of the reasons we like the way Thematic has broken up the files into separate areas of concern because the mixing of PHP and HTML code never turns out pretty or readable. It is best to keep this information separate and in maintainable file sizes.

Creating your own theme control panel is outside the scope of this book, but it is definitely a great feature to have and most of the premium theme frameworks are including this functionality. Having a theme control panel helps your WordPress theme bridge that gap from blogging engine to full-fledged content management platform for the average user. As a coder, WordPress is easily extendible through the code and the vast WordPress functionality, but for the average user, who is probably your client, not having to deal with code is crucial.

Search.php

The search template file is really a misnomer. This template is actually the search engine result page (SERP). The search form itself is called `searchform.php`, which is covered in the next section. The concept of a search engine result page is pretty self-explanatory. It is going to show the results of what the visitor looked for, by default in reverse chronological order. Chapter 10 covers some of the weaknesses with the built-in search functionality of WordPress and addresses some alternatives to enhance the user experience.

That is all the basic Sandbox search template does. This is fine if there are results, but if not, it shows a new search form, where you might want to include your own (see the next section).

You can do a couple things to your search engine result page to improve on the default. First, you do not want your results page to be a dead end if there are not any results. Plugins are available to offer related searches or spelling variation searches based on what was initially entered. This will make the search itself behave more like a traditional search engine.

Still, if you do not have any results, offer up some alternative content that the visitor might be interested in. This might be a good place for a tag cloud or a list of your most popular content. Plugins are available for showcasing your most popular content or you could create a custom query, but you would have to decide what your metrics are.

For some sites we have built, the top content was essentially a known issue. In this case we created a special post category and made a new loop to show only this category in the SERP page.

If you do have results, some people like to see the search terms highlighted in the search engine results page. The Sandbox theme uses `the_excerpt()` to display the content excerpt in the results. This is where you will make some changes to highlight the search terms.

Replace this line:

```php
<?php the_excerpt( __( 'Read More <span class="meta-nav">&raquo;</span>',
'sandbox' ) ) ?>
```

with the following snippet:

```php
<?php
$excerpt = get_the_excerpt( __( 'Read More <span class="meta-nav">&raquo;
        </span>', 'sandbox' ) );
$keys = explode(" ",$s);
$excerpt = preg_replace('/('.implode('|', $keys) .')/iu',
        '<span class="searchTerm">\0 </span>',$excerpt);
echo $excerpt;
?>
```

Because `the_excerpt()` echoes the content directly to the rendering, you have to use the plugin API function `get_the_excerpt()`, which returns a string instead, but does not support appending the Sandbox function content to it. Run this string through the regular expression `replace` to put `span` elements around all the search terms and then echo this out to the rendering. In your CSS you can add a nice rule to highlight these `span` elements to match your theme.

Finally, if your visitors did not find what they were looking for after reviewing the search results, rather than forcing them to scroll back up to the top, you can provide a second search form at the bottom to refine their search. After the results loop, add something like:

```
<h2>Not seeing what you're looking for?  Try again</h2>
<?php get_search_form(); ?>
```

Chapter 10 discusses improving the way search works through plugins and some alternatives.

SearchForm.php

The generic search form is pulled from the WordPress core template files and is pretty basic looking. In cases where your theme needs a customized search input field, create a new template named `searchform.php` because Sandbox does not include this template. This form can then be styled to match the rest of your theme. The search widget automatically uses this template to include this form in your regular templates with the following code:

```
<?php get_search_form(); ?>
```

The basic Search form could look like this:

```
<div id="search">
   <label for="s">Search:</label>
   <form id="searchform" method="get" action="/index.php">
      <div>
          <input type="text" name="s" id="s" size="15" /><br />
          <input type="submit" value="Search" />
      </div>
   </form>
</div>
```

Note that because this same form could be used in the unordered lists of the sidebar as well as wherever else you may include it, the HTML markup may need to be adjusted; most notably, changing the enclosing `<div>` to be `<li>`.

Another option is for special-case search forms, often seen in the nameplates of sites, is to create a traditional PHP `include` for the search form. Make sure the filename is not one of the reserved filenames for the template engine, and then include it in the appropriate place in your other template:

```
<?php include($bloginfo['template_directory'].'includeThis.php'); ?>
```

Remember to use the `bloginfo[]` array to keep the theme portable. We have also used this method to comply with the DRY principle when there are consistent elements across multiple pages, but outside of the header and footer templates. WordPress itself does an excellent job of enforcing DRY through the variety of page templates, assuming you as a developer stick to the rules. But there are always more ways to skin a cat and traditional PHP rules can help out here. Often we use this functionality to keep the template sizes manageable.

Other Files

Here are some other files that polish off your theme. For the Manage Themes Control Panel, you will want to include a screenshot for easy visual recognition of your theme. Create an image file to represent your theme that is 300 pixels wide by 225 pixels tall and save it as a PNG. GIF and JPG are also accepted and preferred in that order. Traditionally this image is an actual screenshot of your site using your theme. The remainder of the information for each theme on the Manage Themes page comes from your `style.css` header information.

The Sandbox theme includes several language files and is ready out of the box for localization. Some of this was covered in the previous functions section of this chapter. However, if you intend to launch your site in multiple languages, pay attention to the special considerations involved. Localization and internationalization are well outside the scope of this book. Just bear in mind that the Sandbox theme supports this functionality when you need it.

CUSTOM PAGE TEMPLATES

Occasionally you will have a specific page that requires a unique layout, relative to the rest of your web site. This could be a contact page, or it could be that each product on a brochure web site has its own specific page. Maybe using a general `page.php` template is not going to meet the needs of your site, because each page has its own distinctive qualities. Possibly, you have widgets you would like to display on certain pages and not others, although you could probably accomplish this with a plugin like Widget Logic. Or perhaps you are integrating a third-party web application into your WordPress site. This is where page templates step in.

You can assign page templates to a page using the Write panel in the admin Control Panel. WordPress will assign which page template to use when displaying your content following the already established specificity pattern. For example, if your page is assigned a page template, this will be selected because it is the most specific option. If the default page template is set, the traditional `page.php` template discussed earlier will be used to render your content. Finally, if neither of those templates is available, WordPress will use your `index.php` template.

In Figure 8-5 you can see several page templates to choose from, including the two default page templates for archives and links, discussed later, and the two added as examples, Boring and Fancy.

FIGURE 8-5: Selecting the page template

When to Use Custom Page Templates

Many reasons exist for having custom page templates in your site. Custom page templates are a very powerful tool to add to your arsenal, and when used effectively they can extend the breadth of your site immensely. A simple example is to create page templates for unique product pages, where the sidebar of each product page has unique data and links specific to that product. Like everything in WordPress, there are many ways to achieve this functionality, but sometimes, creating custom page templates is a simple, straightforward method to achieve the results you desire. And often, simplest is best.

Another simple example is to create a custom page template that uses an iFrame HTML element to include a third-party web application. Depending on the exact needs and aspirations of the site (not to mention budget), this can be a quick and dirty way to integrate two sites into one. The caveats to this method are the same as you would usually find when using iFrames, which are bookmarking and competing look and feels. But admittedly, we have used this method before because sometimes the quick and dirty is all that you need.

More complex examples include integrating different web applications into your WordPress site. For example, a page template could be used to create a custom order page that posts directly back into your ecommerce package. This would be a nightmare to set up and maintain inside the WordPress Control Panel, but when using custom page templates, it is all in the code, and you still get the gooey goodness of WordPress to wrap it all in.

In real life, we have used custom page templates for event calendaring and registration. In one example we had already built an expansive education class offering web applications for searching and displaying courses as well as registering for attendance either in person or via the Web. This system had been in place for several years and was heavily used. The simplest way to integrate this education registration system into our WordPress client sites was to create custom page templates.

In essence, we extended the existing registration system with some REST web service commands. Then, we created a set of custom page templates that communicated with the web services but displayed the contents locally inside the WordPress site wrapper, using the local style sheet. Although setting up the page templates was daunting at first, the benefits in the end were enormous. One, we continued to use the existing system that corporate staff was already knowledgeable and trained on. Two, we extended the registration options to multiple sites, therefore increasing the potential audience. Three, even though the registrations were spread across multiple web properties, they were still centralized into the one system. And four, the education system matched the look and feel of the local web site because it utilized the local theme of the WordPress site.

How to Use Custom Page Templates

Creating the custom page template themselves is really easy. The goal of the templates and making the templates achieve the goals is what really complicates the matter.

To create a page template, copy an existing template that is similar to the new template you are going to make, usually this is the `page.php` template. Name this new template file whatever you want and keep it in your `theme` directory. However, in our development shops, we tend to follow a convention that page templates are named `t_templatename.php`. That is, they are prefixed with the `t_` so that we can easily distinguish between traditional template files and individual page templates, although the name of this file really does not matter as long as you avoid the reserved filenames.

To make your new template a page template you must include a special comment section at the top of the file:

```php
<?php
/*
Template Name: Fancy Page Template
*/
?>
```

This must be in the first couple of lines of your file for WordPress to scan and register as a page template. In practice, the only thing above this stanza is the source code control comment.

The name of your template can be anything you want. It should be meaningful, but not too long, because WordPress will use this PHP comment to populate the drop-down box in the Control Panel. Your page template is now registered with WordPress.

The remainder of your page template can be whatever you need to accomplish your page template goals. You can, and most likely should, use the built-in WordPress functions like `get_header()` and `get_footer()` as well as the content gatherers. Basically you can do whatever you need to do here, just remember you will have to sleep in the bed that you made.

For example, if you remove the dynamic WordPress sidebar generation and replace it with static HTML, you have also removed all the functionality from the Control Panel to manage widgets on this page template. It would be a better practice to register a new widget area on this page template and continue to use the Control Panel to manage this content.

Keep in mind that page templates are not restricted to displaying page information. You could create a page template that displays a traditional post loop or do something that is completely unrelated to the WordPress content. Then just leave the page text editor blank, or use it to write instruction notes to yourself.

Stock Sandbox Page Templates

The Sandbox theme comes standard with two page templates for use on your site. The names of these templates can be confusing, because they are related to existing WordPress templates or functionality

The first page template that comes with the Sandbox theme is `archives.php` (note: it is plural). Instead of showing posts from the archive, the archives page template is more of an overview of all the content on your web site showing both archives by category and archives by month with respective links.

This page template could easily be expanded to include archives by author:

```
<li id="author-archives">
    <h3><?php _e( 'Archives by Author', 'sandbox' ) ?></h3>
    <ul>
        <?php wp_list_authors() ?>
    </ul>
</li>
```

You could also add a tag cloud. The WordPress tag cloud was added in WordPress 2.3. Tag clouds change the size of each tag based on the quantity of its use in your content. This would only be beneficial if you were running a current version of WordPress and you tagged your content. By default, the `wp_tag_cloud()` function displays as unstructured anchor tags, so you could pass a formatting parameter to the function to render an unordered list like the other section on this page template.

```
<li id="tag-archives">
    <h3><?php _e( 'Archives by Tag', 'sandbox' ) ?></h3>
    <p><?php wp_tag_cloud('format=list'); ?></p>
</li>
```

`Links.php` is the second page template that comes standard with the Sandbox theme. Traditionally, the links that have been added in the Control Panel are used in a special links widget in a sidebar. The Links page template extends this functionality into a page, so rather than having your links stuck off to the side, you can easily have a separate page with all these bookmarks in them.

This is very useful when using WordPress as a CMS, and the site has links to different sets of resources. In practice you could set up link categories for the site administrator to populate and then build custom page templates for each category. For example, a site discussing the virtues of WordPress might have resource pages with links to various supporting web sites; perhaps one for themes and one for plugins. Using a custom page template, the site administrator populates and organizes the links in the Control Panel. Then he creates WordPress pages for each link category and assigns the appropriate page template. Each page template only pulls the bookmarks for the specified category.

```
<?php wp_list_bookmarks('category=6' ); ?>
```

The easiest way to find a category ID number is to hover over the link category name in the Edit Control Panel and look in the status bar at the bottom of the browser window. Note that link categories are different than post or page categories.

Custom page templates are a very powerful tool. Truly, if you cannot fit your content into the predefined template types, you always have this last trick up your sleeve to make a custom page template and override everything. This is also a great way to add special non-WordPress functionality to your web site.

THEME HIERARCHY AND CHILD THEMES

So far in this chapter we have advocated making a local copy of the Sandbox theme, renaming it and making your custom theme in that new directory. This is a good way to get started with theme creation and is how many development teams work today. This method works for us because we know exactly where our template files and CSS files are that need to be edited. The whole theme is self-contained, which minimizes our workflow and deployment efforts and the Sandbox core theme does not update very often — not that it's perfect, but it is very solid.

However, changes are afoot and the future is now. With the release of WordPress 2.7, child themes became a functional reality. While you could implement child themes prior to WordPress 2.7, it was not until template file inheritance was included that child themes became a viable development option. Child themes let you take an existing theme or theme framework and use the best parts of it, then extend and modify it, license permitting, to meet your own theme's needs while maintaining future updates to the parent theme. After you have the basics of theme development down, we highly recommend picking a theme framework you are comfortable with (a few are covered in the next section) and creating child themes. Child themes are the future of theme development for WordPress.

This concept is pretty revolutionary for several reasons. First, it certainly opens the door for theme frameworks. Starting with a solid foundation, like the Sandbox theme, you can now make countless variations on the theme simply through inheritance. The Sandbox theme is very plain, and intentionally so, but by using child themes, you can inherit all the CSS semantic hooks and microformat gooey centers and build your own candy shell around it, basically taking the best parts and making a new creation.

Second, updates to the parent theme will not overwrite your customizations. Previously, when you made modifications to your copy of the theme, you had to keep track of the changes you made so that you could reapply them when the theme was upgraded. This can be somewhat automated via a source code management solution, but it is arduous at best, when it works. And there is always the day when you forget to make a modification to the updated files.

Third, this led the way for auto-updating themes in the Theme Manager. Occasionally theme templates are vulnerable to security exploits like cross-site scripting. Using a properly inherited child theme means the parent theme can auto-update to address security issues while not affecting your child theme. This creates a more secure implementation for your site.

There are a couple of caveats here. The functionality that keeps your child theme customizations unaffected works both ways. If you override a particular template file with your own customizations, any enhancements to the parent template file of the same name will not cascade to your unique file. In practice, this could create a false sense of security, where you may have copied a poorly coded template file to modify, and then changes were made to the parent version but your file is unaffected and still vulnerable. This would not only apply to security amendments but would also apply to any feature enhancements. That is, child themes do not totally remove you from the code management process.

In addition, there is a little bit of CSS overhead here. Generally, a child theme builds upon the CSS of the parent theme. And in truth that is exactly how CSS is designed to work, hence the word *cascading* in the name. So, for this to work in child themes, the child theme has to include the CSS from the parent theme, even the rules that get overridden in the child theme. That means that the byte weight of the CSS in your child theme may be quite a bit larger than what you actually use in the browser, but you have to transfer it all anyway.

That all said we do believe child themes are a fantastic feature of WordPress, and we absolutely anticipate using this methodology in the very near future. Certainly the benefits of maintaining a pristine theme framework and then extending that theme to individual sites continues to build on the benefits of a common theme vernacular of CSS and functions, as well as the other benefits mentioned previously. Again, using child themes is the future for WordPress theme development and is the best practices recommendation.

Take a look at how child themes actually operate and what is required in making your first child theme. The first thing you need to do is find the theme you are using as the parent. Your parent theme does not have to be labeled a theme framework. You can extend any theme as long as it meets the following conditions:

➤ The licensing permits you to extend or modify the theme.

➤ The parent theme is not a child theme itself.

This example continues to build on the venerable Sandbox theme. As alluded to earlier in the chapter, to make your custom theme a child theme of another theme, you must add a line to the header information of your `style.css` file. This line informs WordPress of the location of the parent theme. Therefore, the variable in the comment should be the folder name of the theme and, though it depends on the server, is best to be case-sensitive. In this instance we are adding the line:

```
Template: sandbox
```

To illustrate this, the entire header comment block from our sample child theme reads:

```
/*
Theme Name: A Sandbox Child Theme
Theme URI: mirmillo.com
Description: A sample sandbox child theme
Author: David Damstra
Author URI: mirmillo.com
Template: sandbox
Version: 1.0
*/
```

As covered previously, having the `style.css` file with the properly formatted header information in your uniquely named folder registers your theme with WordPress.

The next step is to import the CSS from the parent theme, so that your custom theme has base rules to work with. Additionally, import the layout from the examples folder:

```
/* import the base sandbox styles  */
@import url('../sandbox/style.css');

/* use the two-column with sidebar on right layout from the /examples/ folder  */
@import url('../sandbox/examples/2c-r.css');
```

Note that the Sandbox `styles.css` file also imports the two columns with left-hand sidebar layout. Although this later import will override the previous one, you may want to comment out the layout import in the Sandbox style sheet to reduce overhead. This is a change you will always have to make when you update the parent Sandbox theme, should you choose to make it. If your child theme is using the `2c-l.css` example layout, you can ignore this `import` line.

 This would also be a great place to import any CSS frameworks you have opted to include in your design, such as Yahoo! YUI, Blueprint, or the many worthwhile others, perhaps even your own.

At this point, you can activate your theme in the WordPress appearance Control Panel. You have a fully functional child theme of the Sandbox theme. It will not look like much, because it is in essence a practical copy of the parent theme. The remainder of your style sheet operates like traditional CSS where you can override previous rules through the CSS rules of precedence, including the order in which they are listed — because your custom ones appear later, they will take precedence — or via specificity.

Again, working with CSS is outside the scope of this book, but for the sake of example, you'll extend your child theme a little bit. As we said, we cannot stand the black Times New Roman font on a white background. It is a pet peeve, but in our opinion it looks unfinished. You will update your child theme with a nice pink background, change the font and make the links hot pink. It will be beautifully hideous. Here's what the complete `style.css` file might look like:

```
/*
Theme Name: A Sandbox Child Theme
Theme URI: mirmillo.com
Description: A sample sandbox child theme
Author: David Damstra
Author URI: mirmillo.com
Template: sandbox
Version: 1.0
*/

/* import the base sandbox styles */
@import url('../sandbox/styles.css');

/* Two-column with sidebar on left from the /examples/ folder  */
```

```css
@import url('../sandbox/examples/2c-1.css');

body {
    background: #E0A3BD;
    color: #333;
    font: 100%/1.5 calibri, arial, verdana, sans-serif;
}

a, a:link ,a:link ,a:link, a:hover {
    background:transparent;
    text-decoration:underline;
    cursor:pointer
}
a:link {color:#D74C4C}
a:visited {color:#F91DFC}
a:hover,a:active {color:#FFF688}
```

From here on out, Firebug (or the inspector that comes with your browser of choice) is your best friend. Use the inspector to see the current style rules applied to various elements and make the appropriate changes in your child theme's CSS file. Again, remember to follow the precedence and specificity rules of CSS.

Your child theme can be as simple or complex as you make it. You can create a completely unique theme by simply editing the style sheet, as we have done previously. Or your child theme can turn into a complete new theme with all new templates, although this most likely defeats the purpose of using a child at all.

Here is how it works. When WordPress makes a decision on which template file to use, first it scans your child theme directory for that file. If that file does not exist, the parent theme directory is scanned. WordPress will prefer your template files over those of the parent theme, which means you can override the functionality of specific templates while maintaining the core of the parent theme. Or, your child theme could introduce custom page templates, but the foundation templates are pulled from the parent. There is a wide scope of opportunities here, although keep in mind the previously mentioned limitations.

The easiest way to accomplish this is to copy the template file you want to modify from the parent theme directory into your child theme directory and then modify as needed.

For example, the author template in the Sandbox theme is perfectly functional, but suppose you want to add the author image to this template. This is pretty easily accomplished by using the Gravatar service from Automattic, assuming your authors have set up gravatars.

First, copy the author.php template from the Sandbox into your child theme directory. Second, edit your child copy to include the gravatar code. It might read something like this:

```php
<?php get_header() ?>
<div id="container">
    <div id="content">
        <?php the_post() ?>
        <h2 class="page-title author">
            <?php printf( __( 'Author Archives: <span class="vcard">%s</span>',
            'sandbox' ), "<a class='url fn n' href='$authordata->user_url'
            title='$authordata->display_name' rel='me'>
            $authordata->display_name</a>" ) ?>
```

```
</h2>
        <span style="float:right; padding: 5px; background: #fff;
                  border: 1px solid #333;">
          <img alt="<?php echo $authordata->display_name; ?>"
          src="http://www.gravatar.com/avatar/
          <?php echo md5( strtolower(get_the_author_email()) ); ?>.jpg?s=256" />
        </span>
        <?php
        $authordesc = $authordata->user_description;
        if ( !empty($authordesc) ) {
            echo apply_filters( 'archive_meta', '<div class="archive-meta">' .
            $authordesc . '</div>' );
        }
        ?>
```

Notice the new `<span>` before the author description. That coupled with our fledgling style sheet renders like Figure 8-6.

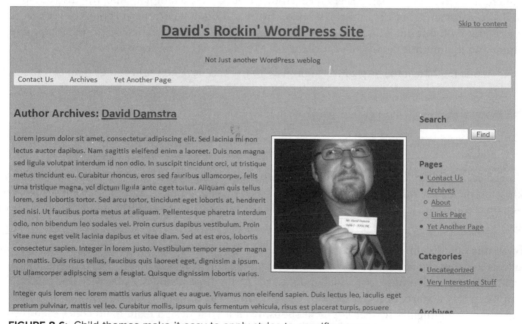

FIGURE 8-6: Child themes make it easy to apply styles to specific pages.

You can further extend our child theme with your own `functions.php` file. WordPress automatically includes the parent theme's functions, but in addition, it also includes your child theme functions. You do have to be conscientious about function naming. Be very careful not to create functions in your own theme that have the same name as a parent theme function. If you need to override functionality, it is advised that you make a new function in your own theme and adjust the template files as necessary to call your function instead.

Suppose you wanted to override the `sandbox_globalnav()` function from the Sandbox theme, similarly to what we did earlier in the chapter. Create a new function, with a unique name, in your child theme functions file that accomplishes your goals. Then copy the `header.php` template from the Sandbox theme into your theme and edit the function call to invoke your new function instead.

As an example, take the author photo example and refactor the gravatar image generation code into a function for use in multiple places. We created a `functions.php` file in our child theme directory and inserted the following code:

```php
<?php
/* this is my child themes functions */

function ddamstra_showGravatar($authordata, $size=100) {
    if ($size < 80 ) { $size = 80; }
    if ($size > 512) { $size = 512; }
    echo '<img alt="'.$authordata->display_name.'
        " src="http://www.gravatar.com/avatar/'.
        md5( strtolower($authordata->user_email)).'.jpg?s='.$size.'" />';
}
```

This function receives the `$authordata` object from the `author.php` template and will also accept an optional size parameter, but defaults to 100 pixels wide. Additional parameters could be set according to the gravatar API, but this suffices for now. A couple of constraints are then set on the image size for maximum and minimums. Finally, it echoes the HTML back to the template.

The next step is to change the `author.php` template to use this new function rather than call the web service directly:

```php
<span style="float:right; padding: 5px; background: #fff; border: 1px solid
#333;">
    <?php ddamstra_showGravatar($authordata, 200); ?>
</span>
```

As you can see, child themes are yet another powerful tool in the WordPress theme arsenal. You can quickly get a theme up and running using an established theme as a base, and then modify and extend only what is required to create your own theme, all the while future proofing the upgradeability of your foundation theme.

Although this functionality has been around for the last several releases of WordPress, it was not until WordPress 2.7 that the child theme system was fully implemented. This really is a game changing feature, and not one that has been widely publicized. At the time of this writing very few tutorials exist on using this feature, but we expect by the time you read this, child themes may be a common method for creating themes for development shops. Even if your design team hand codes each theme from scratch, the benefits of having a foundation to start from increases efficiencies due to commonly implemented features being already, and consistently, implemented, as well as having the familiar CSS and markup vocabulary that your team is intimately familiar with. Regardless of whether your parent theme is one of the popular theme frameworks or something you have developed in house, the benefits are tangible.

PREMIUM THEMES AND OTHER THEME FRAMEWORKS

Thus far in this chapter we have espoused the virtues of the Sandbox theme and used it in most of the examples. But certainly it is not the only theme or theme framework out there and may not be the best match for you or your development team.

As we have stated, Sandbox works really well for teams of seasoned PHP developers. Some of these other themes we will look at briefly include another layer of abstraction in them or a flurry of functions in the `functions.php` file. Generally, this abstraction brings the ability to modify the theme into the WordPress Control Panel. This may be ideal for certain clients who are not PHP savvy and want that control delegated to the site administrator rather than the developers.

The best way to make a choice here is to try them out and kick the tires. Find a theme or theme framework that fits your coding style and needs and then run with it. Remember you can make child themes or modify themes to meet your needs (license permitting, of course) from basically any theme out there, but with the new child theme functionality in WordPress 2.7 there has been a growth spurt in theme frameworks. We take a cursory look at some of the more popular theme frameworks, at the time of this writing, here. Many are out there, so be sure to look around.

Please keep in mind various terms are thrown about with regard to themes. Magazine themes and premium themes mean different things to different people. Sometimes premium means the theme costs money, other times it means it includes an administration control panel. Some themes that are available for a fee are called commercial themes. Theme frameworks generally mean they were developed to be built upon. Though they may stand by themselves, they are intentionally written for extension.

Revolution Theme

The Revolution theme was a pioneer in WordPress themes and really raised the bar to change theme development standards. Revolution was one of the first themes to embrace the magazine theme style that helped WordPress transcend the blog stereotype and become a viable CMS solution. Magazine-style themes made WordPress look less bloggy and more like a traditional web site. In addition, the Revolution theme was one of the early commercial themes.

The Revolution theme has since been retired and is no longer available in its original incarnation. At the time of this writing, Brian Gardner, the creator of the theme, was working on a theme refresh and offering a new version of it called Magazine theme and offered through his company StudioPress online at `http://studiopress.com`.

Hybrid Theme

The Hybrid theme framework by Justin Tadlock is free, but charges a club membership fee for access to the theme documentation, tutorials, and support forums. This theme includes a nice control panel to toggle various features and CSS hooks on and off. The Hybrid theme has several ready-made child themes available.

This theme also appears to be a descendant of Sandbox and has rich CSS hooks throughout the posts and body tags. It also includes nine widget-ready areas and a whopping eighteen custom page templates in the stock installation. These custom page templates cover a variety of use cases and really add to the theme, if you know how to use them.

Finally, the Hybrid theme also includes a custom write panel for posts and pages to complete specific fields that are used in the templates to enhance the SEO of your site.

You can find more information about the Hybrid theme at `http://themehybrid.com/`.

Thematic Theme

Thematic is a theme framework developed by Ian Stewart. The Thematic theme is a free theme with a decent breadth of existing child themes already available. Child themes are available both free and commercial. Thematic also includes a minimal administration control panel to modify limited information.

Two features really stand out. First, this theme's ancestry includes the Sandbox theme. The rich semantic CSS hooks that are found in Sandbox have been brought into Thematic and extended. Second, this theme includes thirteen widget-ready areas. Similar to the OpenHook plugin for the Thesis theme, this allows the site administrator to put content in various places of the page, but better than Thesis, it uses widgets.

You can find more information about the Thematic theme at `http://themeshaper.com/thematic/`.

Thesis Theme

The Thesis theme framework is a very powerful commercial theme created by Chris Pearson that offers both personal and developer licenses, each with lifetime updates. The foundation focuses heavily on typography and a very flexible layout. What really stands out with Thesis is the theme control panel. This control panel puts the control of the layout in the hands of the site administrator or designer, who do not have to get their hands into the code. The Thesis Design Options Control Panel controls many CSS settings and layout settings without touching the template files. This theme could work out very well for a designer or administrator who does not know PHP, HTML, and CSS. Of course, the more the administrator knows, the more power that is available to him.

The Thesis theme also includes a set of hooks to put custom code in various locations of the page. This could be a very powerful feature for an administrator who knows a little HTML but does not want to, or does not know how to, adjust the template files. You would not want to touch the template files in Thesis anyway; all the changes are stored in the database.

You can find more information about the Thesis theme at `http://diythemes.com`.

Sandbox Theme

The Sandbox theme by Andy Skelton and Scott Allan Wallick is the grandfather of the WordPress theme frameworks and many of these other themes bear some resemblance to it. The Sandbox theme does not have all the bells and whistles of the page templates and the custom widget-ready areas, but it never meant to. The Sandbox theme focuses on the CSS hooks and what can be done with CSS alone, really in a CSS Zen garden sort of way. Its best feature is the markup it provides.

You can find more information about the Sandbox theme at `http://www.plaintxt.org/themes/sandbox/` and `http://code.google.com/p/sandbox-theme/`.

Partial Themes

Recently there have been some partial themes for sale. Partial themes are really just a customized template files. For example, one site does not sell a whole custom theme, but rather only the comments portion of the theme. It is a pretty interesting idea, and the samples we saw looked very nice.

But it remains to be seen whether they will merge into a cohesive look and feel with the remainder of your theme, or if it will look like a patchwork of different partial themes that are glued together. Maybe we are on to a new quilt theme idea.

In this chapter we covered how to use themes to organize, structure and present your content. Your theme is the face of your site, and no matter how good your content is, this presentation is what really seals the deal on the user experience. An amateurish looking theme can hurt the credibility of your site, while a sharp, great looking theme can enhance the whole experience. In the next chapter we will look at taking external content sources and incorporating them into your WordPress site to further develop quality of your content and the user experience.

Content Aggregation

WHAT'S IN THIS CHAPTER?

➤ Learn how to get your content noticed.

➤ Understand how to import various sources into your WordPress site.

➤ Discover ways to push content from your WordPress site to other locations.

➤ Gain an understanding of different advertising methods to monetize your web site.

With the rise of social web sites, your own web site is not the only place on the Web to find you. Nowadays, you most likely participate in several different social networking applications, each catering to a different audience — your friends, family, or professional acquaintances, or people who share a common interest on a specific topic. Whatever the case, there is no one place to find you online, except maybe Google. What if you want to aggregate all these different interactions into a single point of contact? Enter the idea of a *lifestream*.

This chapter is about getting content from external locations — typically, but not always social networking web sites — into your web site and conversely taking your own content and publishing it out through social sites or feeds. In particular we will cover Facebook, Twitter and subscription feeds, as they are the most common. We'll also consider how to utilize other content sites with their own APIs like Google maps and how you can use the WordPress API to integrate other sources.

WHAT IS A LIFESTREAM?

Simply put, a lifestream is the amassed collection of your activity from different locations and social networks into one place. Because each social network you participate in either has different audiences due to the nature of the participants or caters to a specific niche, it may make sense for the content of your participation to spread beyond the walls of the one location.

You have to make some choices. Is all content going to go everywhere? Do you have to keep work and social audiences separate? Is content going to be syndicated from every site to every site? This is most likely not possible, or desired, so will you have one place to aggregate your participative content? Obviously for the purposes of this book, your WordPress site is that one place.

The next step is to determine which sources you will aggregate into your blog. You could participate in so many different ones that this can be a tough decision. One thing to consider is who your audience is. Realize that once you put something on the public Internet, it is always out there and will probably be discovered.

Another consideration is which web sites actually have a mechanism or conduit to facilitate getting this content into your WordPress pages. Many offer web services to promote the spreading of information, but others (notably Facebook) are sealed off and will only take information in, although Facebook is opening up more and more with its Facebook Connect initiative. This covers the mechanism for assembling external sources; using a prebuilt API provided from the source web site that can push the content, code or a plugin on your WordPress site to pull the information or some other custom method.

What services and content do you want to include? For example, Delicious and Digg enable you to share references or interesting links with others. Flickr enables you to show your latest uploaded photos in your site, and YouTube has a service for doing the same for video. You can post what music you are currently listening to if you participate at Last.fm. Probably the most common is posting your current activity via Twitter. Business users can integrate with LinkedIn and other job posting sites. A business site can extend its functionality simply by combining various web resources into one site.

You will also have to decide how much of the content you are going to collect. Are you intending to completely syndicate the content and republish the whole piece, or are you planning to tease at one location and drive traffic to the other. Additionally, on what schedule? Do you want daily digests of information from various sources or near real time re-publishing?

GETTING NOTICED

You might want to aggregate your online participations into one spot for many reasons. The primary reason is for personal branding and getting noticed; whether by design or not, this is the root reason. Personal branding is guarding and reinforcing your public image online through these various resources for professional reasons, for example if you are a freelancer, or for personal reasons, vanity or otherwise.

Promoting your online identity is one of the major reasons to amass your online interactions into one place. You can use this to showcase your professional involvement a community or profession. This can showcase your expertise in many ways as well as spread your audience to different groups. It can really function as a type of business networking among different audiences.

Even if you're not using a public persona for business purposes, this same reason applies to your hobbies or your personal passion. If you participate in social networks for home beer brewing, why not aggregate those activities into one location? If you attract attention because of your witty insight or accurate and knowledgeable information, this is one way to become recognized as an expert in your field of interest. A nice side effect of this behavior is that the links help the popular search engines find you, which is covered in Chapter 10.

Another reason for collecting different information into one site is simply about how easy it is for others to find that information. For example, if your site functions as a family grapevine or business news aggregator it could be difficult for a family member or a possible client to keep tabs on all the different locations that you participate in. If you tweet about your baby's first steps, will your mom ever see it? Does she even know what Twitter is? Well, she probably does now that Oprah is on it, but can she keeps tabs on all the different places this news could be broadcast? In the same vein, how will clients know to check your latest YouTube promotional video if they do not know it is even available? Collecting this information into a primary source brings all these different data points in front of your audience's eyes. And in the end, it drives traffic to your site rather than away from it, because your site becomes the one true source.

This is a classic "long tail" content problem, and worth discussing a little more. Your web site is just one source of content in hundreds of millions out there. But the people you intersect and actively communicate with, and the closure of the set of those people's friends and families, builds an audience: Your audience. Aggregating your content is about building this audience by "showing up" in multiple places with appropriate content, context and granularity of updates. Tweeting about recent blog posts, or importing blog post summaries into Facebook, for example, are easy ways to spread the word. Incorporating professional organizations that strengthen your own professional reputation furthers this goal.

SOCIAL MEDIA BUTTONS

A great way, perhaps the best way, to get your content noticed and generate more traffic to your site is to use the power of the social networking sites. First, you have to have good, interesting content on your site. But, unlike *Field of Dreams*, if you built it, they will not necessarily come. You have to advertise. Of course, an ambitious and loyal visitor may take the link to your content and submit it to the Internet at large, but why not make it even easier?

Adding social media buttons to your WordPress site makes it easy for readers to include your content in their rankings, ratings or aggregations, whether through the nerd-core Technorati or the more mainstream Digg. Getting consumers to share their preferences and point back to your content is the core idea of the "long tail" of content; without recommendations from similarly like-minded people, your content never gets discovered. This is true for music, movies, or blogs.

The Sociable plugin (`http://wordpress.org/extend/plugins/sociable/` and `http://yoast.com/wordpress/sociable/`) currently maintained by Joost de Valk does just this. The Sociable plugin supports links to nearly 100 different social networking sites for your visitors to share your content. This plugin is very configurable and has a great admin control panel. You can configure which sites are enabled for sharing, allowing you to tailor it for your audience or just your own preferences. There are also several options for controlling the placement of the social networking icons on your site as well as some additional styling options.

The default options provide a nice Share and Enjoy snippet at the bottom of each post as shown in Figure 9-1.

Most admirable about this plugin is the simplicity. Out of the box, it just works, and it works as advertised. Visitors can read some of your great content and decide to share it on Digg. All they have to do is click the Digg icon and log in to Digg. It is that simple.

However, there are really two sides to this topic. One is taking your content and spreading it out to the social networks, such as Slashdot, Digg, or Reddit — which is what the Sociable plugin does. The other is linking to your own personal profiles on these sites from your own site.

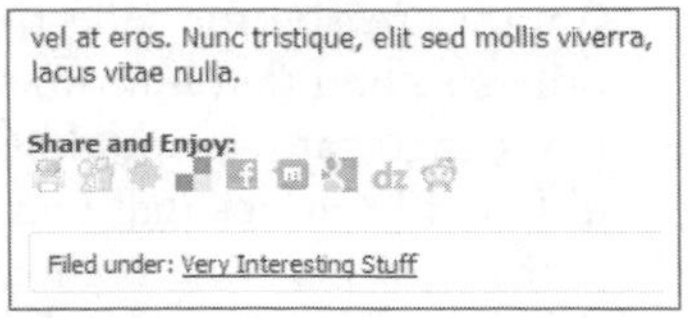

FIGURE 9-1: Sociable social networking button under a WordPress post

Linking to your social networking profiles from your own site reinforces the idea of using your site as the hub. It validates your profiles as being truly you and representative of your online voice. Connecting these profiles together is a double-edged sword because not only does it certify your profiles and solidify your online reputation, but it also links profiles from separate audiences together. It is a choice you will have to make, which is pretty much the caution expressed throughout this entire chapter.

Validating your community profiles is a great thing if you are using your online presence for a professional endeavor. It's advertising how involved you are and in what capacities. Affirming your identities from your main site is like a trust system. This takes some doubt from your visitor and you do not have to deal with Twitter "Verified Accounts" or changing your name to the @theRealDavidDamstra Honest.

You can link to your profiles pretty easily by editing the template files or using an HTML widget. In general, these links do not change very often, if at all. Nevertheless, some nice plugins handle all the hard work for you.

For example, the Social Media Page plugin (`http://wordpress.org/extend/plugins/social-media-page/` or `http://www.norton42.org.uk/294-social-media-page-plugin-for-wordpress.html`) by Philip Norton supports more than 100 social media sites. Once installed, all you have to do is fill in your username information and the links are built for you. You can then use the plugin's smart tag in a post or page or a widget to show the links. Figure 9-2 shows an example of the widget.

Making a social media page is pretty easy. Create a new page. It can be titled anything you want. In the content editor, switch to the HTML view; this step is critical. Then in content, simply use:

```
<!-- social-media-page -->
```

This smart tag will be replaced by links to all of your enabled social media networks. It is a nice way to centralize all your online presences into one easy-to-manage page.

Many plugins can achieve similar results. Check them out and make your own evaluation.

FIGURE 9-2: Social Media Page sidebar widget

SIMPLE SOCIAL NETWORKING BADGES

There are two different ways to integrate external social networking sites into your own site, and they have very different impacts on your content site. We want you to be able to distinguish between the two, and be able to decide when you may want one over the other.

The first is what we are calling "simple social networking badges." These are snapshots of your participation in an external site, at a specific moment in time. That is they are ephemeral and change as frequently as you log activity on the external site. Examples of these badges could be sidebar widgets showing your latest tweet or your current Facebook status.

These simple social networking badges showcase your membership in other social sites, but they do not contribute to the content on your own site. They are more decorative than substantive, even if your participation on the other site is extensive.

The second case is actually taking the content, or a portion of it, from the external location and republishing it on your WordPress site. This gives the content a life of its own, and on your own terms. Specifically, you are not relying on the third party to preserve your content, but also making your own copy in your own database, making it your personal responsibility to maintain.

Both the snapshot and republishing use cases have value, but you should recognize the difference in the permanence and longevity of the different approaches. We will cover both use cases in this chapter.

Using social networking badges creates a positive feedback loop around your WordPress blog. Ideally, if you get people following you on Twitter or Facebook, they're more likely to click through to your "listed web site" to read your output in longer and larger form. People who read your blog may also want to follow your shorter or unrelated updates on other sites; in both cases you're relying on the network effort of "friends of friends" to drive interest in your content.

COLLECTING EXTERNAL CONTENT

You have weighed the pros and cons of aggregating your online reputation into your WordPress site. The next question is how are you going to do it? And which sites are you going to include?

Basically, you can only include sites that have an API to permit the consumption of the data. That is not entirely true; you could code up a spider that logs into the remote site and harvests the information you want, but that would be pretty obscure and not fun to maintain long term. For the purposes of this book we are going to focus on exposed APIs.

The first option to integrate services is to read the API documentation and create a plugin or other function to consume and convert the information into something WordPress can use, such as a post. Because the underlying architecture of WordPress is PHP, you can use whatever PHP tricks you have up your sleeve and code a nice solution. For more information about plugin development, see Chapter 7. In truth, you do not even have to use PHP; you could use an intermediary language and interface with the WordPress table directly.

Generic XML Feed

Let's take a look at a simple example for integrating a generic XML data source into your WordPress site. What you'll do here is take an XML formatted feed, and consume it using PHP code. You'll then convert it into a format suitable for a post on WordPress. In this case, you're taking each node of the XML and making an individual post. Finally, you'll make the WordPress post using the built in WordPress API. This is an automated way of taking the external source that generates the XML and make new posts, just as if you were hand retyping it in the WordPress Dashboard. This is an example that could be used for any XML source, but for this example we will use Twitter, which has a well-documented and simple-to-use API. Again, we are focusing on extracting the content and repurposing it for use in your WordPress site. This is not like the Twitter badges covered in the previous section which show the current Twitter updates. Those badges are more decoration than content and nothing persists on your site. This example turns tweets into posts. Getting the latest tweets for a single user in XML format is simple (assuming you have PHP5 with SimpleXML):

```
$twitterUser = "mirmillo";
$url = "http://twitter.com/statuses/user_timeline/$twitterUser.xml";
$xml = new SimpleXMLElement(file_get_contents($url));
header("Content-type: text/xml");
echo $xml->asXML();
```

Create a new PHP file with the above code (substitute your own Twitter account), and place it on a web server. If you use a web browser and view the served page, you will see the last 20 or so tweets from your account in a nice XML format. This gives you a chance to see what you're working with. Remember, we are only using Twitter as an example; this could be any structured XML.

Rather than echoing this XML, you would in turn parse it and use the WordPress XML-RPC to create new posts. Unfortunately, the XML-RPC is phenomenally not documented. And, for some strange reason there is not a built-in WordPress API function for creating a new post, so you have to use the metaWebBlog API. Google will be your friend here.

Here is a simple example using the XML-RPC with the built-in WordPress client. First, you will retrieve the XML feed into a local variable on your site. Next you will include the built in XML-RPC client that comes with WordPress. This will allow you to create the new posts.

```
$twitterUser = "mirmillo";
$url = "http://twitter.com/statuses/user_timeline/$twitterUser.xml";
$xml = new SimpleXMLElement(file_get_contents($url));

include('../../../wp-includes/class-IXR.php');
$client = new IXR_Client('http://localhost/wordpress/xmlrpc.php');
```

Depending on your needs, you may want to sort your tweets by date or keep track of the last one posted. In order to keep this example simple, we will skip that. The next step is to loop over the XML nodes and pull the appropriate information that make up a WordPress post. The XML-RPC format for a new post is an associative array with title and description key/value pairs. There are other keys you can use to populate other WordPress fields should you need them. However, if you do not provide them, WordPress will fill in the blanks with defaults from your configuration.

```
foreach ($xml->status as $status)
{
    /* set up the post - there are many more keys you can include */
    $content['title'] = "Tweet from $status->created_at";
    $content['description'] = "<p>".$status->text."</p>";
```

Next, you will take this associative array and use the XML-RPC client to make a new WordPress post. Again, there is not a built-in way to do this in WordPress, so you use the `metaWeblog.newPost` method.

```
    /* post the tweet */
    $client->query('metaWeblog.newPost', '', 'admin', 'password', $content, true);
    if ($client->message->faultString)
    {
        echo "Failure - ".$client->message->faultString."<br />";
    } else {
        echo "Success - ".$status->text."<br />";
    }
```

Putting it all together, from retrieving the XML feed, instantiating the local XML-RPC client, formatting the data and creating the post, here is the file in its entirety:

```
$twitterUser = "mirmillo";
$url = "http://twitter.com/statuses/user_timeline/$twitterUser.xml";
$xml = new SimpleXMLElement(file_get_contents($url));

include('../../../wp-includes/class-IXR.php');
$client = new IXR_Client('http://localhost/wordpress/xmlrpc.php');

foreach ($xml->status as $status)
{
    /* set up the post - there are many more keys you can include */
    $content['title'] = "Tweet from $status->created_at";
    $content['description'] = "<p>".$status->text."</p>";
    /* post the tweet */
    $client->query('metaWeblog.newPost', '', 'admin', 'password', $content, true);
    if ($client->message->faultString)
    {
        echo "Failure - ".$client->message->faultString."<br />";
    } else {
        echo "Success - ".$status->text."<br />";
    }
}
```

This file can be placed in the active theme folder of your WordPress installation. By placing it here, you can access it directly without messing with core files and your upgrade path. You would also want to set up some sort of cron job to make this trigger automatically depending on how often you want to aggregate. This method is a departure from using the WordPress Dashboard to generate content. In this case you are prompting the creation of the new posts without invoking WordPress directly. To make this work, you will need to access the URL of the PHP file you just created in a browser, which will kick the import process off. Once you have this manual process working, you can then set up a scheduled task via your operating system's built in mechanism, such as cron, to launch the import on a regular basis.

What is really nice about the XML-RPC method is that there is no WordPress overhead involved. It accomplishes the goals outside of the WordPress framework, yet integrates the content appropriately. This method uses the application stack of PHP and the cron job, and only relies on WordPress for the XML-RPC client. It's similar to posting from an external editor that invokes the XML RPC API to send its content to WordPress and have it turned into a post.

Alternatively, you could accomplish something similar with a full-fledged plugin and use the built-in WordPress API. For example, a traditional plugin could use `wp_insert_post()`, which is well documented in the codex and may provide you more flexibility. But in order to use the plugin method you will need to load all the database connectivity and API features. For more information on writing a plugin, check out Chapter 7. We'll explore a Twitter-specific plugin that performs this function in the next section.

Consuming XML to aggregate the content into your own posts is pretty simple. If you do not find a plugin that already exists to import your content, you can do it yourself with relative ease. You could create an XML-RPC consumer for each XML interface you want to aggregate into your WordPress site. If you designed it properly you could probably even reuse some of the code and keep it relatively lightweight. This flexibility allows you to consume nearly any type of XML feed, manipulate it and import the content.

Integrating Twitter

Even though we just used Twitter as an example of how to integrate any XML feed, let's look at how you could integrate Twitter specifically. Twitter is currently the poster child for open web service APIs. The Twitter API is well documented and easy to use. In addition, it has tons of features. All of this makes integrating your Twitter activities with your WordPress installation a breeze. As such, there are several things you can do with Twitter integration. For example, you can show your latest tweets in a sidebar widget; this is an example of a simple social media badge. You could archive each tweet as its own WordPress post, or get fancier and have daily or weekly archives. You could grab specific tweets and use them in your header to create a dynamic first impression. Or finally, you could reverse the integration and automatically tweet every time you publish a new blog post.

The Twitter Tools plugin (`http://wordpress.org/extend/plugins/twitter-tools/`) by Alex King does almost all of this. And it is all contained in one plugin with a simple control panel so you can pick and choose how you want to use it.

For example, showing your latest tweets in the simple social networking sidebar widget is straightforward functionality with this plugin. First, install the plugin on your WordPress site and activate it. Using the new Twitter Tools dashboard, configure your Twitter username and password. Next, save your settings and jump over to the Widgets control panel. You will notice a new widget for Twitter Tools. This widget, by default, will show your last three tweets. Drag this widget to the appropriate sidebar for your theme to enable it. The benefit of this method is that it is trivially simple to implement; turn it on and it's there. The downside is the transitive nature of this type of integration. You may generate some interest in people to follow you on Twitter, but it does not provide lasting content for your personal site.

Twitter Tools can also convert each individual tweet into a post. Depending on how you use Twitter, this can be a nice way to back up, or archive your tweets on your own site. For example, if you use Twitter to create notes to yourself, having WordPress convert these to posts will give you the simplicity of Twitter, but then include the power of the structured content in WordPress.

An alternative approach would be to publish your tweets as asides intermingled around your regular blog posts. Think of asides in the same context as comments you make in the course of conversation that aren't related to the main topic at hand. In this case, because they are originating from Twitter, they would be single-line posts, which make them ideal for asides. Simply take the tweets from Twitter and create new posts in a special category. Your theme would have to handle this special logic to create the right "asides" feel: shown in a sidebar, or highlighted, to differentiate them from the main narrative of your blog posts. Once you have the tweets making new posts, this could be as simple as using the Sandbox theme discussed in Chapter 8 and some creative CSS:

```
category-twitter h2, .category-twitter .entry-date,
.category-twitter .entry-meta {
    display:none;
}
.category-twitter .entry-content p {
    background: #22739E url('images/twitter.png') 5px 5px no-repeat;
    color: #fff;
    padding: 2px 5px 2px 25px;
}
```

If you're publishing each tweet to its own individual post, Twitter Tools also has the capability to create daily or weekly digests. This is particularly interesting when you use Twitter to capture moments of your day through tweets. The hook with Twitter is how easy it is to use, and yet, because of the size restriction you are forced to keep your posts short — hence microblogging. In this case, you are telling the daily story of your life in a series of small takes. Allowing WordPress to import them creates another form of the same narrative. It is no different from writing an entire post entry and publishing it, except this way is self-assembled from the microblogging format used by Twitter.

One more feature of Twitter Tools is to reverse the integration; that is, tweet when you publish a new post. This feature has to be explicitly enabled in the Twitter Tools dashboard. Once turned on, Twitter Tools will automatically tweet on your behalf that a new post has been published and will include a link to your article. For some people this is a nice alternative to RSS syndication, which we will look at later in the chapter.

Alex King's Twitter Tools plugin is very powerful and covers a broad spectrum of Twitter integration possibilities. However, sometimes you may need to do something unique, or something that a plugin was not designed for. Maybe you just have a different itch than the plugin author. Let's take a look at how you could show your latest tweet as part of your WordPress header, without using a plugin. This would function similarly to a Facebook current status and would be like a "What I am doing right now" visual hook in the masthead of your web site. To accomplish this, you'll create a special function that will retrieve the latest tweet from your Twitter timeline. We should note that Twitter does impose rate limits on the number of times the Twitter API can be accessed per hour, so depending on your traffic levels, you may want to consider augmenting this function with caching or rate limiting of your own to avoid triggering these limits.

The first step is to create the function that will retrieve your latest tweet. This functionality would be best placed in your functions.php file. You will notice some similarity to the previously discussed example for integrating a generic XML feed. We are using the same API, just fine tuning what is being retrieved, and abstracting it into a unique function. Here is the function:

```
function ddamstra_getLatestTweet($twitterUser = "mirmillo") {
    $url = "http://twitter.com/statuses/user_timeline/$twitterUser.xml?count=1";
    $xml = new SimpleXMLElement(file_get_contents($url));
    $status = $xml->status->text;
    return $status;
}
```

This function gets the text of the latest tweet from Twitter. It only retrieves one tweet, as seen in the query string of the URL. This status text is then returned to the function caller. Next, you will need to access this information by calling the function. In your `header.php` template file, you can add some code to the latest tweet:

```
<div id="header">
    <h1 id="blog-title"><?php bloginfo('name') ?></h1>
    <div id="blog-description"><?php bloginfo('description') ?></div>
    <div id="twitter-current"><?php echo ddamstra_getLatestTweet(); ?></div>
</div><!-- #header -->
```

Supplement this sample with a simple link to your Twitter account and you have added a nice touch of personality to your site. Assuming, of course, that your audiences overlap and you are a responsible Twitter user.

The Twitter API is very robust and open. You can do pretty much whatever you want with it; you just need to read the documentation and this is what makes playing with the Twitter API so much fun. The result is tons of plugins to integrate with Twitter including posting to Twitter from the WordPress Control Panel, adding a "tweet this" to your blog posts to encourage visitors to spread your word. There is even a plugin to add Twitter information to comment posts and one to use Twitter pictures in lieu of gravatars.

Google Maps

Google Maps, or really any mapping service, is a commonly requested item. If you have any intention of clients actually visiting your place of business, or want them to attend a certain event, you need to provide directions. Online mapping and direction services like Google Maps are ubiquitous for this now. It is hard to remember how we found our way around town before, but at the same time we now have the social benefit of location-aware services.

Anyway, you want to add a map to your site. Google provides a nice mechanism to simply embed a map in your site using its tools. You can find this in the top right of the Google Maps page. Copy the code and paste it into your WordPress post or page. It is that simple and it works.

But, what if you need a whole bunch of maps for your site? For example, if you are a site focusing on local events and happenings this manual process would work, but it is time-consuming and inefficient. Brad Williams (yes, one of us authors) made a plugin just for that called Post Google Map (http://webdevstudios.com/support/wordpress-plugins/post-google-map-plugin-for-wordpress/ and http://wordpress.org/extend/plugins/post-google-map/).

Once you enable this plugin and enter your Google API key, you'll have a new section in your write panels. This new section allows you to relate addresses with each post or page and automatically creates an associated Google Map. This map can be displayed either in a sidebar widget or can be embedded right in the content using a WordPress shortcode. Figure 9-3 is an example of a post with the map embedded.

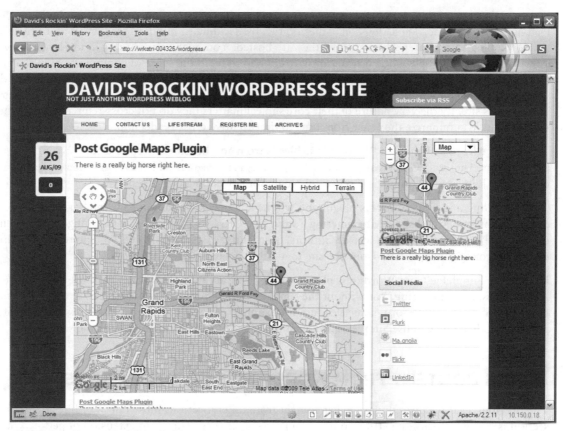

FIGURE 9-3: Example of Google Maps integration

It works well and is immensely useful for a site that offers local news, restaurant reviews, or any other location-based information. It also has some nice features such as being able to switch out the markers on the map from various stock markers or you can even upload your own. Multiple addresses can be associated with the same post, meaning if you were reviewing a restaurant that had multiple locations, you could place each location in the same map.

Integrating RSS and ATOM Feeds

For us, RSS is becoming the glue that ties many sites together. Despite its shaky start and competing standards, RSS is a solid means to communicate certain information between different sites.

One reason you might want to import RSS feeds from another site into your own is to create your own RSS aggregator site like a "Planet" (a la http://planet.wordpress.org/) or like Google Reader. RSS is an easy way to keep tabs on multiple sites in an easy-to-digest location. Make sure you have permission to republish the content; consult a lawyer if you have questions. Also, make sure you are courteous and cache the feeds. Your web site should not adversely affect the performance of another.

If the originating content is your content, or content you have permission to repurpose, building a feed aggregator is fine. Typically, companies do this by deciding to build a "planet" of all of their employee blogs, no matter where or how they are hosted. You might also do this if you have a few quasi-independent people who all want to share content to build the sense of community akin to early points about getting noticed. Finally, you could do this if you have more than one blog and periodically want to post a summary of "what's going on over in XYZ land." For example if you run a food site and a sports site. By the very nature of their core subject matters they do not cross-reference each other, but each could summarize the other from time to time to drive cross-readership.

The easiest way to consume an RSS or ATOM feeds from another site for republishing in your site is to use a plugin. The FeedWordPress plugin (`http://wordpress.org/extend/plugins/feedwordpress/`) by Charles Johnson is a simple and powerful plugin for consuming these feeds.

After installing and activating this plugin you will have a new set of administration dashboards to configure the syndicated sites. After entering a valid feed URL, you have options to configure scheduling of when the feed is re-visited, as well as, authors, posts and tag information. This plugin really simplifies the means to republish content from one site to another via RSS or ATOM feeds.

Finally, the SimplePie Core WordPress plugin is a PHP library that gives you a bit more control over feed processing and filtering, but without the simpler-to-use interface. If you want to extract content from an RSS feed and perform some cleanup, for example removing images or resorting items before publishing, then you can use SimplePie as a container for your PHP content processing scripts.

PUSHING CONTENT FROM WORDPRESS TO OTHER SITES

The previous section covered ways to get content from other locations into your WordPress site. This section is going to focus on getting your content into other sites. This is an extension of getting your site noticed, and really focuses on using WordPress as the hub of your content generation. WordPress is designed to be a publishing platform and it excels at it, so using your WordPress as the source site has its advantages.

Feeding RSS into Other Sites

As covered previously, WordPress can easily import a RSS feed and republish it. But WordPress also can be the source of the RSS feed. One of the killer features of WordPress is it generates an RSS feed for which ever view you are looking at, automatically.

Besides your traditional "latest posts" RSS feed, WordPress also makes a RSS feed for each category, tag, author and post comments. To see this at work, browse to any category, tag or author view of a WordPress site and add `/feed` to the end of the URL. You will see the RSS feed for that particular taxonomy.

This allows you to control which information you are viewing in your own RSS subscription to the site. It actually gives you fine-grained controls that you can now tweak in your RSS reader of choice. Also combine this with the previous example using the FeedWordPress consumer plugin.

A great use of this is to update one WordPress site, and feed multiple locations. For example, we have a policy where news articles are published across multiple WordPress sites. A great solution to avoid having to publish the same content many times is to use these tuned RSS feeds. In this case, we publish news to a central WordPress site, publishing the content once, and selecting specific categories for the post to be published in. These categories in turn, map to the individual child sites. The child sites use FeedWordPress to consume only the category RSS feed for their precise news feed and republish the article. This provides us one central location to update the content, but the content is then published on a multitude of sites.

Feeding WordPress into Facebook

Whereas Twitter is so open and easy to use, on the flip side is Facebook. Also immensely popular, Facebook is the new walled garden of online communities. Various roads exist into Facebook, but very few to get data out. This makes integrating your WordPress site with Facebook somewhat more of a challenge. There are no plugins to take your current Facebook status and post it on WordPress. (Although you can work around this by using Twitter to update both Facebook and your site.) Despite all the press about the Facebook platform, you are limited in what you can do, unless you are pushing data to your Facebook profile.

In Facebook, you can feed your site's posts (or any RSS feed) into your notes stream. It is really easy, actually, because it is a built-in feature of Facebook and really has nothing to do with WordPress. Here is what you do:

1. Log in to your Facebook account.
2. Click Setting in the top right (assuming Facebook has not changed the layout again).
3. Click Application Settings.
4. Click Notes.
5. Click the link in the upper right that reads "Import a Blog."
6. Read the warnings and disclaimers.
7. Key in your RSS feed URL. Given your regular URL, Facebook can probably determine your RSS feed URL itself.
8. Review the content import and click the Accept button.
9. Your WordPress posts are now in your Facebook stream.

These notes have all the features of regular Facebook note content. That is, people can comment and mark them as "liked." This process works for individual Facebook accounts as well as for Facebook "Pages." If you have multiple blogs, or wish to separate your blogging life from your personal life, create a Facebook Page for your blog, import the WordPress content into the Page's Notes application, and use the Facebook social network to drive "fans" to it.

There are a few downsides to pushing your blog content to Facebook:

➤ It impacts your viewer statistics as seen by your WordPress site counters, because Facebook viewers aren't accessing the WordPress site with the statistics hooks.

➤ Comments on Facebook notes do not syndicate back to your blog, so you've fractured your discussion and have comments in two places.

➤ Once a note is imported, you can't edit it, so Facebook becomes a write-once replica of your blog.

One middle road is to use your Facebook page (individual or blog-oriented) for summaries of blog entries, or to highlight that you've posted something new. This drives readers outside of Facebook's walled garden back to your single content source.

A second option is to integrate with Facebook Connect. Facebook Connect currently is mostly about authentication — specifically using your Facebook credentials to sign in to other web sites like Digg or your WordPress site, although the long-term goals include much more functionality.

With the Facebook Connect plugin (`http://www.sociable.es/facebook-connect/`) by Javier Reyes, visitors will be able to log in to your WordPress using their Facebook credentials. On your WordPress site, they will have specially formatted usernames that include their Facebook Profile ID. However, their full name will be properly formatted and their web site URL will be their Facebook public profile page. It takes several steps to get this plugin up and running, including signing up (if you are not already) for the Facebook Developer program.

However, once this plugin is set up, it does have some interesting features, including showing some of the recent visitors and the comments they leave on your WordPress site are also displayed back in Facebook. In short, this is a pretty powerful plugin that uses what limited functionality is available in the Facebook Connect platform.

Although Facebook is enormously popular, and shows no signs of slowing down, at the time of this writing, it's a serious data stream dead end. Definitely weigh the benefits of what pushing data into Facebook gets you, and make sure it is in line with your goals. The key point here is that if you are relying on your WordPress site to measure content, interest and traffic, but you also publish into Facebook, you are going to miss some fraction — possibly a large fraction — of your audience. This impacts your statistics for some ad sites, and if you're counting on click-throughs, you lose the ad display credits.

ADVERTISING

When using your web site to sell a product or service, or gain potential customers for your business, your WordPress installation is more overhead than profit center. On the other hand, blogs with large readerships often drive non-trivial advertising rates, picking up the online equivalent of local or national newspaper display ads. In this section, we'll look at various aspects of the money game, from configuring ad boxes to becoming an affiliate merchant site.

If you're wondering what this section is doing in the middle of a content aggregation discussion, it's because advertising is a syndication issue. You're either taking someone else's idea of an attractive, keyword-specific ad and placing it in your content stream, or you are putting your own ads into someone else's display slots.

Monetizing Your Site

There are a number of ways to monetize your WordPress site: display ads from one of the larger online advertising agencies such as Google or Yahoo, become an affiliate of an online merchant like Amazon that offers commissions on click-throughs that result in product sales, or sell specific sponsorship or banner space on your blog to an interested party. When you go down the commercial route, however, you're also making an explicit decision to cede some of the design and display value of your site over to a third party.

Passive monetization of your content is nice, and some truly popular blogs do throw off enough advertising revenue to fund small companies, but for the average blogger, advertising is going to be more about catching an occasional click-through. It's critical to have reasonable expectations of how much advertising revenue your blog can generate, because you're trading off aesthetics and display space for advertisement placements, with little control over the products and graphics styles represented.

Advertising monetization ranges from the pay-per-click model, where you get paid each time a viewer clicks on a displayed ad, to the pay-per-view or pay-per-day model, where you earn income for simply displaying the ad or placing an ad on your site for some specified time period. Google AdSense fits the first model, where Google's ad syndication service establishes a price per click based on keywords and content, and then matches available advertisers to available slots based on Google's defined market pricing and advertiser budgets. Project Wonderful is an example of the pay-per-day model, where you offer predefined ad boxes to potential advertisers, and Project Wonderful runs a continuous auction for each day of display. You get the same income whether or not anyone clicks on the ads.

In all models, the value of advertising slots offered on your WordPress site is proportional to the popularity of your site and the probability of a view or click-through. If you don't have a variety of content that's regularly updated, your ads will tend to cluster in the equivalent of late-night local cable television commercials. Similarly, if the thought of a weight-loss ad sitting under your blog post discussing the "fat tone" of a jazz guitarist's solo offends your sensibilities or detracts from the seriousness of your musical musings, consider passive monetization of your site using an affiliate or referral program like Amazon Associates that pays you a fee for each referred purchaser.

Compounding these issues is the path users take to find your content; advertising is carried on your hosted WordPress site, but not in content republished through Facebook or aggregated on other sites. If your site is read through an RSS feed, make sure you consider choosing an advertising manager that places ads in feeds as well as in the generated HTML for your blog.

Setting Up Advertising

Placing advertising on your site is no different than laying out a print page with a mix of editorial and commercial content: Decide how many ads you want, where they are going to be placed, and what potential content conflicts you want to avoid. This is as much a design as a technical process, because you have to pay attention to the eventual page presentation and tone of the content when displayed with advertisements.

Using Advertising Plugins

Before running ads on your site, you need to create an account with one of the popular ad syndication services. Generally this means that you have to create a login, describe your blog, demonstrate some minimum competence in terms of content, and provide payment information. In return, you get an advertising client identifier, and usually a slot (or ad) identifier. If you're using Google AdSense, for example, you can create multiple channels for your advertising slots, perhaps tying different channels to different categories or parts of your blog, or using one channel for each of several different blogs. The client identifier is tied to you as a payment entity; the channels describe different display destinations for ads and may be wildly different in terms of their content, size, shape, and going click-through rates.

Advertising Manager (http://wordpress.org/extend/plugins/advertising-manager) is the most popular plugin for handling ad placement and inventory within WordPress. It supports Yahoo, Google, and the emergent OpenX, among other ad services, and it has a wealth of configuration options that account for terms of service, like limiting Google AdSense impressions to three per page. Figure 9-4 illustrates some of the configuration options available for Google AdSense with this plugin.

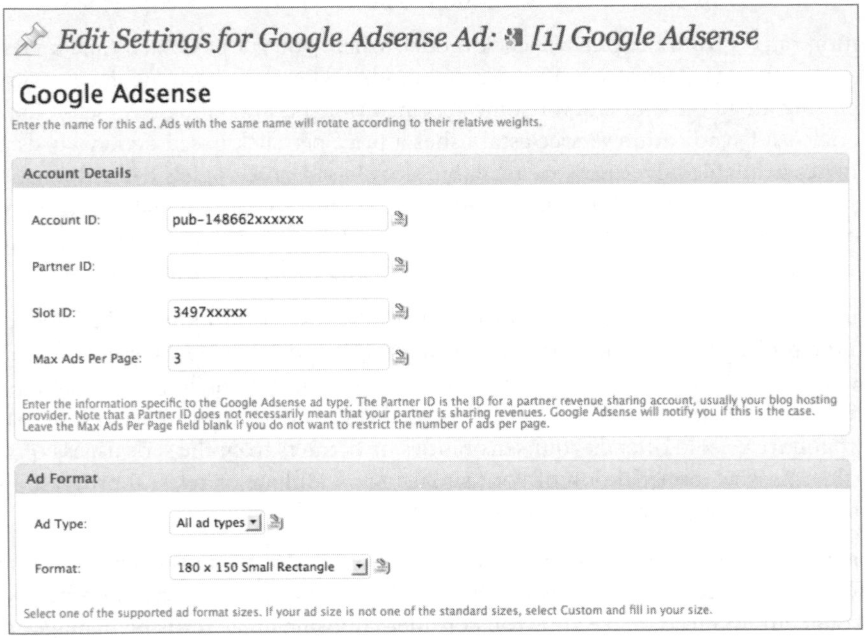

FIGURE 9-4: Advertising Manager for Google AdSense

After installing the plugin, configuration is as simple as choosing the ad service, copying your account and slot information into the control panel, and choosing the display specifics to govern the size and shape of ad boxes. Once the plugin is initialized, you'll see an "Insert Ad ... " drop down menu in the WordPress post editing pane, allowing you to insert ads selectively in posts. When you click on the drop-down, you'll insert the smart code [ad#Google Adsense] into your post; this is best done at the end of the post for readability and user happiness.

If you want to exert explicit control over what is being advertised on your site, rather than handing that option off to an ad syndication service, you can take over the advertising management process using the Author Advertising Plugin. This plugin creates a database within your WordPress MySQL instance for advertising content, allowing you to have each WordPress author attach ads to their individual posts, with the WordPress administrator having editorial control over the ad images, content, and placement. If you want to set up site sponsorships, where someone pays you for a spot that shows up in the header, footer or sidebar, or you want to sell simple display ads that rotate through the site using your own rate card and payment schedule, this plugin gives you the most control over the insertion of ads into your site.

Manual Advertising Placement

The advertising plugins work very well if you want to attach ads to each post, or have them show up in the header or footer of every page. The plugin architecture that we covered in Chapter 7 handles filtering of post code to replace the smart codes with a JavaScript template to call your advertising service, or inserts the appropriate script in the theme's content files. If you'd like finer grain control over ad placement, such as more tightly integrating them into some theme elements, then you'll need to hand-edit the appropriate files and insert the advertising script code.

We won't go through every permutation of editing theme files to insert ad boxes, as this effort is a derivative of the theme creation discussion in Chapter 7. In general, if you're adding an advertising box to your header or footer, then it's going to go just below the last `<div>` in the file, so as not to interfere with other theme elements. In a sidebar, the ad box should be a separate list element, with the ad box code surrounded by `<li>` and `</li>` HTML tags.

The manually insertion process isn't much different than adding a Facebook badge or Twitter bug to your sidebar, as the ad box code is automatically generated by your advertising manager site. For example, if you're using Google AdSense, the control and configuration pages for AdSense let you choose the shape of the ad (rectangular or square), the size of the display box, and the color scheme used. The final step in the ad configuration shows you a small chunk of JavaScript that you copy and paste into your WordPress file. In the example code snippet we've blocked out the Google ad client and ad slot identifiers, but you can see the relative simplicity of the ad display process. The script calls Google's ad syndication engine with information about the destination (your ad client information), the size, and a slot identifier that Google uses to account for ad displays in terms of different "channels" that you set up within their configuration system:

```
<script type="text/javascript"><!--
google_ad_client = "pub-1486xxxxxxxx";
/* 300x250, created for Professional WordPress */
google_ad_slot = "0789yyyyy";
google_ad_width = 300;
google_ad_height = 250;
//-->
</script>
<script type="text/javascript"
src="http://pagead2.googlesyndication.com/pagead/show_ads.js">
</script>
```

Note that the variables defined in the JavaScript are exactly the same values you would have entered in the AdSense plugin. The other somewhat obvious point is that every time you display a Google ad, you're calling Google's syndication service to decide which ad to insert, and waiting for it to return the image and text. This has a nominal impact on your site's perceived performance, unless Google is particularly taxed and your blog display is slowed by the advertising generation.

Hand-editing and insertion of ad boxes from other services is equally simple. Project Wonderful's JavaScript code is even more compact (again we've edited out the personally identifying information):

```
<!-- Beginning of Project Wonderful ad code: -->
<!-- Ad box ID: 45xxx -->
<script type="text/javascript">
<!--
var pw_d=document;
pw_d.projectwonderful_adbox_id = "45xxx";
pw_d.projectwonderful_adbox_type = "6";
pw_d.projectwonderful_foreground_color = "";
pw_d.projectwonderful_background_color = "";
//-->
</script>
<script type="text/javascript"
src="http://www.projectwonderful.com/ad_display.js"></script>
<!-- End of Project Wonderful ad code. -->
```

Project Wonderful has a non-JavaScript version of the advertising box built around calls to their ad manager with parameters for each element in the box. It's the preferred version of the service, because disabling JavaScript in the browser has become a trend. If many of your web site readers turn off JavaScript code, this slightly more verbose ad box still lets you display ads. The bottom of the ad box shows you the current auction rate for that ad slot.

You'll also find a Project Wonderful-specific plugin, Plugin Wonderful (http://wordpress.org/extend/plugins/plugin-wonderful), that allows you to insert Project Wonderful ads into your sidebars using widgets. Plugin Wonderful also creates a new template tag that calls out to the Project Wonderful ad server, giving you the ability to insert ads using the template structures and theme constructs discussed in Chapter 5 and Chapter 8.

Where you put the ads and their shape and style are co-dependent. If you are going to add a stack of ad boxes to your sidebar, then a single column of ad boxes with multiple rows is best; ensure that the width of the ads fits within the sidebar width used by your theme. Opt for a header or footer approach and a single row of multiple ad slots, or a short multi-row matrix fits best. The size of your advertising box also governs what type of ads fit within it: leaderboard ads that span the entire width of the display page won't work in a sidebar, and are least visually difficult when there's only one per ad box. Project Wonderful lets you define multiple ad boxes per site, so if you want to mix and match ads of different geometries, consider wide, single-row boxes for headers and footers and the skyscraper or tall matrix approach for stacks of buttons or square ads in sidebars or under blog posts.

Dealing With Conflict

Conflict between commercial and editorial content probably dates back to the first newspaper that carried advertising. Within the context of this book, we'll only look at two potential types of conflicts: ads you don't want in your space, and advertising platforms that don't want others in their space.

Undesirable ads run the gamut from unrelated products to things that you find offensive. Part of the issue is how the advertising managers decide to match ad campaigns to available advertising slots: keywords and context from the content itself are matched against those keywords that the ad campaign chooses. If you find yourself writing about food, eating, and the resulting weight gain, perhaps in an off-hand manner, don't be surprised if the weight loss ads start showing up under your blog posts. Perhaps your best defense here is a good offense: write regularly, keep your site dynamic and updated, and use tags and the search engine optimization techniques discussed in Chapter 10 to best present your content to advertising managers.

All media vehicles that carry advertising have their own standards of business conduct, such as not running two commercials for competing businesses in the same advertising break. Online advertising services impose their own terms of service on their channels, typically limiting the number of ads that can be placed per page, the types of pages in which ads can appear (not in e-mail, or not on pages that encourage viewers to click away in a thinly veiled click fraud scheme). When you use Google AdSense, you are free to display other ads on your site, provided they are differentiated in color and style to avoid confusion with Google's displayed ads. On the Google AdSense configuration page, pick a color palette for those ads that is distinct from that used by your theme, and then whatever ad slots your theme controls will have distinct borders and backgrounds. If your theme has a widget or slot earmarked for advertising, use that for self-hosted, sponsorship or rotating banner type ads, and let the Google AdSense plugin manage the per-post or per-page boxes, being careful not to mix different advertising platforms in the same part of your display page where they could be confused.

Advertising has been a part of public visual media since the dawn of television and highway billboards. As a site administrator, developer and content creator, you need to decide how and where you want to commercialize your work, and if the aesthetic and editorial efforts are worth the potential financial return.

PRIVACY AND HISTORY

Whether you are creating a business site or a personal site, aggregating your various online interactions into your WordPress site creates the benefit of one true source of your online presence. This makes it easier for your clients, potential clients, family, or random admirers to track what is currently happening with you.

However reasons also exist as to why you would not want to create a lifestream. The obvious reason is the complete opposite of the reasons to create a lifestream — privacy. The main reason for lifestreaming is for discoverability and getting noticed. What makes you discoverable, however, is putting it all out there. Sometimes, for your personal information, this is not what you want.

Privacy should be a concern for anyone publishing information on the Internet. Google caches anything it can find; so does the Internet Archive. There is not anything nefarious about that, but just be aware that once it is out there and discoverable, it is potentially always out there. There is no "are you sure?" button to click. To quote an old Usenet warning:

> *This program posts news to thousands of machines throughout the entire civilized world. Your message will cost the net hundreds if not thousands of dollars to send everywhere. Please be sure you know what you are doing. Are you absolutely sure that you want to do this?*

While the actual financial impact may not be true anymore, if it ever was, you can see this concern of "no going back" has been around a long time on the Internet. The short story is to take a deep breath before you publish something into the ether, because you do not know its lifespan. Once you say it on the net, it is said forever. We don't yet know how kids are going to react when they realize their entire life from birth to this afternoon has been permanently documented on Twitter, Facebook and personal web sites. Long term, it could potentially be far more embarrassing than that picture of you in the bathtub as a baby.

When putting it all out there, you have to be careful. You hear stories about employees being fired because of Facebook — they call in sick and then post stories on their Facebook page about playing hooky and fooling the boss. Posting inappropriate pictures on Flickr can have a lasting effect on your reputation. Certainly within five minutes of interviewing new employees and reading their resumes, many human resources specialists are on search engines and social media sites looking for information about them. Often you can find details that you are not allowed to ask about in a traditional interview. It is an augmented background check of sorts.

The lesson here is that lifestreaming is not for everyone. You have to consider your goals and which streams to include. For better or worse, aggregating all this content onto your WordPress sites makes it all public and easily accessible, but a well-managed online persona can enhance your business or personal reputation. Finally, having your entire online information centrally located can enhance the user experience and build trust at the first impression.

10

Crafting a User Experience

WHAT'S IN THIS CHAPTER?

➤ Understand the principles of the user experience.

➤ Learn the benefits of usability and usability testing.

➤ Recognize how to optimize your site for search engines.

➤ Find out how to improve the built in WordPress search.

The last two chapters have been about creating and presenting your great content to the user. In truth, those two chapters are really about your own goals — how you want the site to look and function and what content you are presenting. But it is not all about you. What about the visitors to your site? This is where the user experience factors in.

Up to this point, we have focused on how to create a site and manage its content. Now the question is — is the site going to attract and retain viewers (users) because of the mechanics and decisions put in place? Because we are dealing with people and their unique perceptions, it is an entirely non-deterministic exercise.

The user experience covers more than what an actual person sitting at a browser in Middle America thinks. Indirectly, web spiders, search engines, and service consumers such as RSS readers, are also your users. Your site needs to be designed and structured so that all classes of users benefit and have a great experience.

USER EXPERIENCE PRINCIPLES

User experience is a topic that is open to interpretation; everyone sees it a little differently. But some good guidelines are available. Some of these ideas are common sense, or seem to be. They all strive to establish that balance between aesthetically pleasing and usable to the end user. These are not hard-and-fast decrees that must be followed. Humans are soft and these guidelines need to flex to meet the needs.

Here are some basic questions to ask:

➤ Does your site have a consistent look?

➤ Is the design helpful or hurtful?

➤ Is your content easy to find and access?

➤ Is your content well structured?

➤ Is your site reasonably quick to load?

This list itemizes the pillars of the user experience. How you choose to use them, or in what combination, is really what this chapter is about. The following sections delve into these topics for a little more clarity.

Consistent Navigation

This is almost a no-brainer these days; it is difficult to not have a consistent look and feel with WordPress themes. You want your visitors to be aware that they are consistently using your site, independently of the path taken to get there. That means having a coherent look and feel to your site — such as a masthead and dependable global navigation.

That does not mean that different sections cannot have their own flair, but it needs to be coherent. It will be very disorienting for a visitor to read some of your content on one page and then click through to the next page with a totally different look and feel to it. Visitors will think they have left your site and you will not get credit for the great content you have created.

Likewise, each page in your site should have a dependable global navigation. Dependable means it does not change and does not move. Visitors should be able to explore your content without fear of getting lost. It may sound silly to a technologist like you, but the average user has a different relationship with technology. This global navigation is a safety line for your visitors to get back to where they came from.

Good global navigation also tells visitors where they are in the site. Specifically setting an "active" item in the menu and making it clear that it is lit up, or somehow distinguished from the rest of the global navigation. This enables a visitor to glance at the navigation and immediately see where they are in your site with respect to the other sections or pages. The Sandbox theme does this automatically; when you use the built-in `sandbox_globalnav()` function you will automatically receive a `current_page_item` class in your menu items like so (this is the rendered HTML):

```
<li class="page_item page-item-27 current_page_item">
  <a title="Register Me" href="/register-me/">
    Register Me
  </a>
</li>
```

Alternatively, if you are creating navigation yourself using WordPress's built-in `is_page()` function, you can achieve the same result (this is the PHP code in the template file):

```
<li class="benefits
  <?php if(is_page('benefits')) { echo "current_page_item";}?>">
    <a title="benefits" href="/benefits/">
      Benefits
    </a>
</li>
```

In both cases some nice CSS on the `current_page_item` class would differentiate this menu item from the rest. We are firm believers in the user feedback functions of the anchor element. First, mousing over the element should provide some sort of feedback beyond switching the cursor to a hand. Usually this means a highlight or darkening of the font, background, or border. Second, the currently active navigation section should be similarly delineated, but different. These two tenets, when used together, create a nice global navigation that visually presents a multitude of information on where the visitor is in relation to the rest of the site and where he can go to read more. Some sample CSS might be:

```
div#menu li a {
  background: #333;
  color: #efefef;
  display: block;
  padding: 5px 10px;
  text-align: center;
  text-decoration: none;
}

div#menu li a:hover {
  background: #EE5900;
}

div#menu li.current_page_item a {
 background: #841BD5;
}

div#menu li.current_page_item a:hover {
 background: #A80499;
}
```

This works in Firefox and Internet Explorer 6 through 8. In Figure 10-1 you can see how this plays out in the web browser. If you browsed this site in real life you would see that the global navigation across the top is in the same place on each and every page of this test web site. You will also notice that this screenshot is of the "A Page" menu item, and that navigation item is visibly different from the other menu items to indicate that it is the active page.

Notice we are referring to it as *global* navigation. That does not mean that every page in your site has to be listed in the main menu. It can, but it does not have to. Sections can have a local navigation block once you are inside them, but the main sections should be accessible via the main menu. This is what makes navigation dependable. It reinforces what the visitor can expect on your site and the methods used to navigate it.

A consistent style and dependable navigation comfort your visitor and reinforce the validity of your content.

Visual Design Elements

Specifically, are the visual assets of your site helpful or distracting to the user? Does the theme reinforce the persona you are portraying with your content or detract from it? This is another one of those topics that are open to personal interpretation. Photos and colors have differing subjective responses from different people, but the overall impression of your site should match the general content.

For example, a business site should not have a bubble-gum pink theme if it wants to be taken seriously; unless, of course, the site is selling toys or bubble gum. At the other extreme, there has recently been a bit of backlash against the use of pink to denote sites or content addressing women's health issues; over-use degrades its impact and importance if blindly applied. Visual design should reflect the brand and brand values you are trying to develop with your WordPress site.

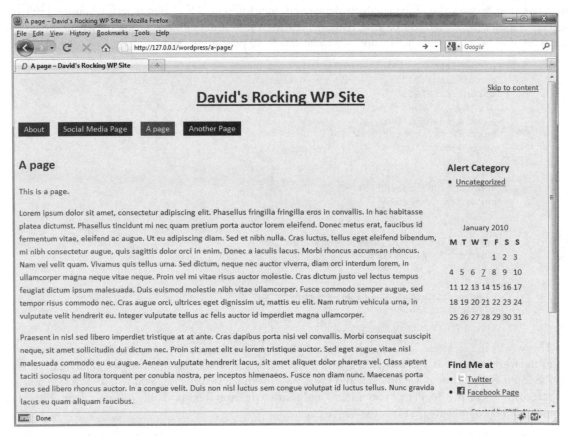

FIGURE 10-1: Active navigation

Colors evoke different feelings. Blue instills trust, which is why it is so prevalent in business logos. Orange suggests new technology and is often used in the telecom industry. Color and branding is a whole topic unto itself, but just consider that pink ponies may not be the way to market your bank, and skulls and crossbones may not be the way to market your children's furniture site.

This topic is pretty difficult to gauge. It is a very emotional topic and often marketing takes over rather than common sense. For example, many of us have worked for clients who were bound and determined that every time they added a new item to the index page that it was the most important thing on the page. That meant that every design element was oversized and blinking, causing the whole page to become nausea inducing. Sort of along the same lines as laundry detergent, if every brand is ultra-new-super-improved, are they not really all the same again?

One design theory that that works well when working up a new mockup is to toil away at the composition. Build up layers of elements working toward the end goal. Once you are happy with what you think could be the final mockup, remove an element. Kick it back one rung and use that. This is a variation on the less-is-more approach.

Take for example, this mockup being created in Adobe Photoshop in Figure 10-2. You will notice in the layers palette on the right side that all the components that make up the mockup are broken into individual layer groups. During the development of this mockup, each graphic element was composed using this method. This enables them to be moved and changed easily without interfering with other layers. You will also notice that a couple of the layer groups are currently turned off. You can tell because the little eyeball icon is not there next to them. This is because when creating this mockup, we tried both of the graphic elements in those layers and deemed them to be too much. Turning them off, kicking it back a notch, created what we felt was a stronger layout.

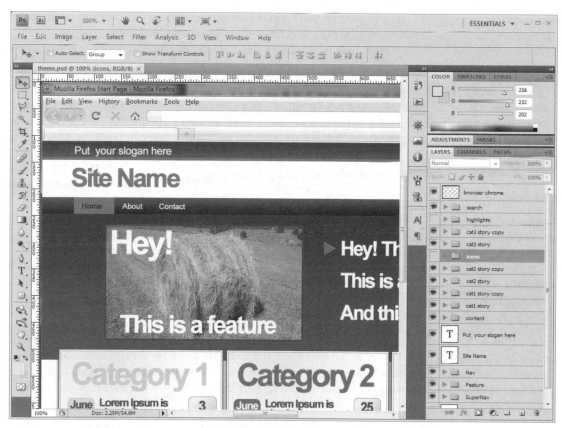

FIGURE 10-2: Mockup being created in Photoshop

Making Content Easy to Find

With a successful site you will reach a point where you have a substantial body of content. Often, the visitor to your site does not categorize or organize content mentally in exactly the same manner as you do. Therefore, there should be multiple paths to get to all content in your site. This increases the likelihood that visitors will be able to find what they are looking for. This is an excellent reason for having categories, tags, and calendar-based archives templates. Having these templates covers three popular ways in which people remember "where something was." They also serve as a way to drive more content interaction and consumption, exposing your thoughts (as the creator) on content sorting.

WordPress assists in this strategy right out of the box. First and foremost your site should have a dependable global navigation, as mentioned previously. WordPress encourages this in its native structure, but how you actually build and organize the navigation is up to you.

Second, WordPress does come with a built-in search functionality. Although it can be improved, as discussed later in this chapter, some search is better than no search. Tagging your content helps with search.

Third, WordPress offers many alternative views of the content. Either with special templates or by simply using the default index template file (see Chapter 8, "Theme Development," for more information on template files), WordPress can offer up your content by date, category, title, author, or through several other variations. Creative use of these templates and other custom loops offers another vector into your content. The catch here is that this method also serves duplicate content, which the search engines discourage, but we cover that later in this chapter.

Fourth, many plugins are available for "related posts." Adding a related posts list to the bottom of a post is another method for providing a way to find your content. This is particularly effective if you have already piqued the interest of your reader with one set of content. Offering similar content is a great idea, and it is a way to provide more information on the subject that can be useful to your visitor.

Site Load Times

Back when dialup was the most prevalent connection speed, web developers were extremely conscientious about the weight of the page and how long it took to load. But as broadband access has increased, developers have become much more lax about it. CSS files have bloomed as new selectors and styles are added rather than merged with existing styles. AJAX and JavaScript libraries have been included, sometimes more than one JavaScript library, just to achieve neat-o gee-whiz effects. iFrames, web services, and other third-party components all add to the bloat of an HTML document. Multiple database queries to gather information slow down the page on the server side.

Is the time to load still a factor to consider? It should be. Just because the access speeds are faster does not mean we should not consider optimizations in the code. However, never optimize too early in the process. Premature optimization slows down the development and deployment of your site. This is a delicate balance between getting things done and out the door and optimizing them so the launch is successful.

Page load times should be a consideration when developing your site. A nicely optimized site loads much quicker than one that was put together by someone who does not understand the implications.

This can be a complex issue: think about all the aspects that affect load times of your web site. There are the obvious ones that you should be familiar with, including the number and sizes of images, the number of JavaScript libraries being used, and to what effect. Consider also your integrations with third party sites, such as using a few too many Facebook badges with status and fan updates, or multiple hotlinked images from image hosting sites. What happens when these remote locations are slow to respond, or worse, do not respond at all? Does your site's response time get held up because of something outside your control? Think about the "tree" of performance dependencies that you create by referencing other sites. That does not mean to not use them at all, but recognize how they can affect your own site's performance.

Firebug is an excellent tool for working through optimizations and network bandwidth on your site. In addition, Yahoo! and Google each have Firebug add-ons for helping improve your page speed with YSlow (http://developer.yahoo.com/yslow/) and Page Speed (http://code.google.com/speed/page-speed/), respectively.

A caveat with YSlow and Page Speed is these are two tools provided by Internet power houses. These sites likely see more traffic in an hour than you see all year. The problems and speed issues that they need to address are not the same types of issues that you need to address. YSlow always recommends a Content Delivery Network (CDN). Sure, a CDN distributes your assets across a geographically diverse set of servers to increase reliability and reduce latency, but does your site really need this? Do you really need to incur the costs? It is a developer choice, but in short, your site is probably not on the same scale as Yahoo!.

You need to pick and choose your battles in the area of site load times. Here's a quick checklist of things to consider, starting with the low-hanging fruit:

➤ Optimize your graphics and pick the right DPI, color depth, and format.

➤ Standardize your JavaScript library and use only one. Measure the benefits of packing and minifying your JavaScript and CSS. Those efforts may not improve page load times.

➤ Evaluate the number of external references made, whether hotlinking an image or including a Facebook badge with a status update.

➤ Be sensitive to MySQL database performance on your hosting site. Because every page or post displayed involves database queries, make sure you're not over-taxing the expected performance of your hosting option. Plugins that store content in the database give you flexibility, but also add to the database query burden when you're generating page output.

➤ Caching your output may be a viable solution; we cover that more in Chapter 11, "Scalability, Statistics, Security, and Spam." You will have to weigh the deployment options and come up with a solution to meet your site's scale requirements and deployment obstacles.

Using JavaScript

One more thing about using JavaScript in your web design: you may be tempted at times to base your entire site navigation (or another design element) around a super-cool jQuery plugin. The JavaScript may be a really neat effect, but JavaScript should not be the core of your design. jQuery effects should be the sprinkles you put on top of the frosting on the cake. You need to have a solid foundation so that the site still functions and is aesthetically pleasing, even if the JavaScript sprinkles fail. You have to build a site from the bottom up and only add the glitter to a functioning site. Realize that each new JavaScript library and gee-whiz effect you add to your site increases the load time for the end user. Consider if the effect really adds something to your site, or if you are just using it because it looks neat to you.

Furthermore, make sure that your site degrades gracefully if the JavaScript does not work. That is, make your cake still taste good even if my slice does not have any sprinkles on it. If your site relies on JavaScript for some functionality to work, and it is the only way for it to work, your site is not accessible. You have to consider that some visitors will not have JavaScript enabled, or perhaps not even available to them, and your site should be able to elegantly downgrade to support them.

In every case, there is a level of effort or visual trade-off required to improve page load times, and you'll have to measure the work input versus the user experience output improvement.

USABILITY AND USABILITY TESTING

Your client is probably not the end user. Furthermore, your clients do not know what their users really want. For that matter, anyone in the content creation side of things, be they developers or writers, do not know what the eventual users — the readers — really want, unless there is some sort of feedback mechanism, such as testing. Web design is one of those weird trades where everyone thinks they know what is best. Think back to the marketing person who wanted every element to be the most important element on the page, which in the end created a wash of blinking badges.

Your clients generally think they know what their users want because it is what they would want when visiting a site of this nature — that is, the site you are building. This works sometimes. But often, your clients have an intimate knowledge of the topic that their visitor does not have, making it impossible to have an objective opinion.

If you are serious about having a well-crafted user experience, test early and test often. You have to decide what you are going to test and this really depends on what the goals are for your site. For example, an ecommerce site generally wants to sell products. What are the goals of those sites?

> *This story has been used the poster child for usability testing for quite a while now, but it is an interesting anecdote about how changing one button made a $300 million difference during checkout:*
> `http://www.uie.com/articles/three_hund_million_button/`.

How can you apply this type of thinking to testing your own site? Ryan Carson of Carsonified offers a tutorial on doing A/B option testing with WordPress (`http://carsonified.com/blog/business/how-to-do-ab-testing-in-wordpress/`). A/B testing is a nice way to test what works in a real world laboratory. Using the method described by Carson, you have two different version of an actionable web page. Your site will randomly display one version or the other to each visitor. It involves some nice code trickery and provides an easy way to do usability testing on the general public so it does require your site to be live. Carson's method utilizes Google's Website Optimizer and a special plugin to perform his tests. Using the results of the test, you can see which version of your action item performs better. This is, in some ways, also how Google does usability testing — they modify their services on the fly and see what generates actual traffic.

Some other options are to use your family and friends, or call for help on Twitter. This is called *crowd sourcing*.

Any testing is better than no testing. Having a second set of eyes is just a good idea. You do not always have to accept their results and make the changes they suggest, but you should at least consider them. Again, a fresh set of eyes and a new perspective from someone who is not intimate with the site, like you are, is a good idea.

If you do not have a budget, use your family and friends and watch them interact with your site. Seeing how they can find information can isolate places where your design can be improved and listening to their comments will show what is good and bad about the overall feel. Generally, your family and friends represent the average user's computer skills and make a nice test audience.

Likewise, you can solicit help from strangers via social networks. However, the results you get back vary greatly. Generally people will be polite and tell you one or two little things either positive or negative, but rarely will you get a cohesive user test back. It is just too time-intensive for the average Joe.

If you do have a budget, many sites are available that provide you access to user testing agents. Generally with these services you submit your application or site and provide some goals for the user to achieve. You can also select which level of computer literacy you are targeting. The service then contacts its agents, who are average users at home, and using special software the user records a session while trying to accomplish your goals.

We used one of these services last year to test a whole new front-end interface to one of our core web applications (not WordPress related). The resulting videos we received allowed us to watch how the user interacted with the site and provided audio commentary from the users. Some comments were quite overt whereas others required us to interpret the emotions of grunts and "OKs." In the end, the user testing showed us some places that required immediate improvement to make the actions more clear and reinforced some changes we made based on more experienced internal focus groups.

The WordPress team has done some user testing with the Dashboard in the last several releases. It seemed for a while that the administration dashboards were receiving complete overhauls for a couple of revisions, but the newest version is pretty well established after the last set of user testing. WordPress is, by virtue of being community-developed, a terrific example of crowd sourcing, in both development testing and usability. These user tests focused on what features WordPress users used the most and directly led to the development of the QuickPress and other features. This crowd source testing has led to the very usable control panel we have now.

Along these same lines, a little user testing goes a long way in improving the layout and design of your site. It is usually an overlooked aspect because developers are smart people and we know best, but we are also very intimate with the site and the fresh perspective can make your site better if you listen to some of the advice.

STRUCTURING YOUR INFORMATION

How your site is organized is critical to your visitors and to search engine spiders. In general, WordPress does a good job of keeping your content organized. After all, that should be a core function of a Content Management System. However, you do have to put a little thought into the overall structure of your site.

One of the first things we ask clients who want to redesign their site, or develop a new one, is to have them create an outline of the pages or content for the new site. This forces the client to think about the structure and organization of the entire site from a 10,000-foot view. Including what type of content each outline item represents also helps in structuring the overall flow of the site. Using this outline, developers are able to stub out an information architecture of post categories, pages and parent pages that will align with client's outline and make creating the site a smoother operation. This also allows the client to see the layout of the site with dummy copy, like lorem ipsum, early in the process to make any structural changes as needed.

Once upon a time there was a golden rule for web sites that no page in your site should be more than three mouse clicks deep. This was back in the days when dialup connections were the most prevalent form of Internet access. Though we are not fans of deep sites, we are not sure if this rule is still true today. It is not that the attention span of the visitor has increased at all; in fact, it has probably diminished. And certainly broadband is more widespread nowadays, but it is not page load times that are affecting our opinion here.

The short answer is: search has largely replaced top-down navigation. In our opinion, people do not go to a web site's index page and run through the global navigation to find the particular topic, article, or product they are looking for. Rather, they go to a search engine. The search engine provides a link to the exact page, or as close as it can get, regardless of how deep in the site it is.

So, though we still favor "everything in three clicks" as a design rule, it is only because it adheres to the K.I.S.S. methodology and makes your site easier to use. But do not think this is a hard-and-fast rule, and sites are far more complex and encompass more content than they did when this rule was in favor. Putting in effort to make your content easier to find through search engines, and then structuring the content itself with the "three clicks rule" will jointly improve the user experience.

This is also the ideal time to evaluate what the individual pages or sections are titled. Here is a sad truth of web design: no one actually reads your content. In a 2006 study by Jakob Nielson (`http://www.useit.com/alertbox/reading_pattern.html`), the researchers found that visitors scanned the content of a web page in a very fast F-shaped pattern, meaning their eyes scroll down the left-hand side and skim the headers searching for the content they are looking for.

Again, this is not a blanket statement. Obviously, people do read the articles and content on web sites or there would be no reason to have them. But, when you are still trying to attract visitors and get them to stick around on your site, what should you take away from this study?

Headers matter. Headers should be concise and descriptive. Your content should start with the most important and evocative information and then get more in depth. They should also be properly formatted to use the different levels of HTML headers (more on this later). Headers should contain action words. They should be interesting and make visitors want to read your content, assuming that is your goal. Recognizing that visitors are scanning your site, having actions and descriptions in your headers will allow the visitor to get the overall gist of your page, help them find what they are looking for, and possibly entice them to read the rest of the section.

For example, which of these outline structures is more meaningful and interesting?

- ➤ How to use WordPress
  - ➤ Overview
  - ➤ The Technology
    - ➤ Software
    - ➤ Hardware
  - ➤ How to Get Started

Or this:

➤ Publishing your Content on the Internet using WordPress

    ➤ What Steps are Involved?

    ➤ What Do I Need?

        ➤ Installing the Applications

        ➤ Configuring the Server

    ➤ Getting Started Publishing

As you can see, with the first outline, you grasp the general idea of the web site. But the second outline is much more engaging and draws you in with actionable tasks. You can also see the structure of the site, and how it flows.

Remember back in school when you had to write an outline with several levels of headings? This is the same endeavor. Your content should have structure and headings and supporting paragraphs. If a heading intrigues a visitor enough, he will read the supporting paragraphs. If not, he will scan on to the next header. Funny how school actually taught you things you can use in real life, isn't it?

GETTING YOUR SITE FOUND

Search engine optimization (SEO) is how to get your site discovered by the search engines. One of the key ways to do this is by using the permalink structure in WordPress. These search engine–optimized permalinks are one of the key features that actually show up in the results pages of all the search engines. Making them meaningful and descriptive is a must.

Unfortunately, out of the box, the WordPress URL structure uses the query string post identifier format (`http://example.com/?p=100`). For compatibility reasons this is the default because it works across the board on different platforms and servers.

Given the choice in a search engine results page between these two URLs,

    http://example.com/?p=42

or

    http://example.com/this-is-the-information-you-want

which would you choose? The choice is pretty obvious. With the second option the visitor or potential visitor at least has an idea of what they are going to find at the site. This descriptive URL helps with search engines and click throughs since the savvy web user knows to look in the status bar of his browser to see the target site. Therefore we heartily recommend one of the first things you should do when setting up a WordPress site is change the permalink structure, as shown in Figure 10-3. Of course, you have to be on a platform that will support them. Changing the permalink structure was covered in Chapter 2, "Functional Overview." But which one should you pick?

Shorter URLs are generally better because they are easier to type, yet they need to maintain some inherent descriptive nature. Therefore we recommend a custom permalink structure using `/%postname%/`.

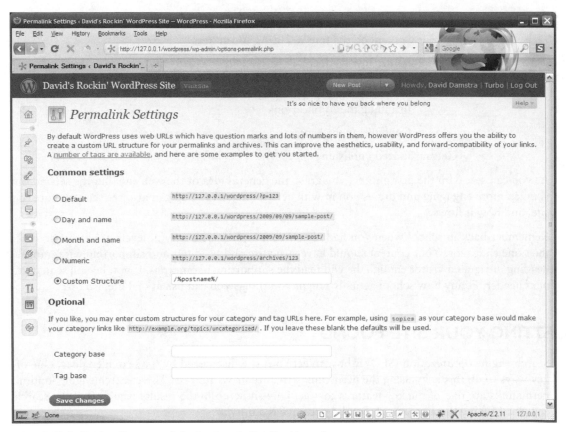

FIGURE 10-3: Setting the permalink structure in the Dashboard

This will use the slug from your post or page and create the nice SEO-friendly URLs referenced in the preceding example.

Additionally, you have two optional fields on this control panel to rewrite the category and tag base URL elements. For example, when you visit a category page in your WordPress site, the URL usually looks something like `http://mysite.com/category/cool-stuff/`. You can replace the word "category" with whatever you key into these optional fields. Occasionally we use just a letter "c" for category and "t" for tag to make the URLs shorter, but some creative uses of these fields can lead to some interesting and meaningful URL structures.

Chris Shiflett has an interesting post on his PHP Security blog (`http://shiflett.org/blog/2008/mar/urls-can-be-beautiful`) *that discusses how URLs can be beautiful. At the time, Chris worked for OmniTI, and the URLs for the new site involved action words that conveyed a very clear meaning. For example:* `http://omniti.com/is/hiring` *and* `http://omniti.com/helps/national-geographic`.

Duplicate Content

Duplicate content hurts. When a search engine is spidering your site, if you have duplicate content, or more specifically, multiple paths to the same content, the search engine may divide up your ranking (and SEO equity) across these multiple pages, diluting your overall ranking for any specific content piece. This section addresses how to keep multiple paths to content from appearing as distinct content views.

WordPress practically encourages duplicate content. Your posts are shown on the index page and on the category page for each category the post is in, each tag creates a tag page for that content, plus your posts are kept in the yearly and monthly archives. So, while this provides you multiple paths to get to your content, which was considered a good thing in a previous section, it also belabors you with duplicate content issues. Duplicate content on your own site may or may not be a bad thing; the jury still seems to be out on it.

But why taunt the search engines? Take this duplicate content issue and flip it around to your advantage. Use the power of WordPress template files to make these alternate views of your content self-reinforcing rather than search engine de-ranking.

Our beloved Sandbox theme does this automatically. For the category, tag, and archive templates, rather than display the whole content and create a duplicate content issue, the template displays the excerpt with a link back to the original content:

```
<div class="entry-content">
<?php
  the_excerpt( __( 'Read More
    <span class="meta-nav">&raquo;</span>', 'sandbox' ) )
?>
</div>
```

This method allows the search engine to see the multiple views of your content but reinforces that the `single.php` view of the post is the original source. This method further validates the need for your theme to have a complete set of templates in order to avoid problems like these.

Alternatively, some plugins are available that add "no-follow" header tags to your site. This may work, but you are relying on the spider to play by the rules, which may not be the case for all spiders. The Duplicate Content Cure plugin available at `http://www.seologs.com/?p=300` does just this by adding this head tag to your category pages:

```
<meta name="robots" content="noindex,follow">
```

 It is hugely ironic that a site named SEOLogs.com uses the ineffective post ID URL structure.

In addition, Google provides a Webmaster Tools site that can provide insight into how the Google spider sees your web site. Use the Google XML Sitemaps plugin from Arne Brachhold available online at `http://wordpress.org/extend/plugins/google-sitemap-generator/`. This creates a XML sitemap for Google to use when indexing your site, which helps the spiders find everything. But Webmaster

Tools also has some other interesting tools and investigative features. For example, under Diagnostics ⇨ HTML suggestions, you can see duplicate content that the spider saw, as shown in Figure 10-4.

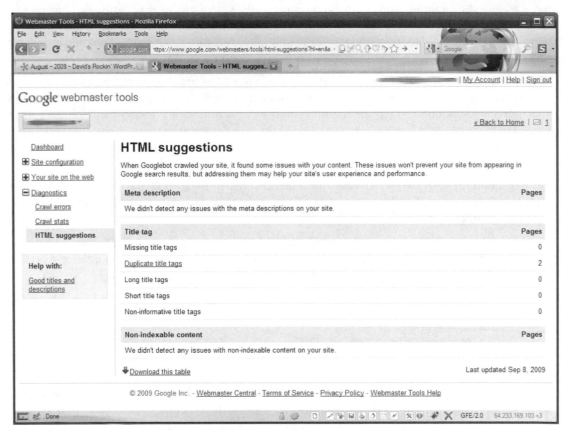

FIGURE 10-4: Google Webmaster tools

Further clicking into the duplicate content suggestion will indicate exactly which pages are causing you problems. In fairness, Microsoft's Bing.com has a similar set of tools that are just as nice.

Additionally, you should edit your robots.txt file. The robots.txt file provides some more guidance to the search engine spiders on what should not be indexed. By default, a spider will aggressively index whatever it can find. The robots.txt file tells the spider what it is explicity not allowed to index. Again, you are relying on the spider to play by the rules, but here is a good start for your robots.txt file:

```
User-agent: *
Disallow: /wp-
Disallow: /search
Disallow: /feed
Disallow: /comments/feed
Disallow: /feed/$
Disallow: /*/feed/$
Disallow: /*/feed/rss/$
Disallow: /*/trackback/$
```

```
Disallow: /*/*/feed/$
Disallow: /*/*/feed/rss/$
Disallow: /*/*/trackback/$
Disallow: /*/*/*/feed/$
Disallow: /*/*/*/feed/rss/$
Disallow: /*/*/*/trackback/$
```

Trackbacks and Pings

Google increases your page rank by counting links to your site. Trackbacks are other sites validating your content. Trackbacks started as a way for one blog to inform its readers that they may be interested in this content from another blog and to let the other site know "hey, I talked about your content and here's the link." They can basically be thought of as comments about your content on a remote site.

By default, WordPress groups comments and trackbacks together, further validating that they are remote comments, but this can often look messy to your reader. A common practice is to separate out the trackbacks from the actual comments in the comment loop. The Sandbox theme does this for you in the default templates using the get_comment_type() function:

```php
<?php if ( get_comment_type() == "comment" ) {
  // do comment display code
} ?>
<?php if ( get_comment_type() != "comment" ) {
  // do ping display code
} ?>
```

The comments will have to be walked in two foreach loops: one for the actual comments and one for the trackbacks. You can review the Sandbox comments.php template file for more information. What this gets you is a clear separation between the active discussion on your site, for your visitors to participate in, and a list of related sites that have also mentioned your content. They can be divided logically and visually, making it easier to digest for the visitor.

Alternatively you could accomplish similar functionality using the built in WordPress functions for listing comments, like so:

```php
wp_list_comments(array('type' => 'comment'));
wp_list_comments(array('type' => 'pings'));
```

Trackbacks must be enabled in the Discussion Settings Administration dashboard as discussed in Chapter 2.

Pings, on the other hand, notify other sites when new information is published. Generally your WordPress site would ping an update service, such as Ping-o-Matic, that you have new content on your site. Likewise, if you are writing about content on another WordPress site, your site may ping that other site to let it know about your content. In this respect, pings are similar to trackbacks.

Pinging update services is a good way to drive traffic to your site. Some sites take the information from these update services and create information link sites about them. The theory is that casual surfers of these sites may discover your content related to a topic they are browsing. In this respect, pinging works very much like a push version of RSS or tweeting your new blog posts.

Signing up to use an update service like Ping-o-matic is really simple to do. Simply browse to their site at `http://pingomatic.com/` sign up your site and it starts working. There is not much to it.

Tags and Content Sharing Sites

Technorati.com was one of the first sites to utilizes these update services and create an aggregation of blogs. Technorati tags enable to put your content into categories at Technorati.com. Basically you insert a tag on your page that points back to Technorati, so that your content is aggregated by tag along with similar posts. Technorati tag functionality is waning in lieu of new notification processes. The Technorati site is not the important add-on to WordPress that it once was, but it is still an easy place to get your content listed with relatively little effort. You now have plenty of ways to advertise new content with the advent of social media sites like Digg, Reddit, and Twitter. For example, in Chapter 9 we covered how to add social networking buttons to your posts, serving as a simple way for you to to effectively crowd source the notification processes through these new aggregators. Having your readers recommend content, and pass it on to tag-oriented sites, improves the changes of your content being found through channels other than search engines.

In practice, we do not use the pinging functionality very much. Rather, we have a custom application that parses the RSS feeds of our various sites and tweets new posts as they are posted. In certain situations, this notification works better.

HOW WEB STANDARDS GET YOUR DATA DISCOVERED

HTML is text markup. That is literally what it means. When it was first developed it had the intention of taking content and marking it up in a consistent and meaningful way. Many different HTML tags accomplish this. It was for scientific and academic use and the majority of content fit this nature.

Eventually the marketers showed up and got their greasy hands involved. They wanted fancy layouts, graphics, sales pitches, and pretty pink ponies. To accomplish this, designers and developers, both good and bad, lost sight of the original markup and used whatever means necessary to create the best looking site on the Web. This included table-based layouts.

In recent years there has been a back-to-basics mentality among the better developers. We're assuming this includes you, because you are reading this book. These developers recognize the power of separating concerns, such as presentation and content, CSS and HTML. They also recognize the advantages of using semantic HTML.

Semantic HTML

POSH stands for plain old semantic HTML. This is the acronym that expresses this back-to-basics mentality in the underlying HTML of web sites. For all the glittery design and flair, developers can use CSS to make it happen. Look at CSS Zen Garden for an example.

Why should your site use POSH? There are a few of reasons. First, it is the best thing for the future Web. Paying it forward, if your site continues to use semantic HTML, browser manufacturers will continue to support it in their browsers.

Second, for the developer, it makes the content easier to validate and maintain. There is much less cruft in a properly semantic HTML document than in one that is coded old style. Consider:

```
<div style="
  background: #F0CCFA;
  border: 1px solid # D894EB;
  color: #f00;
  font-size: 2em;
  margin: .25em 0;
   padding: .5em;">
     This is my subheading
</div>
```

versus:

```
<h2>This is my subheading</h2>
```

And that is not even really old style. This still uses CSS instead of the multiple nested <font> tags that really clutter up the old HTML documents. Valid, lean HTML is easier to maintain. It is that simple.

Speaking of lean, stripping all the cruft out of your HTML can really make your pages load faster. Think of all the extra markup that is moved out of each page load and into a browser-cached CSS file. This can be a significant weight loss on your pages.

The third reason is accessibility. Structuring your HTML semantically increases the likelihood of screenreaders figuring out your content and having it make sense to the visitor.

Finally, valid semantic HTML helps with search engine optimization. Search spiders are not very smart. They do not care how pretty the site looks or the cool new graphic treatment you created. They only care about the content. And they cannot think for themselves.

Semantic HTML conveys the meaning of the text you are marking up. That is why it is called semantic, after all. Using the proper HTML tag for the content is the first step. For example, six levels of headers are available to you in HTML. Using them in the correct order is essential for SEO. Going back to using a site outline, this is how the spider knows the order of your content.

Even if you separate your CSS properly into a style sheet, the spider cannot determine the value of this HTML:

```
<div class="pagetitle">My Site Is About Something Important</div>
```

Whereas if you use the <h1> tag, the spider knows that this is the header for the entire page, and attributes this content with the appropriate weight.

```
<h1 class="pagetitle">My Site Is About Something Important</h1>
```

Following down your content, you should use the appropriate levels of headers for additional content. The general consensus is that each page on your site should only have one <h1> tag to indicate the top level of each rendered page. Conventional wisdom is that this <h1> is reserved for the name of the site and then there can be multiple instances of the other heading levels as needed. The only flaw in this is that the name of your site does not really change, so it is not the <h1> that matters the most for each page. Using headers in this manner makes the <h1> really irrelevant and the <h2> would be the page title describing the rendered page's content. It's easy to can both sides of the argument; you will have to make your own decision.

Images should always have `alt` attributes. This informs the spider what the image is rendering because the spider cannot see the graphic itself. This information is also what screenreaders use.

The `<div>` tag is for blocks of content and the `<p>` is for paragraphs. Use the more meaningful `<em>` and `<strong>` to emphasize and strongly emphasize your content.

Use proper lists to list your data. Ordered lists (`<ol>`) and unordered lists (`<ul>`) are easy ways to convey information to the spider. A properly formatted list is semantically more information to rate than a paragraph filled with `<br />` tags. There is also the lesser known definition list (`<dl>`) element, which is very effective in paired information lists such as frequently asked questions. This list and explanation of HTML attributes can go on and on.

In short, semantic HTML is all about using the proper HTML tag for its intended use. It is worth reading through the W3C specifications and learning the different tags and their purpose. Adding these additional tools to your bag of tricks will make you a better developer, but will also make your pages lighter, more meaningful, and more accessible, all of which are good things for your visitors and your search engine rankings.

Valid HTML

For, you, the developer, valid HTML and valid CSS is just plain easier to maintain. It is a simple fact. If your code is structured correctly, you can get in and out and make the changes you want quicker. We still have some ancient table-based layouts lying around from clients that have never wanted to update the look of their site. If you have not had to work on one of these in a while, it's astonishing to see how hard they were to work on.

Valid HTML also helps in solving cross-browser rendering issues. All developers dread the day they have to test their great looking site in one of the older less standards-compliant browsers. You know which one. It is important that the developer has completely consumed the requisite amount of coffee and moved all sharp objects out of arm's reach before opening this browser for testing. Inevitably, something will not be right. Having validated HTML is the first line of attack when dealing with this browser's rendering challenges. Always start from a clean code before taking measures to make it look reasonable in these browsers. And have hope, maybe, that someday this browser will not be around anymore.

For SEO, it is back to a "spiders are not very smart" problem. Valid HTML makes your content easier for the spider to understand and therefore rank. If your HTML is not properly valid, the search engine can lose the content that is not visible to it while it is looking for the closing tag or attribute. This can severely limit the content that is viewable to the spider and hinder your site's ability to rank. Browsers tend to be more forgiving on invalid HTML and do their best to render what they can, but a spider is working on speed and quantity of content to digest. The spider is just going to breeze past anything it does not understand.

Many resources are available to validate your HTML including the W3C's own Markup Validation Service at `http://validator.w3.org/`. In addition, several Mozilla Firefox extensions provide validation services and Microsoft's Developer Tools for Internet Explorer 8 includes a tool to use the W3C's validator.

Microformats

Microformats are the more complicated brother of POSH. The idea is to add simple tags to HTML that convey contextual information for the HTML content. Once you see how they work, some are an almost natural way of dealing with the content, similar to an implementation of XML in HTML. The microformat convention is to format certain information in HTML so that it is reliable and can be discovered by microformat-enabled tools. For example, you will often see contact information and addresses expressed in a microformat syntax. You might even be using microformats already and not even know it.

For example, the Technorati tags we talked about earlier are microformats. The "rel" attribute on an anchor tag linking to Technorati.com indicates that the page you are linking from has been tagged for Technorati consumption. This is a microformat.

```
<a href="http://technorati.com/tag/wordpress" rel="tag">WordPress</a>
```

Another common microformat that is built into WordPress is the XFN (Xhtml Friends Network). This microformat is simply an attribute you place on links to indicate your relationship with that person. This feature is built in on the Links Control Panel, also known as your blogroll.

Using this handy control panel you can easily add microformat attributes to your link indicating how and where you know the individual you are linking to. For example, consider the settings shown in Figure 10-5.

Those settings will render the HTML as:

```
<a title="WordPress.org" rel="friend colleague muse"
   href="http://WordPress.org">WordPress.org</a>
```

This is a simple yet effective way to create some meaningful information about the link. The key is the simplicity of it. To a web browser, this information does not affect the rendering. In fact, only recently has Internet Explorer even allowed developers to use the rel attribute as a CSS selector.

But imagine the power when a search engine spider or other tool can create a social graph out of the information contained in microformats. You can find more information about the XFN at http://gmpg.org/xfn/.

Another microformat that is gaining traction is the hCard. The hCard microformat is for displaying contact information for a person or organization. The hCard microformat is the HTML rendering of the common vCard format used in e-mail and e-mail address books like Microsoft Outlook and Mac OS X Address Book.

Here is a sample hCard:

```
<div class="vcard">
  <a class="url fn" href="http://mirmillo.com">David Damstra</a>
  <div class="adr">
    <div class="street-address">123 Main Street</div>
    <span class="locality">Grand Rapids</span>,
    <span class="region">MI</span>
    <span class="postal-code">49525</span>
  </div>
  <div class="tel">1-616-555-1234</div>
</div>
```

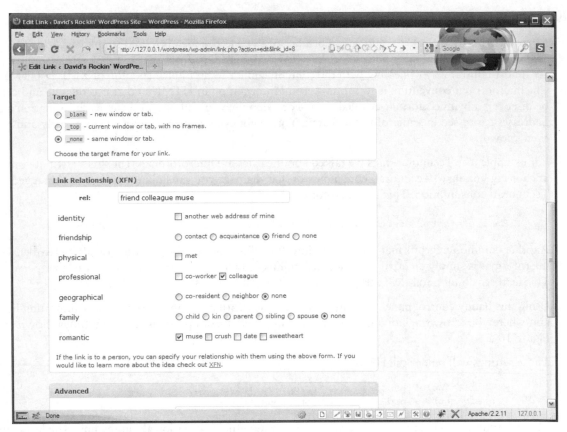

FIGURE 10-5: Editing the XFN of a link

Obviously, the information has been changed so you cannot stalk David. The hCard is one of the most common microformats used. It is very similar to the vCard format used in e-mail and address book software.

Render the preceding hCard on your site and it looks like an innocuous address block. But running this same code through a tool or spider that understands this microformat can lead to much more intelligent use of the information.

Microformats allow external tools to make better use of your blog posts, ideally driving more viewers to your site. Conversely, they make use of external services using metadata in your microformat tagged posts. One example is the GeoMark plugin that converts location information in a post into GEO microformat tags stored as post metadata that is also passed on in RSS feeds of your post.

Currently, search engine spiders do not weight microformatted data any differently than the other content on your site. However, microformats are emerging and gaining traction and eventually, spiders will recognize them and be able to harvest the semantic data included. The bottom line is microformats are becoming the de facto convention for marking up this type of information. So, though it is spidered the same as traditional content, by using the microformat conventions you are working toward future-proofing your content.

Microformats are an investment in the future. They are relatively simple ways to structure specific content so that at a later time this information can be used to do something informative or cool. Hopefully the future holds a time when you can search for a name and find that person's social graph along with it, search for a business and automatically have the contact information logged to your smart phone, or search for a location and time and have an aggregated list of events that are occurring in the vicinity. We are beginning to see the data, so the tools cannot be far behind.

SEARCHING YOUR OWN SITE

So far we have talked about making your site visible and effective in the big search engines by structuring, organizing, and coding your site to raise your listings, or at least get the ranking you deserve. What happens when the visitor gets to your site and uses the built-in on-site search? Do the same rules and guidelines apply?

The answer is yes and no. The SEO principles and practices we have discussed are a solid foundation to build on. They are tried-and-true rules, though the search engines can make up their own rules and change them at whim — we are in the Wild West Internet. The change lies in the built-in WordPress search.

Weaknesses of the Default Search

Out of the box the WordPress search is probably good enough for most small sites. After all, this was how WordPress evolved, and good enough was good enough. But as your site grows, or as you build larger, more prominent sites, good enough is no longer good enough. The default WordPress search has some serious deficiencies for larger sites, and there are a couple of important challenges to be addressed here.

Results are sorted by date, not relevance to the search terms. WordPress loves showing content in chronological order. Chronological posts are the heart of the WordPress blogging engine. So the default search will return results of the search term in reverse chronological order. It suffers from the halo effect.

Even if you have a large, excellently written article about a topic, if newer posts about the same topic exist, the newer ones will get top billing in the results pages. Relevance to the search terms does not matter. There is no weighting in the results for search term counts. The search strictly glances through all the post and page content and if the term appears, it flags it for the results and then spits them out in date order.

This brings us to the next shortcoming. The search only searches some of your site's content. The default search only looks in the post content and page content; not the headlines, not the comments, not the links, not the categories, not the tags, nothing else. You learned earlier that headlines matter, and visitors only read the headlines, so if you're catchy article headline sticks in someone's head and they return to your site to search on some variation of your headline, search may not find it because headlines are not indexed.

Ideally your content supports the catchy headline you made, so eventually your content will be found with search. But there is so much more content to your site that could be used to empower the search to make it more effective or even to broaden the search. After all, it could have been one of your comments that really sparked the interest.

Next, there is no logic to the search. That is, you cannot use any sort of Boolean syntax in the query. The search is a straight up "find this word in the posts" kind of search. Search power users use Boolean syntax all the time to create very refined search engine results. WordPress search does some silly things with these keywords.

For example, try searching on your WordPress site using Boolean keywords in your search string, such as searching for "keyword1 AND keyword2." In this case you want to find content that contains both keywords. You will find that WordPress search treats the "AND" just like any other keywords and will include content that contains all three words, that is, the keywords and the word "AND." Likely you will have no results.

WordPress search handles a Boolean "or" in the same fashion. Try searching for content with either "keyword1" or "keyword2" in it using the search string "keyword1 OR keyword2." Again, WordPress search treats the "OR" just like the actual keywords. Now search for either keyword independently and compare the results. Depending on your site, you will notice that the "OR" search does not contain the same results as the two independent searches combined. After some simple experimentation, you will see that WordPress search does not know how to handle these generic Boolean queries.

Some people complain that the WordPress search does not highlight the search terms in the results. Some places it is handy, other times it does not affect the utility of the search results. This definitely seems like a personal developer choice, which makes it ripe for a plugin. On the other hand, this could easily be handled with some creative PHP and CSS also.

The WordPress search has been good enough, but it does not take advantage of some available tools like MySQL FullText search or other third-party search engines like Lucene or Sphinx. Understandably, WordPress needs to keep the installation process simple and reduce the dependencies on external software packages. This definitely complicates the whole installation. But, if a developer is capable and willing to integrate these other packages, why not let them? Well, the 2009 Google Summer of Code project for WordPress set out to do just that, and we get to this in a moment.

Some of these seem like big deals, and for some developers they certainly are. But search is a pretty personal thing. Different developers want it to have specific functionality or algorithms and because WordPress has a great plugin system, each developer can have what he wants. You can either find an existing plugin or you can write your own to scratch that pesky search engine itch.

Alternatives and Plugins to Help

Obviously, we are not the first to recognize these inadequacies in the default search mechanism. Some very talented developers have set out to create plugins that enhance or replace the built-in search. Many, many plugins are available. Some target specific issues, and others change the whole search process. Following are a some of the more popular search engine plugins for WordPress.

Search Unleashed by John Godley (`http://wordpress.org/extend/plugins/search-unleashed/` and `http://urbangiraffe.com/plugins/search-unleashed/`) sets out to right all that is wrong with the default search. Search Unleashed extends the searchable content to include all the missing content mentioned earlier, but also includes plugin-inserted content. With Search Unleashed you can switch out the search engine to use either MySQL Full Text search or Zend Framework's Lucene implementation. Search Unleashed also performs search term highlighting. Search Unleashed includes a nice Administration Control Panel making managing the settings very easy.

Another popular plugin is Search Everything (`http://wordpress.org/extend/plugins/search-everything/`) by Dan Cameron of Sprout Venture. Search Everything also extends the breadth of the WordPress search to include the different content sources in the index. Search Everything also has settings for search term highlighting and all the settings are managed from an Administration Control Panel.

For the 2009 Google Summer of Code Project, Andy Skelton from Automattic took on student Justin Shreve to improve the built-in WordPress search. The results of the project is a set of plugins that create an API to extend and replace the core search. The first plugin, cleverly called Search API (`http://wordpress.org/extend/plugins/search/`), does exactly what it is named. It creates a new set of API hooks for search plugins to tie into. This plugin also comes with two additional plugins that utilize this new functionality. There is a MySQL FullText engine and a Google Site Search engine, which requires your own Google account. Shreve also created a Sphynx Search Engine plugin that interfaces with the API.

MOBILE ACCESS

This is a hot topic right now, due to an enormous market uptake of smart phones with high speed data services and stores that proliferate fat client applications for these phones There are currently two camps of thought. One is that with the newer browsers on the smart phones, like the Apple iPhone, Google Android, and Palm Pre, can render traditional web sites acceptably fine. The tech savvy users of these devices know that the browser is limited and the screen is small and do not expect a stellar user experience.

The other camp is that we have the technology available to create custom themes for these devices. These themes should hearken back to the lightweight themes of dialup days to conserve the limited bandwidth available. They should be tailored to fit the small screen real estate and focus on the information that the mobile visitor is really looking for — often locations and contact information.

The WPTouch iPhone Theme is actually a plugin that converts your site to look like a native iPhone Application. Let's face it, at the time of this writing, the iPhone is the dominant smart phone. The WPTouch iPhone Theme was created by Dale Mugford and Duane Storey from Brave New Code and is available at `http://wordpress.org/extend/plugins/wptouch/`.

After installing this plugin, your site will automatically detect mobile browsers and offer them your entire site, but in a lightweight, mobile-enhanced theme. This theme uses AJAX requests and other effects giving the illusion of a native application. In addition, WPTouch offers an extensive control panel to manage all the settings.

WPTouch also offers the ability to set a custom index page for mobile browsers. This is a fantastic feature and enables the developer to create a custom page for the quick information that the mobile visitor really needs. In addition to the iPhone widget theme, WPTouch includes the ability to tweak the

CSS to create a theme that matches your traditional site theme. WPTouch also offers the ability for the mobile visitor to select to view the traditional theme.

We are currently automatically enabling this plugin on all of our WordPress installations. One note of caution is that if you are using a caching plugin, discussed in the next chapter, you will have to set it to exclude showing cached content to the mobile browser. Otherwise the caching will supersede the WPTouch browser detection and the traditional theme will be shown.

Mobile themes are an up-and-coming area. As smartphones with reasonably supportable browsers become more commonplace, this type of functionality will become a requirement for all sites. We are starting to see mobile optimized themes pop up all over the place. For example, if you use Alex King's Carrington theme, he has recently launched a mobile version (`http://carringtontheme.com/themes/`).

Now that we've looked at the user experience that makes your site interesting to readers, we'll examine the deployment and manager experience in terms of performance and security.

11
Statistics, Scalability, Security, and Spam

WHAT'S IN THIS CHAPTER?

➤ Adding traffic counters to your web site

➤ Caching your content for higher traffic loads

➤ Keeping your WordPress site healthy and secure

➤ Delegating permissions to your users

The past few chapters have covered how to present your fabulous content in effective and beautiful ways, how to increase the likelihood of visitors finding your content, and how to amass all your various content sources into your home web site. What happens when (if?) this all succeeds? Well, now you have a live and active site, which opens up a whole range of other stuff you have to think about. In this chapter we look at mechanisms to define and measure success, and then deal with the resultant attention you'll get in terms of unwanted content, malicious visitors and the need to scale in response to increasing readership.

STATISTICS COUNTERS

Viewing traffic statistics allows you to see which content on your site is actually bringing visitors in. This shows you what content is working and what is not. In addition, it can show you valuable information about your visitors and their hardware and software setups. Using this information can allow you to tailor your site to accentuate the positive and support your visitors' browsers to create a more pleasant and meaningful experience.

Various statistics packages employ a couple of different methods, and each has its own advantages and disadvantages. Likewise, each vendor puts its own spin on the traffic statistics.

You can gather traffic statistics in a couple of ways. The grandfather in this realm is to parse your log files. Your web server, if configured properly, will create log files for each and every request and error that it handles. Certain statistics packages can parse these logs and create human-consumable information. Some packages even let you download these logs to your local machine and let it do the busy work offline.

The second method is to put a snippet, usually JavaScript, on each page of your site that reports back to a central server, which then accumulates the data and makes it meaningful to you. This method is the current trend.

Each of these packages has an available WordPress plugin. Each package also varies in its specific vernacular. You will have to determine what the truly meaningful metrics are from each package; for example: visitors versus unique visitors, and hits versus page views versus unique page views. Deriving useful information from statistics depends on your goals. If you want more viewers, and are trying to attract attention from Google searches, social network recommendations, and other external aggregators, you may be happy with an increasing number of visitors who look at only one page or spend under a minute per visit on your site. A site that aims for more discussion and community feel should have more return visitors, a longer interval between visitor entry and exit, and multiple pages viewed by each visitor.

AWStats

AWStats is the granddaddy of web traffic statistics. Actually, there was a package that pre-dated this but had many security problems and AWStats took over as the main statistics package.

AWStats is of the log parsing variety of statistics counters. It can be run on the server or you can download the log files to another machine and run it. AWStats requires Perl to run and we have successfully used it on both Apache and Microsoft IIS servers, although it requires a little configuration of the log file formats for IIS. To install and get AWStats up and running automatically for your site, you'll need to be familiar with server administration tasks. Being a log parsing package, AWStats is designed to run automatically in the background via a `cron` job on Unix systems

Because AWStats is a server-side log parsing package it easily tracks the actual request information of your web site. You can extend the information gathered by adding in the special JavaScript tag for AWStats to catch browser-side information such as screensize and browser plugin support for various technologies.

One good thing about AWStats is that it is one of the original open source log parser statistics packages. It has survived so long because it is reliable and free and relatively easy to get going. This also includes many contributed scripts and tidbits of help and support from various sources around the Web. Numerous hosts rely on AWStats and like any good open source software package, there is a robust support community around it.

What is not so good about AWStats is when it messes up. Specifically, it sometimes loses track of dates, mainly because of an unintentional system admin error. In order to provide certain historical information and to process logs quicker, AWStats maintains cache files. If dates get out of order or other time problems exist, these cache files trump any new logs to be parsed and can provide inconsistent data. Basically you have to go back and rebuild all the cache files. Luckily, with some searching you can find some scripts to assist in this. Another complaint with AWStats is the browser agents were not updated for a long time, but this does not appear to be the case anymore.

A couple of different WordPress plugins are available for AWStats, but they are not required to use AWStats on your site. One plugin for this package basically takes the human-consumable information and makes it available on the front end of your site. There is also a plugin that will add the extended information JavaScript to every WordPress page render so that AWStats can capture additional information. Take a look at Figure 11-1, which shows the basic AWStats reporting screen.

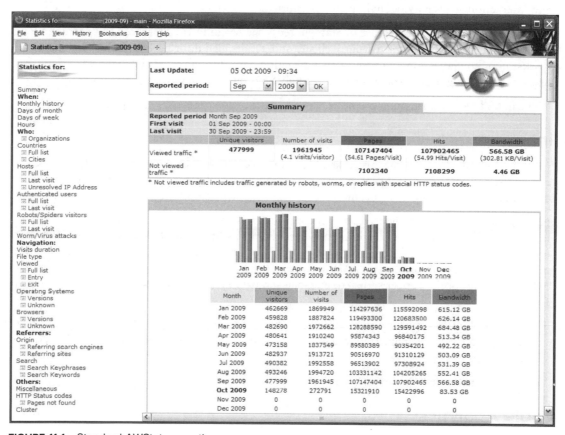

FIGURE 11-1: Standard AWStats reporting screen

You can find more information online at http://awstats.sourceforge.net/.

Statcounter

Remember the days when you put a visitor odometer on your site showing off how many visitors it served? Ah, the glory days of the early Web. Statcounter started off as one of these packages and has since matured into a full-featured web traffic statistics package — although it still offers the functionality of putting the Visitors Served odometer on your site.

Statcounter comes in both free and paid subscriptions depending on the traffic level of your web site and the amount of detail you require for the latest page views. The free package shows detailed information for the last 500 page views. All packages maintain lifetime statistics for your site.

Statcounter works by adding a special JavaScript tag to each page of your site. There is a WordPress plugin to take care of this for you. You will also need to register for an account to get your unique project codes for tracking. Unlike AWStats, which is all self-contained on your hosting server, Statcounter graphs and reports are presented on its site where your JavaScript reports back to. Obviously, users who disable JavaScript aren't going to show up in the recorded statistics, so your actual traffic and interaction levels may be slightly under-reported.

One particularly intriguing feature of Statcounter is the Magnify User feature. This feature allows you to focus in on one visitor to your web site and get detailed information about his browser and workstation configuration and well as his navigation path through your site. This is a pretty neat feature; though make sure you evaluate its implications on your web site's privacy policy.

You can find more information online at `http://www.statcounter.com/`.

Mint

Mint is a hybrid version of the hosted JavaScript tag to create web traffic statistics. It functions, like the current trend in statistics packages, by using a JavaScript tag on the page render that reports back to a centralized server for aggregation and parsing. The twist here is that the central server is your own.

Having the central server under your own control alleviates some privacy concerns about reporting your traffic information to a third party (see the next section on Google Analytics). This also enables you to deploy this type of package in a secured environment, such as online banking. Mint is all self-contained on your own LAMP servers and is written in PHP. The core Mint package can be extended using special Pepper scripts to enhance and extend the functionality. However, Mint is not a free solution.

The official WordPress plugin for Mint will put the necessary JavaScript into your page renders and will also add a special Administration dashboard to view your Mint statistics from within WordPress via an iFrame.

You can find more information at `http://haveamint.com`.

Google Analytics

Google Analytics is currently the big dog in hosted web traffic statistics. It has a clean and generally intuitive user interface for seeing the reported statistics. It works similarly to Statcounter, in that you inject a special JavaScript tag into your rendered page, which reports traffic and browser information to Google for parsing.

And therein lies the rub with this free statistics package. You are reporting all of your traffic information to Google. Many people use Google for nearly everything these days — e-mail, calendar, and web traffic statistics included — though we distrust giving all this information to what could become Big Brother. Though, clearly, people have some trust for Google, in reality they could use the information they get for any number of purposes. Just think of the wealth of information Google has at its fingertips related to browser and OS share, then combine this with the AdSense and keyword information from your site. Today, Google allows you to track campaigns and site "reach" by cross-referencing AdWords and AdSense traffic with Google Analytics data. The amount of data related to web site use and marketing trends is staggering. The trade-off of data access is a business decision you will have to make.

Google Analytics is definitely marketing oriented. Many powerful tools are built in and learning how to use them will greatly benefit the quality of the reported data, including advanced segmentation of your traffic and custom reporting data. For example, we use Google Analytics to track which specific PDFs from our library site get the most traffic, and in e-mail marketing we track which campaigns generate the most clickthroughs. Many resources are available online to extend Google Analytics.

For example, here is the jQuery snippet for tracking outbound document links via Google Analytics. This code is derived from `http://css.dzone.com/news/update-tracking-outbound-click`.

```
/* use jquery to track outbound and file links
 * http://css.dzone.com/news/update-tracking-outbound-click
 */
$("a").click(function() {
    var $a = $(this);
    var href = $a.attr("href");
    // see if the link is external
    if ( (href.match(/^http/)) && (! href.match(document.domain)) ) {
     // if so, register an event
     var category = "outgoing"; // set this to whatever you want
     var event = "click"; // set this to whatever you want
     var label = href; // set this to whatever you want
     pageTracker._trackEvent(category, event, href);
    }
});
var fileTypes = ["doc","docx","xls","pdf","ppt","pptx", "rtf", "txt"];
$("a").click(function() {
    var $a = $(this);
    var href = $a.attr("href");
    var hrefArray = href.split(".");
    var extension = hrefArray[hrefArray.length - 1];
    if ($.inArray(extension,fileTypes) != -1) {
     pageTracker._trackEvent("download", extension, href);
    }
});
```

Tracking outbound traffic is useful if you're trying to use your site as a reference point or expertise repository, and need to know where readers are going for additional information. Getting detail on the types of documents referenced gives you a high-level view of what content flavors are most popular or helpful. Obviously, you can add additional document types if you point users at OpenOffice, PhotoShop, or other file formats.

Many WordPress plugins are available for Google Analytics, which anecdotally serves as a barometer for the popularity of this service. Each offers slightly different functionality, but all essentially do the same thing, which is inject the appropriate JavaScript into the page. Some offer additional features to track the extra events via the control panel. Take a look at Figure 11-2 for a screenshot of the standard Google Analytics dashboard.

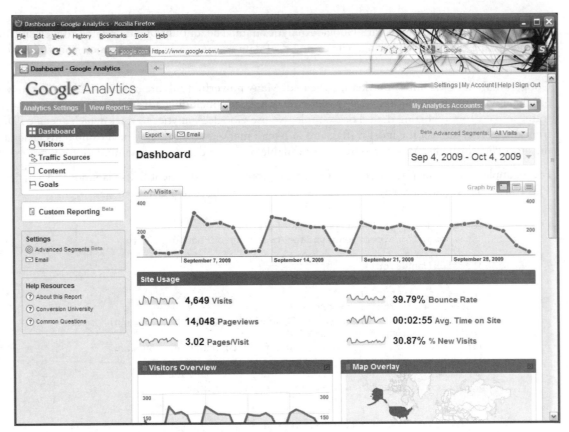

FIGURE 11-2: Standard Google Analytics reporting screen

You can find more information online at `http://google.com/analytics/`.

If the statistics are giving you good news — your site is gaining in popularity, readers are actively participating in discussions, and search engines are sending new users your way — you'll likely want to turn your attention to site scalability. Now we'll look at ways to improve the overall performance the WordPress system components.

CACHE MANAGEMENT

WordPress is a Content Management System, which by its very definition means it creates a dynamically driven site. In today's technology environment that essentially means that the managed content and all of its meta data is stored in a database. Every page request has to access the database to determine which content to be displayed, versus simply fetching HTML files from the web server's local directory. The trade-off in handing over content management to a database is that you are going to take a speed hit in the individual page access in exchange for more powerful persistence, selection and organization tools – those features used within the WordPress Core. Basic computer science comes into play here: when you introduce a new abstraction layer that's slower than the layer above it, you typically introduce a caching mechanism as well to improve average access times.

It helps to think of caching in a sequence of access methods, starting closest to the user and working back to the MySQL database. Each point in the sequence has some caching and tuning that can be done; however, like all performance tuning work, your mileage varies depending upon the access patterns, content types, and actual workload moving through that point in the system. Here is our view of the WordPress caching hierarchy that we'll walk through in the following sections:

➤ **Browser:** Most of your end users' browser performance is going to come from optimized CSS, graphics, and JavaScript libraries. Because these affect the single-page load times, we covered them in Chapter 10's exploration of user experience. Enabling Google Gears, as discussed in Chapter 2, allows some code to be cached locally as well.

➤ **Web Server:** WordPress and its plugins are largely written in PHP, an interpreted language that relies on the web server for an execution container. Improving the web server's PHP caching will speed up some portions of the WordPress user-to-database path.

➤ **WordPress Core:** Caching objects used by WordPress effectively builds a database results cache, the same approach taken by highly scalable, MySQL-based sites like Facebook. Changing some dynamic page generation to static HTML rendering speeds up page access at the expense of possible small windows of update inconsistency.

➤ **MySQL:** Caching objects at the database layer prevents an eventual disk access, turning a query into a memory reference where possible. These options are independent of, and frequently complementary to, enabling a caching plugin within the WordPress Core.

Again, the actual benefit provided by each or any of these approaches depends on many factors, including your hosting provider's database layer, whether you can configure web and database servers yourself, the size, frequency and complexity of database queries, and the overall load on your WordPress installation.

WordPress System Complexity

First and foremost, WordPress is a complex system, and honorably so. WordPress simplifies the process of content management and broadens its core feature set through the plugin system. But providing these various hooks and flexibility comes at the cost of database accesses, PHP processing, handling each plugin's unique requirements, and any special theme prerequisites. Each plugin adds additional overhead to the page rendering, and the quality of code in plugins varies from author to author. Using an execution path analyzer like WinCacheGrind or KCacheGrind, which profiles your application to determine where bottlenecks in the code may occur, you can create a graphic representation of the complexity of a web application. Take, for instance, a plain vanilla WordPress installation using the default theme. Running a simple page load through this profiler and viewing the resulting execution graph, you see something like Figure 11-3.

Even without being able to zoom in and see the details, you can perceive the inherent complexity of WordPress. Each of those boxes represents a function or action in the WordPress Core, including action hooks for linking in plugin and theme functionality.

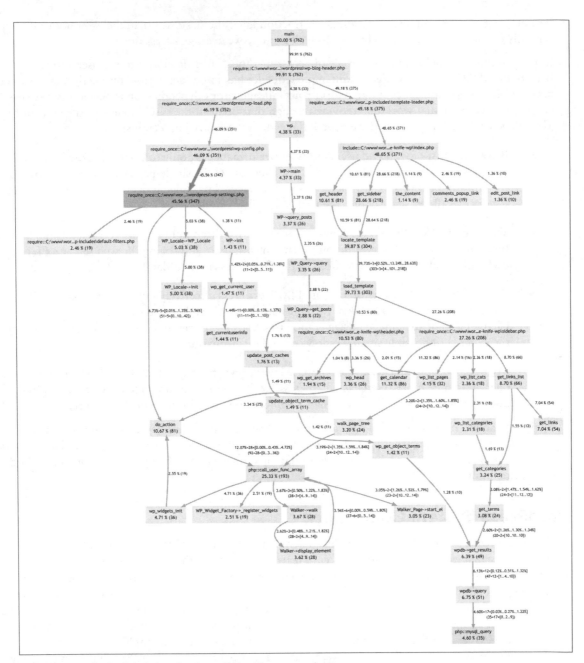

FIGURE 11-3: CacheGrind visualization of WordPress complexity

Each and every thing you add to your site, including that fancy theme control panel that lets you set particular runtime characteristics of your site and plugins that parse your content for related posts, create overhead and more boxes on the execution graph.

Do not get alarmist here and disable plugins and choose overly simple themes. This challenge is not unique to WordPress. The flexibility enabled through WordPress, especially the configurable runtime flexibility of WordPress, which is so powerful, is an expensive operation. The alternative is a statically fixed set of features that require new built-in code to accomplish new features, rather than the versatile plugin architecture of WordPress. Each of those plugins and theme hooks adds functionality and features to your WordPress installation. That is why you enabled them in the first place. Just accept that it is a trade-off in features versus performance, some negligible and some larger.

In practice, your site does not really change that often. You are probably not running the next Twitter through a WordPress installation (though you can build a reasonable facsimile with the p2 theme) and the content does not change every 30 seconds. Leveraging the ideal situation in which your content is viewed significantly more frequently than it's updated, and allowing for minor windows of inconsistent updates, let's look at caching layers from the web server back to the MySQL installation.

Web Server Caching and Optimization

Improving WordPress scalability through the web server layer involves PHP execution optimization and web server configuration changes. In both cases, you'll need administrator level access to the web server configuration files.

We'll work our way back to the MySQL queries and object caching, but no matter how you end up with a list of pages, WordPress relies on PHP to pull the displayed page together and generate its HTML. PHP is an interpreted language. That means for every execution of the code, the code must be interpreted and compiled to machine code that a computer can use. This methodology has pros and cons, and the flame war that would ensue is completely outside the scope of this book. However, you can cache at the PHP execution level with an *opcode cache*.

A PHP opcode cache attempts to bridge the gap between runtime interpreting and full-on compiled code. APC (or Alternative PHP Cache) is one such implementation that works to cache and optimize the intermediate PHP code. This method is completely outside of WordPress and works on the underlying PHP layer of your server, making the actual configuration outside the scope of this book.

To get APC set up you will need full access permissions on your server. Once APC is set up it caches the compiled PHP files that make up the WordPress Core. The biggest downside is that you have to restart the server every time you change a PHP page, specifically the template files in this case. You can find more information about APC at http://us3.php.net/manual/en/book.apc.php. Again, the ability to enable APC and start/stop the web server depends on you having sufficient administrator privilieges.

Caching can be further augmented by using memcache and memcached, also requiring server administration level of implementation. Memcache uses your server's RAM to cache frequently used objects. RAM is significantly faster than file-based operations, and because memcached runs as a local daemon, it is also completely outside of your web server. You can find more information about memcache at http://us3.php.net/manual/en/book.memcache.php and http://memcached.org/.

While we are talking about the PHP level of the WordPress stack, you should also optimize (and secure) your php.ini configuration. PHP has prospered by having so much built-in functionality that it lowers the barriers of entry and empowers developers to just get the task done. This has been the boon and the bane for PHP. Take a look at your php.ini file and disable extensions you are not using. You can always turn them back on.

Also take this opportunity to secure your PHP execution container and help it run faster. Here are some simple settings. There probably are more depending on your setup, which you can likely turn off to improve security and performance:

```
;Hide PHP for security
expose_php = Off
;Turn off for performance
register_globals = Off
register_long_arrays = Off
register_argc_argv = Off
magic_quotes_gpc = Off
magic_quotes_runtime = Off
magic_quotes_sybase = Off
```

Finally, on the system administration level, optimize your web server. In most cases the stock configuration for your web server is designed to handle the most common basic use cases. Certainly, it has not been tweaked to match your specific server's capabilities. Apache, for example, comes with tons of extra modules to handle general-case situations. If you do not use those modules, disable them. This will reduce the overall memory footprint of Apache.

In practice, we have been able to tweak Apache to perform better under restricted resources (like low-memory virtual private servers) by adjusting the Apache PreFork configuration. The default configuration is pretty generous, and depending on your site's traffic and system configuration you can usually pare this down. For example, on a low-traffic site hosted on a low-memory shared server, you could edit your Apache2 configuration file to the following, assuming you are using Apache2:

```
<IfModule mpm_prefork_module>
    StartServers         3
    MinSpareServers      3
    MaxSpareServers      3
    ServerLimit          50
    MaxClients           50
    MaxRequestsPerChild  1000
</IfModule>
```

These settings are for a relatively low-traffic site on a low-memory server. Your results will vary, but these changes anecdotally affected the web server's response time for our WordPress installation. Of course you will have to adjust these settings to meet your own requirements.

Tuning the individual components of the LAMP stack warrants a book unto itself. Like WordPress, the LAMP development stack is very popular because of its flexibility and capability to handle multitudes of different tasks. The management and administration of LAMP components is a required skill for the full stack solution developer. Invest some time learning your tools and how to deploy them effectively.

WordPress Object Caching

The goal of web server caching is to keep frequently accessed files and popular chunks of code in memory and ready to serve or execute. Within WordPress, caching has to deliver a request for a page without going through additional code or database accesses, which really boils down to short circuiting the PHP WordPress core and serving up a static representation of your page directly.

If you search for "WordPress caching," you will find countless results about the built-in object cache. Initially, object caching was WordPress's solution to repeatedly serving up frequently used data, and you will find many references to setting a specific flag, the ENABLE_CACHE flag to be precise, in your configuration file to enable this functionality. Unfortunately, this information is all out of date. It was true for older versions of WordPress, but has been removed in favor of plugins that handle object caching more effectively. Not that WordPress has completely done away with all internal caching, but it only keeps the cache for the current request.

Object caching, as we have already discussed, keeps certain frequently used and expensive data sets in memory. The flexibility of object caching means that when certain information does change, that does not affect the entire cache, but only the objects in cache that actually changed. However, object caching still requires the plugin to execute PHP to determine which aspects of the cache are still valid and also for WordPress to execute the PHP to pull the parts of the page together for rendering. As previously discussed, optimizing your web server's PHP environment and enabling WordPress level object caching are quasi-independent as a consequence.

There may be times when your content is static enough or being served so frequently, that you need to short-circuit the whole PHP and object cache overhead; for example, when your page is being listed in the top echelons of Digg, Reddit, and Slashdot. A good way to do this is to have your page rendered to static HTML and served directly by the web server. After all, this is what the web server was designed to do in the first place.

In our opinion, the best plugin for this WP-Super Cache by Donncha O Caoimh. WP-Super Cache is based on and an improvement of the WP-Cache plugin. (See, this one is SUPER!) WP-Super Cache functions in various modes including writing out static HTML files. However, it does require mod_rewrite for the static HTML files, so this plugin will only work on Apache servers.

WP-Super Cache has an extensive control panel that allows the site administrator to adjust the settings to meet specific needs. It even includes a full lockdown mode that prepares for a heavy traffic spike.

The only fault with WP-Super Cache is that it does its job too well sometimes. On certain occasions we have been frustrated that new content sections were not being added to a site being worked on only to realize later that caching was not disabled before forcing the updates. Another time, we were deploying new mobile themes to a WordPress installation but for some reason the browser was not auto-detecting the mobile browser and displaying the correct theme. After too long troubleshooting user-agents and other issues, it turned out to be the cached files were being served and shortcutting the mobile theme code. This was easily remedied in the WP-Super Cache control panel.

Other caching plugins such as HyperCache are available, with many building on the basic theme of generating HTML for a page and caching it with the URL used to access the page as a key. Each plugin will have variations on cache invalidation and page lifetime policies, and all of them disrupt the general dynamic nature of WordPress page generation. If you're going to change your theme, add new plugins, or otherwise alter the flow of data from MySQL to user browser, either disable WordPress caching until you're sure all of your changes work, or frequently invalidate and flush the cache so that you can see the freshly generated pages as you test.

MySQL Query Cache

While researching for this book we set up a plain-Jane WordPress installation using the default theme and no additional plugins, so essentially an out-of-the-box installation. To render the index page Word-Press used 14 MySQL queries. You have to evaluate your site, but odds are the database-persisted content is not changing quickly enough that you need to make all these database calls for every page load. We discussed the translation of a URL into a MySQL query in Chapter 5 and looked at the underlying data models in Chapter 6, so the volume of database traffic required for the basic index page shouldn't be too surprising.

WordPress caching improves access times to content extracted from MySQL. If you want to further improve MySQL performance, and make it more responsive to queries from the WordPress core, you'll want to explore the MySQL query cache. The MySQL query cache stores the results of `select` statements, so that if an identical query is submitted, the already retrieved results can be immediately pulled from the system RAM and returned. This will significantly increase your response time, as long as your data is not changing that much. If your content is changing you may not see the updates immediately.

It used to be that WordPress' main query to retrieve posts included the current timestamp. Thus it changed every second and defeated MySQL query caching. This has now been optimized so that MySQL query caching can be used.

To enable MySQL query cache you will have to edit your MySQL configuration file on the server, assuming you have adequate permissions at your hosting company to do so. If you edit your MySQL configuration file, you can raise the memory limit. For example:

```
# enable 16 MB cache
query_cache_size   = 16M
```

Be careful not to go overboard here. Allocating too much RAM to MySQL caching will adversely affect other subsystems on your server. It is always a balance. Even just enabling this cache creates a management overhead in MySQL, but generally speaking this trade-off works in your favor.

LOAD BALANCING YOUR WORDPRESS SITE

At some point, you (hopefully) hit the performance limit of a single software stack on one physical server. That's when you may want to load balance your WordPress site with one or more additional servers. It could be for scalability to handle more requests, or as a failover precaution to increase the availability of your site. Whatever the reason, load balancing your site gets you both of these features, but it is a complex issue. We are just going to briefly discuss some of the challenges you will encounter when attempting to load balance a dynamically generated site.

First and foremost, you need a means to load balance. Simply, you can use round-robin DNS and bounce between your servers as needed. This will cause problems, especially with session cookies. You will need a legitimate load balancer to handle this. The load balancer could be a software package like Pound (`http://www.apsis.ch/pound/`) or a full hardware solution like an F5 BIG-IP (`http://www.f5.com/products/big-ip/`). Both will handle the session information and load balancing for you.

The second challenge is keeping your dynamic data in synchronization between your two (or more) web front ends. Consider that your site administrator could effectively log in to either web front end, post new content, and upload a graphic asset to the uploads directory. However, the next request could be load balanced to the other server, where this content may not exist.

Let's look at the uploads directory first. This content is uploaded from the WordPress Dashboard to the uploads directory of that WordPress installation. By default content is uploaded into `/wp-content/uploads/`. However, you can change the uploads directory in your Settings ➪ Miscellaneous Dashboard. Depending on where you set your uploads folder, you could also reap the benefit of having shorter asset URLs.

At this point you have options. One option is to have a shared folder that both web servers can access. Most likely this would be an NFS/Samba share on your third server, which serves as your MySQL server. A second option is to use rsync or a similar tool to coordinate uploads between the two servers and make sure each has the same assets in place.

The second challenge is your dynamic data that is stored in the database. Assuming your database is not the bottleneck and the reason for load balancing, you could use a third server as your database server. Both web servers can then read and write from the same source. This can be a more secure deployment architecture when your database server is not directly addressable on the public Internet, but it also creates a potential single point of failure. Technically, you are only load balancing the front-end web servers in this situation.

Adding a second database server increases the redundancy but introduces the problem of keeping two MySQL database tables in synchronization. MySQL servers can be configured for replication in a master-slave set up. Technically, this again, is not load balancing, because only one server is being accessed at a time, but this type of configuration does provide additional redundancy. Changes to the master MySQL database are replicated to the slave database in near real time via a journaling log. Should the master database fail, the slave has a full set of data for a manual cut over.

Finally, there is also a special WordPress-specific solution for multiple database servers. HyperDB (`http://codex.wordpress.org/HyperDB`) was created by Automattic to handle the requirements of WordPress.com traffic. HyberDB is a full replacement for the built-in WordPress database access layer and includes functionality for using multiple databases, sharding or partitioning your database across multiple servers, and also replication and tiered failover. Unfortunately, the documentation is far from complete.

As you can see, load balancing for performance and high availability is an extremely complex topic. There are countless variations of systems in place to handle a vast expanse of needs and requirements.

This short overview of the topic certainly glances over many nuances and challenges being faced when deploying WordPress into a high-availability environment. Cloud computing and content delivery networks are hot topics right now, and we expect to see WordPress being able to utilize these services for critical aspects and redundancy as those technologies and services mature.

DEALING WITH SPAM

As your WordPress blog gets noticed and generates traffic, it becomes a natural target for spammers. If you're noticing posts on your site that you don't expect, or see users in the Dashboard that you didn't create, you have other security problems that are covered later in this chapter. Most likely, your blog posts will accrete a variety of spam comments as a side effect of being popular.

You can recognize spam by a list of links within the comment or content-free comments saying that the poster enjoying your writing, with an attached URL or source address that invites you to a less-than-reputable destination. In either case, the goal of comment spam is to generate more web content that points back to the spammer's site, taking advantage of the page popularity ranking algorithms used by Google and others that give weight to incoming links. The best way to deal with spam is to simply get rid of it, denying spammers the opportunity to use your site to boost their own visibility.

There are three basic approaches to dealing with the problem: make it impossible for anyone to leave comments, increase the difficulty of a spammer sneaking a comment onto your site, and enable auto-detection of common spam patterns. Obviously, disabling comments (through the Dashboard) is a bit harsh, and defeats the goals of establishing conversation with your readers. On the other hand, if you decide to take this drastic step, remember that changing the settings for posts on the control panel only affects future posts; anything already on your blog will still have comments enabled unless you go through the Dashboard and turn them off individually. If you don't mind an even greater bit of brute-force effort, you can remove the `wp-comments.php` file from the WordPress core, which somewhat unceremoniously puts an end to the ability to comment on your posts.

We recommend something a bit more subtle.

Comment Moderation and CAPTCHAs

One approach to comment spam is to slow down the spammers; however, the simple approach slows down valid commenters as well. You can require commenters to register as site users before being allowed to post comments, as we discuss later in this chapter, but that has the downside of preventing passing-by users from adding their thoughts. It also requires that you stay on top of the user registration, as you may see seemingly valid users that are created purely for the purpose of posting spam to your blog.

Moderation is another tool in the slow-but-don't-stop vein; you can hold all comments for moderation or require all commenters to have a previously approved comment. We covered moderation options in Chapter 2. In effect, you're putting the burden of spam detection on yourself, looking at each comment as it appears and deciding whether to post it to your blog or flush it. Again, an innocuous looking comment may be the approval stepping stone for an avalanche of spam later on from the same user. As with many security mechanisms, the bad guys are continually getting smarter and more automated, and testing the edge protection and response of the systems they want to infiltrate.

A variation of the brute-force and moderation method is to blacklist IP addresses that seem to be the primary sources of spam; the access controls can be put in your .htaccess file as shown in Chapter 4. Again, this is perhaps a bit of hunting bugs with an elephant gun, as you're likely to block valid IP sources from common carriers who are unfortunately home to some low-limit spammers.

Enter CAPTCHA methods — based on a phrase coined at Carnegie Mellon University that ostensibly stands for "Completely Automated Public Turing test for telling Computers and Humans Apart" — that impede spammers' ability to post unwelcome comments by requiring them to enter some additional, dynamic piece of information. There are quite a few CAPTCHA generating plugins for WordPress, all of which add a displayed word or math problem to the end of the comment posting form, requiring the user to enter the correct information before the form is submitted. The simplest of these, the Math Test plugin, displays a two-term addition problem that must be solved by the user. The basic idea is that an automated spamming process won't be able to recognize the distorted words or solve the problems, alleviating the spam at the point of insertion. There's some debate as the effectiveness of CAPTCHAs, with their failure rates suggested as high as 20 percent. You're also adding a step for commenters, albeit a trivial one. If your site attracts a large, non-English speaking audience, CAPTCHAs depending upon wavy English words will be effective, but only in preventing valid comments from frustrated users.

The WP-Spamfree plugin is an inverse CAPTCHA; it tries to ensure that the commenter is using a browser, and not coming in via an automated process. This combination of JavaScript tricks is a variation on the spam impedance theme, and like the others, its effectiveness and user impact will vary depending upon the demographics of your site viewers.

Automating Spam Detection

The first step in automating spam detection is blacklisting certain types of posts or particular words. In the Dashboard's Options ➪ Discussion ➪ Comment Moderation box, you'll find an option to block any comment that contains more than a particular number of links. Don't set this to zero, or anyone who includes their own blog URL in a comment is going to filtered. This cuts down on the obvious spam messages, however. Similarly, adding words to the blacklist like "Vicodin" will eliminate the faux-pharmacy spam, but if you're perturbed by offers of fake Rolexes, don't add "watches" to the blacklist or you'll drop any comment that uses "watches" as a verb as well as a fake product noun. Word blacklists are universally effective in blocking comments with those words, irrespective of context.

Fortunately, WordPress has the Akismet plugin built-in for dealing with comment spam that relies on a crowd sourced blacklist and is transparent to users. Go to http://akismet.com/personal to register for an API key for the service; when you open up the Dashboard and configure the Akismet plugin you'll need this to make sure your instance of WordPress can connect to the Akismet service. Effectively, Akismet takes each comment as posted, runs it through a database of spam comments hosted by Automattic, and decides whether or not to mark the comment as spam. Statistics on the akismet.com site claim that upwards of 80 percent of all comments are spam, and that they have caught and marked more than 14 billion spam comments.

There are other implementations of the Akismet service besides the built-in plugin, and Akismet works on other content management systems as well. The Akismet terms of service ask that you buy a commercial license key if your blog generates over $500 in revenue, ranging in price from $5 to $50 per month.

SECURING YOUR WORDPRESS SITE

Unfortunately, with success and popularity you also become a target. WordPress is a successful and popular platform for web sites and with that comes the attention of the hackers and bad guys. It is simple economics that bad guys looking to build a network of sites will look to the most widespread applications and attack their vulnerabilities. Unfortunately, one of the vulnerabilities with WordPress (similar to PHP) is that because of the low barrier of entry and ease of use, users who are generally not too tech savvy or security minded can utilize WordPress without recognizing the full security ramifications involved.

This portion of the chapter covers some of the basic security principles you should employ when using WordPress. Some of them seem like common sense, but surprisingly are not put into practice on the average site. These are all preventative measures that you need to put into place before you really need them. As Benjamin Franklin said, "An ounce of prevention is worth a pound of cure." The time you spend protecting yourself will pay off should you have to work on cleaning up an exploited web site.

Stay Up-to-Date

Rule number 1 is always stay updated. WordPress developers are constantly working to make Word-Press a better, more secure and stable platform. This is one of the key advantages to open source software. Many developers, each with different skill sets, are looking over the code every day and performing various audits and updates to improve the overall codebase.

Updates often fix security concerns before there are exploits in the wild. In fact, many of the recent exploits have been targeting outdated versions of WordPress while consistently updated sites are immune.

WordPress implemented new notices in the Dashboard letting you know when there is a new version available. Another new feature is the ability to upgrade WordPress directly from the Dashboard. The WordPress team has been working to make upgrading as painless as possible. This new feature lets the site administrator update the WordPress Core right from inside the web interface.

If your web server has the ability to write to the files in your WordPress directories, then the automatic upgrade functionality works. If not, WordPress prompts for your FTP credentials to update the files for you. Both of these situations concern us. In general, your web user should not have write permissions to your entire web root. This is just asking for trouble, especially on a shared hosting platform; realizing, of course, that certain directories such as the uploads folder must be writable by the web user in order to function.

Second, it is not clear how this FTP credential information is stored or used. Although we do not believe anything nefarious is happening, we also do not want to encourage users to key in FTP (an unsecured protocol at that) credentials into any form that asks for it. However, if you do decide to go this route, you can set some WordPress configuration variables in your `wp-config` file that will further automate the FTP process.

There is definitely a balance here between the simplicity of keeping the WordPress Core updated, which is of the utmost importance, and with keeping the web root security intact.

Another new feature is the plugin changelogs, which let you keep tabs on what is actually changing in the new plugin. It is a new feature, and it is up to the plugin developer to keep this information current.

We are starting to see it in some plugins, but it is a new feature and we expect to see more use of it in future releases.

Hiding WordPress Version Information

This section is about concealing which specific version of WordPress you are running from the public eye. Honestly, we are mixed on this one. As WordPress evangelists, we say leave it in there. Say it loud and say it proud. As security conscious users, we say take it out. It is a way for the bad guys to easily find vulnerable sites, so why give it up?

Then again, we also agree with the WordPress developers. For a botnet scanning for vulnerable sites, it does not make sense to waste the time looking for specific WordPress versions, when it can just run the attack against the site. It will take the same amount of time, so why take twice as long? If you are going to get hacked because of your old version of WordPress, hiding the version number is not going to stop it. You should have been upgrading anyway.

In a standard WordPress installation, the version number is shown in the HTML source code as a meta tag for anyone to view source and see. However, if you want to remove this meta tag, there are several plugins that can do it for you. Or you can edit your `functions.php` and at the bottom add:

```
Remove_action('wp_head', 'wp_generator');
```

Also be on the lookout for certain themes and plugins that include version information in your header.

Don't Use the Admin Account

Definitely one of the first things you should do when you set up a new WordPress site is create a new administrator account. Do not use the default admin account.

Think about it. To get full access to your site, all the bad guys have to do is get access to your admin credentials. All they have to guess is your username and password; if you use the default username for the admin, you have already given them half of it.

Create a new user for your admin and delete the default one. If you are using an existing installation, still do this. Attribute all the admin posts to your new account. Just make sure you create the new account first.

Further precautions include limiting the number of login attempts on your WordPress control panel. This can prevent or discourage bad guys from brute force attacking your site. By default, WordPress will allow unlimited invalid login attempts, meaning that an automated script could be whacking away at your site all day long.

The Limit Login Attempts plugin by Johan Eenfeldt looks to remedy that. After a configurable number of invalid login attempts, that IP address is locked out for a specified period of time. This slowdown reduces the attractiveness of your site to an automatic attack script. You can find more information about Limit Login Attempts at `http://wordpress.org/extend/plugins/limit-login-attempts/`.

Furthermore, use good passwords for your account. Yes, we all have hundreds of passwords to remember, but there are tricks to using good passwords including mnemonics and password safes. WordPress has a nice JavaScript indicator when you are setting your password to let you know the quality of it.

Remember, you can pick a good password that is something you remember, or use a secure password-safe application to store it. Your password is your key to your kingdom, so make it a good key.

Change Your Table Prefix

This is another method to obscure the default attack vector. By default new WordPress installations have a table prefix of "wp_". That means every table in your WordPress database has a very predictable name, making it easier for attackers to form an assault on your site. If you are deploying a new site, set something unique for this prefix.

If you are already on an existing site, plugins are available that can handle renaming your tables for you. The WP-Security Scan by Michael Torbert, which we cover later in this chapter, offers the functionality to change your table prefixes for you. Make sure you make a database backup before performing this task, because the implications in case it does not work are quite severe. In addition to altering your table names, you will also have to edit the content in your blog_usermeta and blog_options tables as well as your wp-config file.

Move Your Configuration File

By default the WordPress configuration file is located in the root of your web site. In the event that PHP stops functioning on your web server for any reason, you run the risk of this file being displayed in plain text, which will give up your passwords and database information.

You can safely move the wp-config directory up out of the root directory. This will stop it from ever being accidentally served. WordPress has built-in functionality that will automatically check the parent directory if it cannot find a configuration file.

In some situations on certain hosts this is not an option. The alternative is to set your .htaccess to not serve up the wp-config file. Add the following line to your .htaccess file in the root directory:

```
<FilesMatch ^wp-config.php$>deny from all</FilesMatch>
```

Move Your Content Directory

Since WordPress 2.6 you can move your wp-content directory. This way you can take a large portion of your WordPress installation and move it to a non-default location. Again, this makes hoops for the bad guys to jump through.

Make two additions to your wp-config file:

```
define('WP_CONTENT_DIR', $_SERVER['DOCUMENT_ROOT'].'/mysite/wp-content');
define('WP_CONTENT_URL', 'http://domain.com/mysite/wp-content');
```

Some plugins may have difficulty dealing with a non-standard directory structure. If you are experiencing problems with certain plugins, you can add the following lines to your wp-config file for compatibility:

```
define('WP_PLUGIN_DIR', $_SERVER['DOCUMENT_ROOT']. '/mysite/
wp-content/plugins');
define( 'WP_PLUGIN_URL', 'http://domain.com/mysite/wp-content/plugins');
```

Moving your content directory in and of itself does not make your site more secure. What it does is make the automated tools used by attackers not work on your site. These automated tools are looking for the least common denominator of sites, so essentially, they are looking for stock WordPress configurations with default settings because that will give them the most bang for the buck. Security through obscurity is not security, but it does make your site a less attractive target.

Use the Secret Key Feature

In your WordPress config file are values for hashing salt keys. You should set these to make the encryption on your site stronger. Either make them up or visit https://api.wordpress.org/secret-key/1.1/ and get randomly generated ones.

You can change these keys at any time, but it will force anyone who is logged in to log in again.

```
define('AUTH_KEY',
    'CWTEFSwD/RJ.V.?@cc7C3.pe}|;Ew5yA[Mjwpdvzv90U#q̇1z7Ii5#ZLTiZG]`B{');

define('SECURE_AUTH_KEY',
    'Tl;(0u)<7=]27YQp:eg6wE#4wnwrE671](G|.@RStxDW5y0*Gvy6ita77K48Z<5>');

define('LOGGED_IN_KEY',
    'H8>z8V4m8:!66Em&grave;:j)T| 7>;R6+;+S^+R--XWMB;ywLjvNSIK2RR(C.c-LWVlO>');

define('NONCE_KEY',
    'ja+h9t/UXNjq̇?Ei;H*|q5I</#tw&qYoQtuI+yZxYYZI%oEq̇e,dTBuy>9K;2Q/-{#');
```

Do not use these values; set up your own.

Force SSL on Login and Admin

You can force your visitors and administrators to log in via an SSL encrypted page, assuming you have that set up already. Edit your WordPress config file and add the following flag:

```
define('FORCE_SSL_LOGIN', true);
```

You can also force the entire WordPress Dashboard to be served over HTTPS. Again, edit your config file and add the following line:

```
define('FORCE_SSL_ADMIN', true);
```

Apache Permissions

Permissions will vary depending on your configuration, but a good rule of thumb is set files to be 644 and folders to 755. If you cannot upload to the uploads folder, adjust those privileges alone. Generally, we have the files set to be in the same group as the web server and owned by the local user. For example:

```
drwxr-xr-x 7 davidd www-data  4096 2009-10-07 08:22 wp-content
-rw-r--r-- 1 davidd www-data  1254 2009-08-12 16:19 wp-cron.php
-rw-r--r-- 1 davidd www-data   220 2009-08-12 16:19 wp-feed.php
drwxr-xr-x 7 davidd www-data  4096 2009-06-11 15:39 wp-includes
-rw-r--r-- 1 davidd www-data  1946 2009-08-12 16:19 wp-links-opml.php
```

```
-rw-r--r-- 1 davidd www-data      2341 2009-08-12 16:19 wp-load.php
-rw-r--r-- 1 davidd www-data     21230 2009-08-12 16:19 wp-login.php
-rw-r--r-- 1 davidd www-data      7113 2009-08-12 16:19 wp-mail.php
-rw-r--r-- 1 davidd www-data       487 2009-08-12 16:19 wp-pass.php
-rw-r--r-- 1 davidd www-data       218 2009-08-12 16:19 wp-rdf.php
-rw-r--r-- 1 davidd www-data       316 2009-08-12 16:19 wp-register.php
-rw-r--r-- 1 davidd www-data       220 2009-08-12 16:19 wp-rss2.php
-rw-r--r-- 1 davidd www-data       218 2009-08-12 16:19 wp-rss.php
-rw-r--r-- 1 davidd www-data     21520 2009-08-12 16:19 wp-settings.php
-rw-r--r-- 1 davidd www-data      3434 2009-08-12 16:19 wp-trackback.php
-rw-r--r-- 1 davidd www-data     92522 2009-08-12 16:19 xmlrpc.php
```

Note that this will most likely break some of the "cool" functionality like one-click upgrades, and theme and plugin installations from the control panel. In this case you may have to provide WordPress with the FTP credentials to your site for this functionality to return. See the section "Stay up to Date" in this chapter for more on why this is a concern.

MySQL Credentials

Set your MySQL login and permissions correctly. For the love of all things open source, do not connect your WordPress site to your database with the MySQL root user. Set up a special user for each WordPress site. Make sure it only has access to the database it needs, and make sure it only has the privileges it needs. For example, your WordPress database user never needs to grant access to another user.

Recommended Security Plugins

Being vigilant is an important step in security. You cannot expect what you do not inspect. That is, you cannot expect things to be working, if you do not check in on them periodically. Some plugins help with security maintenance and configuration on your WordPress installation. Just like anti-virus and malware detection on workstations, these tools are here to assist in strengthening your security posture.

WP Security Scan

WP-Security Scan by Michael Torbert, shown in Figure 11-4, provides an overall security scan of your WordPress installation. It checks many of the items listed previously, including WordPress version, table prefix, and absence of the admin account. It also includes a file system scanner to verify that the permissions are set to the recommended settings. WP-Security Scan provides a nice mechanism to make sure the base settings are in line with a good security posture. We look forward to him adding new features in future releases.

You can find more information on WP-Security Scan at http://wordpress.org/extend/plugins/wp-security-scan/.

WordPress Exploit Scanner

WP-Exploit Scanner is another plugin by Donncha O Caoimh. The Exploit Scanner scans your files, posts, and comments for suspicious information. Basically, this is a forensics tool for you to use to make sure your site has not been compromised. This plugin does not remove anything, but creates a list of suspicious content for you to review. The challenge here is that even with the filtered list, you have to have some idea what you are looking for. Running this plugin on my site returns several false positives related to JavaScript from plugins and the WordPress core files.

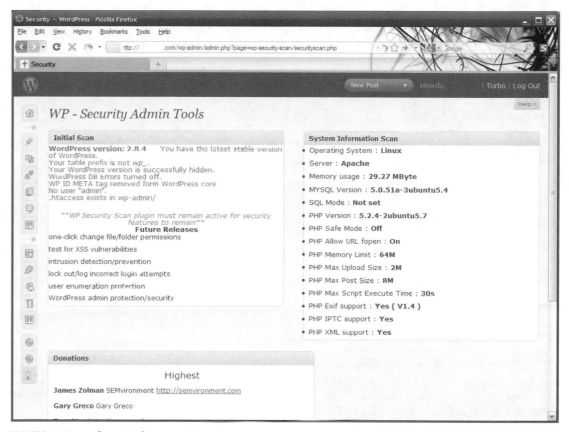

FIGURE 11-4: wp-Security Scan result

You can find more information about the WordPress Exploit Scanner at `http://wordpress.org/extend/plugins/exploit-scanner/`.

WordPress File Monitor

The WordPress File Monitor plugin by Matt Walters, shown in Figure 11-5, looks for files in your WordPress installation that have been added, changed, or deleted. The plugin can be configured to send an e-mail should any file system activity occur. In addition, this plugin can be set to exclude certain directories, like the uploads folder or file-based cache folders.

If file system changes are made this plugin sets a warning in your WordPress Dashboard and also sends you an e-mail to alert you of the changes. This can be very handy in the event that something bad happens, but will also trigger false alarms when you are performing updates. We assume you know when you are doing updates, and therefore can weed these out.

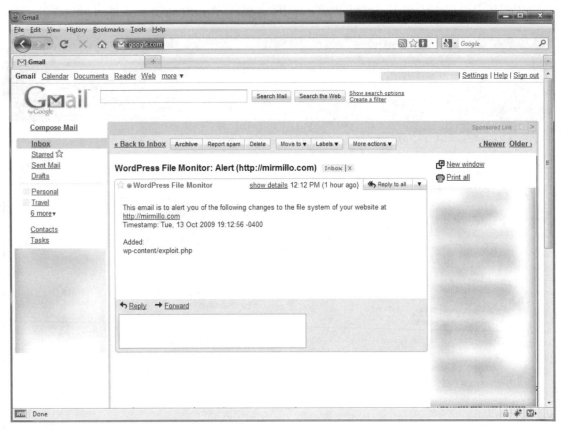

FIGURE 11-5: WordPress File Monitor alert e-mail

You can find more information about WordPress File Monitor at `http://wordpress.org/extend/plugins/wordpress-file-monitor/`.

USING WORDPRESS ROLES

Any smart manager learns how to delegate work, and a site manager should also learn this important skill. The WordPress role system allows you to assign different privileges to different user accounts. WordPress's default roles cover the basics and start to establish a publishing workflow through the fundamental capabilities of each role. These can be further extended through various plugins to create new roles with additional capabilities for specific tasks.

If you are the only person managing your site, you probably do not need roles. It boils down to you, the site administrator, and them, the unregistered masses. This setup, with no ability for new user to register, is a secure way to operate your site. But it also discourages participation. Eventually you may want to open it up to allow regular visitors to log in and reap some additional ease-of-use benefits.

You assign roles to users in the user management dashboard. Each user must be assigned to a role, and your site will have a default role for registered users. Setting each of these appropriately in the dashboard depends on your actual needs and the security permissions you need to delegate.

Subscriber Role

The Subscriber role is essentially the same as a non–logged-in visitor. So why do you need it if this person can read posts and post comments the same as a guest visitor?

There can be a couple of reasons. First, you may want to allow this role for regularly returning visitors. If they are registered they get some advantages such as not having to fill out all the fields to post a comment each time. Second, as a spam control measure, you may only allow registered Subscribers to post comments. This will weed out many of the automated spambots. Finally, certain plugins require this base level for functionality.

Contributor Role

The next step up is the Contributor role. The Contributor role is the first step in delegating responsibilities to your site users. The key item for Contributors is they can create new posts, but they cannot publish them to the site. That requires a higher role. This allows users to contribute information to your site, but you still maintain control over what is actually published. As you can see, this is a fledgling workflow for content publishing.

In addition to creating draft posts, Contributors can also edit their own posts at any time and delete their own unpublished posts. Contributors cannot upload files and images to be used in their own draft posts.

Author Role

Authors are the next role up the hierarchy. Authors are more trusted individuals than Contributors in that they can upload files to be used in their posts and can publish their posts without approval. Likewise, Authors can edit and delete their own published posts.

Authors are restricted to working with their own posts. They can read and comment on any post just like any other user, but they can only modify their own content.

Editor Role

The Editor role introduces two new capabilities. Up until this role we have been restricted to posts, but the Editor role can also work with pages. In addition, the Editor is privileged enough to modify any content on the site.

This role cannot manage users or site settings like themes and plugins, but the actual content is wide open. In practice, this is the role we assign to the client for a managed WordPress install. It provides enough capabilities that the client can manage the day-to-day content of the site, but not so much that he can muck around with the overall site settings and mess things up.

Administrator Role

This is the root level role. Everything in the WordPress Dashboard is open to an Administrator so you want to assign this role carefully. This role can modify users, themes, plugins, and all of the content.

Make sure your Administrator users are security conscious and using good passwords. Also, do not use the default Administrator account. Should bad guys get access to your Administrator account, they will have full access to your site.

Role Overview

Table 11-1 shows a simplified overview of the capabilities assigned to each role. For more exact information about the capabilities of each role, visit the WordPress Codex at `http://codex.wordpress.org/Roles_and_Capabilities`.

TABLE 11-1: Capabilities of Each WordPress Role

Capability	Admin	Editor	Author	Contributor	Subscriber
Manage themes	X				
Manage plugins	X				
Manage users	X				
Manage site options	X				
Moderate comments	X	X			
Manage categories	X	X			
Manage links	X	X			
Manage all posts	X	X			
Manage all pages	X	X			
Manage others' posts	X	X			
Read and manage private posts	X	X			
Read and manage private pages	X	X			
Upload files	X	X	X		
Publish posts	X	X	X		
Delete own published posts	X	X	X		
Edit own posts	X	X	X	X	
Delete own unpublished posts	X	X	X	X	
Read	X	X	X	X	X

Extending Roles

For most cases, the default roles will be enough. However, for certain circumstances there may be the need to extend roles to include more permissions or fine-grained control over content editing capabilities.

The Role Scoper plugin by Kevin Behrens (`http://wordpress.org/extend/plugins/role-scoper/`) is a very powerful tool to manage these access control situations. With this plugin, user access is augmented beyond the default permissions covered previously, with specific access controls related to content-specific settings.

That is, any level of user can have escalated permissions to edit and manage content based on specific categories, pages, or posts. This access permission can go both ways to either enable content modification, or the reverse to remove the ability for a role to read content.

For example, we created a multi–product-line site. Each product line had a product manager responsible for content related to their specific product line. In this case, each product line became a WordPress category. With this plugin, we were able to restrict product managers to be able to only post new content with in their respective categories.

The Role Scoper plugin is a very powerful plugin that allows you to build fine-grained controls. However, it may be more than you need for your particular situation. Many other plugins are available that allow you to supplement the built-in WordPress roles in other ways.

Role definition is key in controlling workflow, at the heart of using WordPress as a full-fledged content management system and in enterprise applications. We'll tackle those topics in the next two chapters.

12

WordPress as a Content Management System

WHAT'S IN THIS CHAPTER?

➤ Defining content management system tasks that are easily performed with WordPress

➤ Configuring WordPress to handle more complex content organization and display

➤ Integrating with interaction vehicles typical of content management systems such as forms, e-mail, and carts

Using WordPress as a content management system (CMS) seems to come up every month on the Web. Run that phrase through a search engine and you will see countless results on the whys, why nots, and hows. It seems that WordPress is trapped with the stigma of being "only" a blogging engine when, as by now you have also discovered, it is so much more.

This chapter defines content management from the perspective of a WordPress system, looks at the major functional areas associated with a CMS and shows how to implement them via Word-Press, and finally points out some areas where WordPress, despite its flexibility and simplicity, is not the best tool for the task.

DEFINING CONTENT MANAGEMENT

"Content management" has become hard to precisely define because it has been applied to a wide array of software tools and systems. On one end of the spectrum you have wikis, with explicit, multi-author editing and version control, but almost no page organization, navigation, or display mechanics. At the other extreme are commercial software packages aimed at the enterprise that handle access control, audit, repository, and community sharing of corporate documents. Clearly there's a difference between the "transactional content management" realm of enterprise document control and self-directed publishing, but trying to pin the content management label on just one or the other ignores the richness of the software tools in those spaces. Since the rise of low-cost, easily used Internet tools, content management has more typically been applied to the systems used to build a site for Internet commerce, featuring online catalogs and customer interaction.

Where does WordPress fit on this spectrum? In the narrowest definition, blog engines are a form of CMS, handling a minimal number of content types (pages and discussion) in a chronological display order. Although WordPress started out as a blogging system, and some popular opinion still tries to pigeonhole it as such, it has the power, flexibility, and resources to perform most, if not all, of the tasks required of a package more typically marketed as a CMS. The mechanics of managing a site, administering users, and bucketing content for structure and distribution aren't specific to blogs or any flavor of content; they require customization, design, and a multi-role delegation system. Hopefully, that's what we have conveyed so far in this book, where we have liberally referred to the "content management" functions of WordPress, and now we can tie the pieces together in a more general CMS view.

Here are the CMS features we discuss:

➤ **Workflow and delegation:** Often the holy grail of the CMS world is enabling multiple authors with minimal technical expertise to control the editing and publishing process. WordPress makes it simple for non-technical users to add content and manage its distribution.

➤ **Content organization:** From mimicking a simple network portal to building complex page hierarchies, content organization involves handling multiple, complex types of content and choosing the appropriate display patterns for each.

➤ **Interactivity:** Mailing lists, forms, discussions, and commerce functions are typical CMS functions that require a bit of WordPress extension.

➤ **Other Content Management Systems:** As a pure blog management system, WordPress can be a powerful editing and content production platform, feeding other content management systems such as Drupal. We also look at areas in which WordPress is not the best choice.

At their core, blogging and content management may have come from different starting points and established their own functional lexicon, but the extensibility, design customization, and diverse developer community around WordPress has blurred the lines between what is "only blogging" and the now in-vogue "enterprise content management." We discuss WordPress in the enterprise in Chapter 13, but as an introduction to the details of implementing full CMS functionality, here is our list of reasons why WordPress should be thought of as a first-tier content management system:

➤ **Simplicity:** From the user interface to content creation, WordPress can be simple or complex to match user skill and deployment requirements.

➤ **Flexibility:** WordPress handles a multitude of site archetypes, from simple reverse-dated blog entries to crowd-sourced, hyperlocal news sites (check out `http://injersey.com`) to hierarchies of fixed and dynamic content showcasing an artist, photographer, or other creative professional.

➤ **Extensibility:** You can find plugins and themes to create a huge variety of visual styles, integrate numerous content types and sources, and simplify the process of going from simple typed content to complex, displayed HTML.

Our goal in covering WordPress as a CMS is to highlight approaches to solving typical content management problems, building on the techniques and examples provided in previous chapters.

We don't want every conversation to start out with a defense of WordPress, by us in these pages or by you in a setting where you are choosing content management tools. Whatever your definition of content management, or your goals for creating a web site that goes well beyond a list of blog entries, the content management process starts with simplifying the workflow.

WORKFLOW AND DELEGATION

One of the primary appeals of a classic CMS is that it simplifies content creation and management. Closely tied to that effort is a separation of duties, such that those users and administrators with editorial control over the content are given access, responsibility, and control over what is actually published through the CMS.

User Roles and Delegation

User management in a CMS has all of the separation of powers and policy creation complexity of politics, government, or standards bodies. You have to allocate roles based on the types and categorization of content you expect, as well as setting boundaries on users' abilities to publish and edit previously published content. In a purely multi-author blog environment, the distinction may not appear that important, but if you're using WordPress as the face of an e-commerce site or for a company's product catalog, multiple departments and approvers typically demand involvement.

We covered Kevin Behrens' Role Scoper plugin in Chapter 11 as part of our security and user management discussion. This plugin allows you to create new roles for your users and assign them very fine-grained permissions. In a CMS environment this would permit you to delegate content generation to different departments and authorize them to make changes only in their respective areas.

Delegation of authority goes up the hierarchy of users, not down from an editor to an individual author. In a typical publishing environment, an editor will be able to dole work out to writers and composition experts, creating a workflow for the finished product that is organized in a tree structure similar to an organizational chart. WordPress mobilizes the leaves in that tree structure: every user that has contributor or author privileges can create content (and upload files, in the case of authors), and manage publishing of their own posts. Deciding how and where to divide responsibilities is a key part of establishing a CMS framework with WordPress:

➤ Be diligent about administrator roles. Give them out like `root` or `sudo` passwords. At the same time, don't confuse editors with administrators. Editors may want to change the way a page appears, or aggregate content differently. Administrators are going to fix themes, core files, and plugins, and each has to be clear about the bounds on their domains.

➤ Treat editors as such. They will be given permission to edit pages, modify the content or status of any posts, and change metadata on the WordPress site. They should be using their editorial roles to manage the work of the authors and contributors as well.

➤ If you really want every piece of content reviewed before it hits the public Web, separate contributors (who cannot publish) from authors (who can publish their own work but not edit that of others). Establishing a contributor class of users ensures that your editors will be busier, but also fully delegates the publishing decisions to those editors.

➤ Note that roles and delegation cover the creative process, not access control to content once published. As soon as it's accessible as a published post, it's public until deleted (and even then, it may be cached or replicated elsewhere through a feed mechanism). In contrast to other content management systems, WordPress does not focus on a mechanism to control access to published content; it's not about intellectual property management or control in the same way a corporate document repository might track access, reference, and auditing.

A wrinkle on the multi-role and multi-user WordPress administration framework is WordPress MU, discussed briefly in Chapter 1. WordPress MU powers WordPress.com, because it allows multiple independent user trees to run independent but co-hosted blogs. This may be attractive if you have independent product groups or multiple brands that each want their own WordPress installations but you are limited (or want to be restrictive) in terms of administrator people power. WordPress MU is in the process of being merged into the WordPress Core, and by WordPress 3.0 it will no longer be a separate distribution.

Workflow

Having established users and their roles, the next step is to clearly establish a workflow for getting content out of people's heads and onto the Web. After a simple editorial user structure, workflow is probably the next most matched term when asking what users associate with mainstream CMS. Two major components to workflow within WordPress exist: post revision history and post control.

Revision history is visible within the Post portion of the Dashboard, where entering edit mode on a post shows you the list of revisions. If you're running a system with multiple authors and editors, where the editors may fine-tune the first writing output, ensure that the editorial staff is using the revision feature to track content added, subtracted, or different between posts revisions. It's effectively source code control for post content, managed within the MySQL database under WordPress.

Though we are big fans of the simple Dashboard, and find it compact yet powerful, some site administrators may find that the interface is too complicated given the technical back-ground of their editor or administrator delegate. Some people freeze up when they have too many options or choices. You can use the WP-CMS Post Control plugin by Jonathan Allbut (`http://wp-cms.com/our-wordpress-plugins/post-control-plugin/`) to turn off unneeded features. This plugin installs a new control panel that allows you to configure the Write Panel to show only the fields you want them to see, as shown in Figure 12-1.

There are many options here, but it is a simple management control. Using this plugin is the admin-istrative control step that's complementary to creating simpler (or more specific) post editing panels, described later in this chapter.

The second part of content workflow is the process of taking posts from the draft state to published state, with stops at "private," "future," and "pending" along the way if warranted. A post written by a contributor will be held as "pending" until published by someone with that permission. Much of the post workflow happens through the Posts tab on the Dashboard, where the status of each post is clearly labeled, and there are menu items for publishing or making other post status changes such as marking a post as private or setting a future publication time.

If you're running a multi-writer WordPress site, remember that all of the content is stored in the same MySQL database, making it easy for other users to see the current state of the content. WordPress provides the `wp_transition_post_status()` function for plugins that want to catch individual post

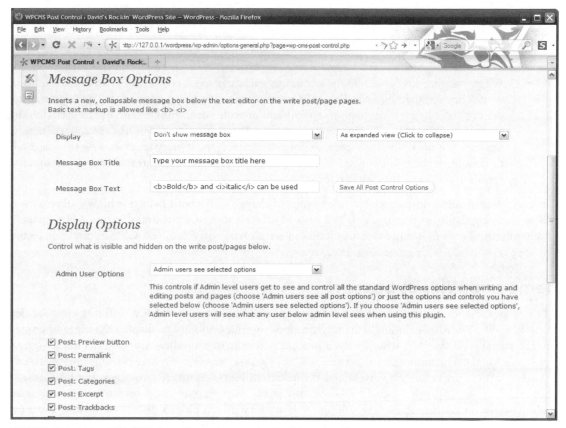

FIGURE 12-1: Using WP CMS Post Control to set the Dashboard options

status changes, either to update a work in progress page or to otherwise signal to other users that a workflow change has propagated.

CONTENT ORGANIZATION

There is an ongoing discussion bordering on a flame war about posts in a WordPress site that is being used as a traditional, static content web site. Posts are an indelible part of WordPress and absolutely have a place and use in any web site, whereas the common argument is that posts are naturally chronological and only time-based content fits this paradigm. Posts can represent any small content block that can be used multiple ways, and part of using WordPress as a CMS involves changing your strategic thinking about what types of content are used to what effect on the site.

Here are three simple examples of using posts for a commerce site:

➤ Create a post for each product that you sell. Comments on the post allow users to offer feedback and recommendations.

➤ Create a category or tag for each product on the site, and then organize posts about the product. The first post in each category should be the product information, and possibly a link to a shopping cart via which to purchase the product — something we cover shortly. Now you can use the posts structure to provide deeper information about each product: why did you offer it? How was it created, defined, or sourced? What other reviews, feedback, or public commentary exists?

➤ When creating a help section for a product, each help topic could be a post. Each help topic would be one small bite-sized piece of content that addresses a specific task or feature, using the tag and category mechanisms to sort and provide navigational guidance to users looking for self-directed help. Comments on the posts allow for users to describe the relative helpfulness of each post. Similarly, though not e-commerce, the jQuery team is using this method to document their API at `http://api.jquery.com` creating a help resource and community resource via comments, all in one.

In every one of these simple examples, we want to change the default behavior of WordPress away from showing the most recent posts, and instead create a mix of static and dynamic "homepage" content reminiscent of a static web site. You can see a variety of WordPress CMS application examples at `http://wordpress.org/showcase/tag/cms`.

Theme and Widget Support

Theme support for content management is key. You're not trying to make WordPress look decidedly non-blog-like but rather finding a theme that gives you the flexibility to display the types of content in the visual style that fits, whether it's a product sales site or an online newsletter. This is a great use case for the Thematic (`http://wordpress.org/extend/themes/thematic`) framework with its thirteen widget areas and powerful child theme extensibility. As an extreme case, the P2 theme (`http://p2theme.com`) developed by Automattic puts a posting panel, real-time updates, and in-line editing right on the homepage, combining the best of Twitter, a blog, a discussion forum, and a news site.

If you're going to be using a theme with widget areas and want to expand the content types available in those sidebar areas, you'll want to leverage the TinyMCE JavaScript-based editor to turn HTML text areas into something more theme-appropriate. The Rich Text Widgets plugin addresses the challenge that default text widgets only support plain old text. When you enable the Rich Text Widget plugin by Jacquet Aymeric (`http://wordpress.org/extend/plugins/rich-text-widget/`) as shown in Figure 12-2, you have a new widget available in your widget control panel. This widget has the built-in TinyMCE editor, so your content creators can put more than text in the sidebar.

You do have to exercise some caution when using this plugin. Usually, your sidebar and other widget-ready areas have fixed widths. With this plugin, your content creator can upload anything into the widget and potentially break the layout of the site. However, this can be remedied with some proper training.

The bundled TinyMCE editor is workable but doesn't support some frequently used features such as adding tables. The TinyMCE Advanced plugin by Andrew Ozz (`http://www.laptoptips.ca/projects/tinymce-advanced/`) steps in and tries to address these shortcomings; however, be forewarned that the more elaborate your widget text, the more opportunity you create to break your site (again) with ill-formatted or rendered tables. Figure 12-3 shows a couple of features turned on, but there are many more.

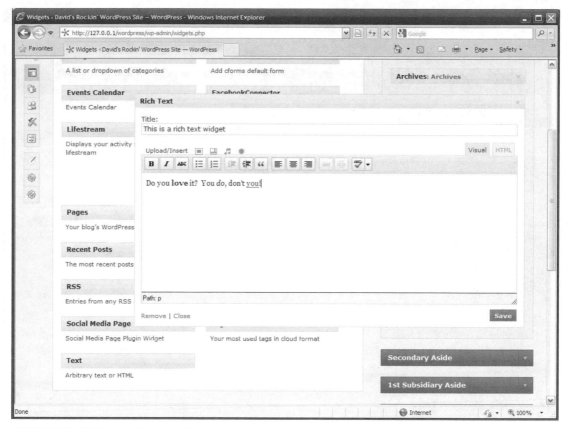

FIGURE 12-2: Editing a rich text widget

Homepages

Remember writing classes where every story had to have a narrative hook? The hook was the point in the story where you established what made your story unique or interesting, and encouraged your reader to keep going. A good narrative hook on a WordPress site will engage the reader and kick off the remainder of your story line, whether it's product-related content, or a mix of static and time-sensitive posts.

The common approach is to set a static homepage. Covered back in Chapter 8, you can do this in several different ways. The easiest is to use the WordPress Reading Settings Dashboard to set a static page for your front, or homepage. In addition, this page could use a page template to modify and distinguish the layout from the rest of your site. You'll need to create a page (not a post) specifically for this purpose, and then use the Dashboard to set it as the front page.

The other option is to use a special WordPress template file to serve as your index page, replacing the default listing of posts. WordPress looks for a template file named home.php in your theme, as also discussed in Chapter 8. Using a template file will afford you more flexibility in the layout and functionality of your index page because you can edit the PHP code directly, choosing, for example,

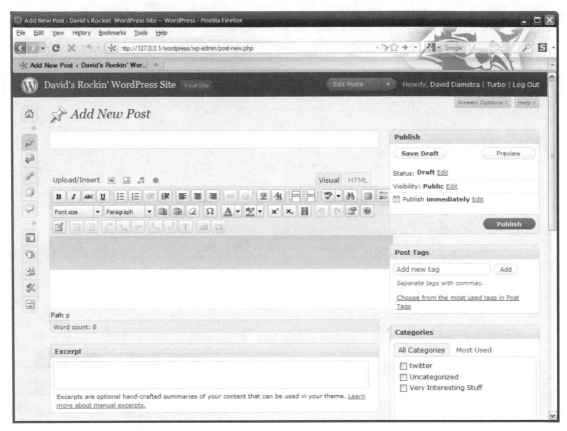

FIGURE 12-3: Using TinyMCE Advanced to edit a post

to list sticky posts or featured products first, and then related content or more recent chronological posts. Using a mix of additional page data fields, and the custom Loop query mechanisms described in Chapter 5, you can hand-tune the selection of content for your homepage as finely as you want.

Featured Content Pages

A good tool for your narrative hook on your static index page is a featured item. This is very common among the magazine-style themes and many web sites. Often, in the top third of the content area you will see a large image area with a headline featuring content from elsewhere in the site. This position is sometimes called the "hero spot" and features prominently on popular web sites. It is a frequently deployed device because it works.

Generally when we deploy a featured item on the index page we like to have several different images and use jQuery (or another JavaScript library) to cycle through them. That way, you are not relying on one hero item to save the day, but putting forth a couple of different ideas, and hopefully one will catch the visitor's eye. The goal here is to feature items managed as posts or media by WordPress so that the editorial staff can control them rather than the site administrator.

The first thing to do is set up a post category for the featured items. For this example, the category is named "Features." We should also note that in other parts of the site, for example, if there is a news section that shows all posts, we will want to exclude this category from those Loops.

The plan is to showcase three random features from the Features category for display. To get this to work on the site, you are either going to edit your home.php template file or make a new page template file for your index page. These code changes will go into that file.

First, you have to get the posts from the database. You can get these posts with a simple WordPress query using the query object:

```
$my_query = new WP_Query("category_name=Features&showposts = 3&orderby=rand");
```

You can tell from the parameters what this object will return (if not, revisit our discussion of using WP_Query objects to build custom Loops in Chapter 5). Then in the content area of the template file, you mix a little HTML for the jQuery to hook into and then loop over the result object:

```
<div id="feature-content">
  <?php
    while ($my_query->have_posts()) : $my_query->the_post();
      echo '<div id="feature-'.$post->ID.'" class="slide" >';
      echo '<div class="feature-post-content">'. $post->post_content .'</div>';
      echo "</div>\n";
    endwhile;
  ?>
</div>
```

What you are doing here is creating a wrapping div to contain the slideshow. Then looping over each post in the query result, you are creating a new div of class "slide" and inside that, a div with the actual post content. When you put this to use, the post content is generally a specifically sized image wrapped in an anchor tag. The post content in the Features category will look similar to this:

```
<div class="feature-post-content">
  <a href="/somepage/">
    <img width="500" height="312" alt="This is a great picture"
    src="/wp-content/uploads/photo.jpg" title=" This is a great picture"
    class="aligncenter size-full wp-image-89"/>
  </a>
</div>
```

Now if you view your site, you will see three stacked images on top of each other. So the next step is to take these posts and use a little JavaScript magic to turn it into a slideshow or carousel. We are big fans of the jQuery Cycle plugin by Mike Alsup (http://malsup.com/jquery/cycle/). Note that this is a plugin for jQuery, and not WordPress. This plugin is really easy to use and has a ton of neat transition options. Using this plugin you can convert the HTML into an autoscrolling slideshow. This JavaScript code goes into the bottom of your page template file where you would normally place your JavaScript.

```
$('#feature-content').cycle({
  fx:     'scrollHorz',
  speed:  500,  //time the transition lasts
  timeout: 5000, //time between transitions
  pause: 1, //stop the show on mouseover
```

```
      random: 0, //random order (our mysql does this already)
});
```

Experiment with the different effects and timing, using the other parameters you can set to create unique results. This same method could be used to showcase some testimonials. Either keep it in a slideshow pattern, as outlined previously, or pull a random post from the testimonial category. Rather than using images as your content, you could have the actual formatted post data.

Content Hierarchy

Building on the featured item concept, most content management systems will allow you to create a hierarchy of content, with content of different types existing in a tree-like structure that eases navigation and allows you to mix static content features with more dynamic content. Another feature of the upcoming WordPress 3.0 release is a full user interface and menu system, giving site administrators the ability to create multi-level menus of pages. Without clicking through menus, WordPress supports built-in and plugin-driven mechanisms to create rich content hierarchies.

One obvious path to a content hierarchy is to use categories and tags to sort posts into related groups. This is useful when you are using posts as the primary content type, and organize equivalent classes of posts by category or unique tag information. In addition, you saw in the previous section of this chapter how posts can be used for featured image content on an index page carousel.

The custom taxonomy features discussed in Chapter 6 provide another way to organize and search posts, giving you even more flexibility when customizing a theme's Loop. This section digs into these custom page and post hierarchies more, providing examples of plugins that let you craft the content management aspects of WordPress to suit your desired site look and feel.

Let's start with a complex navigation challenge: You have a hybrid site that has sections where pages are the obvious content type, but you also have some sections where post categories make more sense. You do not want to manage a hardcoded navigation tree, and implementing menus isn't perfect because the post content is (intentionally) regularly changing.

One solution is the Page Links To plugin by Mark Jaquith (`http://txfx.net/wordpress-plugins/page-links-to/`). This plugin creates a new field on the page Write Panel. Using this field, you can create a page that functions as a redirect to another web page. This enables you to use the `wp_list_pages()` function as your site's global navigation in your template file, but still empowers you to create menu items that can redirect to offsite links. Or, more often, you can now create a menu item as a page, but have it redirect to a post Loop page.

For example, pretend that under your "About Us" menu, you have the traditional history of your company and contact us pages, but you also have a press release page. Press releases make more sense to be implemented as posts, which creates a problem in your navigation. With this plugin, you can create a new page called Press Releases, but have the page link to "/category/press-releases/" instead. You can see how this would be set up in Figure 12-4.

The next challenge with a large site is managing the pages. After a while, your site grows to have multiple pages, under multiple parent pages. This structure is necessary to make your site coherent, as discussed in Chapter 11. Using the built-in Parent pages management is functional, but can get

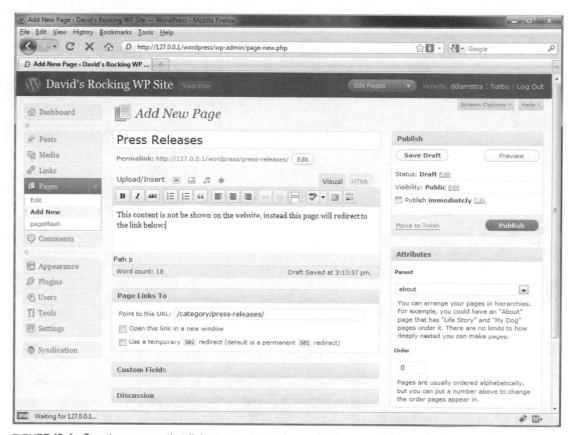

FIGURE 12-4: Creating a page that links to a category loop with the page links to plugin

confusing quickly. And when you need to move pages around, using this method can get quite tedious, as you can see in Figure 12-5.

Enter the PageMash plugin by Joel Starnes (http://joelstarnes.co.uk/blog/pagemash/). PageMash, in all its AJAXy goodness, allows you to move pages around in a drag and drop natural fashion. As you can see in Figure 12-6, pages can be nested and organized in a very intuitive interface. In addition, the plugin will let you hide pages from the wp_list_pages() function, offering even more control over the whole navigation structure of your site.

Assuming you are following our "posts are generic content" lead and are using posts for various types of content in your site, the Yet Another Related Post plugin by Michael Yoshitaka Erlewine (http://wordpress.org/extend/plugins/yet-another-related-posts-plugin/) is a nice add-on. This plugin provides a list of additional content that is possibly related to the

FIGURE 12-5: The Parent pages drop-down selection on a site with just a few pages

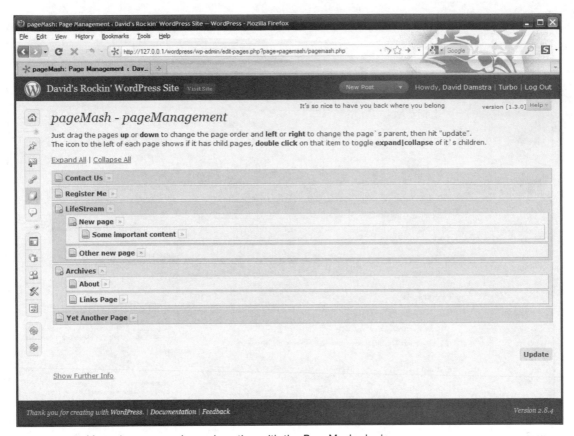

FIGURE 12-6: Managing page order and nesting with the PageMash plugin

current entry. Using this type of functionality will encourage visitors to explore other areas of your site that are of similar interest. In examples like the support center mentioned previously, this plugin would provide additional help topics related to the current issue. In short, using this plugin creates cross-references in your web site among related content.

Finally, you can tie together taxonomy-based page sorting, custom content types, and a simpler Dashboard with the Flutter plugin. Created by the guys at Freshout (http://flutter.freshout.us/) as a way to easily create custom Write Panels and use the custom information in your page templates, Flutter adds superb configuration control to the post Write Panels. Where this plugin really shines is when you have several page or posts in your site that all require comparable information or content for similarly structuring them at rendering time, such as the jQuery API web site, where each and every function has a description, example, and demonstration. Traditionally, in WordPress you would do this with the custom field functionality. Flutter simplifies this process for your content administrators by allowing you to create a specific Write Panel to meet each content type's need.

For example, say you are creating a new site that will have several product information pages. Each product information page will include the product name, a tagline about the product, a thumbnail, and the description. You want them all to look similar, so there is a consistent look across the product line.

With Flutter, you can create a custom Write Panel for these product pages. First, you turn off all the unneeded fields in the standard Write Panel, and then you can add in the custom fields you need. In this example, you create Flutter fields for the thumbnail and the tagline, as shown in Figure 12-7. This is better than custom fields, because you can set what the input labels are and direct the proper content population, which makes it easier for your content administrator.

From here, you can easily access these Flutter fields in your template files. For example, you can create a custom page template and use the Flutter-specific template tags to structure the content appropriately. Your custom page template might include something like this:

```
<div class="post">
  <h2 class="page-title">
    <a href="<?php the_permalink();?>" title="<?php the_title();?>">
      <?php the_title();?></a>
  </h2>
  <div class="content">
    <h3 class="tagline"><?php echo get('tagline'); ?></h3>
    <?php the_content();?>
  </div>
</div>
```

This way, each product page using the product page template will have the product tagline rendered in the exact same HTML context and position, giving you something like Figure 12-8.

As you can see, incorporating the Flutter plugin into your content administration plan and theme design can simplify the whole process of managing structured content. This plugin will force structure to your content input workflow so that all information is consistent, and then by integrating the Flutter template tags into your theme you can keep the front end consistent too. The Flutter plugin has other features beyond custom Write Panels, and in the right situation this is a very powerful plugin.

The Pods CMS plugin by Matt Gibbs (http://pods.uproot.us/) takes structuring data even further. Pods CMS allows you to create new content types above and beyond posts, pages, and custom fields. You can then normalize these new types with relationships among the data. You can use these new content types and relationships in your Pods pages that support special Pods syntax and PHP code. Pods CMS is a much more complex system than the Flutter plugin, but it also is much more powerful.

Finally, WordPress 2.9 started adding support for custom content types by extending the internal API functionality. This is intended to allow for more forms of content beyond the posts, pages, and attachments currently in use. This functionality is expected to be further enhanced in WordPress 3.0.

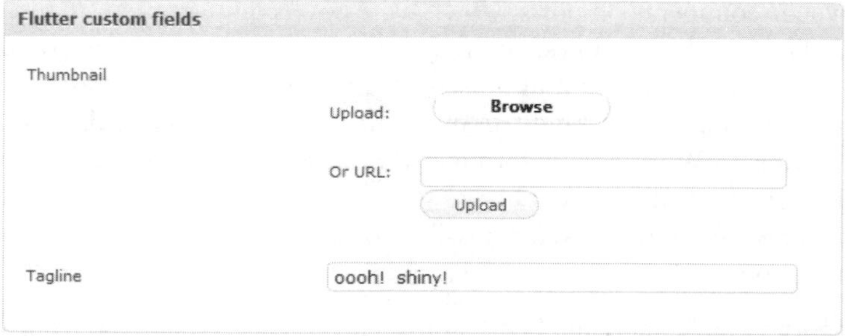

FIGURE 12-7: Flutter custom fields on a write panel

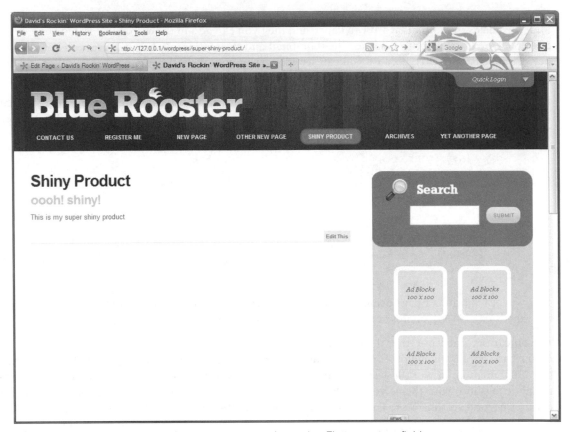

FIGURE 12-8: HTML rendering of custom page template using Flutter custom fields

INTERACTIVITY FEATURES

The most basic interactivity feature is search, discussed in Chapter 10. The other primary user interaction features associated with a CMS are forums, forms, and basic e-commerce features.

Forums

The simplest content discussion type is comments on posts, which were covered in detail in Chapter 2, and in terms of spam comments in Chapter 11. At times, you're going to want to move from content that you create in an attempt to stimulate conversation into user-led and threaded conversation. A forum is an open discussion, most commonly called a bulletin board in the pre-broadband days of the Internet. The easiest way to add forums to WordPress is through bbPress (http://bbpress.org), a WordPress-related project also delivered by Automattic. bbPress will share user data with WordPress, so registered users can participate in forum discussions. It's possible to load them both, and have your forums simply appear as a section of your web site.

Other plugins are available to support forums, including Eric Hamby's Forum Server, derived from WP-Forums. If you want a simple forum feature as a content type, the plugin route is likely to produce an acceptable result. On the other hand, if you want to integrate multiple content management repositories into a single user experience, take a page (literally) from WordPress.org: bbPress powers the Word-Press.org user-generated support area.

Forms

The next challenge for a web site is forms, such as contact forms and other similar web-form-to-e-mail functionality. Countless plugins are available for contact forms, but for a full-featured site, you will eventually have to move beyond this. For the longest time, the cForms 11 plugin by Oliver Seidel (`http://www.deliciousdays.com/cforms-plugin`) has been our regular stand-in. CForms works very well and is extremely powerful. You can customize it to all ends of the earth, but the user interface is very daunting at first. You cannot really hand off CForms to your content administrator to make new forms as needed.

An alternative to CForms is Gravity Forms by RocketGenius (`http://www.gravityforms.com/`). This is the only plugin on this list that costs money to use. But, and we will be honest here, we have a little software crush on Gravity Forms. Gravity Forms lets you create any type of form you need with a simple, easy-to-use AJAXy interface. It is so easy to use, we even show our content administrators how to use it. We do not want to gush too much, but the clean, intuitive interface is truly among the best we have seen among plugins.

In addition to the user interface side, the HTML rendering is top notch. It looks fantastic without any additional styling required. However, should you desire to change the look and feel, the HTML is filled with CSS class and ID hooks for you to use. A final, powerful feature of Gravity Forms is that in addition to the traditional "e-mail the form contents to a specified address" functionality, Gravity Forms also adds a dashboard module that tracks the forms submitted. Although CForms has similar functionality, the usability of GravityForms really justifies the cost.

E-Commerce

If you're building a site with featured products and pages, product tags, and categories, ideally you'd like to sell something. Shopping cart and payment systems integration fill the last category of user interaction. Searching the plugin directory on WordPress.org shows at least a dozen different shopping cart and checkout plugins available. Rather than itemize them all, here's a quick checklist of things to look for:

- ➤ How hard is it to configure the shopping cart? Are you going to be burdening your administrators with minor details like updated discounts, or can content managers handle that task?

- ➤ What kinds of statistics can you get from the cart? Learning how and why users abandon items will help you improve the site, whether it's through more product information or an easier checkout process.

- ➤ What payment systems are supported? If you're not looking for anything more complicated than the ability to accept PayPal payments with a specific product or item number filled in, you can use PayPal button templates and hand-edit them into your pages or sidebars.

OTHER CONTENT MANAGEMENT SYSTEMS

We have illustrated how WordPress is so much more than a blogging platform. It can be used for a wide range of different types of web sites, but aside from what a plugin can offer — which can be substantial — the functionality of the WordPress Core is what it is. Sometimes you want to complement your web site with additional functionality found in other traditional web-based applications, such as forums like bbPress, e-commerce applications, or other CMS solutions.

Given the range of content management systems available, and the fact that most enterprises already have one, if not several, content repositories up and running, it's often useful to integrate WordPress with another CMS. This section takes a brief look at the issues of using WordPress as an external content consumer or producer and when you should not use WordPress as the core of a content management system solution.

WordPress Integration

Integrating an application like WordPress with another content-oriented application requires that you align user management, content packaging, and potentially look-and-feel issues. It's not something easily accomplished with a plugin or theme extension, and typically requires custom bridge code. You will find building blocks in the plugin directory; this section presents a rough outline of the problems to be solved.

How does the external system provide content? Are you getting an RSS feed, in which case you can use the RSS aggregator discussed in Chapter 9 as a starting point, or do you get raw JSON that requires editing and parsing before being turned into a post?

If you have a remote resource URL, can you embed it using an oEmbed (http://oembed.com) provider plugin? oEmbed takes a URL and returns a variety of content types that can be integrated into WordPress themes, allowing them to be displayed without WordPress having to parse the content type. WordPress 2.9 added oEmbed support for a slew of popular web sites and is on track to further expand support in 3.0.

Do you need to manage user credentials between the sites? Do you have to store user login information for the external site (in the WordPress MySQL database, using a table created by your plugin) and if so, how do you handle error conditions like password changes or user deletion in the remote system?

It's possible to treat WordPress as a blog-only engine, producing blog posts for consumption by a CMS like Drupal. In this case, WordPress becomes a component of Drupal, managing its content as the source of the blog posts type but ceding presentation control to the Drupal configuration.

Where Not to Use WordPress

Not every content management problem is a nail waiting to be pounded home by the WordPress hammer. Sometimes you'll need to pick a different tool, or set of tools, for the job:

➤ **Handling rich media:** Streaming video, audio, and images with copious quantities of metadata can be displayed and included in WordPress posts, but if you want to be able to tag and index video files or search images based on their EXIF (Exchangeable Image File Format) tags, you probably want to use a CMS designed for rich media management.

➤ **Backend for Rich Internet Applications:** We're now seeing the next generation of fat clients, also known as Rich Internet Applications, written in Flash, Silverlight, JavaFX, or for the iPhone. They usually expect to talk to a backend data repository or service, rather than a full-featured web site. WordPress eventually emits HTML, not JSON or other data packaging formats most likely consumed by RIAs.

➤ **Simple network storefront:** If you're just building a store, use a storefront builder with shopping cart, payment systems, and product catalog. You'll miss the integration of product discussion, feedback, recommendations, and the ability to describe how and why you're carrying (or have built) a particular product, all of which are possible using the approaches described in this chapter, but sometimes you just need users to be able to click and buy.

➤ **Event and calendar focus:** Several types of sites manage calendars, event registrations, event materials, and notifications or reminders about upcoming calendared items. WordPress does not (yet) have highly functional calendar and event management plugins, making this an area where using Drupal will be simpler out of the box.

➤ **Force-fitting a solution:** If you have to make modifications or changes to the WordPress Core, either you are doing something wrong or more likely, WordPress is not the right solution. When hacking the core WordPress code you break your upgrade path, such that you overwrite any changes you made to the core package files that enabled your specific functionality to work as soon as a new version of WordPress is released. As we stated in Chapter 4, don't hack the core.

➤ **Plugin overload:** Plugins rock, and a large portion of this book has been devoted to identifying appropriate plugins for specific functions or outlining how to create your own for those uses. But you can go overboard. If you are using too many plugins, you hurt the performance of your site and probably make it more fragile due to unknown dependencies between the plugins. Each plugin also increases the resource requirements of your site, specifically, memory and processing power.

WordPress is a powerful content management system with many of the features found in commercial systems that pre-date the blogging craze. In equal parts tribute to its open source roots, strong developer community, and simple extensible design, WordPress has established itself as a tool that goes far beyond a simple blog engine. Chapter 13 looks at enterprise-scale WordPress deployment.

13

WordPress in the Enterprise

WHAT'S IN THIS CHAPTER?

➤ Determining if and how WordPress could benefit your company

➤ Understanding ways to tune your application stack to help WordPress scale to meet traffic demands

➤ Evaluating different corporate authentication integration options

What exactly is enterprise software? Is it more than a marketing term, one that is used to nebulously declare that my software is better than yours? Just like using WordPress for a CMS, we think this topic needs to be put to rest. Obviously, developers are using WordPress as a CMS; you just read a whole chapter about it. Likewise, companies, or enterprises, are using WordPress every day. Just take a look at http://en.wordpress.com/notable-users/ and you see many big names using WordPress as an enterprise solution.

This chapter will look at the motivations for using WordPress in your small or large enterprise. We will also look at the reasons WordPress may not be a good fit. If you decide to take the plunge and try WordPress for your enterprise, we will cover some methods for making it scalable and techniques for integrating authentication and content into a corporate environment. These techniques will also work on a stand-alone site, so even if you are not using WordPress in a corporate environment, many of these approaches will still apply to your site.

IS WORDPRESS RIGHT FOR YOUR ENTERPRISE?

So, again, what exactly is enterprise software? In the most general terms, enterprise software solves a company-wide requirement or need rather than focusing on the necessities of a certain team or department. Often, enterprise software will integrate with other software pieces or business processes, such as a corporate authentication system or a standard for web servers. But frankly, what makes a software package enterprise-worthy depends on your actual enterprise requirements. Clearly, WordPress works for certain businesses, and will most likely work for yours. Following are some reasons why.

Many of these reasons are plain old reasons to use WordPress, or reasons to use WordPress as a CMS, which are essentially one and the same. Look at all the functionality you receive out of the box when you use WordPress. WordPress by its very nature is easy to use, search engine optimized, security aware, and well-maintained, and countless other features have made it so popular today.

For our enterprise, this base functionality is what allows us to create fully functional, professional web sites quickly, whether they are for one of our marketing initiatives, a new brand, or for a department or a client. This standardization, coupled with theme development standardization covered previously, makes our web site infrastructure predictable and manageable, making the development process more efficient and cost effective, all of which are enterprise-worthy goals.

Other reasons why WordPress works in the enterprise environment are the ones covered in the previous chapter about using WordPress as a Content Management System. The primary benefit is the ability to delegate content creation to department owners. There is no way the development team can know the happenings and updates of every department company wide. Furthermore, even if these other departments provided content and relied on the web developers to perform the updates to the sites, the developers could be endlessly occupied with maintenance work. By using WordPress and some select plugins we are able to hand the updates back to the respective departments to manage their own content creation, control, editing, and maintenance cycles.

WordPress is extensible. We have been covering that throughout this entire book. You can extend WordPress in countless different ways by using plugins, and if the plugin that you need does not exist, you can use the plugin API to make your own. This allows you to integrate WordPress into your existing IT infrastructure.

The simplest form of integration is using RSS (really simple syndication), which does not require a plugin. We use RSS throughout the company as a way to organize content coming from different locations and re-use that content in new places. For example, press releases are syndicated from one central site, and by using tags and post categories, these content pieces are broadcast to the individual department sites as needed. This permits our content creators to post once, and publish across a wide array of web sites.

Furthermore, using RSS we are able to publish alerts and other timely news pieces from a central site to various locations around the country for use in their intranets and portals. This provides us a one-stop location to publish, and provides the consumers a one-stop location to review the information.

Other integration pieces could include authorization with an existing identity provider, which we cover later in this chapter, calendaring applications, project management, or system status indicators. Because of the open API, you could integrate anything that you put your time and talents to.

Another reason is cost — you cannot beat the price of WordPress. For the actual outlay of money your company would have to pay to try WordPress in your enterprise, you can afford to give it a try and see if solves some business needs (assuming, of course that you follow good security practices).

WordPress is open source software. That means when you download it, you have everything. There are no magic compiled libraries of which you cannot see the direct functionality. Being open source and completely transparent prevents vendor lock in. Should you decide in the future that WordPress is not the right fit, all of your content is extractable. Sure, Automattic is the brains behind WordPress but with access to all the source code you can always maintain the code should Automattic go away.

Or you could fork the codebase and make your own changes if you do not like the direction Automattic is taking, although other risks are involved here, such as disenfranchising the WordPress community by not respecting the existing licensing. Generally a better approach would be to get involved with the development and direction of WordPress, which is covered in Chapter 15.

WHEN WORDPRESS ISN'T RIGHT FOR YOU

Depending on your circumstances WordPress can be a good fit for your company's needs. But also consider the flip side. There are times when it does not match up with your company's goals, virtues, or culture, or the functionality does not match up with your needs or requirements.

WordPress may not have the exact functionality your company requires. It is not a panacea and cannot be all things to all people. For example, editorial workflows and default permissions are two places that may not line up directly. Plugins exist or are being developed such CoPress.org's Edit Flow Project (`http://copress.org`) and the Role Scoper plugin covered previously, that address these deficiencies. Should you find a requirement that a plugin does not address, perhaps you have actually stumbled across an opportunity to develop one yourself.

This one is not WordPress specific, but a common enterprise concern about free/open source software (FOSS) is that there is no one entity to hold accountable. Sadly this is a reality for some companies. They want someone to hold accountable should something go wrong. In the worst circumstances, this could be you. At the same time, misconceptions about licensing, copyright, copyleft and layering of software still persist in the business and technology communities. We touched on some of these in Chapter 1. Likewise, there is no "go to" for support situations. But if you look around, you can find copious amounts of information on the Internet both good and bad, and there are tons of consultants. (possibly including you, after reading this book). Automattic also offers paid support through its WordPress Support Network (`http://automattic.com/services/support-network/`) for companies that truly want to pay for accountability.

Next, because it is open source software, anyone and everyone can develop for it. When picking plugins you are at the mercy of the developer. Short of doing it yourself, you do not know the quality of the plugin or the developer's credentials and security awareness. So prepare to get your hands dirty and actually evaluate the code you are going to use on your site. Be sure you know what you are getting into with a plugin.

Finally, the last item is the development progression from developing locally, moving to a staging or quality assurance server and then finally deploying to a live production server. In most cases, this progression is not a big deal. Developing themes and plugins locally can easily be deployed through these stages. The challenge really comes into play when you are making drastic content changes on a production site. Aside from multiple imports and exports of the data or database syncing we have yet to find a viable, low-maintenance solution for this challenge. Perhaps it is time to develop a plugin.

SCALABILITY

At some point the question arises, can WordPress scale? And the answer is, of course it can. Just look at WordPress.com statistics (`http://en.wordpress.com/stats/traffic/`). You can clearly see that it is capable. But the actual task of scaling a WordPress installation involves many layers, including the WordPress code, plugins and themes, the PHP version and settings, the web server software and the underlying operating system and finally, the actual server hardware. The key to scaling a WordPress installation is to secure and tune each of these layers.

Performance Tuning

Securing and tuning your WordPress installation was covered back in Chapter 11. Be sure to review that content.We're going to touch on more enterprise-specific issues here, with the assumption that in an corporate technology deployment, you'll have access to the web, database, and file servers that comprise the bulk of your WordPress installation.

Tuning your theme should be part of any theme development process. That process includes checking the file sizes of all images, making sure the JavaScript and CSS are as small as possible, perhaps even minified, and reducing the total number of HTTP requests a browser has to make. Using a tool like YSlow! for the Firebug Firefox add-on (`http://developer.yahoo.com/yslow/`) can help isolate these problems. Our caution about YSlow! is that, though it is a nice tool to determine slowdowns, it was designed by Yahoo! for Yahoo! and even though we are talking about scalability, likely Yahoo!'s sense of scale is bigger than yours. So, take the results with a grain of salt and use some common sense in weeding out the low hanging fruit. Generally, good web development practices will help your theme scale.

For plugins, you have to look at the code. As mentioned previously, it is unlikely that you know the credentials or skill level of the plugin developer or the terms under which it was created. Some plugins are created in a straightforward, get it done style and may not be very efficient, even if they are effective. You can often see this style with multiple SQL queries to get the information required at any given time rather than a thought-out data access plan. If you are making improvements to existing code, notify the creator. Put your enhancements back into circulation so the entire community can prosper.

Scalability really goes hand in hand with performance. The more efficient your web site is, the easier it is to handle more requests and therefore scale. For the PHP layer of the application stack, turn off any PHP functionality you are not using. This is good for performance, security, and scaling. Much of this was covered in Chapter 11 under the subject of security and performance; here the same rules apply for scalability.

In your `php.ini` file, disable any extensions you are not using, like all those extra database extensions. The default `php.ini` file is designed to work for most people. Here we are talking about tuning it to meet your needs and requirements. The following are pretty safe settings to turn off:

```
;Hide PHP for security
expose_php = Off
;Turn off for performance
register_globals = Off
register_long_arrays = Off
register_argc_argv = Off
magic_quotes_gpc = Off
magic_quotes_runtime = Off
magic_quotes_sybase = Off
```

Set your memory allowances to the correct values for your environment and needs. Make sure error reporting is configured properly for the environment — do not show them on the production site.

The next layer up is the web server software. Apache is the most common, but WordPress can run on any number of web server applications. In general, do some research on your web server and the functionality it requires in order to tune its operation. Turn off any module or extra features you are not using. Like PHP, the stock Apache configuration file is designed to work for most people in a general case. It is in their best interest to reduce the amount of effort to get something to work from the get-go. This can be a huge barrier to entry if too much tweaking is needed just to get something to work.

Tuning for scalability is the exact opposite of this general use case scenario. You want to disable as much as possible to make the software as lean as can be, and still serve your sites properly.

Another option for scaling is to consider serving static content from an assets server. This is a specific case of throwing more hardware at the problem, which we look at shortly. In short, using one web server for serving dynamic content and another for serving the static assets, like images and CSS, can reduce the load across the board. Different web servers have different strengths. Moving your static content to a web server using lighttpd or nginx, which are better at serving this type of content, may be more efficient because each web server can be tuned for a more specific function. This will also reduce the load on your dynamic content server, giving it more resources to perform its own duties.

There is also a faux method available here to accomplish similar results. You can serve static assets from a subdomain, even if it is on the same server. Most web browsers are set to download 2 to 4 items in parallel at a time. By moving some of these requests to a subdomain, like `static.mysite.com`, you can trick the browser into effectively doubling the number of items being fetched at a time.

Caching

Caching can occur at this level too. Previously we covered different levels of caching ranging from in-memory cache using Memcache, to the WordPress object cache of frequently accessed information, and the WordPress plugin Super Cache, which bypasses the entire dynamic nature of WordPress altogether and creates static HTML files.

The database level also has several opportunities for optimizations. MySQL has two main storage types for tables: MyISAM and InnoDB. Others are available, but these are the two that MySQL installations have enabled by default.

The ISAM table type was the original storage engine for MySQL. The MySQL team later improved the engine and created MyISAM. MyISAM is a good general-purpose storage engine. It performs better with a table with many reads or many writes, but not both. That is, it is a good for storing or retrieving data, but not ideal for a situation that requires frequent switching between the two. This is also the default table type for WordPress.

InnoDB, on the other hand, provides better concurrency, through row locking and transactional support. InnoDB can use non-locking reads to maximize efficiency and performance. This makes InnoDB a good storage engine for large volumes of data and datasets that are used in both read and write contexts. If you're going to use WordPress in an enterprise where you have many contributing users, or lively discussion of topics posted by a core developer group, the write and update load on the database will be significantly higher than that of an individual blogger who posts weekly thoughts on buildings and food or the Talking Heads.

Switching some of your WordPress tables, such as the highly dynamic ones, like wp_comments, to the InnoDB storage type can create performance improvements, and therefore scalability benefits. Additionally, MySQL also has a configuration file that can be tuned to match your environment.

Regular Maintenance

Finally, your MySQL database needs to be maintained. From time to time you should run checks on your database tables and optimize and repair if needed. Maintaining your database is like changing the oil on your car or defragmenting your hard drive — you have to do it regularly to keep everything running smoothly. This can easily be done through PHPMyAdmin or other MySQL interface. Plugins such as WP-DBManager by Lester Chan (http://wordpress.org/extend/plugins/wp-dbmanager/) allow you to schedule these tasks, as well as backups, and really not have to worry about it again.

Hardware Scaling

Now on to the expensive options, adding more hardware. A default WordPress installation is all encapsulated on one machine. This machine functions as both the web server and database as shown in Figure 13-1. This is the simplest and most basic WordPress hardware scenario. Many sites run this way.

The next option is to split the database and web server functions into two servers, as shown in Figure 13-2. This allows each server to focus on a specific task and is the next logical step when your hardware starts to get taxed by the workload. At the same time, make sure that you account for the independent database and web hosts when you create your WordPress configuration files; you'll need to know the name of the database host because it's no longer the "localhost" with respect to the web server. This is common web application architecture and is very easy to implement with only a few configuration changes. Again, make sure you re-tune your database and web server software to run on their now independent boxes.

FIGURE 13-1: WordPress on one server

Moving forward this can get confusing, and the possibilities are endless, so we are only going to briefly review some common scenarios. Depending on your existing infrastructure, you may have other options available.

You may need to do some investigative forensics to determine your next step. That is, really figure out what the bottleneck is. Regrettably, this can be a reactive plan of attack rather than proactive one. So, while preparing to scale out your site, invest some time in some server monitoring infrastructure.

Generally, the next step in scaling is to load balance your front end web servers, as shown in Figure 13-3. In this scenario you deploy two web servers with identical copies of the WordPress installation and use a single database server to store all the data.

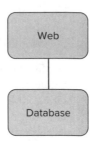

FIGURE 13-2: WordPress on two servers

You have a couple of challenges with this approach. First, you need a load balancing mechanism. This can be a hardware appliance or it could be a software solution. You have many different ones to choose from, and your infrastructure will dictate which you choose.

The second challenge is that you will need to synchronize your `wp-content/uploads` folder. That is, if a content creator uploads media onto one server, because the front ends are load balanced, the next request could pull from the other server where the file does not exist. You have the option of moving the uploads folder to a common location, perhaps on the shared database server, or you could set up a scheduled task to copy the files across. The rsync (`http://www.samba.org/rsync/`) utility would be a good solution for this type of synchronization. You will have to accept that that files will not be there until after the copy has occurred.

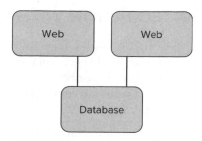

FIGURE 13-3: WordPress with load balanced web servers

The next scenario for scaling means adding a second database server and implementing MySQL replication. You continue to keep the load balanced web servers, but now you have two database servers, as shown in Figure 13-4.

Technically, this does not offer better performance, but it does offer the ability to failover should the database server have a problem. This standby database server is called a hot spare. That means it is on and up to date, but not in current use. Part of scalability is availability. Now, you have two web servers and two database servers, which means you can remove one server from each tier and still have a functioning site.

Putting that second database into active work on the web site is the next layer up. You still have load balanced web servers, but now you can distribute the load on the database servers using MySQL replication, as shown in Figure 13-5. In this situation you want the writes to the database to be written to the master MySQL database, and all the reads to come from the slave MySQL database. This solves the MyISAM challenge where that storage engine excels at reading or writing but not both.

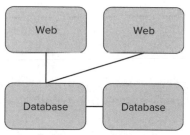

FIGURE 13-4: WordPress with a hot spare database server

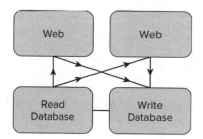

FIGURE 13-5: WordPress with load balanced web and database servers

Finally, another WordPress-specific option to consider is HyperDB (`http://codex.wordpress.org/HyperDB`). HyperDB was designed by Automattic and is a drop-in replacement for the standard WordPress database access layer. It is, however, more powerful than the standard access objects because it can support sharding or partitioning of the WordPress database information across multiple databases. This can permit you to move the highly dynamic data to a more robust server, while the content that is less in flux can be used on a database server with more aggressive caching. HyperDB also supports replication and failover functionality. However, the documentation is sparse, so implementing this solution is not for the faint of heart.

INTEGRATION WITH ENTERPRISE IDENTITY MANAGEMENT

As more applications move to the Web, a common problem is the proliferation of usernames and passwords. This gets compounded by the password constraints to require secure passwords that are difficult to remember. The increase in access credentials is a known concern and there are many ways to deal with it, including using password safe or vault applications, or consolidating credentials into Identity Facilities.

WordPress's extensibility makes integrating with outside identity providers relatively easy, and many plugins do just that. The following sections look at two common methods that can be implemented in a company-wide environment.

LDAP and Active Directory

A common identity provider in a business environment is Microsoft Active Directory (AD), which is a form of the Lightweight Directory Access Protocol (LDAP). Active Directory is what a Windows-based network uses to centrally manage workstation usernames and passwords. It can be much more, but for the purposes of this discussion, we really only care about the username, passwords, and access rights.

Assuming you have this in place already, why not use this same central repository to access your WordPress installation? After all, it is the username and password your users are already using to log in to their workstations. The Simple LDAP Login plugin by Clifton H. Griffin II (`http://wordpress.org/extend/plugins/simple-ldap-login/`) does just that.

Installation is relatively straightforward, like most plugins. However, this plugin does not check whether LDAP is currently enabled in your PHP installation, so before proceeding, edit your `php.ini` file and uncomment the LDAP extension to activate it.

```
//for Windows
extension=php_ldap.dll
//for Linux
extension=ldap.so
```

After restarting your web server to load your new PHP settings, proceed to activate the plugin and visit the plugin settings page. On this control panel you will be able to enter your LDAP settings, and it includes a handy testing section.

The advanced settings are very important for this plugin, as shown in Figure 13-6. Depending on your needs, you will have to carefully consider the Login mode. Since our users were not previously created in WordPress, choosing one of the "Create WordPress accounts" options made sense. You can also use the advanced settings to permit only a specified organizational unit in Active Directory to have login privileges. This is a nice feature to centralize your access and authorization into the already established Active Directory structure.

Several other LDAP/AD plugins are available, so you may want to evaluate them before picking a solution. Be sure to check if the plugin supports secure Active Directory access if that is a requirement of your organization.

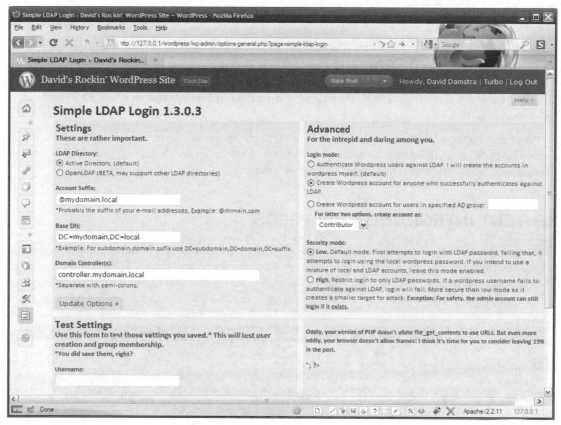

FIGURE 13-6: Advanced settings for the Simple LDAP plugin

OpenID

Active Directory is a specific implementation to a Microsoft-centric network. Commercial LDAP products and their open source OpenLDAP cousin are often used as a common user authorization and authentication system where federation of multiple, department level managed identity systems is required. In either case, this internal enterprise scale authorization is not seen on the wide open Internet.

OpenID was developed as a platform-neutral way to manage authorization in a distributed way. Sounds fancy, does it not? OpenID is set up so that an end user can use the same credentials, in the form of a unique URL and password, and access any application that consumes OpenID for authentication. OpenID is a little different than the traditional username and password credentials most people are used to. With OpenID, you use a unique URL instead of the conventional username. Because it is an open standard, anyone can be an OpenID provider, including many big names on the Web, but you can also become your own OpenID provider.

If your organization does not already have a central authentication or identity facility, OpenID may be a viable option. Otherwise, it is still a nice add-on for your users, because it allows them to manage their own access credentials in their own central location, if they choose to.

The OpenID plugin by the DiSo Development Team (`http://wordpress.org/extend/plugins/openid/`) is a simple way to add OpenID functionality to your site. After activating the plugin, your WordPress login screen and comment screens will be modified to include an OpenID input field, as shown in Figure 13-7.

This plugin includes a settings control panel to manage the specific features including auto-approving OpenID published comments. In addition, this plugin has the ability to change your WordPress installation into being an OpenID provider using your author pages, which is a very nice feature.

CONTENT INTEGRATION VIA FEEDS

In one situation we've encountered, we managed many sites, normally a subdomain for each department. In this example, each department functions as its own business unit. There are alternatives, but for various reasons each site became a unique WordPress installation. One of the challenges we then face is the duplication of content across multiple sites. Maintaining changes across these separate

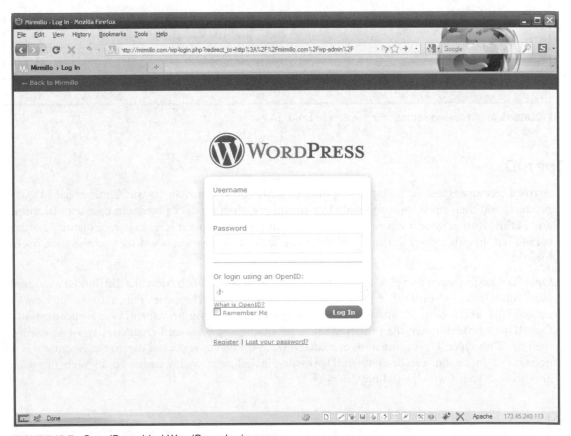

FIGURE 13-7: OpenID enabled WordPress login page

sites means we have to update a specific content piece many times. For example, press releases usually involve multiple departments, or at the minimum, need to be published on the flagship corporate site as well as the individual department site.

In short, the business challenge was to reduce multiple manual updates, which are time-consuming and error-prone. Luckily, we have WordPress. One of the easiest ways to integrate content is by using the built-in RSS (really simple syndication) feeds. This is a core feature of WordPress and we find it is a tool we use all the time.

Our solution was to publish all press releases on a central site. In this case, the parent site became our one true location to publish press releases. Press releases are published just like regular posts, and are then assigned to a specific category for each department.

Each departmental WordPress site has the FeedWordPress plugin (`http://wordpress.org/extend/plugins/feedwordpress/`) by Charles Johnson installed. This wonderful plugin takes any RSS or Atom feed and converts it into posts on the site. Here is where the magic really happens. WordPress automatically creates RSS feeds for any filtered view, such as category, on the originating site. So, for this to work, we use the category RSS feed from original site like `http://example.com/category/press/department/feed`.

Once you get the plugin installed and activated, you simply enter the URL of the originating feed and schedule the syndication to your web site. FeedWordPress has several customizable settings to tailor the category, author and tag information for the incoming feed which makes this a very powerful plugin.

This works well and allows our content creators to publish to one WordPress location yet have the content distribute out to the additional sites, saving time and energy while also improving accuracy and timeliness of the content.

Here is another example of WordPress solving a business need. Our company has two separate web development teams; one focuses on PHP and the other focuses on .NET technologies. In this example, a specification change to a pre existing ASP.NET application required that it contain regularly updated content pieces. In the current development cycle, changing these content pieces meant rebuilding and redeploying the entire application to the multiple load balanced servers each time this content changed.

An alternative was to develop a minimal content management application to integrate with the existing code, and permit content creators to manage the content dynamically. Not through any fault of the developers, but the development time to add this relatively simple system exceeded the constraints of the project (time, resources, money — pick one.)

WordPress excels at content origination. Although we could have installed a new .NET RSS syndicating web application, we chose to capitalize on an existing WordPress site to manage the dynamic content on the .NET application side. The .NET development team simply had to refactor an RSS consumer object to process a specific RSS feed and display the contents in the web application. Our content creators could then use a tool that they were already familiar with to publish the content whenever they needed to. This is a specific example of the Content Management System applications of WordPress discussed in Chapter 14, set in an enterprise context where content publication is the challenging problem.

WordPress certainly can address business needs. Does that mean WordPress is enterprise class software? It does to us. The critical features are WordPress's own inherent characteristics that fulfill certain deficiencies or improve processes in your business coupled with its robust ability to integrate with other services. This uncanny ability for WordPress to both stand alone and blend into an existing infrastructure makes it an ideal problem solver.

14

Migrating To WordPress

WHAT'S IN THIS CHAPTER?

➤ Planning to move an existing site or content pages to WordPress

➤ Choosing among the different import options available

➤ Listing of potential clean-up or manual fine-tuning steps needed to complete a migration

The bulk of this book extols the virtues of WordPress and we hope it has made you more of a WordPress fan, evangelist, and expert. If you're ready, willing, and able to help WordPress conquer the world, but you're not starting with a clean slate, you'll need to migrate existing content into WordPress. Alternatively, if you're adding "Family WordPress expert" to the title of "Family SysAdmin," you're likely to have a queue of friends and family asking you to help them get started.

A variety of reasons exist to move existing content into WordPress:

➤ You want to move from static, time-invariant content to a narrative style. Rather than publishing "brochureware" you want to tell a story, and the timeline element of a blog is the best approach.

➤ You expect comments and discussion around your content and organizing by post (topic) corrals the discussion better than an unstructured bulletin board.

➤ There is sufficient traffic coming to your site that online advertising or sponsorships are economically viable, and you need full control over the platform.

➤ You want to customize the user experience, style, and presentation of your site, or you are in a position to take an existing blog, perhaps hosted by your employer, to a self-hosted environment.

This chapter looks at various ways to move static pages and existing sites to WordPress, implying that you already have content that you need to import. Although WordPress makes it easy to publish content or delegate the writing to other users, gaining a critical mass of pages and posts is essential for generating readership and establishing context for online advertising engines. There's no easier way to get there than by moving your content into a fresh WordPress installation.

PLANNING A MIGRATION

The first step in migrating a site to WordPress is to make a plan. It is equally important — and unexciting — to have a plan. Without a map of all of the components and targets, you'll either lose content or end up repeating steps until your content is imported in some usable fashion. Spending a little time up front to plan will save time in the long run, and definitely reduce future frustrations.

Content Sources

When planning a migration you must decide what data sources you will want to move. Certainly you will want to move the actual content and the related media; otherwise this whole exercise is silly. "Actual content" has many different interpretations, however: Are you moving posts from an existing blog, documents in a word processing system, static HTML from your current site, or some combination of all of these options? We discuss migrating static content briefly in the next section; however, most of this chapter focuses on the bulk import of posts from other blogging systems and building custom import scripts.

When you decide to migrate to WordPress, you have an opportunity to revisit the pages versus posts dilemma covered in Chapter 12. If you are moving a static brochureware web site to WordPress you can probably get away with mapping existing pages to WordPress pages. By thinking outside the box, you may choose to have content on your existing site translate into posts in WordPress. Using a category template page you can replicate the presentation feel of your old site in WordPress and add functionality available through the post structure. Finally, mapping static pages to posts also allows you to add a chronological background to shed light on how an idea or topic developed.

It's possible to migrate from bulletin boards like PostNuke to WordPress, but the conversion from a threaded discussion structure to posts, pages, and comments requires that you carefully plan the disposition of each topic. One common approach is to make each topic a new category, and then organize stories (discussions) into posts in those categories, but you're probably going to end up hand-editing the import script to get the desired result. The custom import script described in this chapter, along with the migration checklist, should help you build a toolset to extract threaded content in a useful form. Chris Samuel's PostNuke to WordPress conversion script (`http://www.csamuel.org/wp-content/uploads/2007/01/pnconvert.txt`) is an outstanding starting point.

Finally, make sure you have the rights to re-use whatever content you are looking to appropriate for your new site. If all of the content is your own, this issue is trivial; but if you have been posting on your employer's blog site, or sharing a blog with co-authors, ensure you have appropriate rights to the content, including copyright, rights to redistribute, and rights for commercial use.

My former employer changed the terms of its corporate blogging platform to accommodate repurposing of blog content. Originally, the corporate site relied on the same copyright agreement implied in employment agreements — whatever you created had the copyright conveyed to the company. The blogging terms of use were later changed to reflect a shared copyright, such that any content that did not contain copyrighted intellectual property such as code fragments or marketing images could be re-used in a form of the employee's choosing. — Hal

Migration Checklist

Migration is never a clean and simple process. Tools will help you automate the vast majority of the work, but the purpose of planning is to be sure you have accounted for all of the content, metadata, and supporting features to capture the desired intent of your migration to WordPress.

Here is a migration checklist:

➤ **Content Identification.** Build a site map, as described in the "Building A Custom Import Script" section of this chapter, to be sure you don't orphan any pages in the process. If you're importing from word processor files, build a file inventory of what you want to capture.

➤ **Media.** Not the theme and presentation graphics, but any actual media assets that are in your content. Do you have any images, graphs, PowerPoint presentations or other linked documents that need to be moved over? Plan ahead of time where you are going to house these assets in the WordPress site. Are you going to follow WordPress convention or keep them in their current directory structure?

➤ **Metadata.** Is there any metadata that describes the content that you also need to move over and reapply, such as tag or category information, or will you let WordPress do the minimum import so you can fine-tune the categories and tags in post-import processing?

➤ **Authors and Users.** Are you moving a single-author or non-attributed web site, or do you need to keep content and author associations? This is a further complicating factor for discussing group migration: are all registered users of the forum also authors?

➤ **Theme and Presentation.** Rarely will an existing site's CSS and presentation HTML translate directly into a WordPress theme. Should you create a new theme for your target WordPress site that attempts to preserve the look and feel of the existing site or are you going to break away and re-launch your new site with a whole new look and feel? You can review Chapter 8, which covers creating a new theme for your site. Also consider whether there is any special or unique content on your site that will require distinctive design concerns.

➤ **Unique Functionality.** Working with financial institution web sites we often run into financial calculators and various applications (like the paper kind you fill out) that will not immediately convert to the new site, or will require individual attention. This could be nearly anything; it could be something that was custom-coded for the web site such as a poll, or a map for directions or CRM integration. Often you can find WordPress plugins that will provide similar functionality for your new site. Or, as we have often said, a strength of WordPress is that you can always write your own plugin. Other times you can use the custom page templates, covered in Chapter 8, to wrap your custom integration code inside of the WordPress framework. This topic is covered more a little later in this chapter.

➤   **Cleanup.** You will need to tweak and fine-tune your content, especially URLs. You will have to visually inspect a fair sampling of your new WordPress site for anomalies. You will want to map old URLs to new URLs so visitors can still find you and search engine results continue to work.

➤   **Launch.** Bite the bullet and launch your new site. No web site is ever done or perfect, but at some point it has to be good enough to let it loose on the web. Remember, shipping is a feature.

Recognize up front that any migration is not going to be perfect. You are moving core web site content from where it was happily living (or perhaps not happily, and that is why you are migrating) to a whole new shell. There is going to be some work involved. We just want to set some expectations — we will look over each step in a little more depth.

Site Preparation

One quick thought before you get into the actual migration. You need a way to work on your new site, while still serving up your content on your old site. How you go about this depends on what resources you have available to you. Setting up your development site, or import playground, also affects your URL structure and may require the manual editing changes discussed in the "Cleaning Up" section of this chapter.

If you're adding content to an existing site, our recommended method is to set up a whole new WordPress instantiation on a new subdomain. For example, if your current site is `http://example.com`, make a new DNS entry and web site host for a subdomain like `http://new.example.com` or `http://test.example.com`. This will make it so you can work on the development site without interrupting your existing site. It will also permit you to use root relative links and make certain steps easier in the long run. On the other hand, if you're establishing a new WordPress site, use the basic installation as your starting point for importing content.

Although you can set up your test environment in other ways, this method can simplify some steps because you are working on what will eventually become your production site. Local development is a good method if you are the only developer working on the site. If you are developing your new site locally, you can use your hosts file to skip all the URL transitions discussed later.

CONTENT IDENTIFICATION

All content migration follows a similar pattern: Extract bits from the existing repository, automate preparation for the new system as much as possible, and import the content, typically repeating that loop as you find steps that require manual editing or fine-tuning. This section identifies and prepares the content that we want to move to WordPress and walks through the three major approaches to WordPress import functions, starting with the fully manual migration of text documents and then exploring the WordPress built-in administrative functions to convert popular blog formats. It concludes with an in-depth development of a custom extraction and import script.

Migrating Text Documents

We define "text documents" as content primarily associated with a word processor for manipulation, and many text documents will end up as pages in your WordPress site. The content isn't static in the sense that it's fixed, but it's not part of the blog narrative.

Brute-force is often the simplest approach here. Copy and paste your text, or export a document as HTML and glue that into a WordPress page. Be warned, however, that most word processing applications insert a huge array of embedded HTML tags, local formatting, and other style elements that make the output page render the way it would as seen from the word processor, but not the way you'd want it to within your WordPress theme structure. If you don't want to strip out all but the most elemental paragraph, table, and link information, consider exporting the file as raw text and then hand-editing it to match the style of your other pages. It's ugly, but so is removing half of the document in the form of HTML directives. Even something as simple as the MacOS TextEdit application uses custom HTML tags for paragraphs if you "Save As" an HTML document. Save your text, without any formatting.

A variation on this theme is merging wiki entries into a blog. Most wikis have their own somewhat arcane syntax, different enough from HTML to make copy and paste time-consuming but not worth automated editing unless you're moving a large wiki. If the wiki is really a collection of topics, it makes sense to migrate the wiki pages to WordPress posts, creating categories for each topic or set of topics and relying on tags to even more finely identify the content. The upside to migrating out of a wiki is that you gain use of the WordPress metadata functions, and can parse comments and discussion into comment threads rather than endless edits to the wiki document; the downside is that you lose the edit history contained in platforms like MediaWiki. If you're running a wiki with a MySQL database as the repository, you can use the custom extract and import script discussed later in this chapter to build a migration tool.

Built-In WordPress Import Tools

For most WordPress users looking to transport content from one home to another, WordPress offers a variety of built-in import facilities. This section covers the basic conversion process and the use of WordPress eXtended RSS (WXR) files for more flexible or powerful data conversion.

Blog Conversion

WordPress offers basic importers for commonly used blogging platforms. You can find these built-in importers on the Import dashboard in WordPress, and you'll find the corresponding PHP functions implementing them in the wp-admin/import folder. The blog conversion tools fall into two main migration categories: they read a file exported by your current blogging platform, or they use the source platform's API set to pull content and re-post it in WordPress. For example, LiveJournal and Blogger are migrated using their APIs, whereas Movable Type, TypePad, and Roller blogs are handled by exporting the blog contents from those platforms into a file that is uploaded and executed by WordPress.

Another option is the Google Blog Converter application (http://code.google.com/p/google-blog-converters-appengine/). This Python application is intended to be exactly what it claims: a converter of different blog formats. Essentially the developers are working to implement each import file format for various platforms using the Blogger import format as a reference point. With this tool you can convert a certain export file from one system into an import file for another system, including WordPress. This tool is also online at `http://blogger2wordpress.appspot.com/`. We've used this tool to successfully convert several web sites to WordPress, but your mileage may vary.

Using WordPress eXtended RSS Files

What if the simple blog-to-blog conversion doesn't work, or doesn't capture enough of the metadata, author information, or other content that you want to migrate? In the most basic case what you are going to do is export your existing content into an XML import file in the WordPress eXtended RSS (WXR) format, which is, as it is named, an extension of the RSS format.

The process for creating a WXR file depends on the starting point for your source content. Some applications have a built in WXR exporter function which will create this file for you. For example, the WordPress Export dashboard will create this file, but this is only useful when moving content from an existing WordPress site to a new one. If your source content does not have this functionality, you can create the WXR file by hand in a text editor. The easiest way to start your WXR file, if you have to create it by hand is to use the sitemap process.

To create a WXR file using a site map, first you need a site map of your source site. Start with a site map created for search engines, or use a whole site link checker like Xenu (`http://home.snafu.de/tilman/xenulink.html` — the site is scary, but the tool works) to create one. This site map will list of all the pages that need to be migrated.

We do so many migrations from static HTML or other random CMS systems that rather than working a migration plan for each site, we built a special PHP application that spiders a web site and builds the WXR for us. Assuming each page is somewhat consistent, this works very well. Using a combination of PHP, curl, and jQuery, we can feed the page list in from the site map, parse the HTML, and gather the content, then write out in WXR format.

Once you have a WXR import file you can then edit it to make any necessary changes to the file prior to importing. You probably will want to read this whole chapter ahead of time so you are aware of the pitfalls that can affect your import and can benefit from some search and replace on the import file rather than hand-editing or fixing each occurrence later.

Because this WXR import file is straight up XML you can edit it in your favorite text editor. This allows you to make some bulk changes to URLs, paths, authors, and anything ahead of doing the import. This can save you a lot of time in the long run, but do not go overboard. WordPress is set up to do an import and can automatically create a lot of information for you based on the import.

When editing the WXR import file you can see how the import content will play out. The nice thing about this format is that it really is extended RSS, so the format is simple. Unfortunately there is not much documentation about it on WordPress.org (`http://codex.wordpress.org/Importing_Content#Importing_from_an_RSS_feed`). There is also some example WXR format to model off of in the Google Blog Converter Google Code web site at `http://code.google.com/p/google-blog-converters-appengine/source/browse/trunk/samples/wordpress-sample.wxr`.

This import file is an easy way to move content from your existing site. As discussed later in this chapter, other ways exist to move sites from other content management systems, but we often find it easier to use the WXR import file method.

Outside of the WordPress built-in migration functions, WXR files represent the fastest pah to get your content moved into WordPress. In many cases automating only the "easy" parts is sufficient to get your new site up and running. Assuming your current site has an Export to WXR, a live RSS feed, or some other export mechanism that you can then hand-edit into a WXR format, this can be your simplest approach.

Building a Custom Import Script

More advanced than a simple WXR migration is to extract entries from an existing content management system that is database (ideally MySQL) based, and attempt a direct data manipulation to migrate the content. In this case you need to have your old and new database tables in the same MySQL database. Then you can run a set of SQL scripts that will read from the old database, transform them appropriately and import the content into the WordPress tables. This method can get tricky because you are juggling several SQL scripts to export, convert, and then import the content; however, it is also the most flexible and powerful approach that operates at the data management level.

Listing 14-1 explores an example script to import data directly into the WordPress database. Take a look at the full source before we break it down.

LISTING 14-1: MySQL Import Script

Available for download on Wrox.com

```php
<?php
//set database connection info for database to import
$hostname = "localhost";
$username = "USERNAME";
$password = "PASSWORD";
$sourcedb = "DATABASE"; // database to import from
$sourcetable = "stories"; // table that stores posts to import
$sourcecomments = "comment"; // table that stores comments to import

//set database connection info for WordPress database
$destdb = "WORDPRESS-DATABASE"; // WordPress database
$wp_prefix = "wp_"; // WordPress table prefix

//database connection
$db_connect = @mysql_connect($hostname, $username, $password)
  or die("Fatal Error: ".mysql_error());

mysql_select_db($sourcedb, $db_connect);

$srcresult = mysql_query("select * from $sourcetable", $db_connect)
  or die("Fatal Error: ".mysql_error());
```

continues

LISTING 14-1 *(continued)*

```php
// used to generate the dashed titles in the URLs
function sanitize($title) {
  $title = strtolower($title);
  $title = preg_replace('/&.+?;/', '', $title); // kill entities
  $title = preg_replace('/[^a-z0-9 _-]/', '', $title);
  $title = preg_replace('/\s+/', ' ', $title);
  $title = str_replace(' ', '-', $title);
  $title = preg_replace('|-+|', '-', $title);
  $title = trim($title, '-');

  return $title;
}

while ($myrow = mysql_fetch_array($srcresult))
{

  //generate post title
  $my_title = mysql_escape_string($myrow['title']);

  //generate post content
  $my_content = mysql_escape_string($myrow['content']);

  //generate post permalink
  $myname = mysql_escape_string(sanitize($my_title));
  //generate SQL to insert data into WordPress
  $sql = "INSERT INTO '" . $wp_prefix . "posts'
(

    'ID' ,

    'post_author' ,
    'post_date' ,
    'post_date_gmt' ,
    'post_content' ,
    'post_title' ,
    'post_name' ,
    'post_category' ,
    'post_excerpt' ,
    'post_status' ,
    'comment_status' ,
    'ping_status' ,
    'post_password' ,
    'to_ping' ,
    'pinged' ,
    'post_modified' ,
    'post_modified_gmt' ,
    'post_content_filtered' ,
    'post_parent',
    'post_type' )
    VALUES
```

```
(
    '$myrow[sid]',
        '1',
    '$myrow[time]',
    '0000-00-00 00:00:00',
    '$my_content',
    '$my_title',
    '$myname',
    '$myrow[category]',
    '',
    'publish',
    'open',
    'open',
    '',
    '',
    '',
    '$myrow[time]',
    '0000-00-00 00:00:00',
    '',
    '0',
    'post' );";

mysql_select_db($destdb, $db_connect);
//execute query
mysql_query($sql, $db_connect);

// load the ID of the post we just inserted
$sql = "select MAX(ID) from " . $wp_prefix . "posts";
$getID = mysql_query($sql, $db_connect);
$currentID = mysql_fetch_array($getID);
$currentID = $currentID['MAX(ID)'];

// retreive all associated post comments
$mysid = $myrow["pn_sid"];
mysql_select_db($sourcedb, $db_connect);
$comments = mysql_query("select * from "
    .$sourcecomments. " where pn_sid = $mysid", $db_connect);
//import post comments in WordPress
while ($comrow = mysql_fetch_array($comments))
{

  $myname = mysql_escape_string($comrow['pn_name']);
  $myemail = mysql_escape_string($comrow['pn_email']);
  $myurl = mysql_escape_string($comrow['pn_url']);
  $myIP = mysql_escape_string($comrow['pn_host_name']);
  $mycomment = mysql_escape_string($comrow['pn_comment']);
  $sql = "INSERT INTO '" . $wp_prefix . "comments'
  (
    'comment_ID' ,
    'comment_post_ID' ,
    'comment_author' ,
    'comment_author_url' ,
```

continues

LISTING 14-1 *(continued)*

```
            'comment_author_IP' ,
            'comment_date' ,
            'comment_date_gmt' ,
            'comment_content' ,
            'comment_karma' ,
            'comment_approved' ,
            'user_id' )
            VALUES
            (
              '' ,
              '$currentID',
              '$myname',
              '$myemail',
              '$myurl',
              '$myIP',
              '$comrow[date]',
              '0000-00-00 00:00:00',
              '$mycomment',
              '0',
              '1',
              '0'
            );";
      if ($submit)
      {
        mysql_select_db($destdb, $db_connect);
        mysql_query($sql, $db_connect)
          or die("Fatal Error: ".mysql_error());
      }
    }


  }

  //Update comment count
  mysql_select_db($destdb, $db_connect);
  $tidyresult = mysql_query("select * from $wp_prefix" . "posts", $db_connect)
    or die("Fatal Error: ".mysql_error());

  while ($myrow = mysql_fetch_array($tidyresult))
  {
    $mypostid=$myrow['ID'];
    $countsql="select COUNT(*) from $wp_prefix" . "comments"
      . " WHERE 'comment_post_ID' = " . $mypostid;
    $countresult=mysql_query($countsql) or die("Fatal Error: ".mysql_error());
    $commentcount=mysql_result($countresult,0,0);
    $countsql="UPDATE '" . $wp_prefix . "posts'
      SET 'comment_count' = '" . $commentcount .
      "' WHERE 'ID' = " . $mypostid . " LIMIT 1";
```

```
        $countresult=mysql_query($countsql) or die("Fatal Error: ".mysql_error());

    }

?>
```

At first glance this looks a little complicated, so let's break it down and discuss each section of the import script:

```
//set database connection info for database to import
$hostname = "localhost";
$username = "USERNAME";
$password = "PASSWORD";
$sourcedb = "DATABASE"; // database to import from
$sourcetable = "stories"; // table that stores posts to import
$sourcecomments = "comment"; // table that stores comments to import

//set database connection info for WordPress database
$destdb = "WORDPRESS-DATABASE"; // WordPress database
$wp_prefix = "wp_"; // WordPress table prefix
```

First you set your database connection info. You also set the table names for the source of the content you plan on importing. This example assumes both the source tables and WordPress tables exist in the same database. Then you set your WordPress tables and table prefix.

Next you need to initialize your database connections as shown here:

```
//database connection
$db_connect = @mysql_connect($hostname, $username, $password)
    or die("Fatal Error: ".mysql_error());

mysql_select_db($sourcedb, $db_connect);


$srcresult = mysql_query("select * from $sourcetable", $db_connect)
    or die("Fatal Error: ".mysql_error());
```

After setting your database connections you execute a query to select the data from your source table. This is the data you are going to import into WordPress as posts. Next you create your sanitize function for creating permalinks. This function removes and replaces any characters that are not legal for URLs and also replaces spaces with dashes to conform to the WordPress permalink structure.

```
// used to generate the dashed titles in the URLs
function sanitize($title) {
  $title = strtolower($title);
  $title = preg_replace('/&.+?;/', '', $title); // kill entities
  $title = preg_replace('/[^a-z0-9 _-]/', '', $title);
  $title = preg_replace('/\s+/', ' ', $title);
  $title = str_replace(' ', '-', $title);
```

```
$title = preg_replace('|-+|', '-', $title);
$title = trim($title, '-');

return $title;
}
```

After your sanitize function is in place you start your `while` loop to loop through the data you are going to import as posts in WordPress:

```
while ($myrow = mysql_fetch_array($srcresult))
{
Next you set variables for your post title, content, and permalink values:
  //generate post title
  $my_title = mysql_escape_string($myrow['title']);

  //generate post content
  $my_content = mysql_escape_string($myrow['content']);

  //generate post permalink
  $myname = mysql_escape_string(sanitize($my_title));
```

Notice you send the values through the `mysql_escape_string` function. This PHP function escapes a string for use in a MySQL query. Next you create the query to insert the post data into the WordPress `posts` table:

```
  //generate SQL to insert data into WordPress
  $sql = "INSERT INTO '" . $wp_prefix . "posts' (
    'ID' ,
    'post_author' ,
    'post_date' ,
    'post_date_gmt' ,
    'post_content' ,
    'post_title' ,
    'post_name' ,
    'post_category' ,
    'post_excerpt' ,
    'post_status' ,
    'comment_status' ,
    'ping_status' ,
    'post_password' ,
    'to_ping' ,
    'pinged' ,
    'post_modified' ,
    'post_modified_gmt' ,
    'post_content_filtered' ,
    'post_parent',
    'post_type' )
  VALUES (
    '$myrow[sid]',
    '1',
    '$myrow[time]',
    '0000-00-00 00:00:00',
```

```
'$my_content',
'$my_title',
'$myname',
'$myrow[category]',
'',
'publish',
'open',
'open',
'',
'',
'',
'$myrow[time]',
'0000-00-00 00:00:00',
'',
'0',
'post' );";
```

As you can see, you set specific values for each row in the `wp_posts` WordPress table. At this point you'll need to match the values you want to import from the source table with the correct table fields in WordPress. The preceding script is just an example showing how that can be accomplished. Next you execute the generated query:

```
mysql_select_db($destdb, $db_connect);
//execute query
mysql_query($sql, $db_connect);
```

After your query has successfully run the source data will start to populate in the WordPress `posts` table. Now you need to import the post comments and associate them with the correct posts. The first step to accomplish this is to load the ID of the post you just inserted, as shown here:

```
// load the ID of the post we just inserted
$sql = "select MAX(ID) from " . $wp_prefix . "posts";
$getID = mysql_query($sql, $db_connect);
$currentID = mysql_fetch_array($getID);
$currentID = $currentID['MAX(ID)'];
```

This is the ID used to associate a comment with a post in WordPress. Next you need to execute a query to retrieve all of the comments from the source table:

```
// retreive all associated post comments
$mysid = $myrow["pn_sid"];
mysql_select_db($sourcedb, $db_connect);
$comments = mysql_query("select * from "
    .$sourcecomments. " where pn_sid = $mysid", $db_connect);
```

Next you start a loop to loop through all of the comments attached to this post and insert into the WordPress comments table:

```
//import post comments in WordPress
while ($comrow = mysql_fetch_array($comments))
{
    $myname = mysql_escape_string($comrow['pn_name']);
```

```
$myemail = mysql_escape_string($comrow['pn_email']);
$myurl = mysql_escape_string($comrow['pn_url']);
$myIP = mysql_escape_string($comrow['pn_host_name']);
$mycomment = mysql_escape_string($comrow['pn_comment']);
```

You also set some variables with the comment data you are going to insert into WordPress. Remember these values will need to be matched to whatever system you are importing from. Next it's time to build the query and insert the comment data in WordPress:

```
$sql = "INSERT INTO '" . $wp_prefix . "comments'
(
  'comment_ID' ,
  'comment_post_ID' ,
  'comment_author' ,
  'comment_author_email' ,
  'comment_author_url' ,
  'comment_author_IP' ,
  'comment_date' ,
  'comment_date_gmt' ,
  'comment_content' ,
  'comment_karma' ,
  'comment_approved' ,
  'user_id' )
  VALUES
  (
    '',
    '$currentID',
    '$myname',
    '$myemail',
    '$myurl',
    '$myIP',
    '$comrow[date]',
    '0000-00-00 00:00:00',
    '$mycomment',
    '0',
    '1',
    '0'
  );";

if ($submit)
{
  mysql_select_db($destdb, $db_connect);
  mysql_query($sql, $db_connect)
    or die("Fatal Error: ".mysql_error());
}
  }
}
```

As you can see you match each value to the correct WordPress table field in the INSERT query. After generating your query you initialize the database connection and execute the query. Remember this is in a loop, so if ten comments exist on this post it will execute this INSERT statement for all ten comments.

The final section of code in the importer updates the `comment_count` value on your posts. When viewing total comments on a post, WordPress does not dynamically generate that number. Instead it's stored as an integer value in the post record. The first step is to load a single post to count comments for:

```
//Update comment count
mysql_select_db($destdb, $db_connect);
$tidyresult = mysql_query("select * from $wp_prefix" . "posts", $db_connect)
  or die("Fatal Error: ".mysql_error());

while ($myrow = mysql_fetch_array($tidyresult))
{
```

You also start a `while` loop to loop through each one of the posts in the WordPress `posts` table. Next you run a `SELECT COUNT` query to count how many comments this single post has:

```
$mypostid=$myrow['ID'];
$countsql="select COUNT(*) from $wp_prefix" . "comments"
  . " WHERE 'comment_post_ID' = " . $mypostid;
$countresult=mysql_query($countsql) or die("Fatal Error: ".mysql_error());
$commentcount=mysql_result($countresult,0,0);
```

Once this code has executed, the variable `$commentcount` will contain the total number of comments attached to this post. The final part is to update the `comment_count` field in the WordPress `posts` table to match this value:

```
$countsql="UPDATE '" . $wp_prefix . "posts'
  SET 'comment_count' = '" . $commentcount .
  "' WHERE 'ID' = " . $mypostid . " LIMIT 1";

$countresult=mysql_query($countsql) or die("Fatal Error: ".mysql_error());

}
```

The `UPDATE` query updates the comment count based on the value of `$commentcount`. This is a loop so it iterates through each post in the WordPress `posts` table and updates the comment count for each post.

Remember, this is an example of how to create a script to do a direct import from a source database table into the WordPress database tables. The individual values set in this script would need to be matched to the appropriate values in your source database tables to import. If you're up to digging around in the WordPress database schema, or have a particularly thorny source data repository to work with, check out the migratedata tool (migratedata.sourceforge.net). migratedata allows you to build a mapping of one database schema to another, creating a SQL file that can be run against your destination WordPress installation. The tool stemmed from a project to convert PostNuke-based sites to WordPress, so the target database schema out of the box is WordPress-centric.

Whichever method you choose to transport your content, the next step is to import into WordPress. We recommend importing into a fresh installation of WordPress. Or, make sure that your import plan includes purging existing content so as to avoid duplicate entries. If you are layering your import on top of existing content you will need to hand-edit your import files or scripts to make sure no conflicts occur.

Next, do a trial import, and see where you end up. Even with up-front planning and consideration there is very little chance you can get it all right on the first try. Review the new site and see what needs to be hand-edited in the script. Again, there will be more "grep-fu" and find and replace fun.

If you are going the WXR route, you can use the WordPress Import dashboard to import this file. An important consideration is the maximum file size and execution time for PHP. If your import file is large, you may need to edit your PHP configuration to increase these timeouts. One way to avoid this problem is using the Advanced Export for WP & WPMU plugin (`http://wordpress.org/extend/plugins/advanced-export-for-wp-wpmu/`). This plugin allows you to break up the export into smaller manageable files based on certain criteria like date range, category or author, reducing the risk of WordPress having memory limit issues during import. The export file can be filtered by date range, author, category, content type, post status, or tag and category terms.

MEDIA MIGRATION

There are really two sets of media and asset files for your site: graphics that make up the theme and site frame, and graphics and documents that are embedded in the content.

We discuss the theme presentation later in this chapter. This section is about moving the media that is embedded in your content portions of the page, for example linked Word documents, PowerPoint Presentations and Adobe PDFs. This also includes any images in your content, like screenshots or graphs. In a traditional WordPress installation, these files are uploaded into your uploads folder and, depending on your configuration, are filed by dates.

Odds are that your existing site is not going to have this sort of directory structure. But, as you know, link structures and naming conventions matter, and if you are moving from Windows to Linux, case now matters too. You have options for moving your content, and how to structure it in the new site. Each migration is different, so you will have to evaluate which method is going to work out best for your case.

Many sites have a top-level folder in the webroot for images, often called `/img/` or `/images/`. The simplest method to move this directory over is just to keep it intact and put it in the top level of your WordPress site. This is primarily copying files from one directory tree on the source server to the new server using a file transfer protocol (FTP) utility and tarball file. Really, we would rather you used a secure file transfer protocol utility (SFTP) to move files, but it all depends on what your server supports. Keeping the original images in the same directory structure on the new server as the old, for example it might be `/pdfs/`, is beneficial because you may not have to remap each image in the content. However, you will see in the cleaning-up stage that changing the URLs is not that difficult, or you could edit the WXR import file ahead of time. This technique may be undesirable because it breaks from the WordPress convention of storing your assets in the `wp-uploads` directory and your media assets will become separated into two different locations when you start using the WordPress Write Panels to upload new images.

The second option is to move all the images into the WordPress uploads folder on the new server. Make sure the target directory choice matches the WordPress configuration; otherwise you are not really using this method effectively. You can change the default upload directory in WordPress under the Miscellaneous dashboard, as covered in Chapter 3. This option pretty much guarantees that you will need to remap every image in your content so you will either need to plan ahead for this in your import scripts, or handle the image URL changes in the clean-up phase.

Yet another option is if the new site still has fully qualified links to images on the old site, you can use the Hot Linked Image Cacher plugin by linewbie (`http://wordpress.org/extend/plugins/hot-linked -image-cacher/`). This plugin searches your WordPress content for link images on remote sites, automatically downloads the images to the local server, and drops them into your uploads folder. Before using this method, you should verify that you have copyright and permission to use these images. In addition this plugin will update your content to link to the local version. You can run this plugin over specific posts of your site or over all the content. Depending on your setup, this could be a real time-saver.

MOVING METADATA

If you need to maintain a certain site structure you should establish that back in the planning phase. If your existing site already has categories and tag information, likely that information will transfer as part of your migration. You will need to pay careful attention that all your information is exact, or the import will make multiple similar categories.

Otherwise, you may just want WordPress to establish new categories for your content during the import. You should review the template files in your theme, and the template file hierarchy discussed in Chapter 8. You may find that some of the structure that you had to manually maintain in the old site is automatically created in WordPress simply through the WordPress site architecture.

Remember to consider your permalink structure and how it relates to your new structured content. Likewise, consider the category base and tag base URLs settings that were covered in Chapter 2. Setting all of these properly on your new site can save you a fair amount of time.

Preserving the site structure or at least the URLs is important if you are moving an established site. Search engines have been indexing your previous site and you have probably made some efforts to search engine optimize the site, so having the search engines' indexed links remain will continue to drive traffic your site.

Even if the default WordPress URL for content is a different link than your original site, you will want to map the old URLs to the new ones. We cover this step in the "Cleaning Up" section of this chapter.

MOVING AUTHORS AND USERS

Most brochureware web sites are author agnostic. That is, you do not really have content attributed to specific site authors, because they are representing a business entity. You can continue with this method, even when using WordPress, which enforces authorship. All you need to do is turn off the author information in your theme.

However, if you are moving from a site that has authorship ingrained, or this is something you want to implement on the new site, you will need to set up your authors in WordPress and attribute the appropriate posts. If you are using the WXR method, your authors can be created for you automatically. If you are using the SQL conversions from another CMS, you will want to carefully build this information into your transformations.

If you are creating a multi-author WordPress site, you may also want to consider the multi-user functionality of WordPress MU which is expected to be merged into the core of WordPress 3.0.

THEME AND PRESENTATION

The presentation of your new site represents the next set of decisions for your migration. Is your new site going to look exactly like your old site or are you making a design change at the same time?

If you are making a design change, you use can an existing theme or build a new theme and not have to dwell on this step too much. Remember to evaluate whether certain content areas need specific, or unique, design considerations. Otherwise, activate your new theme and work out the kinks.

However, if you intend to keep the look and feel consistent across the migration you are most likely in for building a new theme. Usually this is not too much of an undertaking, because most web sites are created with essentially the same building blocks: header, footer, content area, and sidebars. You can pretty easily map these to the proper theme template files.

Nevertheless, you will have to decide if you are going to take your current HTML files and add in the proper WordPress hooks and code, or start with a working WordPress theme, like Sandbox, and style it to match. It really is a mixed bag, and you will have to decide the best path for yourself. For practicality we recommend taking a theme framework and styling it to match your site's look and feel. In the long run, this has worked out better for us.

UNIQUE FUNCTIONALITY

For integration and functionality, there is really nothing to migrate, except for the actual operations — for example, contact forms, event calendars, and polls. Unless you move the existing PHP code to the WordPress site through page templates, your best bet is to find equivalent plugins. There are many plugins for various tasks, you will simply have to pick the one that closely matches your needs, activate and configure it.

CLEANING UP

Even when you are done moving the bulk of the visible content, there is always the final fit and finish work. You have done the heavy lifting and at least have something to look at on the new site. Now you need to go through and review all the content with spot tests and fix any glaring issues and then do some cleaning up and put the final polish on the site.

This section also covers some steps of the "go live" process of launching a site. The balance between when you can make these final changes and when you are still testing can often be difficult to gauge. At some point you have to bite the bullet and make the change. Remember, shipping is a feature.

Though this is called the cleaning-up step, you could be making some drastic changes in this phase, so we recommend doing your first backup of the new WordPress database. The wp-DBManager plugin by Lester Chan (`http://wordpress.org/extend/plugins/wp-dbmanager/`) is an excellent plugin for the job. This plugin allows you to make a backup of the database so you will have this point to roll back to. In addition, this plugin allows scheduling of the backups and some other database tools.

Manual Fine-Tuning

An important pre-launch task is to check all the page links, posts and page names to make sure everything is how you want it. You can tweak all of the relative paths now. You will be changing the fully qualified URL at launch time. This is the time for you to go through the entire site and manually inspect and adjust your imported content. Rarely is a migration import flawless and nearly always your site will require some manual intervention, either because the import was incapable of making the necessary changes or because the effort required to automate, or fix and re-import, is more than simply making the adjustments by hand.

Import Limitations

Be mindful of the PHP memory limit on your server. Because the entire import script file is loaded into memory and executed, you can easily hit low limits. If you have a large number of posts to import, try breaking the source export file into pieces and run the import in sections.

Also, an import cannot catch everything. You will have to manually review all your content. It's time-consuming and painful, akin to being forced to listen to your own recorded voice, but it's worthwhile to get fully up and running on WordPress as well as to ensure that all of your content appears on the other side of the migration.

Updating URLs

If many of the links in your content contain hard-coded test site URLs, you can set these to site relative links to make the launch easier. By default, WordPress uses fully qualified links to reference assets and other pages. Changing these links to site relative means when you make the final DNS switch, you will not have to run this process again; unless of course, you have added new content after this step.

To change some of the common absolute paths that you would encounter in your content you can run some simple SQL queries. Use the SQL page of the wp-DBManager plugin, phpmyadmin, or the command-line MySQL to update them.

Change all the in-site links from absolute to site relative. This query assumes you are running your WordPress site on the test.example.com domain:

```
UPDATE 'wp_posts' SET post_content=replace(post_content,
'href="http://test.example.com/','href="/');
```

This query changes all your absolute image source links to site relative, again assuming you are running your new site on the test.example.com domain:

```
UPDATE 'wp_posts' SET post_content=replace(post_content,
'src="http://test.example.com/','src="/');
```

Now all your internal site links and image sources are root relative, meaning you can check out your site for bad links either manually or with an automated tool and look for missing graphics. It does not matter what your test URL is. This is temporary and allows you to test all your images and graphics on the test site. Again, if you add any new content after this step, WordPress will use fully qualified URLs using the settings in the WordPress Dashboard. As part of launching, you will want to run what is essentially the reverse of this SQL statement to set all the paths to the live URL. This preserves links in RSS feeds and other syndication systems to link back to your full qualified domain name path.

Another method for updating hard-coded URLs in your content is the Search Regex plugin (`http://wordpress.org/extend/plugins/search-regex/`). This plugin adds a powerful set of search-and-replace functionality to WordPress. This plugin also allows you to view the content before and after without making any database changes so you can fully test your methods before pulling the trigger. Regular expression (regex) patterns can also be used for defining search-and-replace rules.

Redirection

This is a very important step. You will want search engines that have previously indexed your site to continue to refer visitors to the same content. You do not want to lose any investment of time and achievement just because you are switching underlying web site platforms. The search spiders do not care how you make your web site, other than being readable to them, but they do care where your content is located. After all, it is the only way they can find you.

You have a couple of options for maintaining your existing URL structure on your shiny new WordPress site, the most basic being permalinks. Depending on how your site was laid out and how the planning phase went you may be able to duplicate the site structure by manually editing the permalink structure of your pages and posts.

If you are running on Apache this is an easy fix. You can use the site map created in the content migration step to build a list of redirects from the old URL to the new WordPress permalink.

A second option is to use an `.htaccess` redirect to map the old URLs to the new URLs. Generally this option is only for Apache web servers with the mod_rewrite module enabled, but some `.htaccess`-like modules exist for IIS servers. The `.htaccess` method is an easy fit if you created a site map back in the planning or import file creation phase. You can easily take this import file and with a small script generate the necessary lines for your `.htaccess` file. Your `.htaccess` then includes the simple one-to-one matching, one match per line, such as:

```
Redirect /about.php http://example.com/services/
Redirect /portfolio.php http://example.com/category/portfolio/
Redirect /cool-article.php http://example.com/2009/10/09/cool-article/
```

Make sure these redirect pairs are listed first in your `.htaccess` file, and make sure you include the WordPress redirect stanza at the bottom of the file. Also make note that if you use the built-in WordPress permalink changer you risk overwriting this file, so make a backup.

Finally, there is a great redirection plugin, aptly called Redirection (`http://wordpress.org/extend/plugins/redirection/`). This plugin, made by John Godley, incorporates your redirect settings directly in the WordPress Dashboard. This can make it very easy for you to set up the necessary redirects if you are unfamiliar with editing `.htaccess` files. The redirection plugin also supports WordPress-based redirects in case your site is not on an Apache host.

This plugin has several other notable features including support for regular expression redirects, 404 logging to track broken links, and several import and export functions. Monitoring your 404 pages is an excellent way to see what you missed in a migration, but will also help you in the long term when you add new content. It will show if you mislinked something in your own site. Reviewing 404 logs is not a fun task, but something that our developers do daily to ensure sites are running fully functional.

LAUNCHING

At some point you have to bite the bullet and launch your new site. You have done all the manual review and automated updates you can, and for better or for worse you are going to make the move to switch sites.

The actual steps for launching your site vary depending on how you did your import and new site development. You may need to make the actual DNS change. If this is the case you will also need to change the URLs in the General Options dashboard of WordPress. Change these URLs to the live site URLs. This will intentionally break the web site rendering. You can temporarily add `define('RELOCATE',true);` to the `wp-config.php` file to regain access to your site. Remember to pull this setting back out when the DNS finally propagates. If you set your internal links to root relative during the testing phase, you can now set them to use your live URL. This is also a final opportunity to validate that your planning and the migration process worked. You should verify each and every page on your web site and double check all functionality.

Some other things to consider when moving your WordPress site to production include enabling privacy settings to make your site visible. Set the admin e-mail address to the proper value. Often if you are moving someone else's site you develop the new site with your own e-mail address so the final user does not get confused. Finalize the database backup plugin to regularly back up the database, or if you have some other backup plan, put it into effect. Likewise confirm the settings of other plugins that should be active in the live site; super cache is a good example. Double-check your 404 handling. Finally, make sure your web traffic statistics, like Google Analytics, are enabled. We usually disable analytics in the development phase.

In conclusion, transitioning a web site to WordPress can seem like a daunting task. However, when you break it down into steps and spend a little time planning up front the process easily falls into place. The real trick is to establish a new development environment with a fresh WordPress installation and then you can iterate over trial imports until you get an import that is far enough along to finish up with some manual fine-tuning. Remember, a little elbow grease will get you a long way and in the end, the long-term reward of using WordPress and all the built-in and plugin functionality will make the endeavor worthwhile.

15

WordPress Developer Community

WHAT'S IN THIS CHAPTER?

➤ Contributing to the WordPress project

➤ Using the Trac software

➤ Working on the WordPress Core using Subversion

➤ Exploring valuable WordPress resources for further learning

The WordPress Community is what truly makes WordPress. As an open source project, Word-Press is continually developed for and by the community and without community support the WordPress project would dry up and eventually development would cease. By getting involved, you can help make WordPress the best open source software package on the market.

This chapter discusses the different methods by which you can contribute to the WordPress project. It also covers some valuable WordPress resources to help expand your knowledge of WordPress and how it works.

CONTRIBUTING TO WORDPRESS

You can contribute to the WordPress project in many different ways. The most obvious way is to help with the source code that powers WordPress. Helping with the code can include finding and testing bugs, creating patches to fix bugs and add functionality, and helping test the patches against the latest WordPress trunk.

Understanding Trac

Trac is the open source bug-tracking and project management software used to develop the WordPress project. You can visit the official WordPress Trac web site at `http://core.trac.wordpress.org/`.

Trac is an easy way to create and discuss tickets regarding WordPress. Whether it is a bug report, feature request, or enhancement, Trac helps in creating these tickets and having discussions around them. Have you ever had a new feature idea that you thought would be perfect for WordPress? The easiest way to start that conversation with the WordPress Core Developer team is to create a feature request ticket in Trac. Have you ever found a bug in WordPress that keeps appearing in every new version? Creating a bug report is the quickest way to get the issue resolved in the next version. Even if you aren't a developer, creating tickets and getting involved in the discussions will ultimately help WordPress grow in a positive way!

Bug Reporting

All software has bugs and WordPress is no different. All open source projects like WordPress need help from the community to identify and fix bugs. Luckily, by utilizing Trac WordPress makes it very easy to report any bugs you might come across.

The first step in reporting a bug is to verify that the bug is in fact a bug in WordPress and not a plugin or theme issue. The easiest way to accomplish this is to post the bug in the WordPress Support Forums. You can also discuss the bug in the #wordpress IRC channel, or post a question to the Testers and Hackers mailing list. Lastly, search Trac to confirm that the bug you are reporting doesn't already exist in Trac. After you have confirmed that the bug exists, it's time to create a new ticket in Trac detailing the bug.

To report a new bug in Trac you first need to log in. The Trac login account is synced with your Word-Press.org account so you can use the same account to login. If you don't have an account you can create a new one at the WordPress.org Support Forums.

After logging into Trac, click the New Ticket link at the top. You'll be presented with a form to fill out to submit the new bug ticket. Fill in the following fields on the new ticket:

➤ **Short Summary:** Short but accurate and informative title summarizing your bug ticket.

➤ **Full Description:** Detailed description of the bug. Include steps to reproduce the bug and add an example URL displaying the bug if possible. Also include platform versions such as operating system, web server, PHP version, MySQL version, and WordPress version.

➤ **Type:** The type of ticket you are submitting. In this case use the default of "defect (bug)" but other options are available.

➤ **Milestone:** The version of WordPress the ticket would apply to. A bug ticket would typically be set to the next minor version of WordPress (2.9.x) whereas a new feature would typically be set to the next major version (3.x). Leave this at the default setting. A core WordPress developer will determine what version to set.

➤ **Version:** The version of WordPress in which the bug was found. This only applies to bug tickets and not new feature requests.

➤ **Keywords:** Tags used to describe your ticket. Some standard keywords are covered in the following section.

➤ **Assign to:** Trac username responsible for fixing the bug. If you plan to fix the bug yourself, you can list your username here.

➤ **Priority:** How critical the issue is. Most bugs should use the default of normal, but critical issues may need to increase this.

➤ **Component:** The component in WordPress where the bug was found.

➤ **Severity:** The significance of the issue. Most bugs would use the default of normal.

➤ **Cc:** You can Cc yourself on all ticket updates by adding your Trac username to this field.

After you have filled in all of the new ticket information, and previewed the ticket to verify it's correct, click the Submit Ticket button to create a new Trac ticket. If you have any attachments to upload, such as a screenshot of the bug, check the box next to "I have files to attach to this ticket." On the following screen you will be allowed to upload any files attachments you would like.

Trac Keywords

In Trac a number of defined keywords are commonly used for WordPress tickets. These keywords are used for reporting to make finding tickets easier. Following is a list of these keywords and their appropriate usage:

➤ **reporter-feedback:** Additional feedback is needed from the ticket creator.

➤ **has-patch:** A solution patch file has been attached to the ticket and is ready to be tested before committing to the Core of WordPress.

➤ **needs-testing:** Someone needs to test the solution.

➤ **2nd-opinion:** A request for a second opinion is needed regarding the problem or solution.

➤ **dev-feedback:** A response is needed from a developer.

➤ **tested:** The patch has been tested. Include as many details as possible including the patch file tested and the environment and versions tested on.

➤ **commit:** The patch has been tested and reviewed by a trusted member of the community and is ready to be committed to the WordPress Core.

➤ **needs-patch:** The ticket has been confirmed and a patch is needed to fix the problem.

➤ **needs-unit-tests:** Unit tests needed to verify and test any patch that may exist.

➤ **needs-doc:** Inline documentation for the code is needed.

By adding the correct keywords your ticket will automatically be included in Trac reports created for WordPress. For example, the has-patch report shows all tickets with the has-patch tag: `http://core.trac.wordpress.org/report/13`. These reports are extremely useful if you want to help contribute to WordPress.

View and Search Tickets

Trac features many different ways to search and filter through the tickets available. To view Trac tickets, click the View Tickets link at the top. The next screen displays multiple predefined searches for filtering tickets. To view all tickets in Trac click the All Tickets link in the Trac menu. The list of all active tickets can be a bit overwhelming because there are usually hundreds of tickets in Trac.

To make Trac more manageable some predefined reports have been created to help filter the tickets down. Following is a list of the most commonly used reports in Trac:

➤ **All tickets:** Displays all tickets in Trac.

➤ **Next Minor Release:** Tickets assigned to the next minor release (3.0.*x*).

➤ **Next Major Release:** Tickets assigned to the next major release (3.*x*).

➤ **Tested / Commit Candidates:** Tickets that have been tested.

➤ **Has Patch / Needs testing:** Lists all tickets with a patch that need to be tested and verified to fix the ticket issue.

➤ **Needs Patch:** Lists all tickets needing a patch.

➤ **Latest Tickets:** Displays the latest tickets submitted to Trac.

➤ **My Tickets:** All tickets created by you.

You can also create your own custom search queries within Trac. To do so, click the small link called Custom Query that appears after you click View Tickets.

By default the Custom Query page displays all open tickets in Trac. To refine this list with your custom query you are going to add a filter. To the right of the screen is a drop-down select box with different filters. For this example select Milestone. After you select Milestone the filter appears under the Filters section across the top of the page. Here you can select the Milestone you want to view tickets for. Select the next version of WordPress to be released to view all tickets assigned to that Milestone, as shown in Figure 15-1.

The number of open tickets is always a good indication of how close the new version of WordPress is to being released. You can add multiple filters to your custom query. For example, you could add a filter for the needs-testing keyword to filter the tickets to show all tickets that need to be tested for the upcoming version of WordPress.

FIGURE 15-1: Custom Query in Trac

Trac Timeline

Trac also features a timeline of all recent activity within the system. This is great for a top-level overview of what changes have happened in Trac daily. You can also filter the date range and ticket status. To view the Trac timeline visit `http://core.trac.wordpress.org/timeline`.

Browsing Source

One of the major advantages of the Trac software is how it integrates with Subversion (SVN). Subversion is the version control software used by WordPress to track code changes and commits. Within Trac you can view the most current version of the WordPress software, which is sometimes referred to as bleeding-edge. To view the current WordPress source, click the Browse Source link in the Trac menu. The current version of WordPress is located in the trunk folder.

Viewing the WordPress source in Trac is extremely useful for seeing new changes made to WordPress. Next to each file the Last Change is listed and linked to the Trac ticket that has details about that change. The Age is also listed showing the date when the file was last edited.

Notice at the very bottom of the page there is a link titled "Download in other formats: Zip Archive." Just click this link to download the entire bleeding-edge copy of WordPress. After downloading WordPress from Trac you can install it on your own server just like a normal installation of Word-Press. This is great for testing out new features in the upcoming version of WordPress. Keep in mind that this is bleeding-edge software so bugs will most likely exist. You wouldn't want to run this version of WordPress on a production web site.

Working on the Core

The WordPress software is built by the community, which means anyone can help contribute to the codebase. When we say WordPress is built by the community it doesn't mean anyone can go edit the WordPress source code. To contribute to the WordPress Core you must create a patch file with your changes and submit that file for review. If accepted your changes will be incorporated into the WordPress Core, and will be included in the next version release. Contributing code edits, bug fixes, and additional functionality is done using Subversion.

We stated rather emphatically in Chapter 4 that you should never hack Core. In this case we aren't actually hacking the Core of a WordPress installation, but rather creating patch files to submit for inclusion into the WordPress software.

Understanding Subversion (SVN)

Subversion is used to make modifications to the current code base and generate patch files. A patch file is a text file that contains the changes that were made to a specific file or files. To work on the WordPress Core you will need to generate patch files and submit them for review. Once a patch file has been accepted as the best fix for the issue it will be committed to the WordPress Core code.

Hook into WordPress Core

The first step in hooking into the WordPress Core is to check out (download) the latest codebase using SVN. To do so, you'll need an SVN client on your development machine. For the rest of this chapter, we'll give examples using the TortoiseSVN client, which is one of the more popular choices for Windows. The WordPress SVN repository is located here at `http://core.svn.wordpress.org/trunk/`. Checking out a repository creates a copy of it on your local machine. This is the copy of WordPress you will modify when fixing bugs and adding new functionality.

Using TortoiseSVN right-click the folder you want to download the WordPress codebase to and select SVN Checkout. Make sure to fill in the SVN repository URL for WordPress and click OK to download the codebase. For more information on using Subversion with WordPress check out `http://codex.wordpress.org/Using_Subversion`.

Create a patch/diff File

Now that you have downloaded the WordPress codebase it's time to make some changes! Pick any file you want to modify and make the appropriate changes as needed. Make sure to save the file after you are finished making edits. Now you need to create a patch file that details the changes you made. To do so, right-click the file you modified and select TortoiseSVN ⇨ Create Patch. A dialog appears allowing you to select the modified files; in this case only one file should appear, so click OK to proceed. Next choose a location to save your patch file and give it a unique name. It's a good practice to name your patch file the same as the file so you edited, so if you modified `wp-config-sample.php`, name your patch file `wp-config-sample.patch`, and click Save. You have just successfully created a working patch file for WordPress! This patch file can be submitted to any Trac ticket as a bug fix or feature recommendation. If the patch is accepted, a Core WordPress Committer will commit your patch file to the Core of WordPress. After a patch you have submitted has been accepted into the WordPress Core you can officially call yourself a WordPress Core Contributor!

Submitting Plugins and Themes

Submitting plugins to the Plugin Directory is the best way to release a plugin to the public. This also holds true for submitting themes to the Theme Directory. Ultimately you want as much exposure as possible for any theme or plugin that you release. Adding your plugin and theme to the appropriate WordPress.org directory is the best way to accomplish this. Remember that both directories are hooked in the admin side of every current installation of WordPress. This means anyone running WordPress can easily install your theme or plugin with just a few clicks.

To submit your theme or plugin visit the official submission page on WordPress.org:

➤   **Plugin Submission:** `http://wordpress.org/extend/plugins/add/`

➤   **Theme Submission:** `http://wordpress.org/extend/themes/upload/`

Here you'll find instructions on the proper submission process for both. The submission process is covered in more detail in Chapter 7, "Plugin Development."

Documentation

Documentation is a thankless job, yet nearly every developer relies on the documentation at some point. A great way to contribute to the WordPress Community is to help keep the documentation updated. Figure that every time a new WordPress release comes out, the documentation needs to be updated to reflect the changes, whether new functionality is added, behavior is modified, or certain aspects are scheduled for deprecation.

Keeping the documentation current is a daunting task, and given the volunteer nature of the project, is sometimes neglected. You can often find out-of-date information in the Codex for WordPress releases from long ago that are no longer best practices, applicable, or even supported.

Documentation updating is not glamorous — it is not the shiny new functionality and features that everyone is excited about — but it is one of the best ways to support the community and help new users. Sometimes, solid documentation is what draws new developers in and helps keep them in the community.

If you are interested in helping out with the WordPress documentation, please subscribe to the Documentation Mailing list at `http://codex.wordpress.org/Mailing_Lists#Documentation`.

SISTER PROJECTS

WordPress has a few different sister projects currently available. These software projects are considered sister projects because some of the codebase is shared with WordPress. Many of the developers behind these projects also contribute to the WordPress project. Sister projects are also built to make WordPress integration simple and easy.

WordPress MU

WordPress MU (WPMU), or multi-user, is a single installation of WordPress that allows for an unlimited number of blogs to be created. This software is the same that is used to power WordPress.com and the millions of blogs it hosts. WordPress MU makes it possible for anyone to host their own blogging community. Visitors can register and create their own blogs within your web site.

As mentioned in Chapter 12, WordPress MU will be merged with the codebase for standard WordPress in version 3.0. This means there will no longer be two separate codebases to download and install. Instead you'll set a flag in the `wp-config.php` file to enable all WordPress MU functionality on your WordPress web site. Currently this new integration of WordPress is being called WordPress MS or Multi Site.

BuddyPress

BuddyPress is a set of plugins and themes that add a social networking layer to WordPress MU. All BuddyPress plugins can be themed to match your current web site design.

Some of the features available include extended profiles, private messaging, friends, groups, wire and activity streams, status updates, forums, and more! Each plugin adds a distinct new social networking feature. All BuddyPress plugins are independent, meaning you can add just the plugins you want and not the entire BuddyPress suite.

bbPress

bbPress is an open source forum software package. The goal of bbPress is to be lightweight, powerful, fast, and easy to use. bbPress has many of the features you would expect from message board software, including a simple interface, customizable templates, and spam protection. bbPress can also run plugins to extend its functionality just like WordPress. bbPress was originally offered as a separate installation package, but has since been ported over to a WordPress plugin, and by the time of the WordPress 3.0 release it should be a core plugin. You can download bbPress at the official Plugin Directory page: `http://wordpress.org/extend/plugins/bbpress/`.

Future Projects

WordPress is growing at an amazing rate and new projects are always popping up. It's hard to imagine what new projects we'll see in the future, but if WordPress has taught us anything it's to expect the unexpected.

RESOURCES

Many different resources are available for WordPress. This section provides a list of the most popular resources that you should be aware of to expand your knowledge of WordPress.

Codex

The WordPress Codex is one of the largest and best resources available for WordPress, and is essentially an online manual for WordPress users. Powered by MediaWiki, the Codex is a wiki-style documentation project, meaning anyone can contribute to the articles and content featured. Featuring tutorials, examples, function references, and much more, the Codex takes you through everything from installation to customization. The official site is `http://codex.wordpress.org/Main_Page`.

Support Forums

The WordPress Support Forum is another great resource. You can visit the support forum at the official URL: `http://wordpress.org/support/`.

The support forum is separated into multiple sections covering many different topics. The quickest way to locate related threads is to search the forum using the search box. There is also a tag cloud powered by hot topics in the forum. This can be a quick way to see what the trending topics are in the forum.

Forum threads can also be tagged with keywords about the post. Any post tagged with the name of a plugin is automatically added as a topic on a plugins detail page. The new forum post will be listed under the "See what others are saying" section in the right sidebar on the plugin detail page, as Figure 15-2 shows.

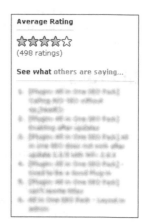

This provides a support forum section for every plugin in the repository. To create a forum post about a plugin, just add the plugin slug as a tag on your post. For example, to create a post about the WordPress Theme Showcase Plugin, you would tag your forum post with "wordpress-theme-showcase-plugin," which is the slug from the plugin URL: `http://wordpress.org/extend/plugins/wordpress-theme-showcase-plugin/`.

Forum posts can also be marked as resolved by the original author. If you post a question and someone replies with a response that helps you resolve your problem, you should mark your post as resolved. This will add the text "[resolved]" to the front of your post topic to let others know the problem has been resolved. This helps other community members find answers to their questions by viewing the resolved threads.

FIGURE 15-2: See what others are saying

The support forum is powered by bbPress, the forum plugin mentioned in the previous section. The support forum uses a separate user account from the Codex, so you will have to create a new user account to start creating new topics.

WordPress Chat

WordPress has some very active chat rooms on IRC (Internet Relay Chat). To join a WordPress chat room you will need to install an IRC client on your computer. Once installed connect to the Freenode server at irc.freenode.net, and once you have connected you can join one or more of the chat rooms listed here:

➤ **#wordpress:** The primary WordPress chat room. Great place to get questions answered quickly and accurately about WordPress.

➤ **#wordpress-dev:** Chat room dedicated to WordPress Core development. Topics are restricted to working on the WordPress code itself and not for general WordPress inquiries.

➤ **#wpmu:** Chat room dedicated to all WordPress MU (multi-user) related conversations.

➤ **#buddypress-dev:** Chat room dedicated to all BuddyPress-related conversations.

➤ **#bbpress:** Chat room dedicated to all bbPress-related conversations.

These IRC chat rooms are a great resource for getting real-time help. Many WordPress experts, including myself, hang out in these rooms regularly and love to help out other WordPress enthusiasts. This is also a great place to expand your knowledge of WordPress.

The WordPress Core developers host a weekly dev chat in #wordpress-dev. This scheduled chat covers a preset agenda of topics regarding the future development of WordPress, and many decisions are made on features and functionality in these weekly chats. The topics typically cover features being developed for the upcoming version of WordPress, but can also cover additional items.

For more information on IRC and WordPress chat rooms visit the official Codex IRC page at http://codex.wordpress.org/IRC. This page details how IRC works, how to download and install an IRC client, how to connect to an IRC server, and also how to join a WordPress chat room.

Mailing Lists

WordPress has multiple mailing lists focused on different topics of the WordPress project. Most mailing lists are two-way conversations, meaning an e-mail is sent to the list with a problem or question, and another member of the mailing list responds with the answer. Anyone subscribed to that mailing list will be able to track the conversation. To register for any mailing list just visit the corresponding join link.

➤ **Announcements:** List for major announcements regarding WordPress. E-mail is very low frequency and one-way, meaning no conversations can take place.

➤ E-mail: wp-docs @lists.automattic.com

➤ Join: Edit your WordPress.org profile and select "Subscribe to WordPress Announcements" under Mailing Lists

➤ **Professional:** List for anyone looking for a professional consultant who specializes in Word-Press. This list is for finding paid WordPress help.

> ➤ E-mail: `wp-pro @lists.automattic.com`
>
> ➤ Join: `http://lists.automattic.com/mailman/listinfo/wp-pro`

➤ **Documentation:** List for coordinating and collaborating on WordPress Codex documentation. If you plan on contributing to the Codex this list is a must join.

> ➤ E-mail: `wp-docs @lists.automattic.com`
>
> ➤ Join: `http://lists.automattic.com/mailman/listinfo/wp-docs`

➤ **Hackers:** Primary mailing list for discussions on extending through plugins or Core code modifications. Many discussions revolve around Core functionality of WordPress.

> ➤ E-mail: `wp-hackers @lists.automattic.com`
>
> ➤ Join: `http://lists.automattic.com/mailman/listinfo/wp-hackers`

➤ **Testers:** Discussions regarding the current nightly, alpha, or beta version of WordPress.

> ➤ E-mail: `wp-testers @lists.automattic.com`
>
> ➤ Join: `http://lists.automattic.com/mailman/listinfo/wp-testers`

➤ **XML-RPC:** Discussions revolving around the XML-RPC topic of WordPress.

> ➤ E-mail: `wp-xmlrpc @lists.automattic.com`
>
> ➤ Join: `http://lists.automattic.com/mailman/listinfo/wp-xmlrpc`

➤ **Support Forum Volunteers:** Discussions involving WordPress Forum Support and providing support to users.

> ➤ E-mail: `wp-forums @lists.automattic.com`
>
> ➤ Join: `http://lists.automattic.com/mailman/listinfo/wp-forums`

➤ **Community Support:** An alternative to the support forum, this mailing list is for anyone needing an answer to a WordPress question.

> ➤ Join: `http://tech.groups.yahoo.com/group/wpgarage/`

➤ **Polyglots:** Conversations revolving around WordPress translators and translation files.

> ➤ E-mail: `wp-polyglots-bounces@lists.automattic.com`
>
> ➤ Join: `http://lists.automattic.com/mailman/listinfo/wp-polyglots`

➤ **SVN Updates:** List for tracking SVN repository updates. E-mail is sent for every update along with information on the changes made. SVN is the version control system WordPress Core developers use to track changes in the WordPress Core files.

> ➤ E-mail: `wp-svn-bounces@lists.automattic.com`
>
> ➤ Join: `http://lists.automattic.com/mailman/listinfo/wp-svn`

➤ **Trac:** List for tracking changes in Trac, the open source bug tracking system WordPress uses for tracking development on the WordPress Core. This is a very high-traffic e-mail list.

> ➤ E-mail: `wp-trac-bounces@lists.automattic.com`

> ➤ Join: `http://lists.automattic.com/mailman/listinfo/wp-trac`

Certain WordPress mailing lists can be high traffic, so it's a good idea to create a rule in your e-mail program to automatically filter WordPress mailing list e-mails to a specific folder. That way you can review the conversations taking place at your leisure.

To subscribe to any of these mailing lists, or for more information, visit the official Codex Mailing list page at `http://codex.wordpress.org/Mailing_Lists`. To view all available mailing lists visit the official Automattic mailing list page at `http://lists.automattic.com/mailman/listinfo`.

External Resources

There are many external resources for WordPress outside of WordPress.org. Following is a list of the most common:

➤ **WordPress Hooks Database:** Web site detailing all hooks (actions and filters) in WordPress by version. Great for referencing latest hook additions when a new version of WordPress is released. `http://adambrown.info/p/wp_hooks`

➤ **PHPXref for WordPress:** Features cross reference code library for WordPress. Use to easily view all variables, functions, classes, and constants used in WordPress. Xref shows where each item is defined as well as where referenced through the WordPress code. `http://phpxref.com/xref/wordpress/`

WordCamp and Meetups

WordPress is powered by the community behind it and because of that the community loves to get together and talk WordPress! This can happen a number of different ways but the two most popular events are WordCamps and WordPress Meetups.

WordCamps are one- or two-day conferences focused on anything and everything WordPress. These events usually have hundreds of attendees and multiple tracks for speakers with a wide array of topics. If you are interested in WordPress at all these are must-attend events. To find a WordCamp in your area visit the official WordCamp Central web site at `http://central.wordcamp.org/`.

WordPress Meetups are smaller local-based gatherings. These are usually informal get-togethers where attendees talk WordPress and share their experiences and knowledge with others. WordPress Meetups are typically held monthly or quarterly. To find a Meetup in your area check out the official WordPress Meetup Groups page at `http://wordpress.meetup.com/`.

WordPress.TV

WordPress.TV is a web site dedicated to videos about WordPress. The web site features tutorials for both WordPress self-installs and WordPress.com. Also featured on WordPress.TV are WordCamp footage and speaker sessions, interviews, and much more. This is a central repository for all videos related to WordPress. WordPress.TV is a great resource for learning more about WordPress through videos. Visit the official site at `http://wordpress.tv/`.

Theme/Plugin Directories

The first place to visit after installing WordPress is the Plugin and Theme Directories. In the Plugin Directory you can download thousands of plugins to add all sorts of amazing functionality to your web site. The Theme Directory features more than a thousand free themes for WordPress that can be used to give your site a new look. Remember both of these directories can be browsed from within your WordPress installation

➤ **Plugin Directory:** `http://wordpress.org/extend/plugins/`

➤ **Theme Directory:** `http://wordpress.org/extend/themes/`

WordPress Ideas

WordPress.org features an Ideas area for gathering ideas for future features in WordPress. Here you can vote on your favorite ideas and view a list of the most popular ideas based on votes. The most popular ideas are usually reviewed before the development of a new version of WordPress and typically a few of them will make it into the new release. You can visit the official Ideas page at `http://wordpress.org/extend/ideas/`.

WordPress Development Updates

Staying informed with the development of WordPress is a great resource for tracking upcoming WordPress changes and features. As new versions of WordPress are developed and released they come with new features and functionality. Understanding what these new features are can help with planning new projects for WordPress. The easiest way to do this is at the official WordPress Development Updates site located at `http://wpdevel.wordpress.com/`.

The WP Devel site uses the popular P2 theme, which is very similar to a Twitter-like theme for WordPress. The site features updates and discussions on the WordPress project. The site is also the location for information regarding the weekly WordPress Developer Chats in the #wordpress-dev IRC channel. The date and time for these meetings is featured in the sidebar. There is also a post detailing the topics for the weekly meeting. Anyone can contribute topics for the meeting by responding to this post.

WordPress Podcasts

Podcasts are a great way to stay informed on the latest news and information on any topic. Currently, four WordPress-centric podcasts are actively being produced.

WordPress Weekly

The WordPress Weekly podcast is a live weekly podcast hosted by Jeff Chandler of WPTavern.com. The show is a roundtable discussion around the top WordPress-related stories of the week. The podcast also features notable members of the WordPress Community for interviews. You can visit the web site at `http://www.wptavern.com/wordpress-weekly`.

WordCast Podcast

The WordCast Podcast is a weekly podcast hosted by Dave Moyer and Kym Huynh. The hosts discuss the latest news in WordPress and the blogging world! They also cover the best looking themes, great plugins, interviews with WordPress Community members, and much more. You can visit the web site at `http://bitwiremedia.com/wordcast/`.

The WordPress Podcast

This is the original WordPress Podcast currently hosted by Joost de Valk. The show is featured on WebmasterRadio.FM and is hosted live with one-on-one interviews with members of the WordPress Community. You can visit the web site at `http://www2.webmasterradio.fm/wordpress-community-podcast/`.

Plugins: The WordPress Plugins Podcast

Plugins is a podcast focused on WordPress plugins. Hosted by Angelo Mandato, this podcast covers one plugin each week. It also features occasional interviews with plugin developers as well as heavy plugin users. This podcast is shorter in length and a normal episode runs approximately 10–15 minutes. The web site is `http://www.pluginspodcast.com/`.

WordPress News Sites

Many different WordPress-related web sites exist. This section provides a list of the most popular WordPress-focused sites for news and information regarding anything and everything WordPress related.

WPTavern.com

The WordPress Tavern is a web site focused on all things WordPress. This includes BuddyPress, bbPress, WordPress.com, and any project under the Automattic umbrella. The Tavern features a very active message board where members discuss the latest news and developments in the WordPress Community. WPTavern.com is also the home of the WordPress Weekly Podcast hosted by Jeff Chandler. You can visit the web site at `http://www.wptavern.com/`.

WPVibe.com

WordPress Vibe is a news web site all about WordPress. The site focuses on two aspects of WordPress: the software and the people who help make WordPress work. WPVibe.com has interviews, plugin reviews, theme reviews, tutorials, and code hacks, all to help you make better use of WordPress. Launched in 2009, it has been one of the newest sites focused on WordPress. You can visit the web site at `http://wpvibe.com/`.

WeblogToolsCollection.com

Weblog Tools Collection (WBTC) is a web site dedicated to blogging, but generally focuses on WordPress-related topics. Home to the popular new Plugin and Theme Weekly release blog posts, WBTC features the latest news and headlines in the WordPress Community. WBTC is also home to the annual WordPress Plugin Competition. You can visit the web site at `http://weblogtoolscollection.com/`.

WPEngineer.com

WPEngineer features tips and tricks, news, and improvements for WordPress. The site features more in-depth tutorials diving into the Core of WordPress and its functionality. These tutorials are focused on intermediate-level WordPress users and developers. You can visit the web site at `http://wpengineer.com/`.

WordPress Alltop

Alltop is basically an RSS aggregator for specific topics. The WordPress Alltop page features news and information from the top WordPress-related web sites. It also lists important WordPress Twitter accounts that are worth following for news and information. You can visit the web site at `http://wordpress.alltop.com/`.

WordPress Planet

WordPress Planet is an aggregation of blogs writing about WordPress. This includes posts from Core contributors and very active community members. This is the same news feed featured on the Dashboard of every default installation of WordPress under the Other WordPress News dashboard widget. Visit the web site at `http://planet.wordpress.org/`.

Planet WordPress

Planet WordPress is also an RSS aggregator that keeps track of bloggers who contribute to WordPress. This feed differs from WordPress Planet in that it extends the WordPress Planet feed with even more bloggers. These bloggers are mainly plugin developers and Core contributors for WordPress. The news feed is maintained by Ozh Richard, a very respected developer in the WordPress Community. The web site is located at `http://planetwordpress.planetozh.com/`.

INDEX

A

action hooks, 127–132
Active Directory (AD), 324–325
AD. *See* Active Directory
additional hardware. *See* hardware, addition of
admin accounts, 289–290
administrators, 34
  WordPress role system, 296
advertising, of content, 242–247
  monetization, 242–243
      pay-per-click model, 243
      pay-per-day model, 243
      pay-per-view model, 243
  setup, 243–247
      conflict resolution, 246–247
      editorial control, 244
      manual placement, 245–246
      plugins, 243–244
Akismet, 32–33
  automated spam detection, 287
All Things D, 3
Allow User Registration option, 33
Alltop, 364
Alternative PHP Cache (APC), 281
Android, 271
Apache Roller, 1, 8
  cache management, 282
  site security, 291–292
APC. *See* Alternative PHP Cache
APIs. *See* Application Programming Interfaces
Application Programming Interfaces (APIs), 74–75
  content aggregation, 233
  Dashboard Widgets, 21, 75
  Google Maps, 238
  HTTP, 75
  Plugin, 74
  Rewrite, 75
  Settings, 75
  Shortcode, 74–75
  Twitter, 238
  Widgets, 74

`archive.php` file, 200–201
  Sandbox theme, 218
assets, in themes, 186
ATOM feeds, 239–240
  republishing form another site, 240
Atom Publishing Protocol, 42
`attachment.php` file, 209–210
audio, insertion of, 29–30
author data, 96
  content migration, 331, 345–346
  WordPress role system, 295
`author.php` template, 34
  theme creation, 210
authors, 34
  core files, 66
`the_author()`, 85
`the_author_meta()`, 85
auto-configuration dialog box, 11
Auto Installer, 36
Automated Browser Activation, 43
Automattic, 33
`AUTOSAVE INTERVAL`, 54
AWStats, 274–275
  reporting screen, 275

B

Bad Behavior plugin, 33
bbPress, 312–313, 357
Behrens, Kevin, 297, 301
Blog Title, 41
Blog Visibility setting, 45
Blogger, 1
  importing from, 40
`bluetrip.org`, 191
BuddyPress, 357
bugs, reporting of, 352–353

C

cache management, 278–284
  HyperCache, 283
  MySQL Query, 284
  objects, 283–284

  optimization, 281–282
    Apache, 282
    APC, 281
    LAMP stacks, 282
    `memcache`, 281
    `memcached`, 281
    opcode cache, 281
    PHP levels, 282
  system complexity, 279–281
    visualization, 280
  web server, 281–282
  WP-Super Cache, 283
caching, 321–322
  InnoDB, 321
  ISAM tables, 321
  MySQL database, 321
Calacanis, Jason, 3
Caoimh, Donncha O., 283, 292
CAPTCHA. *See* Completely Automated Public Turing test for telling Computers and Humans Apart
Carson, Ryan, 256
Cascading Style Sheets (CSS), 265–266
  POSH, 265
  themes, 186
    child, 220–222
    Sandbox, 188–189
  valid HTML, 265
Category to Tag Converter, 27
`category.php` file, 71, 201–202
`the_category()`, 85
CDN. *See* Content Delivery Network
CForms, 313
Chan, Lester, 346
Chandler, Jeff, 362
chat rooms, 359
Checkout Dialog, 179
child themes, 219–224
  CSS, 220–222
  `functions.php` file, 223–224
  page styles, 223
  WordPress 2.7, 219, 224

Cimy User Extra Fields plugin, 35
code. *See also* .htaccess file;
   wp-config.php
  core files, 51, 70–72
     category.php, 71
     formatting.php, 70
     functions.php, 70
     pluggable.php, 70–71
     plugin.php, 71
     post.php, 71
  default directory files, 51
  default files, 51
  downloads, 49–50
    available formats, 50
    locations, 49–50
    Release Archive, 50
    SVN access, 50
  exploration, 50–51
  .htaccess file, 8, 51, 58–61
    configuration control, 60–61
    error logging, 61
    .maintenance file, 61
    permalinks, 45, 58–59
    security, 61
    wp-admin directory, 60
  key file configuration, 51–61
    .htaccess file, 51, 58–61
    wp-config.php, 51–57
  wp-config.php, 51–57
    options, 52–57
    storage location, 52
    table prefixes, 53
    wp-config-sample.php, 9, 14–15
  wp-content directory, 61–63
    media, 63
    plugins, 61–62
    themes, 35, 62
    uploads, 62–63
Codex, for WordPress, 72–76
  APIs, 74–75
    Dashboard Widgets, 21, 75
    HTTP, 75
    Plugin, 74
    Rewrite, 75
    Settings, 75
    Shortcode, 74–75
    Widgets, 74
  controversy, 75–76
  function reference, 73–74
  Lessons Page, 73
  quick index, 73
  as resource, 358
  searches, 72–73
  template hierarchy, 206–207
  term glossary, 73
  uses, 72–73
codex.wordpress.org, 4
comments, 31–33
  administrator approval, 32
  core files, 66
  management, 31–32
    icons, 32
  moderating, 32
  spam, handling of, 32–33
    Akismet, 32–33
    Bad Behavior plugin, 33
    keyword blacklists, 32
    multiple links, 32
  spam moderation, 286–287
comments.php file, 210–211
comments_popup_link(), 85
Completely Automated Public Turing
    test for telling Computers and
    Humans Apart (CAPTCHA), 287
Conditional Tags, 196–197
content, creation and management of, 22–47
  categorization, 26–28
    Category to Tag Converter, 27
    for links, 28
    Most Used, 27
    post categories, 27
    Tag to Category Converter, 27
    tags v., 26–28
  comments, 31–33
    administrator approval, 32
    management, 31–32
    moderating, 32
    spam, handling of, 32–33
  configurations, 41–47
    date settings, 42
    discussion, 44
    emails, for posting, 43
    general settings, 41–42
    media, 44
    miscellaneous, 46–47
    permalinks, 45–46
    privacy, 45
    reading, 42–43
    time settings, 42
    user registration, 42
    writing, 42–43
  extension of, 35–39
    plugins, 38–39
    themes, 35–37
    widgets, 37–38
  links, 25–26
    categorization, 26
    Incoming Links widget, 21
    posts, 22, 24
    saving, 26
    targets, 26
  management, 24–25
    Delete link, 24
    for posts, 24–25
    Posts Edits, 24–25
    Quick Edit link, 24
  media, 28–31
    editing, 30–31
    filters, 30
    insertion of, 29–30
    Media Library, 28
    in posts, addition of, 23
    uploading, 28–29
    uploading of, 28–29
  pages, 25
    creation, 25
    management, 25
  posts, 22–25
    Add New link, 22
    categories for, 23
    creation of, 22–24
    date modification, 24
    image addition, 23
    management of, 24–25
    media addition, 23
    permalinks, 22
    post content box, 23
    Post Edits, 24–25
    publishing, 23
    Quick Edit link, 24
    tags, 23
    visibility variability, 24
  tools, 39–41
    exporting, 40
    importing, 39–40
    Turbo, 40
  trash, 26
  upgrading, 40–41
    backups for, 41
    bulk, for plugins, 41
    links, 41
    notices, 41
  users, 33–35
    administrators, 34
    authors, 34
    contributors, 34
    editors, 34
    images for, 34–35
    management, 33–34
    new user creation, 33
    profile extension, 35
    subscribers, 34
  widgets, 37–38

content aggregation, 229–248
  advertising, 242–247
        monetization of, 242–243
        setup, 243–247
  external content, 233–240
        APIs, 233
        ATOM feeds, 239–240
        generic XML feed, 233–236
        Google Maps, 238–239
        RSS feeds, 239–240
        Twitter, 236–238
  history, 247–248
  lifestream, 229–230
  long tail problem, 231
  for online identity, 230
  privacy, 247–248
  publishing to other sites,
        240–242
        Facebook, 241–242
        RSS, 240–241
  purpose, 230–231
  social media buttons, 231–233
        plugins, 231
        profile linking, 232
        sidebar widgets, 232
        social networking sites,
           231–233
Content Delivery Network (CDN),
  255
content hierarchy, 308–311
  custom taxonomy, 308
  Flutter, 310–312
  page links, 309
  page management, 308–310
  PageMash, 309–310
  Parent pages, 309
  Pods CMS, 311
Content Management Systems (CMS),
  2, 5–7, 299–315
  content creation, 6–7
  content organization, 303–312
        for commerce, 303–304
        featured content pages,
           306–308
        hierarchy, 308–311
        homepages, 305–306
        theme support, 304–305
        TinyMCE editor, 304, 306
        widget support, 304–305
  Dashboard, 6
  definition, 299–301
  Drupal project, 6
  information structuring, 257–259
  interactivity features, 312–313
  Joomla project, 6

Model-View-Controller design
  pattern, 6
  workflow and delegation, 301–303
        post control, 302–303
        revision history, 302
        user roles and delegation,
           301–302
content migration, to WordPress,
  329–349
  author data, 345–346
  cleanup, 346–349
        import limitations, 347
        manual fine-tuning, 347
        redirection, 348–349
        URL updating, 347–348
  content identification, 332–344
        custom import script
           construction, 335–344
        MySQL script, 335–339
        text documents, 333
        WXR files, 333–335
  launch for, 349
  media, 344–345
  metadata, 345
  planning strategy, 330–332
        checklist, 331–332
        cleanup, 332
        content sources, 330–331
        site reparation, 332
  themes, 346
  unique functionality, 346
  user data, 345–346
content pages, featured, 306–308
content sharing sites, 264
the_content(), 84
contributors, 34
  WordPress role system, 295
core files, 51, 65–77
  codes, 70–72
        category.php, 71
        formatting.php, 70
        functions.php, 70
        pluggable.php, 70–71
        plugin.php, 71
        post.php, 71
  Codex, 72–76
        APIs, 74–75
        controversy, 75–76
        function reference, 73–74
        Lessons Page, 73
        quick index, 73
        searches, 72–73
        term glossary, 73
        uses, 72–73
  contents, 65–66

      actions, 66
      authors, 66
      comments, 66
      feeds, 66
      filters, 66
      formatting, 66
      metadata, 66
      pages, 66
      plugins, 66
      posts, 66
      themes, 66
      users, 66
  function features, 67–70
      add_post_meta, 67–68
      global variables, 68
      for serialized data, 69–70
      stripslashes, 69
  hacking of, 76–77
      alternatives, 76–77
      consequences, 76
  inline documentation, 67
  as reference, 66–67
  WordPress community, 355–356
      hooking into, 355
      patch/diff file creation,
         355–356
      SVN, 355
core.svn.wordpress.org/trunk,
  50, 355
Cron Job Activation, 43
cropping, 30
crowd sourcing, 256
CSS. See Cascading Style Sheets
custom Loops, 80–81
custom menus, 135
custom meta boxes, 145–147
custom page templates,
  216–219
  page.php file, 217
  Sandbox theme, 218–219
  selection, 216
  usage, 217–218
custom permalinks, 45–46
custom settings, 140–143
custom taxonomies, 116–120
  admin panel, 117
  content hierarchy, 308
  menu options, 117
  metabox, 118
  name definition, 118
  overview, 116
  use, 119–120
CUSTOM_USER_META_TABLE, 56
CUSTOM_USER_TABLE, 56

D

Dashboard, 19–22
  Admin Menu, 22
    as collapsible, 22
    location, 22
  automated spam detection, 287
  as CMS, 6
  customization, 21
  defaults, 20
  example.com/wp-admin., 19
  first-time login, 16
  screen options, 21–22
    tab location, 21
  site discovery, with permalink
    structure, 260
  widgets, 20–21
    editing, 21
    Incoming Links, 21
    Planet WordPress RSS feed, 21
    plugins, 21, 152–153
    QuickPress, 21
    Recent Drafts, 20–21
    RSS, 21
    WordPress Development, 21
Dashboard Widgets API, 21, 75
  plugins, 152–153
database configuration, 11–16
  dialog box, 11
  installation failure causes, 13
  MySQL, 12–16
    installation failures, 13
    login issues, 14
    mysql_error(), 13–14
    selection errors, 14–15
    table collection, 15
    WordPress v., 15
database configuration dialog box, 11
database management, 103–120. *See
  also* custom taxonomies;
  taxonomies
  configuration, 11–16
    dialog box, 11
    installation failure causes, 13
    MySQL, 12–16
  direct manipulation, 111–114
    phpMyAdmin, 111
    wp_comments, 113–114
    wp_options, 112–113
    wp_posts, 111–112
    wp_users, 113
  schema, 103–105
    attachments, 105
    backward compatibility, 104
    ID fields, 104

revisions, 105
    structure, 104–105
    wp_posts table, 105–106
  tables, 105–111
    complex operations, 108–110
    errors, 110–111
    INSERT statements, 109
    SAVEQUERIES option, 110
    simple queries, 107–108
    UPDATE statements, 109
    wpdb class, 107–108
  taxonomies, 114–120
    custom, 116–120
    default, 114
    definition, 114
    relationships between, 115
    table structure, 115
date settings, 42
db-error.php, 209
DB_COLLATE, 52
default themes, Loop, 83–84
Delete option, trash, 26
Delicious, 230
Digg, 230–231
directories, 9–10
  index.html, 10
  index.php, 10
  public_html, 9
directory constants, 126–127
discussion, 44
Doctorow, Cory, 4, 6
documentation, 356–357
  mailing lists, 360
Don't Repeat Yourself (DRY) theme,
  193–197
downloads, 49–50
  available formats, 50
  locations, 49–50
  Release Archive, 50
  SVN access, 50
Drupal project, 6
DRY theme. *See* Don't Repeat Yourself
  theme
duplicate content, 261–263
  Google Webmaster tools, 262
  plugins, 261
  robots.txt, 262–263
  Sandbox theme, 261

E

e-commerce, 313
Edit Flow Project, 319
Edit User pages, 34
editors, 34

WordPress plugin extensions, 39
  WordPress role system, 295
edit_post_link(), 85
Eenfeldt, John, 289
emails
  configuration, for posting, 43
    Automated Browser Activation,
      43
    Cron Job Activation, 43
    Manual Browser Activation,
      43
  Reading subpanels, 43
  Writing subpanels, 43
environmental data, 97–98
Erlewine, Michael Yoshitaka, 309
error messages, 110–111
  SAVEQUERIES option, 110
  show_errors function, 110
errors. *See* 404.php
example.com/wp-admin., 19
the_excerpt(), 84
Exploit Scanner, 292–293
exporting tools, 40

F

Facebook, 230
  publishing to, 241–242
    Connect plugin, 242
featured content pages. *See* content
  pages, featured
feeds, core files, 66
FeedWordPress plugin, 327
File Monitor, 293–294
File Transfer Protocol (FTP), 36–37
  media migration, 331
  theme installation, 36, 184
  wp-config.php settings, 56–57
filter(s), core files, 66
filter hooks, 128–130
Firebug, 255
  Sandbox theme, 188
Flash uploaders, 28
Flutter, 310–312
  custom fields, 311
FORCE_SSL_LOGIN, 57
formatting, core files, 66
formatting.php, 70
forms, 313
Forum Server, 312
forums, 312–313
FOSS. *See* free/open source software
404.php, 208–209
  db-error.php, 209
free hosting services,3, 7–8

free/open source software (FOSS),319
FS_CHMOD_DIR, 57
FS_CHMOD_FILE, 57
FTP. *See* File Transfer Protocol
functions.php file, 70, 211–214
  child themes, 223–224
  post classification, 212
  Sandbox theme, 211

G

Gardner, Brian, 225
generic XML feed, 233–236
  metaWeblog.newPost, 234
  PHP file, 234
  XML-RPC client, 234–235
getfirebug.com, 188
get_permalink(), 98
get_post_meta(), 101
  parameters, 101
get_posts(), 92–93, 100
get_the_title(), 101
Gibbs, Matt, 311
global variables, 68
  Loop, 95–98
    author data, 96
    environmental data, 97–98
    post data, 95–96
    template tags v., 98
    user data, 96–97
Gnu Public License (GPL), 4–5
  core tenets, 4
  infection of content, 5
  "viral" nature, 4
Godley, John, 270, 348
Google AdSense, 243–244
Google Analytics, 276–278
  reporting screen, 278
Google Blog Search, 21
Google Gears, 40
Google Maps, 238–239
  API, 238
Google Summer of Code Project,
  271
Google Webmaster tools, 262
GPL. *See* Gnu Public License
Gravatars, 34–35
Gravity Forms, 313
Griffin, Clinton H., II, 324

H

hackers, 360
hacking, of core files, 76–77
  alternatives, 76–77
  consequences, 76
Hamby, Eric, 312
hardware, addition of, 322–323
  servers, 322–323
    hot spare, 323
    HyperDB, 323
    load balancing, 322–323
    wp-content/uploads
      synchronization, 323
hCard, 267–268
header.php file, 194–195
  nameplate, 194
headers, 258–259
hero spot, 306
homepages, 197–200
  index.php, 198
  templates, 199
hosting services, 7–8
  Apache Roller, 1, 8
  free, 3, 7–8
  .htaccess file, 8
  lighttpd, 8
  MySQL database, 8
  paid, 3
  URLs, 8
hot spare database server, 323
.htaccess file, 8, 51, 58–61
  configuration control, 60–61
  error logging, 61
  .maintenance file, 61
  permalinks, 45, 58–59
    creation manual, 59
    forward compatibility, 59
    rewriting rules, 59
    SEO, 59
    sharing, 59
    URL redirects, 59
    usability, 59
  redirection of search engines, 348
  security, 61
  wp-admin directory, 60
HTML. *See* Hypertext Markup
  Language
HTTP API, 75
Hybrid theme, 225
HyperCache, 283
HyperDB option, 323
  load balancing, 285
Hypertext Markup Language (HTML),
  264–269
  microformats, 267–269
  POSH, 264–266
    advantages, 264–265
    CSS, 265
    valid, 266
      CSS, 266

I

icanhazcheeseburger.com, 3
Ideas, 362
the_ID(), 84
if statements, 81
image.php file, 206
images, 34–35
  Gravatars, 34–35
  in posts, addition of, 23
  rotation, 30
  scaling, 31
  in themes, 186
import features, 39–40
  from Blogger, 40
  from LiveJournal, 40
  from Moveable Type, 40
  from TypePad, 40
  WordPress-to-WordPress, 40
import script, construction of, 335–344
Inactive Widgets box, 37
Incoming Links widget, 21
  Google Blog Search, 21
index.html, 10
index.php, 9, 10
  first-time administration, 17
  homepages, 198
  theme creation, 191–193
inline documentation, 67
InnoDB, 321
INSERT statements, 109
insertion of media, 29–30
  for audio, 29–30
  Gallery feature for, 29
  shortcode, 29
  for video, 29–30
interactivity features, 312–313
  e-commerce, 313
  forms, 313
  forums, 312–313
internationalization, 124–126
  placeholders, 125
iPhones, 271
ISAM tables, 321
  MyISAM, 321

J

Jaquith, Mark, 308
JavaScript, 255–256
  as statistics counter, 274

Johnson, Charles, 327
Joomla project, 6

K

keywords
  blacklists, 32
  Trac, 353
King, Alex, 237
Kubrik default theme, 184

L

LADP. *See* Lightweight Directory
    Access Protocol
LAMP stacks, 282
LANGDIR, 56
Lessig, Lawrence, 4
licenses, for plugins, 123
lifestream, 229–230
lighttpd, 8
Lightweight Directory Access Protocol
    (LADP), 324–325
  settings, 325
links, 25–26. *See also* permalinks
  categorization, 26
  content and, creation and
      management of, 25–26
    Delete link, 24
    Quick Edit link, 24
  Incoming Links widget, 21
  posts, 22, 24
    Add New link, 22
    permalinks, 22
    Quick Edit link, 24
  saving, 26
  targets, 26
wp_links, 105
Little, Mike, 2
LiveJournal, importing from, 40
load balanced database server,
    323
load balancing, 284–286
  HyperDB, 285
  servers, 322–323
  uploads directory, 285
long tail content problem, 231
Loop, 79–101
  customization, 80–81, 86–95
    adding paging, 89–90
    get_posts() function,
      92–93, 100
    queries, 87–89

    using query_post function,
      90–92
    WP_Query, 86–87
  default themes, 83–84
  definition of, 79
  flow, 81–84
    if statements, 81
    the_post() function, 81–82
    while statements, 82
    WP_query, 82
  functions of, 80–81
  global variables, 95–98
    author data, 96
    environmental data, 97–98
    post data, 95–96
    template tags v., 98
    user data, 96–97
  minimal requirements, 82
  multiple, 81, 94–95
    multi-pass, 95
    nested, 94–95
  MySQL database, 80
  outside of, functions, 98–101
  queries, 87–89
    author parameters, 88
    category parameters, 88
    custom parameters, 88–89
    date parameters, 88–89
    ordering parameters, 88–89
    page parameters, 88
    post parameters, 87–88
    resetting, 93
    tag parameters, 88
    time parameters, 88–89
  template tags, global variables v., 98

M

mailing lists, 359–361
  announcements, 359
  community support, 360
  documentation, 360
  hackers, 360
  polyglots, 360
  professional, 360
  Support Forum Volunteers, 360
  SVN updates, 360
  testers, 360
  Trac, 361
  XML-RPC, 360
.maintenance file, 61
Manual Browser Activation, 43
mapping services. *See* Google maps
media
  configurations, 44

  image sizes, 44
  content management of, 28–31
    Flash uploaders, 28
    insertion, 29–30
    Media Library, 28
    uploading, 28–29
  content migration, 331, 344–345
    FTP, 331
    SFTP, 331
  editing, 30–31
    cropping, 30
    image rotation, 30
    image scaling, 31
    Thumbnails, 31
    undo and redo functionality,
      30–31
  filters, 30
    bulk delete, 30
    bulk edit, 30
    Unattached, 30
  insertion of, 29–30
    for audio, 29–30
    Gallery feature for, 29
    shortcode, 29
    for video, 29–30
  in posts, addition of, 23
  uploading of, 28–29
    with Flash uploaders, 28
    problem-solving for, 28–29
    wp-content directory, 63
Media Library, 28
Meetups, 4, 361
memcache, 281
memcached, 281
menus
  creation, 134–136
    additions to existing menus,
      135–136
    custom, 135
    top-level, 134–135
  page.php file, 205–206
meta boxes, 143–147
  custom, 145–147
metadata
  content migration, 331, 345
  core files, 66
metaWeblog.newPost, 234
Meyers, Eric, 189
meyerweb.com/eric/tools/css/
  reset, 189
microformats, 267–269
  hCard, 267–268
  Sandbox theme, 189
  XFN, 267–268
    editing, 268

Mint, 276
Miscellaneous SubPanel, 46–47
mobile access, 271–272. *See also*
     Android; iPhones; WPTouch
Model-View-Controller design pattern,
     6
Most Used categories, 27
Moveable Type, 1
  importing from, 40
Mullenweg, Matt, 2
multi-pass Loops, 95
multiple Loops, 81, 94–95
  multi-pass, 95
  nested, 94–95
MyISAM, 321
MySQL database, 1
  cache management, for queries, 284
  caching, 321
  configuration, 12–16
     installation failures, 13
     login issues, 14
     mysql_error(), 13–14
     selection errors, 14–15
     table collection, 15
     WordPress v., 15
  downloads, 9
  hosting services, 8
  import scripts, 335–339
  Loop, 80
  site security, 292
  tale names, 8
MySQL import script, 335–339
mysql_error(), 13–14

N

nameplate, 194
nested Loops, 94–95
.NET applications, 327
news sites, 363–364
next_posts_link(), 98–99
Nielson, Jakob, 258
nonces, 157–158
Norton, Philip, 232
number used once. *See* nonces

O

object caching, 283–284
opcode cache, 281
open source software, 318–319
OpenID, 325–326
  login page, 326
options page, 136–143

construction, 138
custom settings, 140–143
Settings API, 136–139
WordPress 2.7, 136
O'Reilly, Tim, 6

P

Page Speed, 255
PageMash, 309–310
page.php file, 204–206
  custom templates, 217
  menus, 205–206
pages, 25
  in content hierarchy, 308–310
     links, 309
     management, 308–310
     Parent pages, 309
  core files, 66
  creation, 25
  management, 25
     Pages Edit link, 25
     Quick Edit link, 25
paid hosting services, 3
Palm Pre, 271
Parent pages, 309
partial themes, 226–227
patch/diff file creation, 355–356
pay-per-click model, 243
pay-per-day model, 243
pay-per-view model, 243
Pearson, Chris, 226
permalinks, 45–46
  custom, 45–46
     static elements, 46
  .htaccess file, 45, 58–59
     creation manual, 59
     forward compatibility, 59
     rewriting rules, 59
     SEO, 59
     sharing, 59
     URL redirects, 59
     usability, 59
  Structure Tags, 46
the_permalink(), 84
php.ini file, 320
phpMyAdmin, 111
Ping-O-Matic, 43
pings, 263–264
placeholders, 125
plain old semantic HTML (POSH),
    264–266
  advantages, 264–265
  CSS, 265
  microformats, 267–269

Planet WordPress, 364
Planet WordPress RSS feed, 21
pluggable.php, 70–71
plugin(s), 121–181. *See also* Plugin
    Directory
  advertising setup, 243–244
     Google AdSense, 243–244
  Bad Behavior, 33
  bulk upgrades, 41
  community directories, 362
  core files, 66
  Dashboard widgets, 21
  Directory, 175–181
  duplicate content, 261
  examples, 160–174
     array values, 168
     default settings, 161
     Post Meta Box, 162–164
     source code, 169–174
     submenu items, 161–162
     widgets, 164–167
  Facebook Connect, 242
  FeedWordPress, 327
  Flutter, 310–312
  hooks, 127–132
     actions, 127–132
     filters, 127–130
  packaging, 121–127
     activate functions, 123–124
     deactivate functions, 123–124
     directory constants, 126–127
     file creation, 122
     header creation, 122
     internationalization, 124–126
     licenses, 123
     listings, 122
  PageMash, 309–310
  Redirection, 348
  Role Scoper, 297
  security, 157–160
     data validation, 158–159
     nonces, 157–158
  settings, 132–143
     array of options, 133–134
     menu creation, 134–136
     option saving, 132–133
     options page, 136–143
  site searches, 270–271
  site security, 292–294
     Exploit Scanner, 292–293
     File Monitor, 293–294
     Security Scan, 292–293
  social media buttons, 231
  spam comments, 32–33
  submission, 356

plugin(s) *(continued)*
  in themes, 186
  Twitter, 236
  for users
      Cimy User Extra Fields plugin,
          35
      Register Plus plugin, 35
  WordPress extension, 38–39
      addition, 38
      directory, 38
      editors, 39
      management, 38
      syntax highlighting, 39
      update notices, 39
      Upgrade Automatically link,
          39
      upgrades, 38–39
      View Version Details link, 39
  WordPress integration, 143–157
      custom tables, 153–155
      meta box creation, 143–147
      shortcodes, 147–148
      uninstallation, 155–157
      widgets, 148–153
  wp-content directory, 61–62
Plugin API, 74
Plugin Directory, 175–181
  new versions, 181
  publishing to, 180–181
  readme.txt file, 176–179
  restrictions, 175
  submission, 175–176
  SVN, 179–180
      branches, 180
      Checkout Dialog, 179
      tags, 180
      trunk, 180
plugin.php, 71
Plugins (podcast), 363
podcasts, 362–363
  Plugins, 363
  WordCast, 363
  WordPress Podcast, 363
  WordPress Weekly, 362
Pods CMS, 311
polyglots, 360
POSH. *See* plain old semantic HTML
post categories, Most Used, 27
post control, 302–303
post data, 95–96
Post Edits link, 24–25
Post Meta Box, 162–164
Post Products widget, 167
post.php, 71
posts, 22–25

Add New link, 22
  categories for, 23
  core files, 66
  creation of, 22–24
  date modification, 24
  image addition, 23
  management of, 24–25
  media addition, 23
  permalinks, 22
  post content box, 23
  Post Edits, 24–25
  publishing, 23
  Quick Edit link, 24
  tags, 23
      meta boxes, 23
  visibility variability, 24
the_post() function, 81–82
previous_posts_link(), 98–99
privacy configurations, 45
  Blog Visibility setting, 45
  robots.txt file, 45
public_html, 9

Q

queries, 87–89
  author parameters, 88
  category parameters, 88
  custom parameters, 88–89
  date parameters, 88–89
  ordering parameters, 88–89
  page parameters, 88
  post parameters, 87–88
  resetting, 93
  tag parameters, 88
  time parameters, 88–89
query_post function, 90–92
  global variables, 91–92
  side effects, 91–92
Quick Edit link, 24–25
  pages, 25
  posts, 24
QuickPress panel, 17–18
  publishing of, 18
QuickPress widget, 21

R

Reading subpanels, 42–43
  Atom Publishing Protocol, 42
  e-mail configurations, 42
      Automated Browser Activation,
          42
      Cron Browser Activation, 42

      Manual Browser Activation,
          42
  Update Services, 43
      Ping-O-Matic, 43
  UTF-8 Unicode, 43
readme.txt file, 176–179
really simple syndication (RSS) feeds,
    239–240
  publishing to other sites, 240–241
  republishing form another site, 240
  in workplace enterprises, 318
Recent Drafts widget, 20–21
Reddit, 232
Redirection, 348
redo functionality. *See* undo and redo
    functionality
Register Plus plugin, 35
Release Archive, 50
Restore option, trash, 26
Revolution theme, 225
Rewrite API, 75
RIAs. *See* Rich Internet Applications
Rich Internet Applications (RIAs),
    314
Richard, Ozh, 364
robots.txt, 45
  duplicate content, 262–263
Role Scoper plugin, 297
role system, 294–297
  administrators, 296
  authors, 295
  capabilities, 296
  contributors, 295
  editors, 295
  extension, 297
  overview, 296
  subscribers, 295
RSS feeds. *See* really simple syndication
    feeds
RSS widgets, 21

S

Samuel, Chris, 330
Sandbox theme, 250
  archive.php file, 218
  creation, 187–189
      CSS, 188–189
  custom page templates, 218–219
  duplicate content, 261
  Firebug, 188
  flaws, 189
  functions.php file, 211, 213
  inspection, 188
  microformats, 189

as premium theme, 226
searchform.php file, 214–215
SAVEQUERIES, 55
SAVEQUERIES option, 110
search engine optimization (SEO) , 259
Search Everything plugin, 271
Search Regex, 348
searchform.php file, 214–215
secure file transfer protocol (SFTP), media migration, 344
Security Scan, 292
semantic HTML. *See* plain old semantic HTML
SEO. *See* search engine optimization
seologs.com, 261
Settings API, 75
  options page, 136–139
setup_postdata(), 100
SFTP. *See* secure file transfer protocol (SFTP), media migration
shortcode, 29
Shortcode API, 74–75
shortcodes, 147–148
showcase loop, 198–200
show_errors function, 110
Shreve, Justin, 271
sidebar widgets, 232
sidebar.php file, 195–196
simple social networking badges, 232–233
single.php file, 203–204
site load times, 254–255
  tools, 255
Skelton, Andy, 226, 271
Slashdot, 232
Sociable plugin, 231
social media buttons, 231–233
  plugins, 231
  profile linking, 232
  sidebar widgets, 232
social media pages, 232
social networking sites, 231–233. *See also* Digg; Facebook; Reddit; Slashdot; Twitter
simple badges, 232–233
spam, 286–287
  Akismet, 32–33, 287
  automated detection, 287
    Dashboard, 287
  Bad Behavior plugin, 33
  CAPTCHAs, 287
  comment moderation, 286–287
  handling of, 32–33
  keyword blacklists, 32

multiple links, 32
plugins, 32–33
Starnes, Joel, 309
Statcounter, 275–276
statistics counters, 273–278
  AWStats, 274–275
    reporting screen, 275
  Google Analytics, 276–278
    reporting screen, 278
  JavaScript, 274
  log file parsing, 274
  Mint, 276
  Statcounter, 275–276
Stewart, Ian, 226
style.css file, 190–191
Subversion (SVN) access, 50
  core files, 355
  core.svn.wordpress.org/trunk, 355
  mailing lists, 360
  Plugin Directory, 179–180
    branches, 180
    Checkout Dialog, 179
    tags, 180
    trunk, 180
  Trac, 354
Support Forum, 358–359
SVN access. *See* Subversion access
syntax highlighting, 39

T

table prefix changes, 290
Tadlock, Justin, 225
Tag meta boxes, 23, 27
Tag to Category Converter, 27
Tagline, 41
tag.php file, 202–203
tags
  categorization v., 26–28
  in posts, 23, 27–28
    meta boxes, 23, 27
  sites, 264
  template, 84–86
the_tags(), 85
taxonomies, 114–120
  custom, 116–120
    admin panel, 117
    content hierarchy, 308
    menu options, 117
    metabox, 118
    name definition, 118
    overview, 116
    use, 119–120
  default, 114

categories, 114
  link category, 114
  tag, 114
definition, 114
relationships between, 115
table structure, 115
template files, 185–186
  custom pages, 216–219
  hierarchy, 186
template tags, 84–86
  common, 84–85
  global variables v., 98
  parameters, 85–86
testers, 360
Thematic theme , 226
Theme Installer, 185
themes, 35–37, 183–227
  child, 219–224
    CSS, 220–222
    functions.php file, 223–224
    page styles, 223
    WordPress 2.7, 219, 224
  in CMS, 304
  community directories, 362
  components, 185–186
    assets, 186
    CSS, 186
    images, 186
    plugins, 186
    template files, 185–186
  content migration, 331, 346
  core files, 66
  creation, 187–216
    additional files, 208–216
    archive.php file, 200–201
    attachment.php file, 209–210
    author.php file, 210
    category name, 200
    category.php file, 201–202
    comments.php file, 210–211
    Conditional Tags, 196–197
    content display, 197–208
    custom page templates, 216–219
    DRY theme, 193–197
    404.php, 208–209
    functions.php file, 211–214
    header.php file, 194–195
    homepages, 197–200
    image.php file, 206
    index.php file, 191–193
    modification of working theme, 187
    Sandbox, 187–189

themes (*continued*)
    `searchform.php` file,
      214–215
    showcase loop, 198–200
    `sidebar.php` file, 195–196
    `single.php` file, 203–204
    `style.css` file, 190–191
    `tag.php` file, 202–203
    template hierarchy, 206–207
    `wp_foot` function, 195
  definition of, 35
  editors, 37
  hierarchy, 219–224
  installation, 36, 184–185
    Auto Installer, 36
    FTP, 36, 184
    Kubrik default, 184
    Theme Installer, 185
    Zip Unload, 36
  management of, 35–36
    new theme activation, 36
    option pages, 36
    `wp-content/themes`
      directory, 35, 62
  partial, 226–227
  premium, 224–227
    Hybrid, 225
    Revolution, 225
    Sandbox, 226
    Thematic, 226
    Thesis, 226
  purpose, 183–184
  Sandbox, 250
    creation, 187–189
    duplicate content, 261
    Firebug, 188
    flaws, 189
    inspection, 188
    microformats, 189
    as premium, 226
  submission, 356
  upgrading, 36–37
Thesis theme, 226
Thumbnails, 31
time settings, 42
`the_time()`, 85
TinyMCE editor, 304, 306
`the_title()`, 84
Torbert, Michael, 290, 292
Trac, 351–355
  browsing source, 354–355
    SVN, 354
  bug reporting, 352–353
    tickets, 352–353
  keywords, 353

mailing lists, 361
overview, 351–352
search tickets, 353–354
  custom queries, 354
timelines, 354
view tickets, 353–354
trackbacks, 263–264
trash, WordPress content, 26
  Delete, 26
  Restore, 26
Turbo, 40
  Google Gears, 40
Twitter, 233–234, 236–238
  API, 238
  content aggregation, 236–238
  plugin, 236
  Tools, 237
TypePad, 1
  importing from, 40

U

undo and redo functionality, 30–31
Uniform Resource Locators (URLs), 80
  cleanup, 332
  hosting services, 8
  `.htaccess` file redirects, 59
  Loop, 80
  updating, with content migration,
    347–348
    Search Regex, 348
uninstallation, plugins, 155–157
unique functionality, content
  migration, 346
update notices, 39
update password feature, 34
Update Services, 43
  Ping-O-Matic, 43
UPDATE statements, 109
Upgrade Automatically link, 39
upgrades
  content management, 40–41
    backups and, 41
    bulk, for plugins, 41
    links, 41
    notices, 41
  plugins, 38–39
  themes, 36–37
uploads
  media, 28–29
    with Flash uploaders, 28
    problem-solving for, 28–29
    `wp-content` directory, 63
  `wp-content` directory, 62–63
URLs. *See* Uniform Resource Locators

user data, 96–97
  content migration, 331, 345–346
user experience, 249–272
  Firebug, 255
  HTML, 264–269
    POSH, 264–266
    valid, 266
  information structuring, 257–259
    headers, 258–259
  mobile access, 271–272
    WPTouch, 271–272
  principles, 249–256
    content organization, 253–254
    design theory, 252–253
    Sandbox theme, 250
    site load times, 254–255
    visual design elements,
      251–253
  searching for sites, 269–271
    alternatives, 270–271
    default search, 269–270
    plugins, 270–271
  SEO, 259
  site discovery, 259–264
    content sharing sites, 264
    duplicate content, 261–263
    permalink structure, 260
    pings, 263–264
    tags, 264
    trackbacks, 263–264
    URL length, 259–260
  usability, 256–257
    A/B options, 256
    crowd sourcing, 256
    testing for, 256–257
  web standards, 264–269
    microformats, 267–279
    POSH, 264–266
    valid HTML, 266
  workflow, 301–302
user registration, 42
users, for WordPress, 33–35
  administrators, 34
  authors, 34
  contributors, 34
  core files, 66
  editors, 34
  images for, 34–35
    Gravatars, 34–35
  management, 33–34
    `author.php` template, 34
    Edit User pages, 34
    strength indicators, 34
    update password feature, 34

new user creation, 33
  administrator accounts, 33
  Allow User Registration option, 33
profile extension, 35
  Cimy User Extra Fields plugin, 35
  Register Plus plugin, 35
subscribers, 34
UTF-8 Unicode, 43

V

Valdrighi, Michael, 2
valid HTML, 266
  CSS, 266
de Valk, Jjoost, 231
video, insertion of, 29–30
View Version Details link, 39

W

Wall Street Journal, 3–4
  blogs, 3
Wallick, Scott Allan, 226
Walters, Matt, 293
WBTC. *See*
  WeblogToolsCollection.com
WeblogToolsCollection.com, 363
while statements, 82
widgets, 20–21
  in CMS, 304–305
  content management with, 37–38
  editing, 21
  Inactive box, 37
  Incoming Links, 21
  Planet WordPress RSS feed, 21
  plugins, 21, 148–153
    creation, 148–151
    custom, 151–152
    Dashboard, 152–153
    default values, 150
    examples, 164–167
    Post Products, 167
  QuickPress, 21
  Recent Drafts, 20–21
  RSS, 21
  sidebar, 232
  WordPress Development, 21
Widgets API, 74
WordCamp, 3–4, 361
WordCast, 363
WordPress. *See also* cache
  management; code; content

aggregation; Content
Management Systems; content
migration, to WordPress; core
files; Dashboard; database
management; Loop; pages;
plugin(s); Plugin Directory; posts;
Trac; user experience
additional hardware, 322–323
  servers, 322–323
advertising on, 242–247
  monetization, 242–243
  setup, 243–247
cache management, 278–284
  HyperCache, 283
  MySQL Query, 284
  objects, 283–284
  optimization, 281–282
  system complexity, 279–281
  web server, 281–282
  WP-Super Cache, 283
as CMS, 2, 5–7
  Dashboard, 6
  Drupal project, 6
  Joomla project, 6
  Model-View-Controller design
    pattern, 6
Codex, 72–76
  APIs, 74–75
  controversy, 75–76
  function reference, 73–74
  Lessons Page, 73
  quick index, 73
  as resource, 358
  searches, 72–73
  term glossary, 73
  uses, 72–73
common misperceptions, 4–5
  GPL infection of content, 5
  published changes, 5
community, 3–4, 351–364
  codex.wordpress.org, 4
  core files, 355–356
  development updates, 362
  documentation, 356–357
  external resources, 358–364
  Ideas, 362
  internal resources, 358–364
  Meetups, 4, 361
  news sites, 363–364
  plugin directories, 362
  podcasts, 362–363
  theme directories, 362
  WordCamp, 361
  WordPress.TV, 361–362

content integration via feeds,
  326–327
  FeedWordPress plugin, 327
content management, 22–47
  categorization, 26–28
  comments, 31–33
  configurations, 41–47
  extension of, 35–39
  links, 25–26
  management, 24–25
  media, 28–31
  pages, 25
  posts, 22–25
  tools, 39–41
  trash, 26
  upgrading, 40–41
  users, 33–35
  widgets, 37–38
content migration, 329–349
  author data, 345–346
  cleanup, 346–349
  content identification,
    332–344
  launch for, 349
  media, 344–345
  metadata, 345
  planning strategy, 330–332
  themes, 346
  unique functionality, 346
  user data, 345–346
current development, 2–3
database configuration, 11–16
  installation failure causes, 13
  MySQL, 12–16
definition, 1–2
download statistics, 3
  hosted blogs, 3
first posting, 17–18
first-time administration, 16–17
  wp-admin subdirectory, 16
GPL, 4–5
  core tenets, 4
  "viral" nature, 4
history, 2
hosting services, 7–8
  Apache Roller, 1, 8
  free, 3, 7–8
  .htaccess file, 8
  lighttpd, 8
  MySQL database, 8
  paid, 3
  URLs, 8
identity management integration,
  324–326
  AD, 324–325

WordPress (*continued*)
LDAP, 324–325
OpenID, 325–326
inefficient uses, 314–315
initiation, 7
complexity, 7
control, 7
costs, 7
installation, 9–16
administrative information, 12
auto-configuration dialog box, 11
database configuration, 11–16
directories, 9–10
file installation, 9–12
first-time administration, 16–17
platforms for, 9
unconfigured, 10
integration of, 314
load balancing, 284–286
HyperDB, 285
uploads directory, 285
mailing lists, 359–361
multiple servers, 322–323
MySQL database in, 1
operating system user differences, 15
plugins
custom tables, 153–155
extensions, 38–39
addition, 38
directory, 38
editors, 39
management, 38
syntax highlighting, 39
update notices, 39
Upgrade Automatically link, 39
upgrades, 38–39
View Version Details link, 39
integration, 143–157
submission, 356
popularity, 3
QuickPress panel, 17–18
RIAs, 314
role system, 294–297
administrators, 296
authors, 295
capabilities, 296
contributors, 295
editors, 295
extension, 297
overview, 296
subscribers, 295
servers, 322–323

hot spare, 323
HyperDB, 323
load balancing, 322–323
wp-content/uploads synchronization, 323
sister projects, 357–358
site security, 288–292
admin accounts, 289–290
Apache permissions, 291–292
configuration file moving, 290
content directory moving, 290–291
force SSL on login/administrators, 291
hidden version information, 289
MySQL credentials, 292
plugins, 292–294
secret key features, 291
staying updated, 288–289
table prefix changes, 290
Support Forum, 358–359
theme submission, 356
themes, 35–37
definition of, 35
editors, 37
installation, 36
management of, 35–36
upgrading, 36–37
Trac, 351–355
WordCamp, 361
WordCamps, 3–4
wordpress.com, 2, 7
workplace enterprises, 317–327
appropriateness, 317–319
caching, 321–322
content integration, 326–327
costs, 318
extensibility, 318
FOSS, 319
hardware scaling, 322–323
identity management integration, 324–326
multiple servers, 322–323
open source, 318–319
performance tuning, 320–321
popularity, 317
regular maintenance, 322
RSS, 318
scalability, 319–320
server applications, 321
zed1.com, 2
WordPress 2.7, 219, 224
options page, 136
WordPress Development widget, 21

WordPress eXtended RSS (WXR) files, 333–335
applications, 334–335
blog conversion, 333–334
WordPress MU (WPMU), 357
WordPress Planet, 364
WordPress Podcast, 363
WordPress Support Network, 319
WordPress-to-WordPress import feature, 40
WordPress Weekly, 362
wordpress.com, 2, 7
wordpress.org, 3
wordpress.org/download, 49
wordpress.org/latest.tar.qz, 50
wordpress.org/latest.zip, 50
WordPress.TV, 361–362
workflow, in CMS, 301–303
post control, 302–303
revision history, 302
user roles and delegation, 301–302
wp-admin directories, 60
subdirectory, 16
wp-config.php, 51–57
edits, 17
options, 52–57
AUTOSAVE INTERVAL, 54
CUSTOM_USER_META_TABLE, 56
CUSTOM_USER_TABLE, 56
DB_COLLATE, 52
FORCE_SSL_LOGIN, 57
FS_CHMOD_DIR, 57
FS_CHMOD_FILE, 57
FTP settings, 56–57
installation localization, 53
LANGDIR, 56
SAVEQUERIES, 55
secret keys, 52–53
WP_CACHE, 57
WP_CONTENT_DIR, 54
WP_DEBUG, 54–55
WP_HOME, 54
WPLANG, 53, 55–56
WP_MEMORY_LIMIT, 54–55
WP_PLUGIN_DIR, 54
WP_PLUGIN_URL, 54
WP_SITEURL, 53–54
storage location, 52
table prefixes, 53
wp-config-sample.php, 9, 14–15
wp-content directory, 61–63
media, 63
custom, 63

plugins, 61–62
themes, 35, 62
uploads, 62–63
wp-content/uploads,
  synchronization of, 323
WP-Super Cache, 283
WP_CACHE, 57
wp_comments, 105–106
  direct database manipulation,
  113–114
wp_commentsmeta, 105
WP_CONTENT_DIR, 54
wpdb class, 107–108
WP_DEBUG, 54–55
WPEngineer.com, 364
wp_foot function, 195
WP_HOME, 54
WPLANG, 53, 55–56
wp_list_bookmarks(), 98
wp_list_categories(), 98
wp_list_pages(), 98
WP_MEMORY_LIMIT, 54–55
WPMU. *See* WordPress MU
wp_options, 105
  direct database manipulation,
  112–113
wp_page_menu(), 99
WP_PLUGIN_DIR, 54
WP_PLUGIN_URL, 54

wp_postmeta, 105
wp_posts, 105–106
  direct database manipulation,
  111–112
  fields, 106
  post status definitions, 106
wp_posts table, 105
WP_Query, Loop, customization,
  86–87
WP_query, Loop, flow, 82
WP_SITEURL, 53–54
wp_tag_cloud(), 98
WPTavern.com, 363
wp_term_relationships, 105
wp_terms, 105
wp_term_taxonomy, 105
WPTouch, 271–272
wp_usermeta, 105
wp_users, 105–106
  direct database manipulation, 113
WPVibe.com, 363
Writing subpanels, 42–43
  Atom Publishing Protocol, 42
  email configurations, 43
    Automated Browser Activation,
    42
    Cron Browser Activation, 42
    Manual Browser Activation,
    42

Update Services, 43
  Ping-O-Matic, 43
UTF-8 Unicode, 43
WXR files. *See* WordPress eXtended
  RSS files

X

XFN. *See* Xhtml Friend Network
Xhtml Friend Network (XFN),
  267
  editing, 268
XML feed. *See* generic XML feed;
  Twitter
XML-RPC, 360

Y

Yahoo!, 320
YSlow, 255
  CDN, 255
YSlow!, 320

Z

zed1.com, 2
Zip Unload, 36
zombies list, 79